Becoming a Master Student

Tools, techniques, hints, ideas, illustrations, instructions, examples, methods, procedures, processes, skills, resources, and suggestions for success.

ELLIS ™

SIXTH·EDITION

College Survival, Inc., P.O. Box 8306, Rapid City, SD 57709-8306

Library of Congress Number: 91-070102

ISBN: 0-942456-10-6

Sixth edition - second printing

Notice:

Becoming A Master Student was previously titled *Survival Tools for
Students*, and before that, *Survival Tools for College.*

This book is now available in Spanish and is being translated into
other languages as well. Write College Survival, Inc., for more
information.

Printed in U.S.A. on recycled paper in accordance with The Environmental
Protection Agency's Section 6002 RCRA definition of recycled paper.

Acknowledgments

Hundreds of people have directly contributed to this book.

In particular, I acknowledge Doug Toft, Stan Lankowitz, Bill Harlan, Mary Maisey-Ireland, and Larry David for their writing and editing.

For his mastery in design I thank Bill Fleming. For their assistance in design and illustration I thank Mike Speiser, Susan Turnbull, Kathy Rusynyk, Paula Ness and Laurie Ellis Pohlad. I acknowledge Gail Chase, Jim Osborne, and Jayne Erickson for photography.

I thank the staff of College Survival, Inc., for their personal and professional support and particularly the consultants for their expertise in higher education. It is an honor to work with people I love. I also thank my wife, Trisha Waldron, and my friends Barb Churchill and Stan Lankowitz for their contributions to my personal growth. I treasure what I have learned from my children, Sara, Elizabeth, Snow, and Berri, and the constant encouragement of my parents, Maryellen and Ken.

I thank Robbie Murchison for proofreading, Judie Arvites for research and index compilation, and Pat Krosschell for contributing ideas and logistical support. I also thank Karen Marie Erickson, Wayne Zako, and Kirk Witzberger for editing. I acknowledge the administration of National College in Rapid City, South Dakota, for assistance in the development of the student success course that led the way for this book.

The first edition of this book was in large part the creation of students, who taught me about student success while I was supposed to be teaching them. Since that edition, hundreds of thousands of students and thousands of teachers have used it and have dramatically changed this book through their contributions. Many of them have sent suggestions, and my files are packed full of their ideas—so is this book. In particular, I want to thank James Anderson, Judy Maisey, Bob Boyd, Russell Floyd, Linda Duttlinger, Joyce Weinsheimer, Linda Halstead, Bill Norris, and Dee Jankovsky. I also thank the nontraditional students and people from many different cultures and ethnic groups who have raised my awareness about communicating in a way that more people can listen.

To all of you, thank you for assisting me in creating *Becoming a Master Student*.

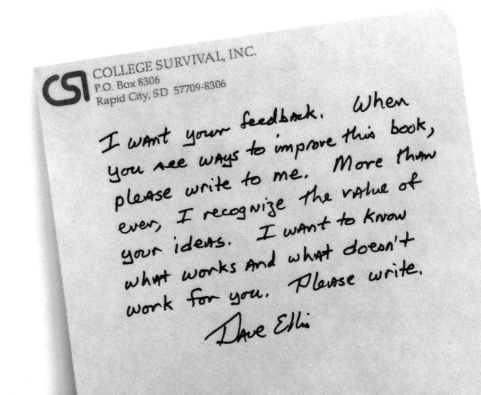

COLLEGE SURVIVAL, INC.
P.O. Box 8306
Rapid City, SD 57709-8306

I want your feedback. When you see ways to improve this book, please write to me. More than ever, I recognize the value of your ideas. I want to know what works and what doesn't work for you. Please write.

Dave Ellis

Table of contents

Introduction

Change and growth take place when a person has risked himself and dares to become involved with experimenting with his own life.
HERBERT OTTO

The human ability to learn and remember is virtually limitless.
SHEILA OSTRANDER and LYNN SCHROEDER

Exercise #1:
Textbook reconnaissance

Start becoming a master student right now by doing a 15-minute "textbook reconnaissance" of this book. Here's how:

First, read the table of contents. Do it in three minutes or less. Next, look at every page in the book. Move quickly. Scan headlines. Look at pictures. Notice forms, charts, and diagrams.

A textbook reconnaissance shows you where a course is going. It gives you the big picture. That's useful because brains work best when going from the general to the specific. Getting the big picture before you start makes details easier to recall and understand later on.

Your textbook reconnaissance will work even better if, as you scan, you look for ideas you can use. When you find one, write the page number and a two-word description of it in the space below. The idea behind this technique is simple: It's easier to learn when you're excited, and it's easier to get excited about a course if you know it's going to be useful, interesting, or fun.

When you have found five interesting ideas, stop writing and continue your survey. Remember, look at every page, and do it quickly. And here's another useful tip for the master student: Do it now.

    Page Number   *Description*

1.

2.

3.

4.

5.

This book is worthless.

The first edition of this book began with that sentence.

MANY STUDENTS THOUGHT THIS WAS A TRICK to get their attention. It wasn't. Others thought it was reverse psychology. It wasn't that, either. Still others thought it meant that the book was worthless if they didn't read it. It's more than that.

The book is worthless even if you read it, if reading is all you do. What was true of that first edition is true of this one. Until you take action and use the ideas in it, *Becoming a Master Student* really is worthless.

Before you stiffen up and resist, the purpose of this sales pitch is not to separate you from your money. You already bought the book. Now you can get something for your money by committing yourself to take action—in other words, commit yourself to become a master student. Here's what's in it for you.

Pitch #1: You can save money now and make more later.

Start with money. Your college education is one of the most expensive things you will ever buy. Typically, it costs students $30 to $70 an hour to sit in class. (See Exercise #31 on page 266.) Unfortunately, many students think their classes aren't even worth 50 cents an hour.

As a master student, you control the value you get out of your education, and that value can be considerable. The joy of learning aside, college graduates make about $700,000 more during their lifetimes than their non-degreed peers. It pays to be a master student.

Pitch #2: You can rediscover the natural learner in you.

Joy is important, too. As you become a master student, you will learn how to learn in the most effective way possible, by discovering the joyful, natural learner within you.

Children are great natural students. They learn complex skills such as language, quickly, and they have fun doing it. For them, learning is a high-energy process involving experimentation, discovery, and sometimes broken dishes. Then comes school. For some students, drill and drudgery replace discovery and dish breaking. Learning can become a drag. You can use this book to reverse that process and rediscover what you knew as a child—that laughter and learning are not mutually exclusive.

Sometimes learning does take effort, especially in college. As you become a master student, you will learn how to get the most out of that effort.

Pitch #3: You can choose from hundreds of techniques.

Becoming a Master Student is packed with hundreds of practical, nuts-and-bolts techniques. And you can begin using them immediately. For example, during your

Textbook reconnaissance on page vi you practiced three powerful learning techniques in one 15-minute exercise. (If you didn't do the Textbook reconnaissance, it's not too late to get your money's worth from page vi. Do it now.) If you doze in lectures, drift during tests, or dawdle on term papers, you can use the ideas in this book to become a more effective student.

Not all these ideas will work for you. That's why there are so many of them in *Becoming a Master Student.* You can experiment with the techniques. As you discover what works, you will develop a unique style of learning that you can use for the rest of your life.

Pitch #4: You get the best suggestions from thousands of students.

The concepts and techniques in this book are not here because learning theorists, educators, and psychologists say they work. They are here because tens of thousands of students from all kinds of backgrounds tried them and say they work. These are people who dreaded giving speeches, couldn't read their own notes, and couldn't remember where the ileosecal valve was. Then they figured out how to solve those problems, which was the hard part. Now you can use their ideas.

Pitch #5: You can learn about you.

The process of self-discovery is an important theme in *Becoming a Master Student.* Throughout the book you can use Discovery Statements and Intention Statements for everything from organizing your desk to choosing long-term goals. Studying for an organic chemistry quiz is a lot easier with a clean desk and a clear idea of its importance to you.

Pitch #6: You can use a proven product.

The first five editions of this book were successful for tens of thousands of students. In schools where it was widely used, the dropout rate decreased as much as 25 percent and in some cases, 50 percent. Student feedback has been positive. In particular, students with successful histories have praised the techniques in this book.

Pitch #7: You can learn the secret of student success.

If this sales pitch still hasn't persuaded you to actively use this book, maybe it's time to reveal the Secret of Student Success. (Provide your own drum roll here.) The secret is, there are no secrets. The strategies and tactics that successful students use are well known. You have hundreds of them at your fingertips right now, in this book.

However, what makes them work is action. Without it, the pages of *Becoming a Master Student* are just 2.1 pounds of expensive mulch. Add your participation to the mulch, and these pages are priceless.

Journal Entry #1
Discovery Statement

Success is a choice. Your choice. And to get what you want, it helps to know what you want. That is the purpose of this Journal Entry.

Select a time and place when you know you will not be disturbed for at least twenty minutes. (The library is a good place to do this.) Relax for two or three minutes, clearing your mind. Then complete the following sentences and keep writing. Write down everything you want to get out of school. Write down everything you want your education to enable you to do after you finish school.

When you run out of things to write, stick with it just a bit longer. Be willing to experience a little discomfort. Keep writing. What you discover might be well worth the extra effort.

You can begin choosing success right now by choosing a date, time, and place to complete this Journal Entry. Write your choice here:

Date:

Time:

Place:

What I want from my education is . . .

_____

_____

_____

_____

When I complete my education, I want to be able to . . .

_____

_____

_____

_____

_____

I also want . . .

_____

_____

_____

Journal Entry # 2
Discovery Statement

On a separate piece of paper, write a description of a time in your life when you learned or did something well. This situation need not be related to school. Describe the details of the situation, including the place, time, and people involved. Describe how you felt about it, how it looked to you, how it sounded. Describe the physical feelings you associate with the event. Do the same for emotions.

How to get the out of this

1. Rip 'em out. The pages of *Becoming a Master Student* are perforated because some of the information here is too important to leave in the book and some of it your instructor may want to see. For example, Journal Entry #1 asks you to write some important things you want to get out of your education. To keep yourself focused, you could rip that page out and post it on your bathroom mirror, or some place where you'll see it several times a day.

You can re-insert a page by just sticking it into the spine of the book; it will hold. A piece of tape will fix it in place.

2. Skip around. You can use this book in several different ways. Read it straight through, or pick it up, turn to any page and find an idea you can use. Look for ideas you can use right now. If you're having trouble listening to boring lectures, skip directly to "Notice your environment" on page 126 in Chapter Five: Notes. If you suspect alcohol might be getting in the way of your education, read "Addiction—The truth" on page 244 in Chapter Nine.

3. If it works, use it.

If it doesn't, lose it. If there are sections of the book that don't apply to you at all, skip them. Even some techniques that do seem relevant might not work for you. However, when you are committed to getting value from this book, even an idea that seems irrelevant or ineffective at first can turn out to be a powerful tool. Topics that aren't relevant now may be just what you want next year or three years from now. Asking "How can I use this?" can turn almost anything into a valuable experience.

4. Rewrite this book. Here's an alternative strategy to the one above. If an idea doesn't work for you, rewrite it. Change the exercises to fit your needs. Create a new technique by combining several others. Create a technique out of thin air! Ask questions, then find the answers. And don't forget to send in the results. Your ideas may appear in the next edition.

5. Put yourself into the book. As you read about techniques in this book, invent your own examples, starring yourself in the title role. For example, as you were reading the explanation of Exercise #1 on page vi, you might have pictured yourself using this technique on your world history textbook. Sometimes it pays to let your mind wander.

6. Work with others. Talk with your classmates about what works and what doesn't. Peer pressure is often characterized as negative. You can turn that idea around. Form a group of students who support each other to master the art of learning.

most book

7. Yuk it up. Going to school is a big investment. The stakes are high. It's OK to be serious about that, but you don't have to go to school on the deferred-fun program. A master student celebrates learning, and one of the best ways to do that is to have a laugh now and then.

8. Own this book. Write your name and address on the first page of this book now, and don't stop there. As you complete Journal Entries and exercises you create a record of what you want to get out of school and how you intend to get it. Every time your pen touches a page, you move closer to becoming a master student.

9. Do the exercises. Action makes this book work. To get the most out of an exercise, read the instructions carefully before you begin. To get the most out of this book, do all the exercises. More importantly, avoid feeling guilty if you skip some. And by the way, it's never too late to go back and do those.

10. Get used to a new look. This book looks different than traditional textbooks. *Becoming a Master Student* presents major ideas in magazine-style articles. You will also discover lots of lists, blurbs, one-liners, pictures, charts, graphs, cartoons, and even a joke or two.

Exercise #2
Commitment

This book is worthless without your action. One powerful way to begin taking action is to make a commitment. Conversely, without commitment, sustained action is unlikely. The result is a worthless book. Therefore, in the interest of saving your valuable time and energy, this exercise gives you a chance to declare your level of involvement up front. Choose the number from one to ten that reflects your commitment to using this book. Write the number in the space provided at the end of the list.

1. "Well, I'm reading this book right now, aren't I?"

2. "I will skim the book and read the interesting parts."

3. "I will read the book and think about how some of the techniques might apply to me."

4. "I will read the book, think about it, and do the exercises that look interesting."

5. "I will read the book, do exercises, and complete some of the Journal Entries."

6. "I will read the book, do exercises and Journal Entries, and use some of the techniques."

7. "I will read the book, do most of the exercises and Journal Entries, and use some of the techniques."

8. "I will study this book, do most of the exercises and Journal Entries, and use many of the techniques."

9. "I will study this book, do all of the exercises and Journal Entries, and experiment vigorously with most of the suggestions in order to discover what works best for me."

10. "I promise to get value from this book, beginning with Exercise #1: "Textbook reconnaissance," even if I have to re-write the sections I don't like and even if I have to invent new techniques of my own."

Enter your commitment level and today's date here:
Commitment level_____   Date_____

If you selected commitment level 1 or 2, you might consider passing this book on to a friend. If your commitment level is a 9 or 10, you are on your way to terrific success in school. If you are somewhere in between, experiment with the techniques and if you find they work, consider returning to this exercise and raising your level of commitment.

Chapter

1 First Step

You either change things or you don't.
Excuses rob you of power and induce apathy.
AGNES WHISTLING ELK

In oneself lies the whole world, and if you know how
to look and learn, then the door is there and the key is in
your hand. Nobody on earth can give you either that key
or the door to open, except yourself.
J. KRISHNAMURTI

No one can make you feel inferior without your consent.
ELEANOR ROOSEVELT

Journal Entry #3
Discovery Statement

Preview this chapter and discover something you want to learn. Choose a technique or specific idea that you can use to get immediate, practical benefit. Write what you've chosen and the benefit you expect to get in the space below.

The technique I choose to learn about is . . .

The benefits I will get from using this technique are . . .

In this chapter . . .

The first step toward any kind of mastery is finding out where you are now and where you want to go. That's the focus of this chapter.

First Step: Truth is the key to mastery explains the power of telling the truth about your abilities, and it offers a path beyond current limitations as a student.

Exercise #5: The Discovery Wheel is like a camera pointed at you. After completing it, you may see in yourself many qualities of a master student.

The Discovery and Intention Journal Entry System lets you focus your energy so you can actually use less of it while gaining more skills.

How to change a habit offers ways to get past barriers to your success in school—and how to use the ideas in this book.

Motivation—or "I'm just not in the mood" suggests some ways to nudge yourself out of procrastination.

Stay tuned to these networks, and The art of re-entry—Going back to school as an older student suggest how you can participate fully in academic life.

Power Process #1: Ideas are tools suggests that you believe nothing you read in this book. You may bruise your philosophical muscles.

Reading ***The master student*** can help you define your goals—as well as reveal qualities that you already possess.

This chapter also suggests: ***Maybe it's your breath, Deface this book***, and that ***"F" is for feedback, not failure***.

Exercises in this chapter give you a chance to discover where you are and where you want to be.

First Step: Truth is a key to mastery

THE FIRST STEP TECHNIQUE IS SIMPLE: Tell the truth about who you are and what you want. End of discussion. Now, proceed to Chapter Two.

Well, it's not quite that simple.

The First Step is one of the most powerful tools in this book. It magnifies the power of all the other techniques. It is a key to becoming a master student.

Unfortunately, a First Step is easier to explain than it is to use, and it's not that easy to explain. "Telling the truth" sounds like pie-in-the-sky moralizing, but there is nothing pie-in-the-sky about a First Step. It is a practical, down-to-earth way to change behavior. No technique in this book has been field-tested more often or more successfully—or under tougher circumstances. Just ask almost any recovering alcoholic.

A fundamental principle of Alcoholics Anonymous is that alcoholics must tell the truth about their drinking before they can begin to change. This is an essential ingredient in AA's "First Step" and in its entire Twelve Step program. Today, people recovering from addictions to food, drugs, sex, work, and whatever else human beings can abuse, employ the same principle. They use First Steps to change their behavior for one reason: First Steps work.

Compared to conquering addictions, training to be a master student is a snap. But let's be truthful. It's not easy to tell the truth about ourselves. We might have to admit that we're afraid of algebra or that we never complete term papers on time. It's tough to admit weaknesses.

For some people, it's even harder to admit strengths. Maybe they don't want to brag. Maybe they're attached to poor self-images. The reasons don't matter. The point is, using the First Step system in *Becoming a Master Student* means telling the truth about your good qualities, too.

Making this technique work also means telling the truth about what you want.

Sounds easy, you say? Many people would rather eat nails. If you don't believe it, find three fellow students and ask them what they want to get out of their educations. Be prepared for hemming and hawing, vague generalities, and maybe even a helping of pie-in-the-sky a la mode.

On the other hand, if one of them tells you she wants a degree in journalism, with double minors in earth sciences and Portuguese, so she can work as a reporter covering the environment in Brazil, chances are you've found a master student.

The details of her vision are a clue to her mastery. Goals are more powerful when they are specific. So are First Steps, whether they are verbal or written. For example, if you want to improve your note-taking skills, you might write: "I am an awful note-taker."

It would be more effective to write: "I can't read 80 percent of the notes I took in American Constitutional History last week, and I have no idea what was important in that class."

Be just as specific about what you want. You might declare, "I want to take legible notes that help me predict what questions will be on the final exam."

In Exercise #5: "The Discovery Wheel" and Journal Entry #3 you can take a giant First Step. You can tell the truth about what kind of student you are and what kind of student you want to become. If that prospect puts a knot in your stomach, that's good. Notice that knot. It is your friend. It is reminding you that telling the truth about yourself takes courage, which is an important characteristic of a master student.

Your courage will be rewarded. The Discovery Wheel and the rest of the exercises in this book are your First Steps to tapping resources you never imagined you had.

No kidding. It's just that simple. The truth has power.

You ought to be in movies!

When this book works, it's not like *going to* the movies, it's like *being in* the movies. The distinction is important. People in theaters watch. People in movies act, and action is the key to getting what you want in school. That's why doing the exercises in this book—as opposed to just reading them—is essential.

These exercises invite you to write, touch, feel, move, see, search, ponder, speak, listen, recall, choose, commit, and create. You might even sing and dance. Learning works best when it involves action. People learn best when, along with their brains, they use their arms, legs, eyes, ears, and noses in the process.

True education is not about cramming material into your brain. Education is the process of expanding your capabilities, of bringing yourself out into the world. Doing the exercises brings you into the heart of that process.

Exercise #3
Taking the first step

The purpose of this exercise is to give you a chance to discover the positive as well as negative aspects of yourself. It is the most difficult exercise in this book. To make the exercise worthwhile, do it with courage.

Some people suggest that looking at negative aspects is counter to positive thinking. Well, perhaps. Positive thinking is a great technique. So is seeing the truth, especially when we see the whole picture—even though a realistic picture of ourselves may include some extremely negative points.

If you admit that you can't read, and that's the truth, then you have taken a strong, positive first step to becoming a successful reader. On the other hand, if you say that you are a terrible math student, and that's not the truth, then you are programming yourself to accept unnecessary failure. The point is, tell the truth.

This exercise is similar to each Journal Entry - Discovery Statement appearing throughout this text. The difference is that in this case you don't write your discoveries in the book for reasons of confidentiality.

Be brave. If you approach this exercise courageously, you are likely to write down some things you don't want others to read. You may even write down some truths about yourself that could get you into trouble. Do this exercise on separate pieces of paper, then hide or destroy them.

To make this exercise work, follow these three suggestions:

1. Be specific. It is not effective to write, "I could improve my communication skills." Of course you can. Instead, write down precisely what you can do to improve your communication skills. For example, "I can spend more time really listening while the other person is talking, instead of thinking about what I'm going to say next."

2. Look beyond the classroom. What goes on outside of school often has the greatest impact on your ability to be an effective student.

3. Be courageous. This exercise is a waste of time if done half-heartedly. Be willing to risk. Sometimes you may open a door that reveals a part of yourself that you didn't want to admit was there. The power of this technique is that once you know "it" is there, you can do something about it.

Part 1
Time yourself, and for ten minutes, write as fast as you can and complete the following sentences with anything that comes to mind. Complete each sentence at least ten times. If you get stuck, don't stop; just write something—even if it's crazy.

It is ineffective when I . . .
It doesn't work when I . . .
I could change . . .

Part 2
When you have completed the first part of the exercise, review what you have written and cross off things that don't make any sense. The sentences that remain represent possible goals for your experience as a master student.

Part 3
Here's the tough part. Time yourself, and for ten minutes, write as fast as you can. Complete the following sentences with anything that comes to mind. As in Part 1, complete each sentence at least ten times and just keep writing, even if it sounds silly.

I am very good at . . .
It is effective when I . . .
Something very positive about me is . . .

Part 4
Review your list and circle the things that really fit. This is a good list to keep for those times when you question your own value and worth.

One way to become a better student is to grit your teeth, grunt, and try harder. There is another way. You can use the Discovery and Intention Journal Entry System to increase your effectiveness with the least possible struggle. It's a way to focus your energy, and it's closely related to the idea of taking a First Step.

The Discovery and Intention Journal Entry System is a little like flying a plane. Airplanes are seldom exactly on course. Human and automatic pilots are always checking and correcting the heading. The resulting path looks like a zigzag. The plane is almost always flying in the wrong direction, but because of constant observation and course correction, it arrives at the right place.

The same system can be used by students. In fact, you have already used it if you completed Journal Entries on pages 3 and 6. (If you haven't, consider doing one right now.) Journal Entries throughout this book

are labeled either "Discovery Statement" or "Intention Statement." Each Journal Entry will contain a short set of directions and a space in which you can write.

Through Discovery Statements, you can learn "where you are." They are a record of what you learn about yourself as a student—both strengths and weaknesses. Discovery Statements also can be declarations of what you want, descriptions of your attitudes, statements of your feelings, transcripts of your thoughts, and chronicles of your behavior.

Intention Statements can be used to alter your course. They are statements of your commitment to do a specific task, to take a certain action. An intention arises out of your choice to direct your energy toward a particular goal.

The purpose of this system is *not* to get you pumped up and excited to go out there and try harder. Discovery and Intention Statements keep you focused on what you want and how you intend to get it.

The Journal Entry process is a cycle. You can write Discovery Statements about where you are and where you want to go. Then you can write Intention Statements about the specific steps you will take to get there. Then you can write Discovery Statements about whether you completed those steps and what you learned in the process, followed by more Intention Statements, and so on. Sometimes the statements will be long and detailed. Usually they will be short, maybe just a line or two. Practice it, and the cycle can become automatic.

Don't panic when you fail to complete an intended task. Straying off course is normal. Simply make the necessary corrections. Miraculous progress may not come immediately. Do not be concerned. Stay with the cycle. Use Discovery Statements to get clear about your world and what you want out of it. Then use Intention Statements to direct your actions. When you notice progress, record it.

The following statement might strike you as radical, but it is true: It often takes the same amount of energy to get what you want in school as it takes to get what you don't want. Sometimes getting what you don't want takes even *more* effort. An airplane burns the same amount of fuel flying away from its destination as it does flying toward it, so it pays to stay on course.

You can use the Discovery and Intention Journal Entry System to stay on your own course and get what you want out of school. Consider the guidelines for Discovery Statements and Intention Statements on pages 14 and 15, then develop your own style. Once you get the hang of it, you might discover you can fly.

Exercise #4
Deface this book

Some books should be preserved in pristine condition. This isn't one of them.

There are valid reasons for not writing in any book. For one thing, it decreases the resale value. However, the benefit of writing in your books far outweighs that consideration.

Becoming a Master Student is about learning, and learning is an active pursuit, not a passive one. Something happens when you reach out and touch a book with your pen. When you make notes in the margin, you can hear yourself talking with the author. When you doodle and underline, you can see the author's ideas take shape. You can even argue with an author, or create your own ideas.

That's the way this book works. To find out more, turn the page. (Please come back to this exercise.)

To complete this exercise, find something you agree with or disagree with on this page and write a short note in the margin. Or draw a diagram. Better yet, do both. Chapter Five: Notes, contains tips to help make notes in textbooks more effective, but for this exercise, let creativity be your guide. Have fun.

Begin defacing now.

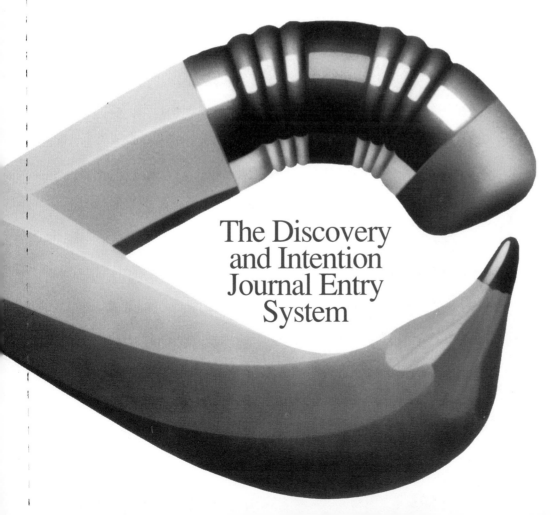

The Discovery and Intention Journal Entry System

GOAL

One way to become a better student is to grit your teeth, grunt, and try harder. There is another way. You can use the Discovery and Intention Journal Entry System to increase your effectiveness with the least possible struggle. It's a way to focus your energy, and it's closely related to the idea of taking a First Step.

The Discovery and Intention Journal Entry System is a little like flying a plane. Airplanes are seldom exactly on course. Human and automatic pilots are always checking and correcting the heading. The resulting path looks like a zigzag. The plane is almost always flying in the wrong direction, but because of constant observation and course correction, it arrives at the right place.

The same system can be used by students. In fact, you have already used it if you completed Journal Entries on pages 3 and 6. (If you haven't, consider doing one right now.) Journal Entries throughout this book

are labeled either "Discovery Statement" or "Intention Statement." Each Journal Entry will contain a short set of directions and a space in which you can write.

Through Discovery Statements, you can learn "where you are." They are a record of what you learn about yourself as a student—both strengths and weaknesses. Discovery Statements also can be declarations of what you want, descriptions of your attitudes, statements of your feelings, transcripts of your thoughts, and chronicles of your behavior.

Intention Statements can be used to alter your course. They are statements of your commitment to do a specific task, to take a certain action. An intention arises out of your choice to direct your energy toward a particular goal.

The purpose of this system is *not* to get you pumped up and excited to go out there and try harder. Discovery and Intention Statements keep you focused on what you want and how you intend to get it.

this pencil is twisted into the shape of the sign infinity. It represents the continual process of discovery and intention that is recommended in the article. the process of growth is neverending, as is journaling and discovering where we are ... and intending to change.

The Journal Entry process is a cycle. You can write Discovery Statements about where you are and where you want to go. Then you can write Intention Statements about the specific steps you will take to get there. Then you can write Discovery Statements about whether you completed those steps and what you learned in the process, followed by more Intention Statements, and so on. Sometimes the statements will be long and detailed. Usually they will be short, maybe just a line or two. Practice it, and the cycle can become automatic.

Don't panic when you fail to complete an intended task. Straying off course is normal. Simply make the necessary corrections. Miraculous progress may not come immediately. Do not be concerned. Stay with the cycle. Use Discovery Statements to get clear about your world and what you want out of it. Then use Intention Statements to direct your actions. When you notice progress, record it.

The following statement might strike you as radical, but it is true: It often takes the same amount of energy to get what you want in school as it takes to get what you don't want. Sometimes getting what you don't want takes even *more* effort. An airplane burns the same amount of fuel flying away from its destination as it does flying toward it, so it pays to stay on course.

You can use the Discovery and Intention Journal Entry System to stay on your own course and get what you want out of school. Consider the guidelines for Discovery Statements and Intention Statements on pages 14 and 15, then develop your own style. Once you get the hang of it, you might discover you can fly.

But i'll feel guilty!

The point!

Exercise #4
Deface this book

Some books should be preserved in pristine condition. This isn't one of them.

There are valid reasons for not writing in any book. For one thing, it decreases the resale value. However, the benefit of writing in your books far outweighs that consideration.

Becoming a Master Student *is about learning, and learning is an active pursuit, not a passive one. Something happens when you reach out and touch a book with your pen. When you make notes in the margin, you can hear yourself talking with the author. When you doodle and underline, you can see the author's ideas take shape. You can even argue with an author, or create your own ideas.*

That's the way this book works. To find out more, turn the page. (Please come back to this exercise.)

To complete this exercise, find something you agree with or disagree with on this page and write a short note in the margin. Or draw a diagram. Better yet, do both. Chapter Five Notes, contains tips to help make notes in textbooks more effective, but for this exercise, let creativity be your guide. Have fun.

Begin defacing now.

HELLO AUTHOR! SOMETIMES I DON'T AGREE!

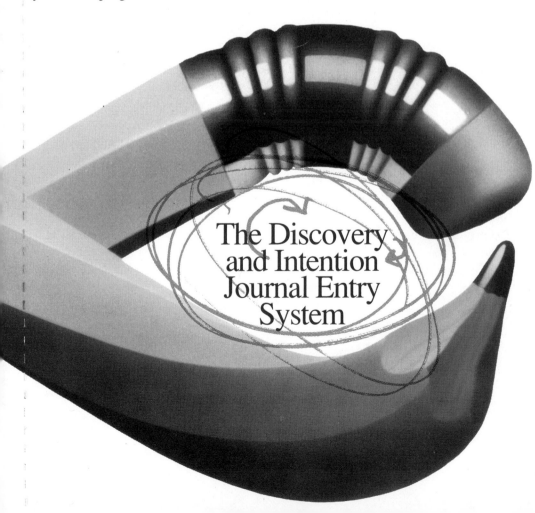

The Discovery and Intention Journal Entry System

Seven Discovery Statement guidelines

1. Discover what you want.

All of us have more energy when what we're doing leads to what we want. Many students quit school simply because they are unclear about what they want. Writing it can make it clear.

2. Record the specifics.

Observe your actions and record the facts. If you spent 90 minutes reading a spy novel instead of your anatomy text, write about it and include the details, such as when you did it, where you did it, and how it felt. Actions tell the truth about life.

3. Notice your inner voices and pictures.

We talk to ourselves constantly in our heads, and our minds manufacture pictures faster than television.

When you notice internal chatter getting in your way, write down what you are telling yourself. If this seems difficult at first, just start writing. The act of writing can trigger a flood of thoughts.

Our mental pictures are especially powerful. Picturing yourself flunking a test is like rehearsing to do just that, and resisting or ignoring negative images can make them even more powerful. One way to deflate negative images is to describe them in detail.

4. Notice physical sensations.

When you avoid a certain kind of accounting problem, note the physical symptoms—a churning stomach, perhaps, or shallow breathing or yawning. Record your observations quickly, as soon as you make them.

Also notice how you feel when you function well. If you discover your stomach churns less early in the morning, you can adjust your schedule. Use Discovery Statements about how you feel to pinpoint exactly where and when you learn most effectively.

5. Use discomfort as a signal.

When you are writing a Discovery Statement and you begin to feel uncomfortable, bored, or tired, that may be a signal that you are about to do valuable work. Stick with it. Tell yourself you can handle the discomfort just a little bit longer. You will be rewarded.

6. Suspend self-judgment.

When you are discovering yourself, be gentle. If you continually judge your behaviors as "bad" or "stupid" or "galactically imbecilic," sooner or later your mind will revolt. Rather than put up with the abuse, it will quit making discoveries. Be kind.

7. Tell the truth.

"The truth will set you free" is a cliche. It has been said so often, people say it without thinking about what it means. Practice this concept and you might find out why the phrase is so well-worn. The closer you get to the truth, the more powerful your Discovery Statements will be.

And remember, telling the truth requires courage and vigilance. Don't blame yourself when you notice you avoid the truth. Just tell the truth about it.

There's freedom in the truth.

Seven Intention Statement guidelines

1. Make your intentions positive.

Instead of writing, "I will not fall asleep while studying accounting," write, "I intend to stay awake when studying accounting."

Also, avoid the word "try." Trying is not doing. When we hedge our bets with "try" we can always tell ourselves, "Well, I *tried* to stay awake." The result is, we fool ourselves into thinking we succeeded. We also rob ourselves of the opportunity to fail. The willingness to risk failure is one mark of a master student.

2. Make intentions small and keepable.

Give yourself the opportunity to succeed. Break large goals into small, specific tasks you can accomplish quickly. The most effective Intention Statements describe action you intend to take within 24 hours. If you want to get an A in biology, ask yourself, "What can I do today?" You might choose to study biology for an extra hour. Make that your intention.

Experience success by choosing your intentions with care. Set goals you can accomplish.

3. Use observable criteria for success.

Choose goals that can be measured. Rather than writing, "I intend to work harder on my history assignments," write, "I intend to study history from 7 to 9 p.m. on Monday, Tuesday, and Thursday. I intend to spend one hour reviewing my class notes, and I intend to make summary sheets of my reading." Then, when you review your progress, you can determine more precisely whether you accomplished what you intended.

4. Set timelines.

Timelines can focus your attention, especially if used in conjunction with suggestion number two. For example, if you are assigned a term paper, break the assignment into small tasks and set a precise timeline for each one. You might write, "I intend to select a topic by 9 a.m. Wednesday." And remember, you create timelines for your own benefit, not to make yourself feel guilty.

5. Be careful of intentions that depend on others.

Your intention might depend on the actions of other people. If you write that you intend for your study group to complete the assignment by Monday, your success depends on other students. Such intentions can be powerful. They can also fail if others do not perform. Make such intentions carefully, then ask for the assistance of the people they depend on.

6. Anticipate self-sabotage.

Be aware of what you might do, consciously or unconsciously, to undermine your intentions. If you intend to study differential equations at 9 p.m., notice when you sit down to watch a two-hour television movie at 8 p.m. If associating with people who value academic success helps you reach your goals, notice who you choose to spend time with.

7. Identify your rewards.

Rewards that are an integral part of a goal are the most powerful. For example, your reward for earning a degree might be the career you want.

External rewards are valuable, too, such as a movie or an afternoon in the park. These rewards work best when you're willing to withhold them. If you intend to take a nap on Sunday afternoon whether you finish your English assignment or not, the nap is not an effective reward.

Another way to reward yourself is to sit quietly after you have finished your task and savor the feeling. Notice how your body feels when you have done a good job. One reason success breeds success is that it feels good.

How to Change a habit

When people talk about how difficult it is to change a behavior they don't like, they often resort to an explanation: "Well, that's just my nature." Often what's implied by this statement is: "And because it's my nature, don't expect me to change."

Perhaps none of us can do much about human nature, especially our individual natures. It could be that we're pretty much stuck with them. Yet the "It's just Human Nature" school of thought robs us of the opportunity to change. There's another perspective we can take—one that opens up far more possibilities for the quality of our lives.

Instead of talking about human nature, we can talk about habits. We can speak of our ability to control habits. We can change habits by eliminating unwanted ones and adding new ones. People stop smoking, drinking, and eating fattening desserts. People also start to exercise, fasten seat belts, and develop scores of other effective habits.

Thinking about ourselves as creatures of habits instead of creatures defined by our nature gives us power, because we are not faced with the monumental task of changing our very nature. Rather, we can take on the difficult yet doable job of changing our habits.

Success in school and life is largely a matter of cultivating effective habits. Ineffective habits can be changed. Following are some steps in changing a habit.

Tell the truth

If you completed the First Step exercise in this chapter, you already know about telling the truth. The Discovery Statements you write throughout this book are also examples of truth telling.

Facing the truth about any habit—from falling asleep in class to cheating on tests—frees people. Without taking that step, our efforts to change may be as ineffective as rearranging the deck chairs on the *Titanic*. Telling the truth allows us to see what's actually sinking the ship.

When we admit what's really going on in our lives, our defenses are down. We're open to help from others. The support we need to change the habit has a place to enter.

Choose one new behavior at a time

Keep in mind that the new habit you choose does not have to make headlines. It can be a simple, small change in behavior. Suppose that you usually forget people's names after meeting them for the first time. This is a habit you want to change. You can decide to apply a new habit in its place: After being introduced to someone, use that person's name once during the next minute of conversation.

Note that there are many other techniques for remembering names. You could choose any of them. Often, however, it's most effective to focus on one technique in the beginning. That can make the process of change more manageable.

Commit to use the new behavior

After choosing a new habit, promise to use it and make a plan for when and how. Answer questions such as these:

When will I apply the new habit?

Where will I be?

Who will be with me?

What will I be seeing, hearing, touching, saying, or doing?

How, exactly, will I think, speak, or act differently?

As an example, take the person who always snacks when she studies. Each time she sits down to read, she positions a bag of potato chips within easy reach. For her, opening a book is a cue to start chewing. Snacking is especially easy given the place she chooses to study: the kitchen. She chooses to change this habit by studying at a desk in her bedroom instead of the kitchen table. What's more, she plans to store the potato chips in an inconvenient place, a shelf she can't reach without standing on a chair. And every time she feels the urge to bite into a potato chip, she decides to drink from a glass of water instead.

Making a plan has a magical power—the power to transform a hazy idea into a true *intention*. With a plan, we move from, "Gee, that's a good idea; I should try it sometime" to "I will change. You can stake your life on it."

Affirm your intention

You can pave the way for a new behavior by clearing a mental path for it. To do so, see yourself carrying out your plan. Before you apply the new behavior, rehearse it in your mind. Mentally picture what actions you will take, and in what order.

Say that you plan to improve your handwriting when taking notes. Imagine yourself in class with a blank notebook poised before you. See yourself taking up a finely crafted pen. Notice how comfortable it feels in your hand. See yourself writing clearly and legibly. You can even picture how you will make individual letters—the e's, i's, and r's. Then, after class is over, see yourself reviewing your notes and taking pleasure in how easy they are to read.

Such scenes are more vivid if you include all your senses. Round out your mental picture by adding sounds, textures, and colors.

You can also speak about yourself in a way that supports change. People who are frustrated with their memory skills, for example, often refer to themselves negatively: "I'd forget my head if it weren't screwed on." Instead, they could say, "I haven't forgotten that fact. I just don't recall it right now. Wait a few minutes and it'll come back to me."

In short, you can act as if your intention is already a reality, as if the new habit is already a part of you. *Be the change you want to see*—today. In some cases, this may be enough to change the old habit completely.

Get feedback and support

This is a crucial step and a place where many plans for change break down. It's easy to practice your new behavior with great enthusiasm for a few days. After the initial rush of excitement, however, things can get a little tougher. We begin to find excuses for slipping back into an old habit: "One more cigarette won't hurt." "I can get back to my diet tomorrow." "It's been a tough day. I deserve this martini."

One way to get feedback is to bring other people into the picture. Ask others to remind you when you are changing your habit. If you want to *stop* an old behavior, such as cramming for tests, then it often works to tell everyone you know that you intend to stop. When you want to *start* a new behavior, though, consider telling only a few people—those who will truly support your efforts. Starting new habits may call for the more focused, long-lasting support that close friends or family members can give.

Support from others can be as simple as a quick phone call: "Hi. Have you started that outline for your research paper yet?" Or it can be as formal as a support group that meets once weekly to review everyone's goals and action plans.

You are probably the most effective source for your own support and feedback. You know yourself better than anyone else and can design a system to monitor your behavior. You can create your own charts or diagrams to track your behavior or you can write about your progress in your journal. Figure out a way to monitor your progress.

Practice, practice, practice...without reproach

Act on your intention. If you fail or forget, let go of any self-judgment. Just keep practicing the new habit and allow whatever time it takes to make a change.

Accept the feelings of discomfort that may come with a new habit. Keep practicing the new behavior, even if feels unnatural. Trust the process. You will grow into the new behavior. Keep practicing until it becomes as natural as breathing. However, if this new habit doesn't work, simply note what happened (without guilt or blame), select a new behavior, and begin this cycle of steps again.

Going back to square one doesn't mean you've failed. Even when you don't get the results you want from a new behavior, you learn something valuable in the process. Once you know how to change one habit, you know how to change *any* habit.

**Journal Entry #4
Intention Statement**

Choose one behavior you want to change. Review the article "How to change a habit." Then select one or two suggestions and declare how you will use them to change your behavior.

I intend to . . .

_____

_____

_____

_____

IS FOR
FEEDBACK,
NOT FAILURE
From The Search for
Solutions *by Horace
Freeland Judson
Copyright 1980 by
Playback Associates.
Reprinted by permission
of Holt, Rinehart and
Winston, Publishers.*

Feedback is one of the fundamental facts of life and ideas of science, yet only in the last fifty years have we recognized its all-pervasive presence. The idea is simple: A feedback mechanism registers the actual state of a system, compares it to the desired state, then uses the comparison to correct the state of the system. Feedback is goal-oriented, definite. A feedback process tells living cells when to manufacture proteins and when to stop. Sometimes the goal is something as dynamic as an equilibrium. An explosion of the rabbit population is followed by a growth in the lynx population is followed by a collapse of the rabbit population is followed by a collapse of the lynx population—a feedback loop that maintains the balance of nature. In modern technology, feedback is the essence of automation. It runs lathes, lands airplanes, steers rockets. The economy is a huge, slow-moving, multiple feedback system. So is democracy. Fast or slow, movement is the essence of feedback. It implies purpose and progress. Like a walker on a high wire, it continually achieves and re-achieves balance in order to achieve something beyond balance. It can never rest.

Motivation
or "I'm just not in the mood"

The terms self-discipline, willpower, and motivation are often used to describe something missing in ourselves. Often we invoke these words to explain another's success. "If I were more motivated, I'd get more involved in school." "Of course she got an A. She has self-discipline." "If I had more willpower, I'd lose weight."

However, we can stop looking outside ourselves for these mysterious qualities. We can say that we're already motivated and disciplined, lacking only certain skills that come from practice. Perhaps what we call "motivation" is just a habit. The advantage of this view is that you don't have to reform yourself overnight. All that's needed is to practice a new habit. The following suggestions offer ways to develop the habit of motivation.

Promise it
Motivation can come simply from being clear about our goals and acting on them.

Say that you want to start a study group. Then commit yourself to inviting people and setting a time and place to meet. Promise your classmates that you'll do this, and ask them to hold you accountable. Self-discipline, willpower, motivation—none of those mysterious characteristics need to get in your way. Just make a promise and keep your word.

Befriend your discomfort
Sometimes keeping your word means doing a task you'd rather put off. The mere thought of doing laundry, reading a chapter in a statistics book, or proofreading a paper can lead to discomfort. In the face of such discomfort, we can procrastinate. Or, we can use this barrier as a means to get the task done.

Begin by investigating the discomfort. Notice the thoughts running through your head and speak them out loud: "I'd rather walk on a bed of coals than do this." "This is the last thing I want to do right now."

Also observe what's happening with your body. For example, are you breathing faster or slower than usual? Is your breathing shallow or deep? Are your shoulders tight? Do you feel any tension in your stomach?

Once you're in contact with your mind and body, stay with the discomfort a few minutes. Don't judge it as good or bad. Accepting the thoughts and body sensations robs them of their power. They may still be present, but in time they will stop being a barrier for you.

Discomfort can be a gift—an opportunity to do valuable work on yourself. On the other side of discomfort lies mastery.

Change your mind—and your body
You can also get past discomfort by planting new thoughts in your mind or changing your physical stance. For example, instead of slumping in a chair, sit up straight. Or, stand up. You can also get physically active by taking a short walk. Notice what happens to your discomfort.

Every feeling registers in the body in some way. For example, when we're happy, we're likely to smile. The reverse might also be true: When we smile, we're likely to feel happy.

Experiment with this idea. If you're about to meet with someone you can't stand, then walk up to that person and shake her hand vigorously. If you feel like dozing off instead of reading, then open the book and flip through the pages as if you're excited to get started. These very motions might change your attitude toward the task at hand.

Work with thoughts, too. Replace "I can't stand this" with "I'll feel great when this is done," or, "Doing this will help me get something I want."

Sweeten the task

Sometimes it's just one aspect of a task that holds us back. That means we could stop procrastinating by merely changing that aspect. If distaste for your physical environment keeps you from studying, then change the environment. Reading about social psychology might seem like a yawner when you're alone in a dark corner of the house. Moving to a cheery, well-lit library could sweeten the task. So could sandwiching the task between things you enjoy. For example, brainstorm topics for a research paper after seeing friends and before you go to a movie.

Talk about how bad it is

One way to get past negative attitudes is to take them to an extreme. When faced with an unpleasant task, launch into a no-holds-barred gripe session. Pull out all the stops. "There's no way I can start my income taxes now. This is a catastrophy of global proportions, an absolute disaster. This is terrible beyond words...."

Griping taken this far can introduce its own perspective. It shoes how self talk can transform mere inconveniences into crises.

Turn up the pressure

Sometimes motivation is a luxury. For example, pretend that the due date for your project has been moved up one month. Raising the stress level slightly can move you into action. Then the question of motivation seems beside the point, and meeting the due date moves to the forefront.

Adopt a model

One strategy for succeeding at any task is to hang around the masters. Find someone you consider successful and spend time with her. Observe this person and use her as a model for your own behavior. You can "try on" this person's actions and attitudes, looking for tools that feel right for you.

Compare the payoffs to the costs

Cramming for tests, eating poorly, forgetting to exercise—each of these behaviors has a payoff. Cramming might give people more time that's free of commitments. Neglecting exercise can give people more time to sleep.

One way to let go of such behaviors is to first celebrate them—even embrace them. We can openly acknowledge their payoffs.

This can be especially powerful when we follow it up with the next step—determining the costs. For example, skipping a reading assignment gives you time to go to the movies. However, you won't be prepared for your class and you'll have twice as much to read next week.

Maybe there is another way to get the payoff (going to the movies) without paying the cost (skipping the reading assignment). You might choose to give up a few hours of television and read instead.

Comparing the costs and benefits of any behavior can fuel our "motivation." We can choose new behaviors because they align with what we want most.

Do it later

At times, it's effective to save a task for later. For example, writing a resume can wait until you've taken the time to analyze your job skills and write career goals. This is not a lack of motivation—it's planning.

When you do choose to "do it later," turn this decision into a promise. Estimate how long the task will take and schedule a specific date and time for it in your calendar.

Let it go

Sometimes "not being motivated"—not feeling like it—carries a message that's worth heeding. An example is the student who majors in accounting but seizes every chance to be with young children. His chronic reluctance to read accounting textbooks may not be a problem. Instead, it may reveal his desire to major in elementary education. His original career choice might have come from the belief that "real men don't teach kindergarten." In this case, "lack of motivation" signals a deeper wisdom trying to get through.

The art of re-entry—
Going back to school as an older student

If you're returning to school after a long break from the classroom, there's no reason to feel out of place. Returning adults and other nontraditional students are already a majority in some schools.

Being an older student puts you on strong footing. With a rich store of life experience, you've got a sound basis for choosing your educational goals. Based on that experience, you can ask questions and make connections between course work and daily life. Many instructors will especially enjoy working with you.

You can succeed at re-entering the classroom. Following are some suggestions:

Plan your week
Many older students report that their number one problem is time. One solution is to plan your week. By planning a week at a time instead of just one day, you get a bigger picture of your roles as student, employee, and family member. Sort out high-priority tasks from lower priorities. Schedule specific times for the important items.

For many more suggestions on managing time, see Chapter Two.

Get to know younger students
You share a central concern with younger students: succeeding in school. It's easier to get past the "generation gap" when you remember this. So consider pooling resources with younger students. Share notes, form study groups, swap job-hunting tips, or edit each other's term papers.

Get to know other returning students
Introduce yourself to other older students. Being in the same classroom gives you an immediate bond. You can exchange work and home phone numbers with these people. Build a network of mutual support. Some students even adopt a "buddy system," pairing up with another student in each class to complete assignments and prepare for tests.

Find common ground with instructors
Many of the people who teach your classes may be juggling academics, work, and family lives, too. That gives you one more way to break the ice with instructors after class or during office hours. It's during these conversations that some of your most powerful learning may take place.

Enlist your employer's support
Employers often promote continuing education. Further education can increase your skills in either a specific subject or in working with people. That makes you a more valuable employee or consultant.

Let your employer in on the plan. Point out how the skills you gain in class will help you meet work objectives. Or offer informal "seminars" to share what you're learning in school.

Get extra mileage out of your current tasks
You can look for specific ways to merge your work and school lives. Some schools will offer academic credit for work and life experience. Likewise, your company may reimburse employees for some tuition costs or even grant time off to attend classes.

Experiment with combining tasks. For example, when you're assigned a research paper, choose a topic that relates to your current job tasks. And if you take training programs or professional seminars through work, choose topics that will reinforce your course work.

Look for child care

For some students, returning to class means looking for child care outside the home. Many schools offer child care at school for reduced rates for students. Even schools that don't offer this service may provide you with a list of child care providers close to school.

Review your subjects before you start classes

Say that you're registered for trigonometry and you haven't taken a math class since high school. Then consider brushing up on the subject before classes begin. Also talk to future instructors about ways to prepare for their classes.

Prepare for an academic environment

If you're used to an efficient corporate setting, school life may present some frustrations. A lack of advanced computer systems may slow down your class registration. Faculty members may take a little longer to return your calls or respond to letters, especially during holiday and summer breaks. Knowing the rhythm of academic life can help you plan around these events.

Be willing to let go of old images about how to study

Many older students find it effective to view their school assignments exactly as they would view a project at work. They use the same tactics in the library as on the job, which often helps them learn more actively. Also consider using modern tools, such as computers, to complete study tasks. These include word processing for writing papers and databases for doing research.

"Publish" your schedule

After you plan your study and class sessions for the week, post your schedule in a place where others will see it. You can treat this as a game. Make your schedule look like an "official" document. Designate open slots in your schedule where others can sign up for "appointments" to see you. Encourage the people you live with to do this, also

Share your educational plans

The fact that you're in school will affect the key relationships in your life. Committing to classes and studying may prompt feelings of guilt about taking time away from others. You can prevent problems by discussing these issues ahead of time.

Another strategy is to actively involve your spouse, partner, or close friends in your schooling. Offer to give them a tour of school and introduce them to your instructors. Attend plays and concerts together. Your school may also sponsor activities where family members are specifically invited.

Take this a step further and ask the key people in your life for help. Ask them to think of ways they can support your success in school and commit to those actions. Make education a joint mission that benefits you all.

Journal Entry #5
Intention Statement

Review Exercise #1: Textbook reconnaissance. Consider the articles in this book that you thought might be valuable. Choose the one from which you think you can get the most immediate, practical benefit, and scan that article until you come to a specific technique you can use. Write an Intention Statement in this space concerning how you will use that technique within the next week. Include when you intend to use it.

For example, if you listed the article called "When reading is tough", you could use any of the techniques suggested for difficult reading assignments. If you have a tough computer science course, you might choose to form a support group to discuss reading assignments. In that case, you might write, "I intend to contact four other students after class tomorrow about forming a group to study computer science."

The study technique I choose is . . .

The time(s) I intend to use it is (are) . . .

Exercise #5
The Discovery Wheel

The Discovery Wheel is an opportunity to tell the truth to yourself about the kind of student you are and what kind of student you want to become. This is not a test. There are no trick questions, and the answers will have meaning only for you.

Here are two suggestions to make this exercise more effective:

First, think of it as the beginning of an opportunity to change. There is another Discovery Wheel at the end of this book. You will have a chance to measure your progress, so be honest about where you are now.

Second, lighten up. A little laughter can make self-evaluations a lot more effective.

Here's how the Discovery Wheel works. By the end of this exercise, you will have filled in a circle similar to the one on this page. This circle is a picture of how you see yourself as a student. The closer the shading comes to the edge of the circle, the higher the evaluation. In the example, the student has rated her reading skills low and her note-taking skills high.

It is dangerous, however, to think of these evaluations in terms of "higher" and "lower" if those designations reflect a negative judgment. The Discovery Wheel is not a picture of who you are. It is a picture of how you view your abilities as a student today.

To begin this exercise, read the statements on pages 23-25 and award yourself points for each one using the guidelines below. Then add up your point total for each section and shade the Discovery Wheel on page 26 to the appropriate level.

5 points - This statement is always or almost always true of me.

4 points - This statement is often true of me.

3 points - This statement is sometimes true of me (about half the time).

2 points - This statement is seldom true of me.

1 point - This statement is never or almost never true of me.

1. _____ I start each school term highly motivated, and I stay that way.

2. _____ I know what I want to get from my education.

3. _____ I enjoy learning.

4. _____ I study even when distracted by activities of lower priority.

5. _____ I am satisfied about how I progress toward achieving goals.

6. _____ Studying is important and I allow adequate time for it.

7. _____ I am excited about the courses I take.

8. _____ I have a clear idea of the benefits I expect to get from my education.

_____ Total score (1) Motivation

1. _____ I periodically refine my long-term goals.

2. _____ I regularly define short-term goals.

3. _____ I write a plan for each day and each week.

4. _____ I assign priorities to what I choose to do each day.

5._____ I plan review time so I don't have to cram before tests.

6. _____ I plan regular recreation time.

7. _____ I adjust my study time to meet the demands of individual courses.

8. _____ I have adequate time each day to accomplish what I plan.

_____ Total score (2) Planning

1. _____ I am confident in my ability to remember.

2. _____ I remember people's names.

3. _____ At the end of a lecture, I can summarize what was presented.

4. _____ I apply techniques that enhance my memory skills.

5. _____ I can recall information when I'm under pressure.

6. _____ I remember important information clearly and easily.

7. _____ I can jog my memory when I have difficulty recalling.

8. _____ I can relate new information to what I've already learned.

_____ Total score (3) Memory

1. _____ I preview and review reading assignments.

2. _____ When reading, I underline or highlight important passages.

3. _____ When I read, I ask questions about the material.

4. _____ When I read textbooks, I am alert and awake.

5. _____ I relate what I read to my life.

6. _____ I select a reading strategy to fit the type of material I'm reading.

7. _____ I take effective notes when I read.

8. _____ When I don't understand what I'm reading, I note my questions and find answers.

_____ Total score (4) Reading

5 points

This statement is always or almost always true of me.

4 points

This statement is often true of me.

3 points

This statement is sometimes true of me (about half the time).

2 points

This statement is seldom true of me.

1 point

This statement is never or almost never true of me.

1. _____ When I am in class, I focus my attention.

2. _____ I take notes in class.

3. _____ I am aware of various methods for taking notes and choose those that work best for me.

4. _____ My notes are valuable for review.

5. _____ I review class notes within 24 hours.

6. _____ I distinguish important material and notice key phrases in a lecture.

7. _____ I copy material the instructor writes on the board or overhead projector.

8. _____ I can put important concepts into my own words.

_____ Total score (5) Note taking

1. _____ I feel confident and calm during an exam.

2. _____ I manage my time during exams and I am able to complete them.

3. _____ I am able to predict test questions.

4. _____ I can examine essay questions in light of what I know and come to a new and original conclusion during a test.

5. _____ I adapt my test-taking strategy to the kind of test I'm taking.

6. _____ I understand what essay questions ask and can answer them completely and accurately.

7. _____ I start reviewing for tests at the beginning of the term and review regularly.

8. _____ My sense of personal worth is independent of my test scores.

_____ Total score (6) Test taking

1. _____ I have flashes of insight, and solutions to problems appear to me at unusual times.

2. _____ I plan writing assigments, create first drafts, and revise them to get clear final drafts.

3. _____ When I get stuck on a creative project, I use specific methods to get unstuck.

4. _____ I know how to prepare and deliver effective speeches.

5. _____ I use brainstorming to generate solutions to a variety of problems.

6. _____ I am confident when I speak before others.

7. _____ I see problems as opportunities for learning and personal growth.

8. _____ I am willing to consider different points of view and alternative solutions.

_____ Total score (7) Creativity

1. _____ I develop and maintain mutually supportive relationships.

2. _____ I am candid with others about who I am, what I feel, and what I want.

3. _____ Other people tell me that I am a good listener.

4. _____ I communicate my upset and anger without blaming others.

5. _____ I am aware of my cultural biases and open to understanding people with different backgrounds.

6. _____ I am able to learn from various instructors with different teaching styles.

7. _____ I have the ability to make friends and create valuable relationships in a new place.

8. _____ I am open to being with people I don't especially like in order to learn from them.

_____ Total score (8) Relationships

1. _____ I have enough energy to study and still fully enjoy other areas of my life.

2. _____ I exercise regularly.

3. _____ My emotional health supports my ability to learn.

4. _____ If the situation calls for it, I have enough reserve energy to put in a long day.

5. _____ I accept my body the way it is.

6. _____ I notice changes in my physical condition and respond effectively.

7. _____ I am in control of the alcohol and drugs I put into my body.

8. _____ The food I eat contributes to my health.

_____ Total score (9) Health

1. _____ I budget my money and I am in control of my personal finances.

2. _____ I am confident that I will have enough money to complete the education I want.

3. _____ I have a clear picture of the financial resources available to me to pay for my education.

4. _____ I can make a little money go a long way.

5. _____ My education supports my long-range financial goals.

6. _____ I repay my debts on time.

7. _____ My sense of personal worth is independent of my financial condition.

8. _____ I make regular deposits to my savings account.

_____ Total score (10) Money

Exercise #6
Maybe it's your breath

The way you breathe affects the way you think, and the way you think affects the way you breathe. A good supply of oxygen to the brain is essential for focused concentration. Next time you find your mind wandering, take a short break and do the following exercise. Read all the directions, then take a moment to practice this technique.

1. Sit up in your chair in a relaxed position, head straight and hands uncrossed in your lap.

2. Close your eyes and take twenty or thirty seconds to relax. Let go of any tension in your face, neck, and shoulders.

3. Inhale, breathing deeply into your abdomen. Your stomach will expand when you breathe deeply.

4. When you have filled your lungs with air, pause; purse your lips as if you were about to whistle; then exhale evenly and forcefully through the small hole between your lips.

5. At the end of your exhalation, pause, then push out the last bit if remaining air in three short, forceful puffs.

6. Repeat this process three to five times.

7. When finished, sit quietly for a minute, observing the rise and fall of your abdomen as you breathe normally.

1. _____ I can effectively use libraries to find the resources and information I want.

2. _____ I am aware of the services offered by my school and know how to use them.

3. _____ I use my job or other activities outside of school as learning experiences.

4. _____ I take on projects that can make a difference in other people's lives.

5. _____ I know where to get help in my community for a variety of problems.

6. _____ My relationships with friends, family, and others support my educational goals.

7. _____ I think of my mistakes as valuable opportunities to learn.

8. _____ I see the world's problems as opportunities for me to participate and contribute.

_____ Total score (11) Resources

1. _____ I see learning as a lifelong process.

2. _____ I relate school to what I plan to do for the rest of my life.

3. _____ I learn by contributing to others.

4. _____ I revise my plans as I learn, change, and grow.

5. _____ I am clear about my purpose in life.

6. _____ I know that I am responsible for my own education.

7. _____ I take responsibility for the quality of my life.

8. _____ I am willing to accept challenges even when I'm not sure how to meet them.

_____ Total score (12) Purpose

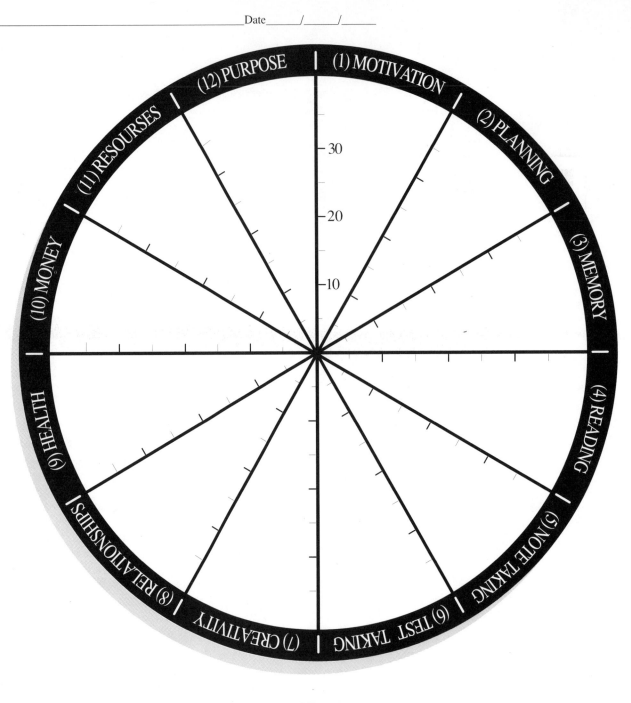

Filling in your Discovery Wheel

Using the total score from each category, shade in each section of the Discovery Wheel. Use different colors if you want. For example, you could use green to denote areas you want to work on. When you have completed the wheel, move on to Journal Entry #6 on the opposite page.

Journal Entry #6
Discovery Statement

Now that you have completed your Discovery Wheel, spend a few minutes with it. Get a sense of its weight, shape, and balance. How would it feel if you ran your hands around it? How would it sound if it rolled down a hill? How would it look? Would it roll at all? Is it balanced? Make your observations without judging the wheel "good" or "bad." Simply be with the picture you have created.

After you have spent a few minutes studying your Discovery Wheel, complete the following sentences. Don't worry if you can't think of something to write. Just write whatever comes to mind. Remember, this is not a test.

This wheel is an accurate picture of my ability as a student because . . .

My self-evaluation surprises me because . . .

The two areas in which I am strongest are related because . . .

The areas in which I want to improve are . . .

I want to concentrate on improving these areas because . . .

Journal Entry #7
Intention Statement

In the space below, select one of your discoveries from Journal Entry #6 and plan how you intend to benefit from it.

To gain some practical benefit from this discovery, I will. . .

Stay tuned to these networks

School can be a frightening place for new students. Minorities, older students, commuters, and people with disabilities can feel excluded. Some people attend classes for years and still feel like they're standing on the outside, looking in.

You don't have to be a stranger to school life. Networking is one way to break through the barriers that keep students isolated.

Webster defines "networking" as "the making of social contacts and the trading of information." The term most often is applied to business, but education can be a social enterprise, too. In fact, it works better that way. Students who overcome feelings of isolation increase their chances of staying in school and succeeding. Networks also prepare students for the work world, where most projects involve teamwork. You can begin networking immediately. Here are some techniques you can use.

1. Introduce yourself to classmates. Get to class early and break the ice by discussing the previous assignment, or stay late and talk about the lecture.

2. Plan to meet people. Write an Intention Statement promising to meet three new people each week. Plan who these people will be and how and when you intend to meet them.

3. See your instructor. If you feel lost in a class, make an appointment to see your instructor outside of class. You might discover a human being who wants you to succeed.

4. Form a study group. Peer pressure can be positive. Study with students who excel, and also look for partners from different racial, ethnic, religious, or socioeconomic backgrounds. Diversity will add depth to your group and stimulate everyone's thinking. (For more ideas, see "Study with people" on page 168.)

5. Join a support group. People with common problems can share solutions. Many schools have support groups for everything from dealing with prejudice to overcoming addictions to even learning computer software.

6. Join a club. Your membership in the Spanish club can support your success in Spanish class. A computer users group, a chess club, a Bible study group, or an Islamic student association can put you in touch with potential friends.

7. Join a professional society. Many professional societies have student chapters. Examples include the International Association of Business Communicators, Sigma Delta Chi (for journalists), and the American Society for Training and Development. You can meet people and get career guidance, too.

8. Perform! Try out for a play or join a band. This can be a good way for non-

traditional students to get involved in school activities. Members of the Bagpipe Club will be so glad to see a fellow piper, they won't care how old you are.

9. Join a political organization. Both major political parties and many minor ones have student organizations. And like the Bagpipe Club, they will be eager to have you participate.

10. Play ball! You don't have to be a world-class athlete to play sports. As a matter of fact, keeping fit is one of the marks of a master student. Most schools have intramural leagues. Many have clubs for runners, bicyclists, hikers, rock climbers, wheelchair basketball players, and other athletes. Instruction is often available, too.

11. Find a mentor. A mentor is an advisor or coach. She can be anyone you trust—another student, a graduate student, a teacher, or a person in the community. Mentors can coach you in study skills, career skills, etc. They also can teach by example, which is one of the most powerful and persuasive ways to teach. Be clear about your reasons for choosing a mentor. Avoid selecting someone just because that person is like you in age, race, or social class. Choose someone who can make a difference in your life.

12. Use school media. School newspapers can alert you to interesting activities and people. Radio stations and bulletin boards can be a source of information about clubs, support groups, political organizations, and social activities. Also, check the school catalog and directory.

13. Hang out at the student union. The student union or activities center often is a hub for social activities, special programs, and free entertainment. Clubs and organizations often meet there, too.

14. Study at the library. It's quiet, it's comfortable, and it's a good place to meet other serious students.

15. Use student services. These include career planning and placement centers, counseling services, financial aid offices, student health services, and student advocates. Many of these services are free to students. Going to school puts you in contact with an extraordinary network of services. All that remains is for you to use them.

Ideas are tools

THERE ARE MANY IDEAS in this book. Don't believe any of them. Instead, think of them as tools. For example, you use a hammer for a purpose—to drive a nail. When you use a new hammer you might notice its shape, its weight, and its balance. You don't try to figure whether the hammer is "right." You use it. If it works, you use it again. If it doesn't work, you get a different hammer.

This is not the attitude most people adopt when they encounter new ideas. The first thing most people do with new ideas is measure them against old ones. If a new idea conflicts with an old one, the new one is likely to be rejected.

People have plenty of room in their lives for different kinds of hammers, but they tend to limit their capacity for different kinds of ideas. A new idea, at some level, is a threat to their very being—unlike a new hammer, which is simply a new hammer.

This is natural. All of us have a built-in desire to be right. Our ideas, we think, represent ourselves. And when we identify with our ideas they assume new importance in our lives. We put them on our mantles. We hang them on our walls. We wear them on our T-shirts and display them on our bumpers. We join associations of people who share our most beloved ideas. We make up rituals about them, compose songs about them, and write stories about them. We declare ourselves dedicated to these ideas. Sometimes, we are even willing to die for them.

Some ideas are worth dying for. But, please note: This book does not contain any of those ideas. The ideas on these pages are strictly "hammers."

Imagine someone defending a hammer. Picture this person holding up a hammer and declaring: "I hold this hammer to be self-evident. Give me this hammer or give me death. Those other hammers are evil. There are only two kinds of people in this world: people who believe in this hammer and infidels."

That picture is ridiculous, but it makes a point. This book is not a manifesto. It's a tool box. If you read about a tool that doesn't sound "right" or one that sounds a little goofy, remember that the ideas here are for using, not believing. Suspend your judgment. Test the idea for yourself. If it works, use it.

If it doesn't, don't.

A word of caution: Any tool—whether it's a hammer, a wrench, or a study technique—is designed to do a specific job. A master mechanic carries a variety of tools because no single tool works for all jobs. If you throw a tool away because it doesn't work in one situation, you won't be able to pull it out later, when it's just what you need.

If an idea doesn't work for you, and if you are satisfied you gave it a fair chance, file it away. It might come in handy sooner than you think.

And remember, this book is not about being right. Even the "Ideas are tools" idea is not "right." It's a hammer...(or maybe a roto punch.)

The master student

In 1482, Leonardo da Vinci wrote a letter to a wealthy baron, applying for work. In excerpted form, he said, "I can contrive various and endless means of offense and defense . . . I have all sorts of extremely light and strong bridges adapted to be most easily carried . . . I have methods for destroying every turret or other fortress . . . I will make covered chariots, safe and unassailable . . . In case of need I will make big guns, mortars, and light ordnance of fine and useful forms out of the common type. . ." And then, he added, almost as an afterthought, "In times of peace I believe I can give perfect satisfaction and to the equal of any other in architecture . . . I can carry out sculpture . . . and also I can do in painting whatever may be done." The Mona Lisa, for example.

This book is about something that cannot be taught. It's about becoming a master student.

A master is a person who has attained a level of skill that goes beyond technique. For a master, methods and procedures are automatic responses to the needs of the task. Work is effortless; struggle evaporates. The master carpenter is so familiar with her tools they are part of her. To a master chef, utensils are old friends. Because these masters don't have to think about the details of the process, they bring more of themselves to their work.

Mastery can lead to flashy results—an incredible painting, for example, or a gem of a short story. In basketball, mastery might result in an unbelievable shot at the buzzer. For a musician, it might be the performance of performances, the night when everything comes together.

More often, the result of mastery is a sense of profound satisfaction, well-being, and timelessness. Work seems self-propelled. The master is in control by being out of control. She lets go and allows the creative process to work. That's why after a spectacular performance, it is often said of an athlete or a performer, "She was playing out of her mind."

Likewise, the master student is one who "learns out of her mind." Of course, that statement makes no sense. Mastery, in fact, doesn't make sense. It cannot be captured with words. It defies analysis. Mastery cannot be taught, only learned and experienced.

Examine the following list of characteristics of master students in light of your own experience. The list is not complete. It merely points in a direction. No one can teach us to be master students because we already are master students. We are natural learners by design. As students, we can discover that every day.

As you read, look for yourself.

A master student is:

Inquisitive

The master student is curious about everything. By posing questions she can generate interest and aliveness in the most mundane, humdrum situations. When she is bored during a biology lecture, she thinks to herself: "I always get bored when I listen to this instructor. Why is that? Maybe it's because he reminds me of my boring Uncle Ralph who always told those endless fishing stories. He even looks like Uncle Ralph. Amazing! Boredom is certainly interesting." Then she asks, "What can I do to get value out of this lecture, even though it seems boring?" And she finds an answer.

Able to focus attention

Watch a two-year-old at play. Pay attention to the eyes. That wide-eyed look reveals an energy and a capacity for amazement that keeps his attention absolutely focused in the here and now. The master student's focused attention has that child-like quality. The world, to the child, is always new. Because the master student can focus attention, to him the world is always new.

Willing to change

The unknown does not frighten the master student. In fact, she welcomes it— even the unknown in herself. We all have pictures of who we think we are, and these pictures can be useful. They also can prevent learning and growth. The master student is open to changes in her environment and changes in herself.

Able to organize and sort

The master student can take a large body of information and sift through it to discover relationships. He can play with information, organizing pieces of data by size, color, order, weight, and a hundred other categories.

Competent

Mastery of skills is important to the master student. When she learns mathematical formulas, she studies them until they become second nature. She practices until she knows them cold, then practices an extra few minutes. She also is able to apply what she learns to new and different situations.

Joyful

More often than not, the master student is seen with a smile on his face—sometimes a smile at nothing in particular other than amazement at the world and his experience of it.

Able to suspend judgment

The master student has opinions and positions, and she is able to let go of them when appropriate. She realizes she is more than her thoughts. She can quiet her internal dialogue and listen to an opposing viewpoint. She doesn't let judgment get in the way of learning. Rather than approaching discussions with the attitude, "Prove it to me and then I'll believe it," she asks, "What if this were true?" and explores possibilities.

Energetic

Notice the student with a spring in his step, the one who is enthusiastic and involved in class. When he reads, he often sits on the very edge of his chair, and he plays with the same intensity. He is a master student.

Well

Health is important to the master student, though not necessarily in the sense of being free of illness. Rather, she values her body and treats it with respect. She tends to her emotional and spiritual health, as well as to her physical health.

Self-aware

The master student is willing to evaluate himself and his behavior. He regularly examines his life.

Responsible

There is a difference between responsibility and blame, and the master student knows it well. She is willing to take responsibility for everything in her life— even for events that most people would

MASLOW'S *QUALITIES OF A SELF-ACTUALIZING PERSON*

Abraham Maslow was a psychologist who worked on a theory of psychological health rather than sickness. Maslow studied people whom he called "self-actualizing," which means, in part, healthy and creative. He listed traits he found in self-actualizing people (ranging from Abraham Lincoln to Albert Einstein). These characteristics also describe the master student.

THE SELF-ACTUALIZING PERSON:

- Reality oriented
- Accepting of herself and others
- Spontaneous
- Problem-centered rather than self-centered
- Detached and needing privacy
- Independent
- Fresh, rather than stereotyped, appreciation of people
- Had a mystical or spiritual experience
- Identify with the human race as a whole
- Has a few deep, intimate relationships
- Democratic values
- A philosophical rather than bitter sense of humor
- Creative resources
- Resistant to conformity
- Transcendent of his environment.

"blame" on others. For example, if she is served cold eggs in the cafeteria, the master student chooses to take responsibility for getting cold eggs. This is not the same as blaming herself for cold eggs. Rather, she looks for ways to change the situation and get what she wants. She could choose to eat breakfast earlier, or she might tell someone in the kitchen that the eggs are cold and request a change. The cold eggs might continue. Even then, the master student takes responsibility and gives herself the power to choose her response to the situation.

Willing to risk

The master student often takes on projects with no guarantee of success. He is willing to participate in class dialogues at the risk of looking foolish. He is willing to tackle difficult subjects in term papers. He welcomes the risk of a challenging course.

Willing to participate

Don't look for the master student on the sidelines. She's in the game. She is a player who can be counted on. She is willing to make a commitment, and she can follow through.

A generalist

The master student is interested in everything around him. He has a broad base of knowledge in many fields and can find value in them that is applicable to his specialties.

Willing to accept paradox

The word "paradox" comes from two Greek words, *para* (beyond) and *doxon* (opinion). Thus, a paradox is something which is beyond opinion or, more accurately, something that may seem contradictory or absurd yet may actually have meaning. For example, the master student can be totally committed to managing money and reaching her financial goals. At the same time, she can be totally detached from money, realizing that her real worth is independent of how much money she has. The master student recognizes the limitations of the mind and is at home with paradox. She can accept that ambiguity.

Courageous

The master student admits his fear and fully experiences it when appropriate. For example, he approaches tough exams as an opportunity to explore feelings of anxiety and tension related to the pressure to perform. He does not deny fear—he embraces it.

Self-directed

Rewards or punishment provided by others do not motivate the master student. Her motivation to learn comes from within.

Spontaneous

The master student is truly in the here and now. He is able to respond to the moment in fresh, surprising, and unplanned ways.

Relaxed about grades

Grades make the master student neither depressed nor euphoric. She recognizes that sometimes grades are important, and grades are not the reason she studies. She does not measure her value as a human being by the grades she receives.

Intuitive

The master student has a sense that is beyond logic. He has learned to trust his feelings, and he works to develop that sense.

Creative

Where others see dullness and trivia, the master student sees opportunities to create. She can gather pieces of knowledge from a wide range of subjects and put them together in a new way. The master student is creative in every aspect of her life.

Willing to be uncomfortable

The master student does not place comfort first. When discomfort is necessary to reach a goal, he is willing to experience it. He can endure personal discomfort and can look at unpleasant things with detachment.

Accepting

The master student accepts herself, the people around her, and the challenges that life offers.

Willing to laugh

The master student might laugh at any moment, and her sense of humor includes the ability to laugh at herself.

Hungry

Human beings begin life with a natural appetite for knowledge. In some people it soon gets dulled. The master student has tapped that hunger, and it gives him a desire to learn for the sake of learning.

Willing to work

Once inspired, the master student is willing to follow through with sweat. Genius and creativity, she recognizes, are mostly the result of persistence and work. When she is in high gear, the master student works with the intensity of a child at play.

The master student in you

The master student is in all of us. By design, human beings are learning machines. We have an innate ability to learn, and all of us have room to grow and improve.

It also is important to note the distinction between "learning" and "being taught." Human beings can resist being taught anything. Carl Rogers goes so far as to say that anything that can be "taught" to a human being is either inconsequential or just plain harmful. What is important in education, Rogers asserts, is learning. And everyone has the ability to do that.

Unfortunately, people also learn to hide that ability. As they experience the pain sometimes associated with learning, they shut down. If a child experiences feeling foolish in front of a group of people, he could learn to avoid those situations. In doing so, the child restricts his possibilities.

Some children "learn" that they are slow learners. If they learn it well enough, their behavior comes to match that label.

As people grow older, they accumulate a growing list of ideas to defend, a fat catalog of experiences that tell them not to risk learning.

Still, the master student within survives. To tap that resource you don't need to acquire anything. You already have everything you need. Every day, you can rediscover the natural learner within you.

 **Journal entry #8**
Discovery Statement

After reading "The master student," consider your own strengths and list the qualities of a master student that you observe in yourself.

This is no easy task. Most of us are competent self-critics, but we tend to discount our strong points. If you get stuck trying to complete this Journal Entry, warm up by brainstorming all your good points on a separate sheet of paper. Remember to consider experiences both in and out of school.

The master student qualities I observe in myself include . . .

In the space below, write a specific example of how you model one of these qualities.

Benjamin Franklin,

printer, author, philanthropist, inventor, statesman, diplomat, and scientist was born in 1706 and died in 1790.

In each chapter of this text there is an example of a person who embodies several qualities of a master student. None of these men and women have all the characteristics suggested in this book, but all of them demonstrate the courage and dedication to the process of becoming a master student.

As you read about the master students in this book and others like them, ask: How can I use this? Also look for the qualities in these people that you already have. You can do so even when a profile of a master student seems dated or unrelated to your life. Look for the timeless qualities in the people you read about. Many of the strategies used by master students from another time or place are tools you can use. Reading about others often reminds us of what's possible for ourselves.

No list of master students can be complete. The master students in this book were chosen because they demonstrate novel ways to learn—not because they are the best or only role models. Round out the profiles in this book with other master students you've read about or know personally. As you meet new people, look for those who excel at learning. The master student is not a vague or remote ideal. Rather, master students move freely among us. In fact, there's one living inside your skin.

The following quote is from Benjamin Franklin's memoirs, available in L. Jesse Lemisch's *Benjamin Franklin: The Autobiography and Other Writings* (New York: Signet Classic, 1961), 28-29, by permission of the Regents of the University of California, Berkeley. Reprinted by permission.

A question was once somehow or other started between Collins and me on the propriety of educating the female sex in learning and their abilities for study. He was of the opinion that it was improper and that they were naturally unequal to it. I took the contrary side, perhaps a little for dispute sake. He was naturally more eloquent, having a greater plenty of words, and sometimes, as I thought, I was vanquished more by his fluency than by the strength of his reasons. As we parted without settling the point and were not to see one another again for some time, I sat down to put my arguments in writing, which I copied fair and sent to him. He answered and I replied. Three or four letters on a side had passed, when my father happened to find my papers and read them. Without entering into the subject in dispute, he took occasion to talk with me about my manner of writing, observed that though I had the advantage of my antagonist in correct spelling and pointing (punctuation) . . . I fell far short in elegance of expression, in method and in perspicuity—of which he convinced me by several instances. I saw the justice of his remarks and thence grew more attentive to my manner of writing, and determined to endeavor to improve my style.

About this time I met with an odd volume of *Spectator*. It was the third. I had never before seen any of them. I bought it, read it over and over, and was much delighted with it. I thought the writing excellent and wished if possible to imitate it. With that view, I took some of the papers, and making short hints of the sentiment in each sentence, laid them by a few days, and then without looking at the book, tried to complete the papers again by expressing each hinted sentiment at length and as fully as it had been expressed before, in any suitable words that should occur to me. Then I compared my *Spectator* with the original, discovered some of my faults, and corrected them. But I found I wanted a stock of words or a readiness in recollecting and using them, which I thought I should have acquired before that time if I had gone on making verses; since the continual search for words of the same import but of different length to suit the measure, or of different sound for the rhyme would have laid me under a constant necessity of searching for variety, and also have tended to fix that variety in my mind, and make me master of it. Therefore I took some of the tales in the *Spectator* and turned them into verse, and after a time, when I had pretty well forgotten the prose, turned them back again. I also sometimes jumbled my collections of hints into confusion, and after some weeks endeavored to reduce them into the best order before I began to form the full sentences and complete the paper. This was to teach me method in the arrangement of the thoughts. By comparing my work afterwards with the original, I discovered many faults and corrected them; but I sometimes had the pleasure of fancying that in certain particulars of small import I had been lucky enough to improve the method or the language, and this encouraged me to think that I might possibly in time come to be a tolerable English writer, of which I was extremely ambitious.

1. Give at least two examples of First Steps that Benjamin Franklin wrote about in his autobiographical excerpt.

2. What is the benefit of writing Discovery Statements?

3. When this book works, it's like going to the movies. True or False. Explain your answer.

4. Our internal chatter and mental pictures can get in our way. What is one way to deflate negative images?

5. Whether you are a traditional or a nontraditional student, describe at least three suggestions given for older students returning to school that you could use.

6. The guidelines for writing Discovery Statements do *not* include:

   (A) Record the specifics.
   (B) Notice your inner voices and pictures.
   (C) Notice physical sensations.
   (D) Trust expectations about what you will discover.
   (E) Use discomfort as a signal.

7. List at least five guidelines for writing Intention Statements.

8. The suggestions for changing a habit do *not* include:

    (A) Tell the truth.
    (B) Choose one new behavior at a time.
    (C) Affirm that you can change your basic nature.
    (D) Commit to use the new behavior.
    (E) Get feedback and support.

9. Briefly describe at least three ways that you can network with others.

10. In order for the ideas in this book to work, Power Process #1 suggests believing in them. True or False. Explain your answer.

Journal Entry #9
Discovery Statement

Review what you learned in this chapter and complete the following Discovery Statement:

In reading and doing this chapter, I discovered that I . . .

_____

_____

_____

_____

Journal Entry #10
Discovery Statement

Did you get what you wanted from this chapter? If you didn't, write down in this space what you wanted to get and didn't.

_____

_____

_____

_____

Journal Entry #11
Intention Statement

Write a plan about something specific that you learned and intend to use from this chapter. Include how and when you intend to use it.

I intend to use the following strategy . . .

_____

_____

_____

In order to use this strategy, I will . . .

_____

_____

_____

I will do this by _____(date and time)

Chapter

2 Time

Even if you are on the right track,
you'll get run over if you just sit there.
WILL ROGERS

Dost thou love life, then do not squander time,
for that's the stuff life is made of.
BENJAMIN FRANKLIN

Journal Entry #12
Discovery Statement

After previewing this chapter, complete the following sentence:
What I want from this chapter is ...

_____

_____

_____

_____

_____

_____

_____

_____

_____

_____

_____

_____

_____

In this chapter . . .

Time is a resource like no other. *You've got the time* explains an attitude you can take toward this unique resource—one that can help you get jobs done quickly without sacrificing quality.

Time management need not be an obsession. *Twenty-five ways to get the most out of now* tells how to find the right time, the right place, and the right environment for learning.

The people we live with can sometimes feel like a barrier to our success in school. It doesn't have to be that way. *Studying with children underfoot* suggests how you can study *and* enjoy your kids.

Develop the skill of staying in the moment with *Power Process #2: Be here now*. This is one of the most powerful tools in this book—one that can increase your effectiveness at doing almost anything.

It's often said that 80 percent of the benefit in time management comes from getting 20 percent of the items on your to-do lists done. *The ABC daily to-do's or Working your A's off* suggests how you can get at that top 20. *Gearing up: Using a long-term planner* takes this process a step further.

Other quick ideas include *The Seven-day anti-procrastination plan, How to plan your time,* and *The polyphasic thinker*.

Exercises in this chapter allow you to experience the satisfaction of reaching a goal.

You've got the time

THE WORDS "TIME MANAGEMENT" can call forth images of restriction and control. You might visualize a prune-faced Scrooge hunched over your shoulder, stopwatch in hand, telling you what to do every minute. Bad news.

Good news: You *do* have enough time for the things you want to do. All it takes is learning a few ways to manage time.

Time is an equal opportunity resource. All people, regardless of gender, race, creed, or national origin have exactly the same number of hours in a week. No matter how important you are, no matter how rich or poor, you get 168 hours to spend each week—no more, no less.

Time is also an unusual commodity. It cannot be saved. You can't stockpile time like wood for your stove or food for the winter. It can't be seen, felt, touched, tasted, or smelled. You can't sense time directly. Even brilliant scientists and philosophers aren't sure how to describe it.

Because time is so elusive, it is easy to ignore. That doesn't bother time at all. Time is perfectly content to remain hidden until you are nearly out of it. And when you are out of it, you are out of it.

Time is a nonrenewable resource. If you are out of wood, you can chop some more. If you're out of money, you can earn a little extra. If you're out of love, there is still hope. If you're out of health, it can often be restored. But when you're out of time, that's it. When this minute is gone, it's gone.

Time seems to pass at varying speeds. Sometimes it crawls and sometimes it's faster than a speeding bullet. On Friday afternoons, classroom clocks can creep.

After you've worked a 10-hour day, reading the last few pages of an economics assignment can turn minutes into hours. A year in school can stretch out to an eternity. At the other end of the spectrum, time flies. These are magic times when you are so absorbed by what you're doing that hours disappear in minutes.

You can manage this commodity so you won't waste it or feel regretful about how you spent it.

Approach time as if you are in control. Sometimes it seems that your friends control your time; your boss controls your time; your teachers or your parents or your kids or somebody else controls your time. Maybe that is not true. When you say you don't have enough time, you may really be saying that you are not spending the time you *do* have in the way that you want.

Time management gives you a chance to spend your most valuable resource in the way you choose. Start by observing how you use time.

You can do so in the next exercise.

Exercise #7
The Time Monitor/
Time Plan

The purpose of this exercise is to transform time into a knowable and predictable resource. You can do this by following a two-phase cycle of monitor-plan, monitor-plan, monitor-plan. . .

This exercise takes place over two weeks. During the first week, you can monitor your activities to get a detailed picture of how you spend your time. Then you can plan the second week thoughtfully. Monitor your time during the second week, compare it to your plan, and discover what changes you want to make in the following week's plan. Before you plan a week, read the suggestions for time planning on pages 50-51.

Monitor your time in 15-minute increments, 24 hours a day, for seven days, recording how much time you spend sleeping, eating, studying, traveling to and from class, working, watching television, listening to music, sitting in lectures, taking care of the kids, running errands—everything.

If this sounds crazy, hang on for a minute. This is not about keeping track of the rest of your life in 15-minute intervals. Complete the monitor-plan cycle only for as long as it is useful to you. Most of us have little idea where our time really goes. This exercise offers us an opportunity to find out how we spend our time, our lives.

The point is to become conscious of how you use time. When you know how your time is spent, you can find ways to adjust and manage it so that you spend your time doing the things that are most important to you. Monitoring your time is a critical First Step toward putting you in control of your time.

Some students choose to track their time on 3x5 cards, calendars, or computer software designed for this purpose. You may even develop your own form for monitoring your time.

1. Getting to know the Time Monitor/Plan

Look at the Time Monitor/Time Plan following page 44. Notice that each day has two columns, one labeled "plan" and another labeled "monitor." The first week, use only the "monitor" column. After that, you use both columns simultaneously to continue the monitor-plan process.

Here is an idea that is an eye-opener for many students. If you think you already have a good idea of how you manage time, then guess how many hours you spend in each of the categories listed on page 44. Do this before your first week of monitoring. After you monitor, see how close you were.

To become familiar with the form, look at the example on this page. When beginning an activity, write it next to the time you begin and put a line just above that spot. Round off to the nearest 15 minutes. If, for example, you begin eating at 8:06, enter your start at 8:00. Over time, it will probably even out. In any case, you will be close enough to realize the benefits of this exercise. On Monday, the student in this example got up at 6:45 a.m. and began to shower and get dressed. He stopped this activity and began breakfast at 7:15. He put this new activity in at the time he began and drew another line just above it. He ate from 7:15 to 7:45. It took him 15 minutes to walk to class (7:45 to 8:00) and he attended classes from 8:00 to 11:00.

Keep your Time Monitor/Time Plan with you every minute you are awake for one week. Take a few moments every two or three hours to record what you've done. Or enter a note each time you change activities.

2. How to remember to use your Time Monitor/Time Plan

It may be easy to forget to fill out your Time Monitor/Time Plan. One way to remember is to create a visual reminder for yourself. You can use this technique for any activity you want to remember.

Relax for a moment, close your eyes, and imagine that you see your Time Monitor/Time Plan, only imagine it with arms and legs and as big as a person. Imagine the form sitting at your desk at home. Picture it sitting in your car or sitting in one of your classrooms. Visualize the form sitting in your favorite chair. Picture it sitting wherever you're likely to sit.

When you sit down, the picture of the Time Monitor/Time Plan will get squashed.

You can make this image more effective by adding imaginary noise. The Time Monitor/Time Plan might scream "Get off me!" Or, since time is money, as the saying goes, you might associate the Time Monitor/Time Plan with the sound of a cash register. Imagine that every time you sit down, a cash register rings.

MONDAY 3/12/			TUESDAY 3/13/	
PLAN	MONITOR		PLAN	MONITOR
	6:45 Get up Shower			Sleep
7:00	7:00		7:00	7:00
7:15	7:15 Breakfast		7:15	
7:30	↓		7:30	
7:45	Walk to class		7:45	Shower
8:00	8:00		8:00	8:00 Dress
8:15	Econ I		8:15	Eat
8:30			8:30	
8:45			8:45	
9:00	9:00		9:00	9:00 Art
9:15			9:15	Apprec
9:30			9:30	Projec
9:45	↓		9:45	
10:00	10:00 Bio I		10:00	10:00
10:15			10:15	
10:30			10:30	
10:45	↓		10:45	
11:00	11:00		11:00	11:00 Data
11:15			11:15	Proces
11:30	Study		11:30	
11:45			11:45	
12:00	12:00		12:00	12:00
12:15	Lunch		12:15	
12:30			12:30	
12:45			12:45	Lunch
1:00	1:00		1:00	1:00
1:15	Eng. Lit.		1:15	
1:30			1:30	work
1:45			1:45	
2:00	2:00 Coffeehouse		2:00	2:00 on book
2:15			2:15	repor
2:30	↓		2:30	
2:45			2:45	
3:00	3:00		3:00	3:00 Art
3:15			3:15	Apprec
3:30			3:30	
3:45	↓		3:45	
4:00	4:00		4:00	4:00
4:15	Study		4:15	
4:30			4:30	
4:45			4:45	Card s
5:00	5:00		5:00	5:00
5:15	Dinner		5:15	Dinne
5:30			5:30	
5:45			5:45	
6:00	6:00		6:00	6:00 Letter t
6:15	Babysit		6:15	Uncle J

3. Analyzing the Time Monitor/Time Plan

After you've monitored your time for one week, group your activities together by categories. The form below includes the categories sleep, class, study, and meals. Another category, "grooming", might include showering, putting on make-up, brushing teeth, getting dressed, etc. "Travel" can include walking, driving, taking the bus, and riding your bike. Other categories could be exercise, entertainment, work, television, domestics, and children. Write in the categories that work for you, and then add up how much time you spent in each of your categories. Make sure the grand total of all categories is 168 hours.

In several months, you may want to take another detailed look at how you spend your life. Combine it with planning your time, following the suggestions in this chapter. This sets up a continuous cycle: monitor, evaluate, plan; monitor, evaluate, plan. When you make it a habit, this cycle can help you get the full benefits of time management for the rest of your life. Then time management becomes more than a technique. It's transformed into a habit, a constant awareness of how you spend your lifetime.

Week of____/____/____

Category	Planned	Monitored
Sleep		
Class		
Study		
Meals		

MONDAY ___/___/___			TUESDAY ___/___/___			WEDNESDAY ___/___/___	
PLAN	MONITOR		PLAN	MONITOR		PLAN	MONITOR
___	___		___	___		___	___
___	___		___	___		___	___
7:00	7:00		7:00	7:00		7:00	7:00
7:15	___		7:15	___		7:15	___
7:30	___		7:30	___		7:30	___
7:45	___		7:45	___		7:45	___
8:00	8:00		8:00	8:00		8:00	8:00
8:15	___		8:15	___		8:15	___
8:30	___		8:30	___		8:30	___
8:45	___		8:45	___		8:45	___
9:00	9:00		9:00	9:00		9:00	9:00
9:15	___		9:15	___		9:15	___
9:30	___		9:30	___		9:30	___
9:45	___		9:45	___		9:45	___
10:00	10:00		10:00	10:00		10:00	10:00
10:15	___		10:15	___		10:15	___
10:30	___		10:30	___		10:30	___
10:45	___		10:45	___		10:45	___
11:00	11:00		11:00	11:00		11:00	11:00
11:15	___		11:15	___		11:15	___
11:30	___		11:30	___		11:30	___
11:45	___		11:45	___		11:45	___
12:00	12:00		12:00	12:00		12:00	12:00
12:15	___		12:15	___		12:15	___
12:30	___		12:30	___		12:30	___
12:45	___		12:45	___		12:45	___
1:00	1:00		1:00	1:00		1:00	1:00
1:15	___		1:15	___		1:15	___
1:30	___		1:30	___		1:30	___
1:45	___		1:45	___		1:45	___
2:00	2:00		2:00	2:00		2:00	2:00
2:15	___		2:15	___		2:15	___
2:30	___		2:30	___		2:30	___
2:45	___		2:45	___		2:45	___
3:00	3:00		3:00	3:00		3:00	3:00
3:15	___		3:15	___		3:15	___
3:30	___		3:30	___		3:30	___
3:45	___		3:45	___		3:45	___
4:00	4:00		4:00	4:00		4:00	4:00
4:15	___		4:15	___		4:15	___
4:30	___		4:30	___		4:30	___
4:45	___		4:45	___		4:45	___
5:00	5:00		5:00	5:00		5:00	5:00
5:15	___		5:15	___		5:15	___
5:30	___		5:30	___		5:30	___
5:45	___		5:45	___		5:45	___
6:00	6:00		6:00	6:00		6:00	6:00
6:15	___		6:15	___		6:15	___
6:30	___		6:30	___		6:30	___
6:45	___		6:45	___		6:45	___
7:00	7:00		7:00	7:00		7:00	7:00
7:15	___		7:15	___		7:15	___
7:30	___		7:30	___		7:30	___
7:45	___		7:45	___		7:45	___
8:00	8:00		8:00	8:00		8:00	8:00
8:15	___		8:15	___		8:15	___
8:30	___		8:30	___		8:30	___
8:45	___		8:45	___		8:45	___
9:00	9:00		9:00	9:00		9:00	9:00
9:15	___		9:15	___		9:15	___
9:30	___		9:30	___		9:30	___
9:45	___		9:45	___		9:45	___
___	___		___	___		___	___
___	___		___	___		___	___

THURSDAY __/__/__		FRIDAY __/__/__		SATURDAY __/__/__	
PLAN	MONITOR	PLAN	MONITOR	PLAN	MONITOR
7:00	7:00	7:00	7:00		
7:15		7:15			
7:30		7:30			
7:45		7:45			
8:00	8:00	8:00	8:00		
8:15		8:15			
8:30		8:30			
8:45		8:45			
9:00	9:00	9:00	9:00		
9:15		9:15			
9:30		9:30			
9:45		9:45			
10:00	10:00	10:00	10:00		
10:15		10:15			
10:30		10:30			
10:45		10:45			
11:00	11:00	11:00	11:00		
11:15		11:15			
11:30		11:30			
11:45		11:45			
12:00	12:00	12:00	12:00		
12:15		12:15			
12:30		12:30			
12:45		12:45			
1:00	1:00	1:00	1:00		
1:15		1:15			
1:30		1:30			
1:45		1:45			
2:00	2:00	2:00	2:00		
2:15		2:15			
2:30		2:30			
2:45		2:45			

SUNDAY __/__/__	
PLAN	MONITOR

THURSDAY		FRIDAY		SUNDAY	
3:00	3:00	3:00	3:00		
3:15		3:15			
3:30		3:30			
3:45		3:45			
4:00	4:00	4:00	4:00		
4:15		4:15			
4:30		4:30			
4:45		4:45			
5:00	5:00	5:00	5:00		
5:15		5:15			
5:30		5:30			
5:45		5:45			
6:00	6:00	6:00	6:00		
6:15		6:15			
6:30		6:30			
6:45		6:45			
7:00	7:00	7:00	7:00		
7:15		7:15			
7:30		7:30			
7:45		7:45			
8:00	8:00	8:00	8:00		
8:15		8:15			
8:30		8:30			
8:45		8:45			
9:00	9:00	9:00	9:00		
9:15		9:15			
9:30		9:30			
9:45		9:45			

MONDAY __/__/__	
PLAN	MONITOR

———	———
———	———
7:00	7:00
7:15	
7:30	
7:45	
8:00	8:00
8:15	
8:30	
8:45	
9:00	9:00
9:15	
9:30	
9:45	
10:00	10:00
10:15	
10:30	
10:45	
11:00	11:00
11:15	
11:30	
11:45	
12:00	12:00
12:15	
12:30	
12:45	
1:00	1:00
1:15	
1:30	
1:45	
2:00	2:00
2:15	
2:30	
2:45	
3:00	3:00
3:15	
3:30	
3:45	
4:00	4:00
4:15	
4:30	
4:45	
5:00	5:00
5:15	
5:30	
5:45	
6:00	6:00
6:15	
6:30	
6:45	
7:00	7:00
7:15	
7:30	
7:45	
8:00	8:00
8:15	
8:30	
8:45	
9:00	9:00
9:15	
9:30	
9:45	

TUESDAY __/__/__	
PLAN	MONITOR

———	———
———	———
7:00	7:00
7:15	
7:30	
7:45	
8:00	8:00
8:15	
8:30	
8:45	
9:00	9:00
9:15	
9:30	
9:45	
10:00	10:00
10:15	
10:30	
10:45	
11:00	11:00
11:15	
11:30	
11:45	
12:00	12:00
12:15	
12:30	
12:45	
1:00	1:00
1:15	
1:30	
1:45	
2:00	2:00
2:15	
2:30	
2:45	
3:00	3:00
3:15	
3:30	
3:45	
4:00	4:00
4:15	
4:30	
4:45	
5:00	5:00
5:15	
5:30	
5:45	
6:00	6:00
6:15	
6:30	
6:45	
7:00	7:00
7:15	
7:30	
7:45	
8:00	8:00
8:15	
8:30	
8:45	
9:00	9:00
9:15	
9:30	
9:45	

WEDNESDAY __/__/__	
PLAN	MONITOR

———	———
———	———
7:00	7:00
7:15	
7:30	
7:45	
8:00	8:00
8:15	
8:30	
8:45	
9:00	9:00
9:15	
9:30	
9:45	
10:00	10:00
10:15	
10:30	
10:45	
11:00	11:00
11:15	
11:30	
11:45	
12:00	12:00
12:15	
12:30	
12:45	
1:00	1:00
1:15	
1:30	
1:45	
2:00	2:00
2:15	
2:30	
2:45	
3:00	3:00
3:15	
3:30	
3:45	
4:00	4:00
4:15	
4:30	
4:45	
5:00	5:00
5:15	
5:30	
5:45	
6:00	6:00
6:15	
6:30	
6:45	
7:00	7:00
7:15	
7:30	
7:45	
8:00	8:00
8:15	
8:30	
8:45	
9:00	9:00
9:15	
9:30	
9:45	

THURSDAY ___/___/___

PLAN	MONITOR
———	———
———	———
7:00	7:00
7:15	
7:30	
7:45	
8:00	8:00
8:15	
8:30	
8:45	
9:00	9:00
9:15	
9:30	
9:45	
10:00	10:00
10:15	
10:30	
10:45	
11:00	11:00
11:15	
11:30	
11:45	
12:00	12:00
12:15	
12:30	
12:45	
1:00	1:00
1:15	
1:30	
1:45	
2:00	2:00
2:15	
2:30	
2:45	
3:00	3:00
3:15	
3:30	
3:45	
4:00	4:00
4:15	
4:30	
4:45	
5:00	5:00
5:15	
5:30	
5:45	
6:00	6:00
6:15	
6:30	
6:45	
7:00	7:00
7:15	
7:30	
7:45	
8:00	8:00
8:15	
8:30	
8:45	
9:00	9:00
9:15	
9:30	
9:45	

FRIDAY ___/___/___

PLAN	MONITOR
———	———
———	———
7:00	7:00
7:15	
7:30	
7:45	
8:00	8:00
8:15	
8:30	
8:45	
9:00	9:00
9:15	
9:30	
9:45	
10:00	10:00
10:15	
10:30	
10:45	
11:00	11:00
11:15	
11:30	
11:45	
12:00	12:00
12:15	
12:30	
12:45	
1:00	1:00
1:15	
1:30	
1:45	
2:00	2:00
2:15	
2:30	
2:45	
3:00	3:00
3:15	
3:30	
3:45	
4:00	4:00
4:15	
4:30	
4:45	
5:00	5:00
5:15	
5:30	
5:45	
6:00	6:00
6:15	
6:30	
6:45	
7:00	7:00
7:15	
7:30	
7:45	
8:00	8:00
8:15	
8:30	
8:45	
9:00	9:00
9:15	
9:30	
9:45	

SATURDAY ___/___/___

PLAN	MONITOR

SUNDAY ___/___/___

PLAN	MONITOR

Journal Entry #13
Discovery Statement

By analyzing the results of one week of monitoring my time I discovered that . . .

_____

_____

I want to spend more time on . . .

_____

_____

I want to spend less time on . . .

_____

_____

_____

I was surprised that I spent so much time on . . .

_____

_____

_____

I was surprised that I spent so little time on . . .

_____

_____

_____

I had strong feelings about (describe the feeling and the situation) . . .

_____

_____

_____

THE POLYPHASIC THINKER

The polyphasic thinker isn't really paying attention to his telephone conversation because he's reading the newspaper. And he won't remember what he read because he's shaving and brushing his coffee as he takes a bite of his ham and cheese on rye, which will be a lump in his gut in an hour, in part because he ate it while he was on the phone.

The polyphasic thinker thinks he's getting lots done. What he's really getting is indigestion. He might accomplish more by doing one thing at a time and really doing it.

With this warning in mind, remember that no rule is absolute. Sometimes choosing to do two or more things at once can be effective—even necessary. The key word is "choose." When you choose, you're still in command of your attention. For example, you might study while doing laundry. You might ask your children to quiz you with flash cards while you fix dinner.

Polyphasic behavior is a problem when it is done unconsciously, out of habit. If you notice yourself with a telephone in one hand and a newspaper in the other, call time out. Ask yourself if your polyphasia is necessary. And remember to stop and enjoy that ham and cheese on rye.

How to plan your time

PLAN	MONITOR
6:45 Shower Dress	Get up
7:00	7:00 Shower
7:15 Eat	7:15 Dress
7:30	
7:45 Travel	Travel
8:00 Class	8:00 Class
8:15	
8:30	
8:45	
9:00	9:00
9:15	
9:30	
9:45	
10:00	10:00
10:15	
10:30	
10:45	
11:00 Study	11:00 Breakfast
11:15	
11:30	
11:45	
12:00 Lunch	12:00 Study
12:15	
12:30	relax
12:45 Relax	
1:00 Class	1:00 Class
1:15	
1:30	
1:45	
2:00	2:00
2:15	
2:30	
2:45	
3:00 Exercise	3:00 Coffeehouse with friends
3:15	
3:30	
3:45	
4:00 TV	4:00 Exercise
4:15	
4:30 Study	
4:45	
5:00	5:00 Eat Dinner
5:15	
5:30 Eat	Dinner
5:45 Dinner	
6:00	6:00
6:15	
6:30 Study	
6:45 Group	
7:00	7:00
7:15	
7:30	
7:45	
8:00 Laundry	8:00
8:15	
8:30	
8:45	
9:00 Study	9:00

PLAN	MONITOR
6:30 Exercise	
7:00 Shower	7:00
7:15 and dress	
7:30 Eat	
7:45	
8:00 Study	8:00
8:15	
8:30	
8:45 Travel	
9:00 Class	9:00
9:15	
9:30	
9:45	
10:00 Library	10:00
10:15	
10:30	
10:45	
11:00 Class	11:00
11:15	
11:30	
11:45	
12:00 Eat &	12:00
12:15 Relax	
12:30	
12:45	
1:00 Shopping	1:00
1:15	
1:30	
1:45	
2:00 Travel	2:00
2:15 Study	
2:30	
2:45	
3:00 Class	3:00
3:15	
3:30	
3:45	
4:00 TV & Relax	4:00
4:15	
4:30	
4:45	
5:00	5:00
5:15	
5:30 Dinner	
5:45	
6:00 Shower	6:00
6:15 Dress	
6:30	
6:45	
7:00 PARTY	7:00
7:15	
7:30	
7:45	
8:00	8:00
8:15	
8:30	
8:45	
9:00	9:00

1. Schedule fixed blocks of time first. Start with class time and work time, for instance. These time periods are usually determined in advance. Other activities must be scheduled around them. Then schedule essential daily activities like sleeping and eating. No matter what else you do, you will sleep and eat. Be realistic about how much time you take for these functions.

2. Include time for errands. The time we spend buying toothpaste, paying bills, and doing laundry is easy to overlook. These little errands can destroy a tight schedule and make us feel rushed and harried all week. Plan for them and remember to allow for travel time between locations.

3. Schedule time for fun. Fun is important. Brains that are constantly stimulated by new ideas and new challenges need time off to digest them. Take time to browse aimlessly through the library, stroll with no destination, ride a bike, or do other things you enjoy. Recreation deserves a place in your priorities. It's important to "waste" time once in a while.

4. Set realistic goals. Don't set yourself up for failure by telling yourself you can do a four-hour job in two hours. There are only 168 hours in a week. If you schedule 169 hours, you lose before you begin.

5. Allow flexibility in your schedule. Recognize that unexpected things will happen, so plan for the unexpected. Leave some "holes" in your schedule; build in blocks of unplanned time. Consider setting aside time each week marked "flex time" or "open time." These are hours to use for emergencies, spontaneous activities, catching up, or seizing new opportunities.

6. Study two hours for every hour in class. It's standard advice that you allow two hours of study time for every hour you spend in class. Students making the transition from high school to higher education are often unaware that more is expected of them. If you are taking 15 credit hours, plan to spend 30 hours per week studying. The benefits of following this rule will be apparent at exam time.

This guideline is just that—a guideline, not an absolute rule. Consider what's best for you. If you do the Time Monitor/Time Plan exercise in this chapter, note how many hours you actually spend studying for each hour of class. Then ask how your schedule is working. You may want to allow more study time for some subjects.

Also keep in mind that the "two hours for one" rule doesn't distinguish between focused time and unfocused time. In one four-hour block of study time, it's possible to use up two hours for phone calls, breaks, daydreaming, and doodling. Quality time counts for as much as quantity.

7. Avoid scheduling marathon study sessions. When possible, study in shorter sessions. Three three-hour sessions are far more productive for most people than one nine-hour session. In a nine- or 10-hour study marathon, the percentage of time actually spent on task can be depressingly small. With 10 hours of study ahead of you, the temptation is to tell yourself, "Well, it's going to be a long day. No sense getting in a rush. Better sharpen about a dozen of these pencils and change the light bulbs." In the nine-hour sitting you might spend only six or seven hours studying, whereas three shorter sessions will likely yield much more productive time.

When you do study in long sessions, stop and rest for a few minutes every hour. Give your brain a chance to take a break.

Finally, if you must study in a large block of time, work on several subjects and avoid studying similar subjects back to back. For example, if you plan to study sociology, psychology, and computer science, sandwich the computer course between psychology and sociology.

8. Set clear starting and stopping times. Tasks often expand to fill the time we allot for them. Saying "It always takes me an hour just to settle into a reading assignment" may become a self-fulfilling prophecy.

An alternative is to plan a certain amount of time for that reading assignment, set a timer, and stick to it. People often discover they can decrease study time simply by forcing themselves to read faster. This can usually be done without sacrificing comprehension.

The same principle can apply to other tasks. Some people find they can get up 15 minutes earlier and still feel alert throughout the day. Plan 45 minutes for a trip to the grocery store instead of one hour. Over the course of a year, those extra minutes can add up to hours. Over a lifetime, they can add up to days.

Feeling rushed or sacrificing quality is not the aim here. The point is to push ourselves a little and discover what our time requirements really are.

9. Plan for the unplanned. The best-laid plans can be foiled by the unexpected. Cars break down in winter. Children and day care providers get sick. Subway trains go out of service. Electricity goes off and freezes alarm clocks in the distant past.

That's when it pays to have a back-up plan. You can find someone to care for your children when the babysitter gets the flu. You can plan an alternative way to get to work. You can set the alarm on your watch as well as the one on your nightstand. Giving such items five minutes of careful thought today can save you hours in the future.

25 *ways to get the most out of now*

The following time management techniques are about when to study, where to study, how to handle the rest of the world, and things you can ask yourself when you get stuck. As you read, underline, circle, or otherwise note the suggestions you think you can use.

Pick two or three techniques to use now. When they become habits, come back to this article and pick a couple more.

When to Study

1. Study difficult (or boring) subjects first.

If your chemistry problems put you to sleep, get to them first, while you are fresh. We tend to study what we like first, yet the courses we find most difficult often require the most creative energy. Save the subjects you enjoy for later. If you find yourself avoiding a particular subject, get up an hour early to study it before breakfast. With that chore out of the way, the rest of the day can be a breeze.

Continually avoiding a subject might indicate a trouble area. Further action is called for. Clarify your feelings about the course by writing about those feelings in a journal, talking to the instructor, or asking for help from a friend or counselor. Finding a study group or tutor could turn the situation around. Consistently avoiding study tasks can also be a signal to re-examine your major or course program.

2. Be aware of your best time of day.

Many people learn best in daylight hours. If this is true for you, schedule study time for your most difficult subjects when the sun is up.

Unless you grew up on a farm, the idea of being conscious at 4 a.m. might seem ridiculous. Yet many successful business people begin the day at 5 a.m. or earlier. Athletes and yogis use this time, too. Some writers complete their best work before 9 a.m.

Getting up that early is like jumping in an icy mountain lake. After the initial shock, your body comes alive.

Early morning is a beautiful time. The world is quiet. Inner voices are less insistent. Spiritual leaders of all persuasions recommend pre-dawn as a time of meditation and prayer. The mind is better able to focus before it is assaulted by the jangle of telephones, traffic, and Top 40 tunes.

Some people experience the same benefits by staying up late. They flourish after midnight.

If you aren't convinced, then experiment. When you're in a time crunch, get up early or stay up late. The new benefits you discover might even include seeing a sunrise.

The key point is to find time when learning feels best. If early morning doesn't work for you, find out what time is better.

3. Use waiting time.

Five minutes waiting for a bus, 20 minutes waiting for the dentist, 10 minutes between classes—waiting time adds up fast. Have short study tasks ready to do during these times. For example, carry 3x5 cards with facts, formulas, or definitions and pull them out anywhere.

Also use time between classes or breaks during work to review class notes or notes on reading you have done. A solid review of a lecture can be completed in 15 minutes, and even five minutes can be valuable if you are prepared.

A tape recorder can help you use commuting time to your advantage. Make a cassette tape of yourself reading your notes. Then play these tapes in a car stereo as you drive or listen through your earphones as you ride on the bus or exercise.

Where to study

4. Use a regular study area.

Your body and your mind know where you are. When you use the same place to study, day after day, they become trained. When you arrive at that particular place, you can focus your attention more quickly.

Avoid eating, watching television, playing ping-pong, or changing diapers where you study. Use your study area for study and make it a ritual.

5. Study where you'll be alert.

In bed, your body gets a signal. For most students, it's more likely to be, "Time to sleep," rather than, "Time to study!" For that reason, don't sleep where you study. Just as you train your body to be alert at your desk, you also train it to slow down near your bed.

Easy chairs and sofas are also dangerous

places to study. Learning requires energy. Give your body a message that energy is needed. Put yourself into a situation that supports that message.

6. Use a library.

Libraries are designed for learning. The lighting is perfect. The noise level is low. Materials are available. Entering a library is a signal to quiet the mind and get to work. Most people can get more done in a shorter time at the library. Experiment for yourself.

How to handle the rest of the world

7. Pay attention to your attention.

Breaks in concentration are often caused by internal interruptions. Your own thoughts jump in to tell you another story about the world. When that happens, notice the thoughts and let them go.

Perhaps the thought of getting something else done is distracting you. One option is to handle that task now and study later. Or write yourself a note about it or schedule a specific time to do it.

8. Agree with living mates about study time.

This includes roommates, parents, spouses, and kids. Make the rules clear, and be sure to follow them yourself. Explicit agreements—even written contracts—work well. One student always wears a colorful hat when he wants to study. When his wife and children see the hat, they respect his wish to be left alone.

9. Get off the phone.

The telephone is the perfect interrupter. People who wouldn't think of distracting you might call at the worst times because they can't see you. It can be easy for you to rationalize interrupting your study for a phone call. After all, it wasn't your fault the phone rang, and besides, you don't want to be rude.

You don't have to be a telephone victim. If a simple "I can't talk, I'm studying" doesn't

25
*ways to get
the most
out of now*

work, use dead silence. It's a conversation killer. Or, short circuit the whole problem: Unplug the phone. Get an answering machine or study at the library.

10. Learn to say no.

This is a timesaver and valuable life skill for everyone. Many people feel it is rude to refuse a request. But saying no can be done effectively and courteously. Others want you to succeed as a student. When you tell them that you can't do what they ask because you are busy educating yourself, most people will understand.

Notice how others misuse your time. Be aware of repeat offenders. Ask yourself if there are certain friends or relatives who consistently interrupt your study time. If avoiding the interrupter is impractical, send a clear message. Sometimes others don't realize they are breaking your concentration. A gentle reminder should do it. If your message doesn't work, there are ways to make it more effective. (See "Sending" on page 206.)

11. Hang a "do not disturb" sign on your door.

Many hotels will give you one free, just for the advertising. Or you can make a creative one. They work. Using signs can relieve you of making a decision about cutting off each interruption—a timesaver in itself.

12. Get ready the night before.

Completing a few simple tasks just before you go to bed can help you get in gear faster the next day. If you need to make some phone calls first thing in the morning, look up those numbers, write them on 3x5 cards, and set them near the phone. If you are set to drive to a new location, make note of the address and put it next to your car keys. Or, if you plan to spend the afternoon writing a paper, get your materials together: dictionary, notes, outline, paper and pencil (or disks and computer). Pack your lunch or gas up the car. Organize the diaper bag, briefcase, or backpack.

You can expand this process to getting ready for the next week or even for the month. You could, for example, plan all your meals for the next month and take one day to cook and freeze them. Then, all you would need to do for the next four weeks is thaw and heat your meals.

13. Call ahead.

Often we think of talking on the telephone as a prime time-waster. Used wisely, the telephone can actually help you manage time. Before you go shopping, call the store to see if it carries the item you're looking for. If you're driving, call for directions to your destination. A few seconds on the phone can save hours in wasted trips and wrong turns.

14. Avoid noise distractions.

To promote concentration, avoid studying in front of the television and turn off the stereo. Many students insist that they study better with background noise, and that may be true. Some students report good results with carefully selected and controlled music. The overwhelming majority of research indicates that silence is the best form of music for study.

At times noise may seem out of your control. A neighbor or roommate decides to find out how far he can turn up his stereo before the walls crumble. Meanwhile, your concentration on principles of sociology goes down the tubes.

To get past this barrier, schedule study sessions for times when your living environment is usually quiet. If you live in a residence hall, ask if study rooms are available. Or, go somewhere else where it's quiet, such as the library. Some students have even found refuge in empty restaurants, laundromats, and churches.

Another option is to enforce noise restrictions. Many residence halls have rules about noise. Also, your city might have ordinances about acceptable noise levels in residential areas. Find out if such rules exist and who can enforce them.

Many students learn to study with noise. Remember that attention is an ability that can be trained. For more ideas, see the Power Process "Be here now" on page 64.

15. Notice how others misuse your time.

Be aware of repeat offenders. Ask yourself if there are certain friends or relatives who consistently interrupt your study time. If avoiding the interrupter is impractical, then send a clear message. Sometimes others don't realize they are breaking your concentration. You can give them a gentle yet firm reminder.

Things you can ask yourself when you get stuck

16. Ask: What is one task I can accomplish toward my goal?

This is a useful technique to use on big, imposing jobs. Pick out one small accomplishment, preferably one you can complete in about five minutes, then do it. The satisfaction of getting one thing done often spurs you on to get one more thing done. Meanwhile, the job gets smaller.

17. Ask: Am I being too hard on myself?

If you are feeling frustrated with a reading assignment, noticing that your attention wanders repeatedly, or falling behind on problems due for tomorrow, take a minute to listen to the messages you are giving yourself. Are you scolding yourself too harshly? Lighten up. Allow yourself to feel a little foolish and get on with it. Don't add to the problem by berating yourself.

Worrying about the future is another way people beat themselves up: How will I ever get this all done? What if every paper I write turns out to be this hard? If I can't do this simple calculation now, how will I ever pass the final? Instead of promoting learning, such questions fuel anxiety. They are often based on unrealistic expectations and seldom serve us well.

Labeling and generalizing weaknesses are other ways people are hard on themselves. Being objective and specific will eliminate this form of self-punishment and will likely generate new possibilities. An alternative to saying "I'm terrible in algebra" is to say "I don't understand factoring equations." This suggests a plan to improve.

18. Ask: Is this a piano?

Carpenters who build rough frames for buildings have a saying they use when they bend a nail or hack a chunk out of a two-by-four: "Well, this ain't no piano." It means perfection is not necessary.

Ask yourself if what you are doing needs to be perfect. You don't have to apply the same standards of grammar to review notes that you apply to a term paper. The basketball player who refuses to shoot until the perfect shot is available may never shoot. If you can complete a job 95 percent perfect in two hours, and 100 percent perfect in four hours, ask yourself whether the additional 5 percent improvement is worth doubling the amount of time you spend.

Sometimes it is a piano. A tiny mistake can ruin an entire lab experiment. Computers are notorious for turning little errors into monsters. Accept lower standards only where they are appropriate.

KEEP GOING?

Some people keep going, even when they fail again and again. To such people belongs the world. Consider the hapless politician who compiled this record:

Failed in business	1831
Defeated for Legislature	1832
Second failure in business	1833
Suffered nervous breakdown	1836
Defeated for Speaker	1838
Defeated for Elector	1840
Defeated for Congress	1843
Defeated for Senate	1855
Defeated for Vice President	1856
Defeated for Senate	1858
Elected President	1860

Who was the fool who kept on going in spite of so many failures?

Answer: The fool was Abraham Lincoln.

A related suggestion is to weed out low priority tasks. The to-do list for a large project can include dozens of items. Not all of them are equally important. Some can be done later on, and others could be skipped altogether if time is short. You can manage time more powerfully if you know what the low priority items are and choose whether or not to do them.

Apply this idea when you study. In a long reading assignment, look for pages you can skim or skip. When it's appropriate, read chapter summaries or article abstracts. When reviewing your notes, look for material that may not be covered on a test and decide whether you want to study it. You may want to predict test questions and just study for those questions. If you're doing well in Physics and short on study time for Accounting, consider letting Physics slide for today. Perhaps Physics "ain't a piano" right now.

19. Ask: Would I pay myself for what I'm doing right now?

If you were employed as a student, would you be earning your wages? Ask yourself this question when you notice that you've taken your third popcorn break in 30 minutes. Most students are, in fact, employed as students. They are investing in their own productivity and sometimes don't realize what a mediocre job may cost them.

20. Ask: Can I do just one more thing?

Ask yourself this question at the end of a long day. Almost always you will have enough energy to do just one more short task. If you get in the habit of working until you are done, then doing one more thing, those end-of-the-day tasks will soon add up. The overall increase in your productivity might surprise you.

21. Ask: Am I making time for things that are important but not urgent?

Exercise is an example of something that is important but not urgent. We sometimes neglect areas that are important because we are too busy dealing with situations that are more urgent. It's easy to let crises and last-minute emergencies eat up our time. There are assignments to complete, papers to write, phone calls to return, letters to answer, and errands to run. Most of them seem so urgent that we dare not let them go.

Yet if we spend most of our time putting out fires, we may feel drained and frustrated. This happens when we forget to take time for things that are truly important but not urgent. Examples are regular exercise, reading, prayer or meditation, quality time with friends and family, solitude, traveling, and cooking nutritious meals. Each of these can contribute directly to a long-term goal or life mission. Yet when schedules get tight, it's tempting to let these things go for that elusive day when we'll "finally have more time."

That day won't come until we choose to make time for what's truly important. Knowing this, we can use some of the suggestions in this chapter to free up more time. We can monitor our time and ask if some urgent tasks can be delegated or eliminated altogether. Also, we can list important activities and schedule specific times for them. That way, these activities won't get lost in the shuffle.

22. Ask: Can I delegate this?

Instead of slogging through complicated tasks alone, you can draw on the talent and energy of other people. Busy executives know the value of delegating tasks to co-workers. Without delegation, many projects would flounder or die.

You can apply the same principle. Instead of doing all the housework or cooking yourself, for example, assign some of the tasks to family members or roommates. Rather than making a trip to the library to look up a simple fact, call and ask a library assistant to do it. Or, instead of driving across town to deliver a package, hire a delivery service to do it. All these tactics can free up extra hours for studying.

It's not practical to delegate certain study tasks, such as writing term papers or completing reading assignments. However, you can still draw on the ideas of other people in completing such tasks. For instance, form a writing group to edit and critique papers, brainstorm topics or titles, and develop lists of sources.

If you're absent for a class, find a classmate to explain the lecture, discussion, and any assignments due. Presidents depend on briefings. You can use the technique, too. Briefings have benefits for both parties. You avoid missing something important. And the person who briefs you gets to repeat the material—a task that helps him remember it.

23. Ask: How did I just waste time?

Notice when time passes and you haven't accomplished what you planned. Take a minute to review your actions and note the specific ways you wasted time. We operate by habit and tend to waste time in the same ways over and over again. When you are aware of things you do that kill your time, you are more likely to catch yourself in the act next time. Observing one small quirk may save you hours. One reminder: Noting how you waste time is not the same as feeling guilty about it. The point is not to blame yourself but to increase your skill. That means getting specific information about how you use time.

24. Ask: Could I find the time if I really wanted to?

Often the way people speak rules out the option of finding more time. An alternative is to speak about time with more possibility.

The next time you're tempted to say "I just don't have time," pause for a minute. Question the truth of this statement. Could you find four more hours this week for studying? Suppose that someone offered to pay you $10,000 to find those four hours. Suppose, too, that you will get paid only if you don't lose sleep, call in sick for work, or sacrifice anything important to you. Could you find the time if vast sums of money were involved?

Remember that when it comes to school, vast sums of money *are* involved.

25. Ask: Am I willing to promise it?

This may be the most powerful time management idea of all. If you want to find time for a task, promise yourself—and others—that you'll get it done. To make this technique work, do more than say you'll *try* or that you'll give it your best shot. Take an oath, as you would in court. Give your word.

One way to accomplish big things in life is to make big promises. There's little reward in promising what's safe or predictable. No athlete promises to place seventh in the Olympics. Chances are that if we're not making large promises, we're not stretching ourselves.

The point of making a promise is not to chain ourselves to rigid schedules or impossible expectations. We can also promise to reach goals without unbearable stress. We can keep schedules flexible and carry out our plans with ease, joy, and satisfaction.

At times we can go too far. Some promises are truly beyond us and we may break them. However, failing to keep a promise is just that—failing to keep a promise. A broken promise is not the worst thing in the world.

Promises can work magic.

When our word is on the line, it's possible to discover reserves of time and energy we didn't know existed. Promises can push us to a breakthrough.

Exercise #8
Goal setting

This exercise can show you how to make goals as real as typewriters or chainsaws.

We all have vague, idealized notions of what we want out of life. These notions float among the clouds in our heads. They are wonderful, fuzzy, safe thoughts like "I want to be a good person," "I want to be financially secure," and "I want to be happy." These are great thoughts and great beginnings for more tangible plans. Left in this generalized form, we might be confused about how to use them in choosing what to do this weekend .

In contrast, there is nothing vague or fuzzy about chainsaws. You can see them, feel them, and hear them. They have a clear function.

Goals can operate the same way—if you make them real. The way to do that is to examine them up close. Find out what they look like; listen to what they sound like. Pick them up and feel how heavy they are. That's what this exercise is about. It's a chance to inspect the switches, valves, joints, cogs, and fastenings of one of your long-term goals. You can do this by choosing a long-term goal and breaking it into smaller segments until you have taken it completely apart.

Disassembled, a goal will look different. When you look at it closely, a goal you thought you wanted might not be something you want after all. Or you might discover you need to change directions to accomplish a goal you are sure you want. Either way, you will be able to see how your education relates to your long-term goal.

This exercise is also an opportunity to test your brainstorming skills. You will need a pen, extra paper, and a watch with a second hand. (A digital watch with a built-in stopwatch is even better.) Timing is an important part of the brainstorming process, so follow the time limits. The entire exercise takes about an hour.

Part one: long-term goals

Long-term goals represent major targets in your life. These goals can take five to 20 years to achieve. In some cases, they will take a lifetime. They can include goals in education, careers, personal relationships, travel, financial security— whatever is important to you. What do you want to accomplish in your life? Do you want your life to make a statement? What is it? Include your answers in your long-term goals.

Brainstorm

Begin with an eight-minute brainstorm. For eight minutes, write down everything you think you want to do or be in your life. Write as fast as you can, and write whatever comes into your head. Leave no thought out. Don't worry about accuracy. The object of a brainstorm is to generate as many ideas as possible. Use a separate sheet of paper for this part of the exercise.

Evaluate

After you have finished brainstorming, spend the next eight minutes looking over your list. Think about what you wrote. Read the list aloud. You can even add to it. Look for common themes or relationships between goals. Then, select three long-term goals that are most important to you.

Write these goals in the space provided.

Goal

Goal

Goal

Part two: mid-term goals

Mid-term goals are objectives you can accomplish in two to five years. They include goals such as completing a course of education or achieving a specific career level. These goals usually support your long-term goals.

Brainstorm

Read aloud the three long-term goals you selected in Part one. Choose one of them. Then brainstorm a list of goals you might achieve in the next one to five years that would lead to the accomplishment of that one long-term goal. These are mid-term goals. Spend eight minutes on this brainstorm. Remember, neatness doesn't count. Go for quantity.

Evaluate

Review your brainstorm of mid-term goals, then select three that you think would lead to the accomplishment of the long-term goal you picked. Allow yourself about five minutes for this part of the exercise. Write your selections below.

Goal

Goal

Goal

Part three: short-term goals

Short-term goals are the ones you can accomplish in a year or less. These goals are specific achievements, such as completing a particular course or group of courses. A short-term financial goal probably would include an exact dollar amount. Whatever your short-term goals are, they will require action now or in the near future.

Brainstorm

Review your list of mid-term goals and select one. In another eight-minute brainstorm, generate a list of short-term goals—those you can reach in a year or less that will lead to the accomplishment of that mid-term goal. Write down everything that comes to mind. Do not evaluate or judge. The more ideas you write down, the better.

Evaluate

Review your list of short-term goals. The most effective brainstorms are conducted without judgment, so you might find some bizarre ideas on your list. That's fine. Now is the time to cross them out. Next, evaluate your short-term goals to determine which ones you can accomplish and are willing to accomplish. Select three of these and write them in the space provided.

Goal

Goal

Goal

Part four: next steps

Take a few minutes to reflect on all the goals you selected in this exercise. Look for relationships. Think about what accomplishing these goals can mean to you. Think about how the process of choosing them felt.

To make this process even more powerful, write a list of small, achievable steps you can take to accomplish each short-term goal. Make these steps specific enough to include a timeline. Then return to this list of steps in a few weeks and note your progress.

The more you practice, the more effective you will be at choosing goals that have meaning for you. You can repeat this exercise using the other long-term goals you generated, or you can create new ones. Use the process to make long-term goals real in the here and now.

Gearing up:
Using a long-term planner

Planning a day or week at a time is a powerful practice. Seeing how your days and weeks fit into a larger picture can yield even more benefits. One way to approach long-term planning is to get an overview of your quarter or semester. Using a quarter, semester, or yearly calendar helps you remember upcoming goals and commitments. On this calendar you can enter test dates, lab sessions, due dates for assignments, days classes will be cancelled, and other items that extend beyond the next week or two. Also list interim due dates, such as when you plan to complete the first draft of a term paper. Then, when planning your day or week, scan this calendar to refresh your memory.

Many office supply stores carry academic planners that cover an entire school year. You can also be creative and make your own. A big roll of newsprint pinned to a bulletin board or taped to a wall may do nicely.

Use your academic or yearly planner to mark other significant events, such as:

Birthdays, anniversaries, and other special occasions. Include a "tickler" note well ahead of time to remind you to pick up cards or gifts.

Medical and dental checkups, car maintenance schedules, meetings, luncheons, and other appointments.

Concerts, plays, television, and radio programs you want to enjoy.

Due dates for major bills—insurance, taxes, car registration, credit card and installment payments, medical expenses, taxes, interest charges, and charitable contributions. Use your calendar to keep track of the amounts you actually paid.

Trips, vacations, and holidays.

Consider keeping your yearly calendar for years to come. It can be as revealing and as fun to re-read as a personal journal. This calendar is a snapshot of your life in time. It says a lot about who you were and who you can be.

Week of	Monday	Tuesday	Wednesday	Thursday	Friday	Saturday	Sunday
9,5							
9,12		English Quiz					
9,19			English Paper Due		Speech #1		
9,26		Chemistry Test				← Fun at the	
10,3	BEACH! →	English Quiz			Speech #2		
10,10							
10,17				← NO CLASS →			
10,24							

LONG TERM PLANNER:____/____/____ to ____/____/____

Week of	Monday	Tuesday	Wednesday	Thursday	Friday	Saturday	Sunday
__/__							
__/__							
__/__							
__/__							
__/__							
__/__							
__/__							
__/__							
__/__							
__/__							
__/__							
__/__							
__/__							
__/__							
__/__							
__/__							
__/__							
__/__							
__/__							
__/__							
__/__							
__/__							

LONG TERM PLANNER: ___/___/___ to ___/___/___

Week of	Monday	Tuesday	Wednesday	Thursday	Friday	Saturday	Sunday
__/__							
__/__							
__/__							
__/__							
__/__							
__/__							
__/__							
__/__							
__/__							
__/__							
__/__							
__/__							
__/__							
__/__							
__/__							
__/__							
__/__							
__/__							
__/__							
__/__							
__/__							
__/__							
__/__							

The seven day anti-procrastination plan

Here are seven strategies you can use to eliminate procrastination. The suggestions are tied to the days of the week to help you remember them.

Monday,
Make it meaningful.

What is important about the job you've been putting off? List all the benefits of completing it. Look at it in relation to your goals. Be specific about the rewards for getting it done, including how you will feel when the task is complete.

Tuesday,
Take it apart.

Break big jobs into a series of small ones you can do in 15 minutes or less. If a long reading assignment intimidates you, divide it into two-page or three-page sections. Make a list of the sections and cross them off as you complete them so you can see your progress.

Wednesday,
Write an Intention Statement.

Write an Intention Statement on a 3x5 card. For example, if you can't get started on a term paper, you might write, "I intend to write a list of at least ten possible topics by 9 p.m. I will reward myself with an hour of guilt-free recreational reading." Carry the 3x5 card with you or post it in your study area where you can see it often.

Thursday,
Tell everyone.

Announce publicly your intention to get it done. Tell a friend you intend to learn 10 irregular French verbs by Saturday. Tell your spouse, roommate, parents, and children. Include anyone who will ask whether you've completed it or who will suggest ways to get it done. Make the world your support group.

Friday,
Find a reward.

Construct rewards carefully. Be willing to withhold them if you do not complete the task. Don't pick a movie as a reward for studying biology if you plan to go to the movie anyway. And when you legitimately reap your reward, notice how it feels. You might find that movies, new clothes, or an extra hour on the bicycle are more fun when you've earned them.

Saturday,
Settle it, now.

Do it now. The minute you notice yourself procrastinating, plunge into the task. Imagine yourself at a mountain lake, poised to dive. Gradual immersion would be slow torture. It's often less painful to leap. Then be sure to savor the feeling of having the task behind you.

Sunday,
Say no.

When you keep pushing a task into the low-priority category, re-examine the purpose for doing it at all. If you realize you really don't intend to do something, quit telling yourself that you will. That's procrastinating. Just say NO! Then you're not procrastinating, and you don't have to carry around the baggage of an undone task.

P.S. In some cases, procrastination is positive. Consider the following possibilities.

1. Procrastinate deliberately. You might discover that if you can choose to procrastinate, you can also choose not to procrastinate.

2. Observe your procrastination. Instead of doing something about it, look carefully at the process and its consequences. Avoid judgments. Be a scientist and record the facts. See if procrastination keeps you from getting what you want. Seeing clearly the cost of procrastination may help you kick the habit.

3. Ask yourself whether it's a problem. As one writer put it, "I don't do my best work on deadline. I do my only work on deadline." Some people thrive under pressure, and maybe that style works for you.

POWER PROCESS #2:

Be here now

THIS POWER PROCESS belongs in one of those late-night television ads—the ones in which hyperactive voices, shouting every sentence, describe "amazing," "fantastic," "revolutionary" new tools that chop, slice, dice, catch trout, and fit in your pocket.

The ad might sound like this:

BE HERE NOW! Yes, that's right friends. BE HERE NOW is a revolutionary tool for students. Carry it anywhere. Use it anytime. Get more out of textbooks. Solve problems faster. Take tests better. Can't stay awake in biology? No problem for BE HERE NOW. Millions sold in Europe! Order today! Send $39.99 to Power Process #2, Box 8306 ....

If this power process were sold on late-night television, some people might even buy it. Being right here, right now, is such a simple idea. It sounds obvious. Where else can you be but where you are? When else can you be there but when you are there? The answer is, you can be somewhere else at any time—in your head. It's human nature to live in our heads. When we do, we miss what's happening in the rest of the world.

To "Be here now" means to do what you're doing when you're doing it, and be where you are when you're there. Focus your attention on the here and now.

Leaving the here and now

We all have a voice in our head that hardly ever shuts up. If you don't believe it, conduct this experiment: Close your eyes for ten seconds and pay attention to what is going on in your head. Please do this right now.

Notice something? Perhaps your voice

was saying: "Forget it. I'm in a hurry." Another might have said, "I wonder when ten seconds is up." Still another could have been saying: "What little voice? I don't hear a little voice."

That's the voice.

This voice can take you anywhere, anytime, especially when you are studying. When the voice takes you away, you might appear to be studying, but your brain is at the beach enjoying spring break.

All of us have experienced the voice, as well as the absence of it. When the voice is silent, time ceases to exist. We forget worries, aches, pains, reasons, excuses, and justifications. We fully experience the here and now. Life is magic.

There are many benefits of such a state of consciousness. It is easier to discover the world around us when we are not chattering away to ourselves about how we think it ought to be, has been, or will be. Letting go of inner voices and pictures—being totally in the moment—is a powerful tool for students, and there are techniques you can use to keep yourself closer to the here and now.

Do not expect to be rid of daydreams entirely. That is neither possible nor desirable. Inner voices serve a purpose. They enable us to analyze, predict, classify, and understand events out there in the "real" world. Your stream of consciousness serves a purpose. When you are working on a term paper, your inner voices might suggest ideas. When you are listening to your sociology instructor, your inner voices can alert you to possible test questions. When you're about to jump out of an airplane, they could remind you to take a parachute.

Generally, letting go of these voices can dramatically improve your effectiveness.

Returning to the here and now

The first step toward returning to the here and now is to notice when you leave it. Thoughts have lives of their own, which they seek to preserve at all times. It is useless to fight thoughts with force because the harder you fight them, the harder they fight back. Thoughts want to live. If you doubt this, for the next ten seconds do *not*, under any circumstance, think of a pink elephant. Please begin not thinking about one now.

Persistent image, isn't it? Most ideas are this insistent when you try to deny them or force them out of your consciousness.

For example, during class you might notice yourself thinking about a test you took the previous day, or a party planned for the weekend, or the CD player you want.

Instead of trying to force a stray thought out of your head—a futile enterprise—simply notice it. Accept it. Tell yourself, "There's that thought again." Then, gently return your attention to the task at hand. That thought, or another, will come back. Your mind will drift. Simply notice again where your thoughts take you and gently bring yourself back to the here and now.

Another way to return to the here and now is to notice physical sensations associated with your surroundings. Notice the way the room looks or smells. Notice how the chair feels. Notice the temperature in the room. And bring yourself back to here and now. Do this as often as necessary, calmly, without irritation.

Experiment with noticing your inner voices. Let go of the ones that prevent you from focusing on learning. Practice the process. Be here now. And now. And now.

The here and now in your future

You also can use Power Process #2 to keep yourself pointed toward your goals. In fact, one of the best ways to get what you want in the future is to realize that you do not have a future. The only time you have is right now. The problem with this idea is that some students will think, "No future, huh? Terrific! Party time!" Being in the here and now, however, is not the same as living for today and forgetting about tomorrow.

Nor is the idea "Be here now" a call to abandon goals. Examine this idea closely: Goals exist only in the present.

Goals are merely tools we create to direct our actions right now. Goals, like our ideas of past and future, are useful creations of our minds. They are real only in the here and now.

The power of this idea lies in a simple but frequently overlooked fact: The only time to do anything is now. You can think about doing something next Wednesday. You can write about doing something next Wednesday. You can daydream, discuss, ruminate, speculate, and fantasize about what you will do next Wednesday.

But you can't do anything on Wednesday until it is Wednesday.

Sometimes students think of goals as things that exist in the misty future. And it's easy to postpone action on things in the misty future, especially when everyone else is going to a not-so-misty party.

However, the word "goal" comes from the Anglo-Saxon *gaelan*, which means to hinder or impede, as in the case of a boundary. That's what a goal does. It restricts, in a positive way, our activity in the here and now. It channels our energy into actions that are more likely to get us what we really want. That's what goals are for. And they are useful only when they are directing action in the here and now.

The process of time management works the same way. You can use the Time Monitor/Time Plan on page 42 to look at your past and plan your future. And the purpose of doing that is to give you more power in the here and now.

The idea behind Power Process #2 is simple. When you plan for the future, plan for the future. When you listen to a lecture, listen to a lecture. When you read this book, read this book. And when you choose to daydream, daydream.

Do what you're doing when you're doing it. Be where you are when you're there. Be here now...and now...and now.

STUDYING WITH CHILDREN UNDERFOOT

It is possible to combine effective study time and quality time with children. The following suggestions come largely from students who are also parents. The specific strategies you use will depend on your schedule and the age of your child.

Plan tasks for your child

Silly Putty, Play Doh, Etch-a-Sketch, blocks, coloring books, and other toys can lead your child to creative play. They can also free up study time for you. Gather the toys your child enjoys and keep them on hand. Consider allowing such activities *only* while you study. This might make the activity even more attractive to your children.

You can set up a desk for the child, just like yours, and even offer rewards for getting his "assignment" done. While he colors, plays with stickers, or flips through a children's book, you can review your notes.

Child-proof a room to study in and fill it with toys

Set aside one room or area in your home for children. Remove from it all objects that are unsafe for children, and fill it with your child's favorite toys. The goal is a "child-proof" area, one where children can roam freely and play with minimal supervision. Again, consider allowing the child in this room only while you study. Study time then becomes a reward.

Allow for interruptions

It's possible that you'll still be interrupted, even if you do set up child activities in advance. If so, then schedule the kind of studying that can be interrupted. You could, for instance, write out or review flash cards with key terms and definitions. Or, you could brainstorm titles for a term paper. Save the tasks that require sustained attention for other times, such as after children go to bed or before they wake up.

Build study time into your school schedule

See if you can arrange for time to study at school, before you come home. If you can arrive at school 15 minutes early and stay 15 minutes later, you'll squeeze in an extra half-hour of study time that day. Also look for study times between classes.

Use television creatively

Another option is to use television as a babysitter when you can control the programming. Rent a videotape for your child to watch as you study. If you're concerned about children becoming "couch potatoes," then select educational programs that keep your child active.

See if your child can use headphones while watching television. That way the house stays quiet while you study.

Make it a game

Studying chemistry with a 3-year-old is not as preposterous as it sounds. The secret is to choose the kind of studying that the child can participate in. For instance, use this time to recite. While studying chemistry, make funny faces as you say the properties of the transition elements in the periodic table. Talk in a weird voice as you repeat Faraday's laws. Draw pictures and make an exciting story about the process of titration.

Use kids as an audience for a speech. If you have invented rhymes, poems, or songs to help you remember formulas or dates, teach them to your children. Be playful. Kids are attracted to energy and enthusiasm.

Sometimes children can even act as private tutors. Ask them to hold flash cards for you. Play "school" with your children as teachers and give them questions to ask you.

Ask for cooperation

Tell the child how important studying is to you and how you appreciate his cooperation. Reward him with attention and praise when he is quiet. When they are included in the process, children are less likely to resent school work as something that takes you away from them. Rather, it becomes something you do together.

When you can't do everything, just do something

One objection to studying with children is, "I just can't concentrate. There's no way I can get it all done while children are around." That's OK. Even if you can't comprehend an entire chapter while the kids are running past your desk, you can skim the chapter. Or you could just read the introduction and summary. When you can't get it all done, just get *something* done.

Caution: If you always study this way, your education may be compromised. Supplement this strategy with others so you can complete crucial tasks.

Be outrageous

When in doubt, go for the bizarre. Make studying look fun or unusual to your child. One parent actually sits inside a playpen to do his studying. Meanwhile, his son is *outside* the playpen in a child-proof room, delighted with this reversal of roles.

Attend to your child first

Keep the books out of sight when you first come home. Take 10 minutes to hug your child before you settle in to study. Ask about the child's day. Then explain that you have some work to do. Your child may reward you with 30 minutes of quiet time.

A short time of full, focused attention from an adult is often more satisfying to children than longer periods of partial attention.

Plan study breaks with children

Another option is to take 10 minutes each hour that you study to be with children. View this not as an interruption but as a study break.

Or, schedule time to be with your children when you've finished studying. Let your children in on the plan: "I'll be done reading at 7:30. That gives us a whole hour to play before you go to bed."

Many children love visible reminders that "their time" is approaching. An oven timer works well for this purpose. Set it for 15 minutes of quiet time. Follow that with five minutes of show and tell, storybooks, or another activity for your child. Then set the timer for another 15 minutes of studying, another break, and so on.

Develop a routine

Many young children are lovers of routine. They often feel more comfortable when they know what to expect. You can use this to your benefit. One option is to develop a regular time for studying: "From 4 p.m. to 5 p.m. each afternoon is time for me to do my homework." Let your child know this schedule, then enforce it.

Bargain with children. Reward them for keeping the schedule. In return for quiet time, give your child an extra allowance or special treat. Children may enjoy gaining "credits" for this purpose. Each time they give you an hour of quiet time for studying, make an entry in a chart, put a star on their bulletin board, or give them a "coupon." Let children know that after they've accumulated a certain number of entries, stars, or coupons, they can cash in for a big reward—a movie or trip to the zoo.

Ask other adults for help

This suggestion for studying with children is one repeated throughout this book: Enlist other people in your success.

This can be as simple as asking your spouse, partner, neighbor, or a fellow student to take care of the children while you study. Offer to trade child care with a neighbor: You will take his kids and yours for two hours on Thursday night if he'll take them for two hours on Saturday morning. Some parents start block-wide babysitting co-ops based on the same idea.

Find community activities and services

Ask if your school provides a daycare service. In some cases, these services are available to students at a reduced cost. Community agencies such as the YMCA may offer similar programs.

You can also find special events that appeal to children. Storytelling hours at the library are one example. While your child is being entertained or supervised, you can stay close by. Use the time to read a chapter or review class notes.

Find a playmate

Another strategy is to find a regular playmate for your child. Some children can pair off with a close friend and safely retreat to their rooms for hours of private play. You can check on them occasionally and still get lots of work done.

The ABC daily to-do's

or
Working your A's off

ONE OF THE MOST EFFECTIVE WAYS to stay on track and actually get things done is to use a daily to-do list. While the Time Plan/Time Monitor is a general picture of the week, your daily to-do list is a specific list of things you want to get done within 24 hours. Keep the list with you; cross out items when you complete them; add new items when you think of them.

The advantage of keeping a daily list is that you don't have to remember what to do next. It's on the list. A typical day in the life of a student is full of separate, often unrelated tasks—reading, attending lectures, reviewing notes, working at a job, writing papers, doing special projects, research, errands. It's easy to forget an important job in a busy day. When that job is written down, you don't have to trust your memory.

Keep a to-do list every day. It's best to write out the daily to-do list the night before. That way, when your day begins, so will you. Write everything you want to accomplish on one sheet of paper, a daily planning calendar, a special notebook, or a 3x5 card. Cards work well because you can slip them into your pocket.

Rate each task by priority. One way to do this is to label each task A, B, or C.

A's on your list are those things that are most important. These are assignments that are due or jobs that need to be done immediately. A priorities also include activities that lead directly to your long-, mid-, or short-term goals.

The B tasks on your list are important, but less so than your A's. B's might become A's someday. These tasks are important, but not as urgent. They can be postponed if necessary.

C's do not require immediate attention. C items include things like "shop for a new blender" and "get brochures for next year's vacation." C priorities are often small, easy jobs.

Once you've labeled all the tasks on your list, schedule time for all of the A's. The B's and C's can be done in odd moments during the day when you are between tasks and don't have time to start the next A.

When you use the ABC priority method, you might discover a condition common to students: C fever. This is the uncontrollable urge to drop that A task and begin crossing C's off the list. If your history paper is due tomorrow, you might feel compelled to vacuum the rug, call your third cousin in Tulsa, and make a trip to the store for shoelaces. The reason C fever is so common is that A tasks may be difficult or lengthy, and the risk of failure is higher. Because they are the most important to us, A's can be threatening.

If you notice symptoms of C fever, ask: Does this job really need to be done now? Do I really need to alphabetize my tape collection, or might I better use this time to study for tomorrow's data processing exam?

Use your to-do list to keep yourself on task and working on your A's. Don't panic or berate yourself when you realize that in the last six hours, you have completed 11 C's and not a single A. Calmly return to the A's.

As you complete tasks, cross them off the list. Crossing off things can be fun, a visible reward for your diligence.

Another option is to put each "to do" on its own 3x5 card. This allows for easy sorting of jobs by priority or time.

At the end of the day, evaluate your performance. Look for A's you didn't complete. Look for tasks that repeatedly appear as B's or C's on your list and never seem to get done. Consider changing these to A priority or dropping them altogether. Similarly, you might consider changing an A that didn't get done to a B or C priority item.

Develop your own style. You might find that grouping tasks by categories like "errands" or "reading assignments" works best. Be creative.

And accept mistakes. You might assign A priority to some items that turn out to be true C's. Some of the C's that lurk at the bottom of your list day after day might really be A's. When you keep a list every day, you are more likely to discover these errors before they become problems.

Keep in mind the power of planning a whole week or even two weeks at a time in addition to the daily to-do list. Planning in this way can make it easier to put activities in context—to see how your daily goals relate to long-term goals. Weekly planning can also free you from feeling that you have to polish off your whole to-do list in one day. Instead, you can spread tasks over the whole week.

In any case, make starting a to-do list an A priority.

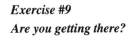

Exercise #9
Are you getting there?

The purpose of this exercise is to let you see how well you are focusing on long-term goals. It's easy to choose long-term goals, commit to them, then forget about them because they seem so far in the future. Yet big goals, like owning a farm, completing a degree, or learning a profession, can be achieved only by stringing together hundreds of small daily goals. This exercise also gives you a chance to look for what barriers are in your way.

Use your completed Time Monitor/Time Plan from page 45 for this exercise. Pick three of your most important long-term goals. You can use the goals you generated in your goal setting exercise on page 58 or you can use others. The first step of this exercise is to write those three long-term goals in the space provided below.

Next, go through the completed Time Monitor/Time Plan and circle everything you did that will eventually lead to the accomplishment of the long-term goals you chose.

Then, write down the activities and the time you spent on them under the appropriate goal.

The final step is your assessment of this data. Write this in the form of a Discovery/Intention Statement. What have you learned about yourself by doing this exercise?

Goal:

Time Spent   *Activities*

Goal:

Time Spent   *Activities*

Goal:

Time Spent   *Activities*

By reviewing my Time Monitor/Plan and my long-term goals, I learned that . . .

Knowing this, I intend to . . .

Malcolm X,

martyred militant, emerged from the heart of the Black ghetto to fight against racial segregation and oppression. At the peak of his power in 1965, his fears of assassination came true.

From The Autobiography of Malcolm X, *by Malcolm X, with the assistance of Alex Haley. Copyright 1964 by Alex Haley and Malcolm X. Copyright 1965 by Alex Haley and Betty Shabazz. Reprinted by permission of Random House, Inc.*

I became increasingly frustrated at not being able to express what I wanted to convey in letters that I wrote, especially those to Mr. Elijah Muhammad. In the street, I had been the most articulate hustler out there—I had commanded attention when I said something. But now, trying to write simple English, I not only wasn't articulate, I wasn't even functional. How would I sound writing in slang, the way I would say it, something such as, "Look, daddy, let me pull your coat about a cat, Elijah Muhammad —"

Many who today hear me somewhere in person, or on television, or those who read something I've said, will think I went to school far beyond the eighth grade. This impression is due entirely to my prison studies.

It had really begun back in the Charlestown Prison, when Bimbi first made me feel envy of his stock of knowledge. Bimbi had always taken charge of any conversation he was in, and I had tried to emulate him. But every book I picked up had few sentences which didn't contain anywhere from one to nearly all of the words that might as well have been in Chinese. When I just skipped those words, of course, I really ended up with little idea of what the book said. So I had come to the Norfolk Prison Colony still going through only book-reading motions. Pretty soon, I would have quit even these motions, unless I had received the motivation that I did.

I saw that the best thing I could do was to get hold of a dictionary—to study, to learn some words. I was lucky enough to reason also that I should try to improve my penmanship. It was sad. I couldn't even write in a straight line. It was both ideas together that moved me to request a dictionary along with some tablets and pencils from the Norfolk Prison Colony school.

I spent two days just riffling uncertainly through the dictionary's pages. I'd never realized so many words existed! I didn't know which words I needed to learn. Finally, just to start some kind of action, I began copying.

In my slow, painstaking, ragged handwriting, I copied into my tablet everything printed on that first page, down to the punctuation marks.

I believe it took me a day. Then, aloud, I read, back to myself, everything I'd written on the tablet. Over and over, aloud, to myself, I read my own handwriting.

I woke up the next morning, thinking about those words— immensely proud to realize that not only had I written so much at one time, but I'd written words that I never knew were in the world. Moreover, with a little effort, I also could remember what many of these words meant. I reviewed the words whose meanings I didn't remember. Funny thing, from the dictionary first page right now, that "aardvark" springs to my mind. The dictionary had a picture of it, a long-tailed, long-eared, burrowing African mammal, which lives off termites caught by sticking out its tongue as an anteater does for ants.

I was so fascinated that I went on—I copied the dictionary's next page. And the same experience came when I studied that. With every succeeding page, I also learned of people and places and events from history. Actually the dictionary is like a miniature encyclopedia. Finally the dictionary's A section had filled a whole tablet —and I went on into the B's. That was the way I started copying what eventually became the entire dictionary. It went a lot faster after so much practice helped me to pick up handwriting speed. Between what I wrote in my tablet, and writing letters, during the rest of my time in prison I would guess I wrote a million words.

I suppose it was inevitable that as my word base broadened, I could for the first time pick up a book and read and now begin to understand what the book was saying. Anyone who has read a great deal can imagine the new world that opened. Let me tell you something: From then until I left that prison, in every free moment I had, if I was not reading in the library, I was reading on my bunk. You couldn't have gotten me out of books with a wedge. Between Mr. Muhammad's teachings, my correspondence, my visitors— usually Ella and Reginald—and my reading of books, months passed without my even thinking about being imprisoned. In fact, up to then, I never had been so truly free in my life.

. . . I have often reflected upon the new vistas that reading opened to me. I knew right there in prison that reading had changed forever the course of my life. As I see it today, the ability to read awoke inside me some long dormant craving to be mentally alive. I certainly wasn't seeking any degree, the way a college confers a status symbol upon its students. My homemade education gave me, with every additional book that I read, a little bit more sensitivity to the deafness, dumbness, and blindness that was afflicting the black race in America. Not long ago, an English writer telephoned me from London, asking questions. One was, "What's your alma mater?" I told him, "Books."

1. What are at least three ways you can control interruptions when you study?

2. It is effective to leave "holes" in your schedule to allow for the unexpected. True or false. Explain your answer.

3. Suppose that after you choose where to focus your attention, your mind wanders. Power Process #2 suggests that one of the most effective ways to bring your focus back to the here and now is to:

   (A) slap your cheek and shout "attention" as loud as you can.
   (B) notice that your thoughts have wandered and gently bring them back.
   (C) sleep.
   (D) concentrate fully and resist the temptation to be distracted.
   (E) indulge your distracting thoughts until they disappear.

4. What are at least five of the *25 Ways to get the most out of now*?

5. In time management terms, what is meant by the question, "Is this a piano?"

6. Within the ABC priority method, define "C fever."

7. Polyphasic behavior is always ineffective. True or false. Explain your answer.

8. Describe at least three of the seven strategies for dealing with procrastination.

9. What two ideas, taken together, led Malcolm X to request a dictionary along with some tablets and pencils for the Norfolk Prison Colony school?

10. Working your A's off refers to:

    (A) a strategy for organizing your study area
    (B) refering to a dictionary when reading unfamiliar material.
    (C) the importance of your physical exercise program.
    (D) accomplishing the top priority items on your to-do list.
    (E) a strategy for studying with children underfoot.

Journal Entry #14
Discovery Statement

After reading and doing this chapter, what did you discover about the way you manage time? Complete the following sentence.

I discovered that I . . .

_____
_____
_____
_____

Journal entry #15
Intention Statement

List one idea or technique you wanted to learn from this chapter and didn't. Then describe what you will do to learn it. I intend to . . .

_____
_____
_____
_____

Journal Entry #16
Intention Statement

Pick two time management strategies and write a short, one-sentence intention statement about how you plan to use each one in the next 72 hours.

I intend to use the strategy of . . .

_____
_____

I intend to use the strategy of . . .

_____
_____

Journal Entry #17
Intention Statement

In the Introduction, you listed what you wanted to get from this book. Choose one of those goals. Then write at least three actions you intend to take within the next 48 hours that could help you accomplish that goal. Make these actions limited and specific—things that you can really accomplish.

_____
_____
_____
_____

Chapter 3
Memory

Memory is the mother of imagination, reason and skill . . . .
This is the companion, this is the tutor, the poet, the library
with which you travel.
MARK VAN DOREN

The true art of memory is the art of attention.
SAMUEL JOHNSON

Journal Entry #18
Discovery Statement

I want the following things from this chapter . . .

In this chapter . . .

This chapter gives you the opportunity to discover your powerful memory and then develop methods to tap it.

You never forget suggests that you already have a powerful memory. The mechanisms you use to recall the names of relatives, how to drive a car, or the meanings of words on this page are the same mechanisms you can use to remember chemistry formulas, economic principles, or medical procedures.

You can take the guesswork out of memory development by using even a few of the suggestions in ***Twenty memory techniques***.

One of the most useful memory skills is explained in ***Remembering names***. You'll never need to fear introductions again.

Mnemonic devices are memory tricks that you can use effectively if you know their pitfalls. Learn how to make up new words, create sentences, and use other devices to improve recall.

Power Process #3: Love your problems is an unusual way to turn problems into opportunities and handle barriers that seem insurmountable.

Also in this chapter are exercises that allow you to discover memory skills you already have: ***Finding your car keys (or anything else)***, ***Set a trap for your memory,*** and ***Be a poet***.

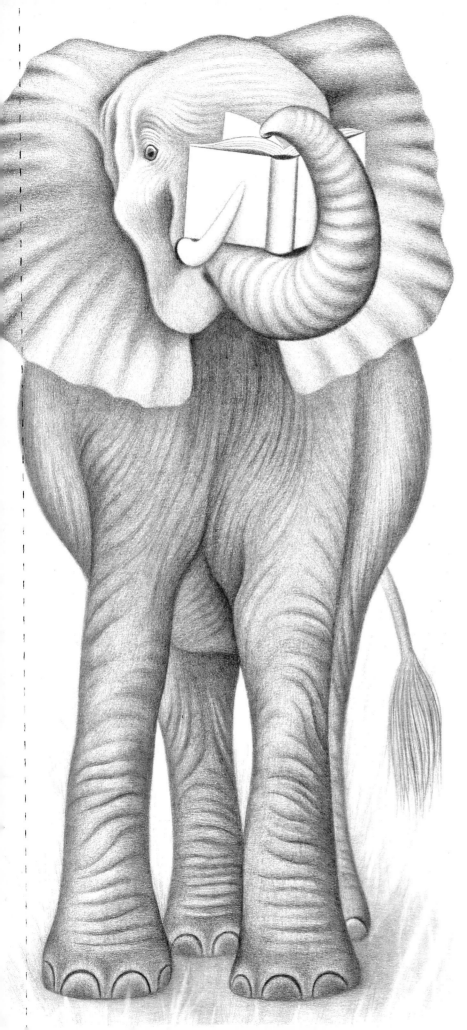

You never forget

THE KEY TO USING YOUR MEMORY more effectively is to realize that–short of injury, disease or death–your brain never loses anything. Once a thought or perception has been input to your memory, it stays there for the rest of your life. What we call "forgetting" is either the inability to recall stored information or the failure to store information in the first place.

For example, during certain kinds of brain surgery, the patient remains conscious. When sections of the brain are stimulated with a mild electrical current, the patient will often remember events of her childhood with absolute clarity. She can recall details she thought were long forgotten–like the smell of her father's starched shirts or the feel of sunlight warming her face through the window of her first grade classroom.

People under hypnosis have reported similar experiences. Some people have been able to recall events that took place shortly after their birth. Working with police, hypnotists have enabled witnesses of crimes to remember vital information, such as license plate numbers.

Once information is stored in memory, it is never forgotten. Sometimes, however, we do have difficulty recalling a piece of information from our memory. The data is still in our heads. We simply can't find it.

Just as often, when we think we have forgotten something, the truth is that we never stored it in our memory in the first place.

Think of your memory as a vast, overgrown jungle. This memory-jungle is thick with wild plants, exotic shrubs, twisted trees, and creeping vines. It spreads over thousands of square miles–dense, tangled, forbidding. Imagine that the jungle is bounded on all sides by impassable mountains. There is only one entrance to the jungle, a narrow pass through the mountains that opens into a small meadow.

In the jungle there are animals, millions of them. The animals represent all the information in your memory. Imagine that every thought, picture, or perception you ever had is represented by an animal in this jungle. Every single event ever perceived by any of your five senses–sight, touch, hearing, smell, or taste–is also in the jungle. Some of the thought animals, like your picture of the color of your seventh grade teacher's eyes, are well-hidden. Other thoughts, like your telephone number or the position of the reverse gear in your car, are easier to find.

There are two rules of the jungle. Each thought animal must pass through the meadow at the entrance to the memory jungle; and once an animal enters the jungle, it never leaves.

The meadow represents short-term memory. It's the kind of memory that you use when you look up a telephone number. You can look at seven digits and hold them in your short-term memory long enough to dial them.

Short-term memory appears to have a limited capacity (the meadow is small), and short-term memory disappears fast (animals pass through the meadow quickly.)

The jungle itself represents long-term memory. This is the kind of memory that allows us to recall information from day to day, week to week, and year to year. Remember that animals never leave the long-term memory jungle.

The following visualizations can help you recall useful concepts about memory.

Visualization #1: A *well-worn path*
Imagine what happens as a thought, in this case we'll call it a deer, bounds across short-term memory and into the jungle. The deer leaves a trail of broken twigs and hoof prints which you can follow. Brain research suggests that thoughts also wear paths in the memory. These paths are called neural traces. The more well-worn the neural trace, the easier it is to retrieve (find) the thought. In other words, the more often the deer retraces the path, the clearer the path becomes. The more often you recall information, and the more often you put the same information into your memory, the easier it is to find.

When you buy a new car, for example, the first few times you try to find reverse you have to think for a moment. After you have found reverse every day for a week, the path is worn into your memory. After a year, the path is so well-worn that when you dream about driving your car backwards you even dream the correct motion for finding reverse.

Visualization #2: *A herd of thoughts*
The second picture you can use to your advantage is the picture of many animals gathering at a clearing–like thoughts gathering at a central location in the memory. It is easier to retrieve thoughts that are grouped together, just as it is easier to find a herd of animals gathered in a clearing than it is to find one deer.

Pieces of information are easier to recall if you can associate them with other similar information. For example, it is easier to remember a particular player's batting average if you associate it with other baseball statistics.

Visualization #3: *Turning your back*
Imagine releasing the deer into the jungle, turning your back on it, and counting to ten. When you turn around, the deer is gone. This is exactly what happens to most of the information we receive.

Generally, people cannot remember 50% of the material they have just read. Within 24 hours, most people can only recall about 20%. That means that 80% of the material is wandering around lost in the memory jungle.

The remedy is simple: Review quickly. Do not take your eyes off the animal as it crosses the short-term memory meadow; and review it soon after it enters the long-term memory jungle. Wear a path in your memory immediately.

Visualization #4: *You are directing the animal traffic*
The fourth picture is one with you in it. You are standing at the entrance to the short-term memory meadow, directing herds of animals as they file through the pass, across the meadow, and into your long-term memory. You are taking an active role in the learning process. You are paying attention. You are doing more than sitting on a rock and watching the animal traffic file into your brain. You become part of the process, and as you do, you take control of your memory.

20memory techniques

Experiment with these techniques to make a flexible, custom-made memory system that fits your style of learning. The 20 techniques are divided into four categories, each of which represents a general principle for improving memory.

Briefly, the categories are:

1) Organize it. Organized information is easier to find.
2) Use your body. Learning is an active process; get all your senses involved.
3) Use your brain. Work with your memory, not against it.
4) Recall it. This is easier when you use the other principles to store information.

The first three categories, which include techniques #1 through #16, are about storing information effectively. Most memory battles are won or lost here. To get the most out of this article, survey the following techniques by reading each title. Then read the techniques. Next, skim them again looking for the ones you like best. Mark those and use them.

Organize it.

1. Learn from the general to the specific.

Imagine looking at a new painting this way. Blindfold yourself. Put a magnifying glass up to your eye. Move your face to within inches of the painting. Now, yank the blindfold off and begin studying the painting, one square inch at a time. Chances are, even after you finished "looking" at the painting this way, you wouldn't know what it is.

Unfortunately, many students approach new courses and textbooks just this way. They feel driven to jump right in and tackle the details, before they get the big picture.

Here is a different approach. Before you begin your next reading assignment, skim it for the general idea. You can use the same techniques you learned in Exercise #1: "Textbook reconnaissance" on page vi.

You also can use this technique at the beginning of a course. Ask someone who has taken it to quickly review it with you. Do a textbook reconnaissance of the reading assignments for the entire course. This technique works best at the beginning of a term, but it's never too late to use it.

If you're lost, step back and look at the big picture. The details might make more sense.

2. Make it meaningful.

A sky diver will not become bored learning how to pack her parachute. Her reward for learning the skill is too important. Know what you want from your education, then look for connections between what you want and what you are studying. If you're bogged down in quadratic equations, stand back for a minute. Think about how that math course relates to your goal of becoming an electrical engineer.

When information helps you get something you want, it's easier to remember. That is one reason it pays to be specific about what you want.

3. Create associations.

The data already stored in your memory is arranged according to a scheme that makes sense to you. When you introduce new data, you can recall it more effectively if you store it near similar or related data.

Say you are introduced to someone named Greg. One way to remember his name would be to visualize another person you know named Greg. When you see the new Greg, your mind is more likely to associate him with a Greg you already know.

(**Parenthetically Speaking** You will find concepts repeated in this book. Some of the most repeated concepts seem, on the surface, to be the simplest. There is a reason for this repetition.

Use your body.

4. Learn it once, actively.

According to an old saying, people remember 90 percent of what they do, 75 percent of what they see, and 20 percent of what they hear.

These percentages might not be scientifically provable, but the idea behind them is sound. Action is a great memory enhancer. You can test this theory for yourself by studying with the same energy you might bring to the dance floor or the basketball court.

When you sit at your desk, sit up. Sit on the edge of your chair, as if you were about to spring out of it and sprint across the room.

Try standing up when you study. It's harder to fall asleep in this position. Some people insist their brains work better when they stand.

Pace back and forth and gesture as you recite material out loud. Use your hands. Get your whole body involved in studying.

These techniques also are great ways to battle boredom. Boredom puts memory to sleep. Wake it up by using your arms and legs as well as your eyes, ears, and voice.

Remember, the main reason people "forget" is that they never really learned it in the first place, even if they think they did. Learning can be deceptive. Most learning, especially in higher education, takes place in a passive setting. Students are sitting down, quiet and subdued.

Don't be fooled. Learning takes energy. When you learn effectively, you are burning calories, even if you are sitting at a desk reading a textbook.

5. Relax.

When we're relaxed, we absorb new information quicker and recall it with greater accuracy. Some courses in accelerated and "whole mind" learning teach relaxation techniques.

Part of this is common sense. Students who can't recall information during a final exam, when they are nervous, often can recite the same facts later, when they are relaxed.

This idea might seem to contradict technique #4, but it doesn't. Being relaxed is not the same as being drowsy, zoned out, or asleep. Relaxation is a state of alertness, free of tension, during which our minds can play with new information, roll it around, create associations with it, and apply many of the other memory techniques. We can be active and relaxed.

Many books, tapes, and seminars are available to teach you how to relax. In addition, relaxation exercises are included in this book. Experiment with these exercises and apply them as you study. "Mellowing out" might do more than lower your blood pressure; it might help you succeed in school.

6. Create pictures.

Draw diagrams. Make cartoons. Use them to connect facts and illustrate relationships. Relationships within and among abstract concepts can be "seen" and recalled easily when they are visualized. The key is to use your imagination.

For example, in physics, Boyle's Law states that the pressure of a quantity of gas is inversely proportional to the volume the gas occupies. That is, if you cut the volume in half, you double the pressure. To remember this concept, you might picture someone "doubled over" using a bicycle pump. As she increases the pressure in the pump by decreasing the volume in the pump cylinder, she seems to be getting angrier.

By the time she has doubled the pressure (and halved the volume) she is "boiling" (Boyle-ing) mad.

Through repetition, learning takes place on a deep level. When concepts become second nature, they are more readily available for use in any situation. So, the book repeats itself. Consider doing the same.

20 memory techniques

Another reason to create pictures is that visual information is associated with a different part of the brain than verbal information. When you create a picture of a concept, you are anchoring the information in two parts of your brain. This increases your chances of recalling that information.

To visualize relationships effectively, create action, such as the person using the pump. Make the picture vivid, too. The person's face could be bright red. Make her ready to "boil." And involve all your senses. Imagine how the cold metal of the pump would feel and how she would sound as she struggled and grunted with it. (She'd have to struggle. It would take incredible strength to double the pressure in a bicycle pump, not to mention a darn sturdy pump.)

7. Recite and repeat.

When you repeat something out loud, you anchor the concept in two different senses. First, you get the physical sensation in your throat, tongue, and lips when voicing the concept. Second, you hear it.

The combined result is synergistic, just as it is when you draw pictures.

That is, the effect of using two different senses is greater than the sum of their individual effects.

The "out loud" part is important. Reciting silently, in your head, can be useful—in the library, for example—but it is not as effective as making noise. Your mind can trick itself into thinking it knows something, when it doesn't. Your ears are harder to fool.

The repetition part is important, too. Repetition is the most common memory device because it works. Repetition blazes a trail through the pathways of your brain, making the information easier to find. Repeat a concept out loud until you know it, then say it five more times.

Recitation also works best when you recite concepts in your own words. For example, if you want to remember, "The acceleration of a falling body due to gravity at sea level equals 32 feet per second per second," you might say, "Gravity makes an object accelerate 32 feet per second faster for each second that it's in the air at sea level." Putting it in your own words forces you to think about it.

Have some fun with this technique. Recite by writing a song about what you're learning. Sing it in the shower. Use any style you want. ("Country, jazz, rock, or rap, when you sing out loud, learning's a snap.")

Or imitate someone. Imagine your textbook being read by Bill Cosby, Madonna, or Clint Eastwood. ("Go ahead, punk. Make my density equal mass over volume.")

Recite and repeat. It's a technique you can use anywhere.

8. Write it down.

This technique is obvious, yet easy to forget. Writing a note to yourself helps you remember an idea, even if you never look at the note again.

You can extend this technique by writing it down not just once, but many times. Let go of the old images of being in elementary school and being forced to write, "I will not throw paper wads" 100 times on the chalkboard after school. Used with items that you choose to remember, repetitive writing is a powerful technique.

Writing engages a different kind of memory than speaking. Writing prompts us to be more logical, coherent, and complete. Written reviews reveal gaps in knowledge that oral reviews miss, just as oral reviews reveal gaps that mental reviews miss.

Another advantage of written reviews is that they more closely match the way we're asked to remember material in school. During your academic career, you'll probably take far more written exams than oral exams. Writing can be an effective way to prepare for tests.

Finally, writing is physical. Your arm, your hand, and your fingers join in. Remember, you remember what you do.

Use your brain.

9. Reduce interference.

Turn off the stereo when you study. Find a quiet place that is free from distraction. If there's a party at your house, go to the library. If you have a strong attraction to food, don't torture yourself by studying next to your refrigerator.

Two hours worth of studying in front of the television might be worth 10 minutes of studying where it is quiet. If you have two hours and want to study and watch television, it's probably better to study for an hour and watch television for an hour. Doing one at a time increases your ability to remember.

10. Use daylight.

Study your most difficult subjects during daylight hours. Many people can concentrate more effectively during the day. The early morning hours can be especially productive, even for people who hate to get up with the sun.

11. Overlearn.

One way to fight mental fuzziness is to learn more than you intended. Students often stop studying when they think they know the material well enough to pass a test. Another option is to pick a subject apart, examine it, add to it, and go over it until it becomes second nature.

This technique is especially effective for problem solving. Do the assigned problems, then do more problems. Find another text and work similar problems. Make up your own problems and work those. When you pretest yourself in this way, the potential rewards are speed, accuracy, and greater confidence at exam time.

12. Escape the short-term memory trap.

Short-term memory is different than the kind of memory you'll need during exam week. For example, most of us can look at an unfamiliar seven-digit phone number once and remember it long enough to dial it. Try recalling that number the next day.

Short-term memory can decay after a few minutes and it rarely lasts more than several hours. A short review within minutes or hours of a study session can move material from short-term memory into long-term memory. That quick mini-review can save you hours of study time when exams roll around.

13. Distribute learning.

Marathon study sessions are not effective. You can get far more done in three two-hour sessions than in one six-hour session.

For example, when you are studying for your American history exam, study for an hour or two, then wash the dishes. While you are washing the dishes, part of your mind reviews what you studied.

Return to American history for a while, then call a friend. Even while you are deep in conversation, part of your mind will be reviewing history.

You can get more done if you take regular breaks, and you can even use them as mini-rewards. After a productive study session, give yourself permission to make a short phone call, listen to a song, or play ten minutes of hide and seek with your kids.

There is an exception to this idea. When you are engrossed in a textbook and cannot put it down, when you are consumed by an idea for a term paper and cannot think of anything else—keep going. The master student within you has taken over.

Enjoy the ride.

14. Be aware of attitudes.

People who think history is boring tend to have difficulty remembering history. People who believe math is difficult tend to have difficulty recalling mathematical formulas. All of us can forget information that contradicts our opinions.

This is not the same as fighting your

attitudes or struggling to give them up. Simply acknowledge them. Notice them. Your awareness can deflate an attitude that is blocking your memory.

One way to befriend a self-defeating attitude about a subject is to relate it to something you are interested in. For example, consider a person who is fanatical about cars. She can rebuild a motor in a weekend and considers that a good time.

From this apparently specialized interest, she can explore wide realms of knowledge. She can relate the workings of an engine to principles of physics, math, and chemistry. Computerized parts in newer cars lead her to data processing. She can study how cars have changed our cities and helped create suburbs, a topic that includes urban planning, sociology, business, economics, psychology, and history.

We remember what we find interesting. If you think a subject is boring, remember, everything is related to everything else. Look for the connections.

15. Choose what not to store in memory.

We can adopt an "information diet." Just as we choose to avoid certain foods, we can choose not to retain certain kinds of information.

Decide what's essential to remember from a reading assignment or lecture. Extract the core concepts. Ask what you'll be tested on, as well as what you want to remember. Then apply memory techniques to those ideas.

16. Combine memory techniques.

All of these memory techniques work even better in combination with each other. Choose two or three techniques to use on a particular assignment. Experiment for yourself.

For example, after you take a few minutes to get an overview of a reading assignment (#1), you could draw a quick picture to represent the main point (#6). Or you could overlearn that math formula (#11)

by singing a jingle about it (#7) all the way to work. If you have an attitude that math is difficult, you could acknowledge that (#14), then you could distribute your math study time in short, easy-to-handle sessions (#13).

Combining memory techniques is like combining sight, sound, and touch when you study. The effect is synergistic.

Recall it.

17. Remember something else.

When you are stuck and can't remember something you know you know, remember something else that is related to it.

If you can't remember your great aunt's name, remember your great uncle's name. During an economics exam, if you can't remember anything about the aggregate demand curve, recall what you know about the aggregate supply curve. If you cannot recall specific facts, remember the example the instructor used during her lecture. Information is stored in the same area of the brain as similar information. You can unblock your recall by stimulating that area of your memory.

A brainstorm is a good memory jog. When you are stumped in a test, start writing down lots of answers to related questions and—pop!—the answer you need is likely to appear.

18. Notice when you do remember.

Everyone has a different memory style. Some people are best at recalling information they've read. Others remember best what they've heard, seen, or done.

To develop your memory, notice when you recall information easily and ask yourself what memory techniques you're using naturally. Also notice when it's difficult to recall information. Let go of the temptation to judge yourself. Instead, be a reporter. Get the facts, and adjust your learning techniques. And remember to congratulate yourself when you remember.

19. Use it before you lose it.

Even information stored in long-term memory becomes difficult to recall if we don't use it regularly. The pathways to the information in our brains become faint with disuse. For example, you can probably remember your current phone number. What was your phone number ten years ago?

This points to a powerful memory technique. To remember something, access it a lot. Read it, write it, speak it, listen to it, apply it—find some way to make contact with the material regularly. Each time you do that, you widen the neural pathway to the material and make it easier to recall the next time.

Another way to contact the material is to teach it. Teaching demands mastery. When you explain the function of the pancreas to a fellow student, you discover quickly whether you really understand the pancreas.

Study groups are especially effective because they put you on stage. The friendly pressure of knowing you'll teach the group helps to focus your attention.

20. And, remember, you never forget.

You might not believe that an idea or thought never leaves your memory. That's OK. In fact, it doesn't matter whether you agree with the idea or not. It can work for you anyway.

Test the concept. Adopt an attitude that says: "I never forget anything. I may have difficulty recalling something from my memory, but I never really forget it. All I have to do is find where I stored it."

Many people use the flip side of this technique and get the opposite results. "I never remember anything," they say over and over again. "I've always had a poor memory. I'm such a scatterbrain." That kind of negative self-talk is self-fulfilling.

An alternative is to speak more positively, or at least more accurately.

Instead of saying, "I don't remember," you can say, "I don't recall right now." The latter statement implies that the information you want is stored in your mind, and that you can retrieve it...just not right now.

We can also use affirmations (see page 314) that support us as we develop our memories. Possibilities include: "I recall information easily and accurately" and "My memory serves me well."

Or even "I never forget!"

NOTABLE FAILURES—

Dr. Milton E. Larson, "Humbling Cases for Career Counselors," Phi Delta Kappan, February 1973, Volume LIV, No. 6; 374.

Creative and imaginative people are often not recognized by their contemporaries. Even more often, they are not recognized in school by their teachers. History is full of examples.

Einstein was four years old before he could speak and seven before he could read. *Isaac Newton* did poorly in grade school, and *Beethoven's* music teacher once said of him, "As a composer he is hopeless." When *Thomas Edison* was a boy, his teachers told him he was too stupid to learn anything. *F. W. Woolworth* got a job in a dry goods store when he was 21, but his employers would not let him wait on a customer because he "didn't have enough sense." A newspaper editor fired *Walt Disney* because he had "no good ideas." *Caruso's* music teacher told him, "You can't sing. You have no voice at all." The director of the Imperial Opera in Vienna told *Madame Schumann-Heink* that she would never be a singer and advised her to buy a sewing machine. *Leo Tolstoy* flunked out of college; *Wernher von Braun* flunked ninth-grade algebra. *Admiral Richard E. Byrd* had been retired from the Navy as "unfit for service" until he flew over both Poles. *Louis Pasteur* was rated as "mediocre" in chemistry when he attended the Royal College. *Abraham Lincoln* entered the Black Hawk War as a captain and came out as a private. *Louisa May Alcott* was told by an editor that she could never write anything that had popular appeal. *Fred Waring* was once rejected for high school chorus. *Winston Churchill* failed the sixth grade.

Exercise #10
Finding your car keys (or anything else)

Pick something you frequently forget. Some people are chronic car key losers or forget to write down checks in their check register. Others forget anniversaries and birthdays.

Pick your forgettable item or task. Then, design a strategy for remembering it. You are on your own, and you are your own best expert. Use any of the techniques in this chapter, research other techniques, or design your own from scratch.

Describe your technique and the results below. In this exercise, as in most of the exercises in this book, a failure is also a success. Don't be concerned with whether your technique will work. Design it, then find out. If it doesn't work, try another technique.

The technique:

The results:

Set a trap for your memory

When you want to remind yourself to do something, link that activity to another event that you know will take place.

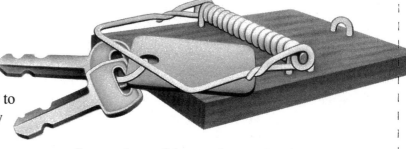

Say you're walking to class and suddenly realize that your accounting assignment is due tomorrow. Switch your watch from your left to your right wrist. Every time you look at your watch becomes a reminder that you were supposed to remember something. (You can do the same with a ring.)

If you empty your pockets every night, put something unusual in your pocket to remind yourself to do something before you go to bed. To remember to call your sister for her birthday, pick an object from the diaper bag—a teething toy, perhaps—and put it in your pocket. That evening, when you empty your pocket and find the teething toy, you're more likely to call your sister.

The key is to pick events that are certain to occur. Rituals like looking at your watch, reaching for car keys, and untying shoes are seldom forgotten. Tie a triple knot in your shoelace to remind you to set the alarm for your early morning study group meeting.

You can even use imaginary cues. To remember to write a check for the phone bill, picture your phone hanging on your front door. In your mind, create the feeling of reaching for the door knob and grabbing the phone cord instead. When you get home and reach to open the front door, the image is apt to return to you. Link two activities together, and make the association unusual.

Another way to remember something is to *tell* yourself you will remember it. Relax and say, "At any time I choose, I will be able to recall . . . ." The intention to remember can be more powerful than any memory technique.

Remembering names

You can use many of the techniques from this chapter to remember names. Here's how some of them can work.

Recite and repeat in conversation. When you hear a person's name, repeat it. Immediately say it to yourself several times without moving your lips. You could also repeat the name in a way that does not sound forced or artificial: "I'm pleased to meet you, Maria."

You can make this fun. When you're alone, recite each name using an unusual or funny voice—for example, Mickey Mouse, Donald Duck, or Mae West.

Ask the other person to recite and repeat. You can let other people help you remember their names. After you've been introduced to someone, ask that person to spell the name and pronounce it correctly for you. Most people will be flattered by the effort you're making to learn their names.

Visualize. After the conversation, construct a brief visual image of the person. For a memorable image, make it unusual. Imagine the name painted in hot pink fluorescent letters on the person's forehead. Or imagine everyone you see as wearing a huge name tag taped to their noses.

Admit you don't know. Admitting that you can't remember someone's name can actually put people at ease. Most of them will sympathize if you say, "I'm working to remember names better. I'm sorry. I forgot yours. What is it again?"

Introduce yourself again. Most of the time we assume introductions are one-shot affairs. If we miss the name the first time, our hopes for remembering are dashed. Instead of giving up, introduce yourself again: "Hello, again. We met earlier. I'm Jesse, and I forgot your name."

Use associations. Link each person you meet with one characteristic you find interesting or unusual. For example, you could make a mental note: "Vicki Cheng—tall, black hair," or "James Washington—horn-rimmed glasses." To reinforce your associations, write them on a 3x5 card as soon as you can.

Limit the number of new names you learn at one time. Occasionally we find ourselves in situations where we're introduced to many people at the same time. "Dad, these are all the people in my Boy Scout troop" or "Let's take a tour so you can meet all 32 people in this department."

As my future daughter-in-law, I'd like you to meet our side of the family."

When meeting a group of people, concentrate on remembering just two or three names. Free yourself of any obligation to remember everyone. Few of the people in mass introductions expect you to remember their names anyway. Another way to avoid memory overload is to limit yourself to just learning first names. Last names can come later.

Ask for photos or lists. In some cases, you may be able to get a photo of all the people you meet. For example, a small business where you apply for a job may have a brochure with pictures of all the employees. Ask for individual or group photos and write in the names if they're not included. You can use these photos as "flash cards" as you drill yourself on names.

If you can't get photos, get a list of names. Look over the list a couple times before you meet these people. Even though their faces will be new, you'll have been exposed to their names.

Go early. Consider going early to conventions, parties, and classes. Sometimes just a few people show up to these occasions on time. That's fewer names for you to remember. And as more people arrive, you can overhear them being introduced to others—an automatic review for you.

Make it a game. In situations where many people are new to each other, consider pairing up with another person and staging a contest. Challenge each other to remember as many new names as possible. Then choose an "award"—such as a movie ticket or free meal—for the person who wins.

Mnemonic devices

It's pronounced ni-'män-ik. *These tricks can increase your ability to recall everything from speeches to grocery lists. Some entertainers use mnemonics to perform "impossible" feats of memory, such as recalling the names of everyone in a large audience after hearing them just once. Waiters use them to take orders from a dozen people without the aid of pad and pencil, then serve food correctly without asking. Using mnemonic devices, speakers can go for hours without looking at their notes. The possibilities for students are endless.*

There is a catch. Mnemonic devices have four serious limitations. First, they don't always help you understand or digest material. Instead of encouraging critical thinking skills, mnemonics only assist rote memorization. Second, the mnemonic device itself is sometimes complicated to learn and time-consuming to develop. It may take more energy to create a mnemonic than to memorize something by using a more traditional memory technique such as repetition. Third, they can be forgotten. Recalling the mnemonic device might be as hard as recalling the material itself. And finally, you may find that mnemonics don't work as well for remembering technical terms in math and science.

In spite of the limitations, mnemonic devices are powerful. There are four general categories: new words, creative sentences, rhymes and songs, and special systems, including the loci system and the peg system.

If you experiment with each, you just might impress your mother-in-law by remembering her birthday and favorite color.

New words

Acronyms are words created by the first letters of a series of words. Examples include NASA (**N**ational **A**eronautics and **S**pace **A**dministration), radar (**ra**dar **d**etecting **an**d **r**anging), scuba (**s**elf-**c**ontained **u**nderwater **b**reathing **a**pparatus), and laser (**l**ight **a**mplification by **s**timulated **e**mission of **r**adiation). You can make up your own words to recall series of facts. A common mnemonic acronym is Roy G. Biv, which has helped thousands of students to remember the colors of the visible spectrum (red, orange, yellow, green, blue, indigo, and violet.) IPMAT helps biology students remember the stages of cell division (interphase, prophase, metaphase, anaphase, and telephase.)

Creative sentences

Acrostics are sentences that help you remember a series of letters that stand for something. For example, the first letters of the words in the sentence "Every good boy does fine" (E, G, B, D, and F) are the musical notes of the lines of the treble clef staff.

Rhymes and songs

Madison Avenue advertising executives spend billions of dollars a year on commercials designed to burn their message in your memory. Coca-Cola's song, "It's the real thing," practically stands for Coca-Cola, despite the fact that it contains artificial ingredients.

Rhymes have been used for centuries to teach children basic facts. "In fourteen hundred and ninety-two, Columbus sailed the ocean blue," or "Thirty days hath September . . . ."

Systems—loci and peg

Use the loci system to create visual associations with familiar locations.

It also helps you to remember things in a particular order.

The loci system is an old one. Ancient Greek orators used it to remember long speeches. Say that the orator's position was that road taxes must be raised to pay for school equipment. His loci visualizations might have looked like these:

First, as he walked in the door of his house, he imagined a large *porpoise* jumping through a hoop. This reminded him to begin by telling the audience the *purpose* of his speech. Next, he visualized his living room floor covered with paving stones, forming a road leading into the kitchen. In the kitchen, he pictured dozens of school children sitting on the floor because they have no desks.

Now the day of the big speech. The Greek politician is nervous. He is perspiring; his toga sticks to his body. He has cold feet (no socks). He stands up to give his speech and his mind goes blank. "No problem," he thinks to himself. "I am so nervous that I can hardly remember my name. But, I can remember the rooms in my house. Let's see, I'm walking in the front door and, Wow! I see the porpoise. Oh, yeah, that reminds me to talk about the purpose of my speech . . ."

Unusual associations are the easiest to remember. This system can also be adapted to locations in your body. You visually link things you want to remember with places inside your skin. The shopping list is remembered when you recall the visualization of a loaf of bread stuck in your brain cavity, a large can of frozen orange juice in your larynx, a bunch of broccoli tucked under your collar bone . . .

The *peg system* employs key words represented by numbers. For example, one-bun, two-shoe, three-tree, four-door, five-hive, six-sticks, seven-heaven, eight-gate, nine-wine, and ten-hen. In order for this system to be effective, these peg words need to be learned well.

You might use the peg system to remember that the speed of light is 186,000 miles per second. Imagine a hotdog bun (1) entering a gate (8) made of sticks (6). Since we tend to remember pictures longer than we do words, it may be easier to recall this weird scene than the numbers one, eight, and six in order.

Exercise #11
Be a poet

Construct your own mnemonic device for remembering some of the memory techniques in this chapter. Make up a poem, jingle, acronym, or acrostic, or use another mnemonic system. Describe your mnemonic device in the space below.

Love your problems
(and experience your barriers

WE ALL HAVE PROBLEMS AND BARRIERS **that** block our progress or prevent us from moving into new areas. We put boundaries on our experiences. We limit what we allow ourselves to be, to do, and to have.

When we bump up against one of our barriers, we usually turn around and start walking along a different path. And all of a sudden, Bump! We've struck another barrier. And we turn away again.

Our barriers might include the fear of speaking in front of a group, anxiety about math problems, or the reluctance to look silly trying to speak a foreign language. We might have a barrier about looking silly when trying anything new. Some of us even have anxiety about being successful.

It's natural to have barriers, but sometimes they limit our experience so much we get bored with life. When that happens, consider the following three ways of dealing with a barrier.

One way is to pretend it doesn't exist. Avoid it, deny it, lie about it. It's like turning your head the other way, putting on a fake grin, and saying: "See, there's really no problem at all. Everything is fine. Oh, that problem. That's not a problem, it's not really there."

In addition to looking foolish, this approach leaves the barrier intact, and we keep bumping into it. We deny the barrier and might not even be aware that we're bumping into it. For example, a student who has a barrier about math might

subconsciously avoid enriching experiences that include math.

A second approach is to fight the barrier, to struggle against it. This usually makes the barrier grow. It increases the barrier's magnitude. A person who is obsessed with weight might constantly worry about being fat. He might struggle with it every day, trying diet after diet. And the more he struggles, the bigger the problem gets.

The third alternative is to love the barrier. Accept it. Totally experience it. Tell the truth about it. Describe it in detail. When you do this, the barrier loses its power. You can literally love it to death.

Suppose one of your barriers is being afraid of speaking in front of a group. You can use any of these three approaches.

First, you can get up in front of the group and pretend you're not afraid. You can fake a smile, not admitting to yourself or the group that you have any concerns about speaking—even though your legs have turned to rubber bands and your mind to jelly. The problem is, everyone in the room will know you're scared, including you, when your hands start shaking and your voice cracks.

The second way to approach this barrier is to fight it. You could tell yourself, "I'm not going to be scared," and then try to

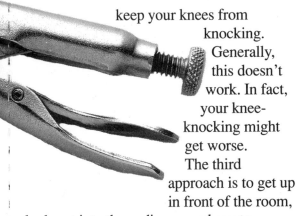

keep your knees from knocking. Generally, this doesn't work. In fact, your knee-knocking might get worse. The third approach is to get up in front of the room, look out into the audience, and say to yourself: "I am scared. I notice that my knees are shaking, my mouth feels dry, and I'm having a rush of thoughts about what might happen if I say the wrong thing. Yup, I'm scared and that's OK. As a matter of fact, it's just part of me, so I accept it, and I'm not going to try to change it. I'm going to give this speech even though I'm scared."

You might not actually eliminate the fear. However, your barrier about the fear—which is what stops you—could well disappear. And you might discover that if you examine the fear, love it, accept it, and totally experience it, the fear itself also disappears.

Applying this process is easier if you remember two ideas:

First, loving a problem is not necessarily the same as enjoying it. Love in this sense means total and unconditional acceptance.

Second, "unconditional acceptance" is not the same as unconditional surrender. Accepting a problem is different than giving up or escaping *from* it. Rather, this process implies escaping *into* the problem—diving into it head first and getting to know it in detail. Often the most effective solutions come when we face a problem squarely, with eyes wide open. Then we can move through the problem instead of around it.

P.S. This technique can also be effective for minor physical ailments. Next time you have a headache, try the experiment of loving your headache. Totally accept and experience the headache.

To do this, sit quietly for a few minutes and look at the headache as if it were an object. First, describe to yourself its exact location in your head. Describe its size. Describe its color, shape, weight, volume, density, and even its smell. How would this headache feel if you rubbed its surface? Is it smooth or rough? Is it hot or cold? Is the pain sharp or dull? Is there a sound associated with it? If the headache had a voice, what would it say?

As you describe the headache, continue to experience it. When you've described every aspect of it you can think of, begin again, starting with the location. Its location and size might have changed. Accept the change and keep describing the headache. Soon, you might notice that the pain has changed into another sensation or disappeared altogether.

Another good way to conduct this experiment is to describe your headache to someone else. Have a friend run through a list of questions such as "Where is your headache?" and "How big is it?"

You can use a similar technique on almost any problem or barrier. When you are willing to love your problems, you drain them of much of their energy.

Journal Entry #19
Discovery Statement

Describe one or two barriers that keep you from getting what you want in school. (First read about barriers as discussed in Power Process #3: "Love your problems" on page 88. If you have trouble identifying a barrier, review the Discovery Wheel you completed in Chapter One.

A barrier I have is . . .

_____

_____

_____

Another block to my growth is . . .

_____

_____

Journal Entry #20
Intention Statement

The following Intention Statement is in three parts.

1. Describe how you could set up circumstances that would allow you to experience the barrier you discovered. What could you do to put yourself right up against the barrier?

_____

To experience the barrier, I could . . .

_____

Also, I could . . .

_____

_____

2. Brainstorm a list of possible benefits or rewards you would enjoy if you let yourself experience away (love to death) the barrier. Do this on 3x5 cards or a separate sheet of paper.

3. This is for the courageous. Pick just *one* circumstance that you intend to set up in order to experience the barrier you have written about. This can be your opportunity to love it to death. Choose a circumstance that you can arrange within the next three days. (For example, if your barrier is fear of speaking in front of a group, the circumstance you could arrange would be asking a question in class or giving a speech.)

I intend to . . .

_____

Journal Entry #21
Discovery Statement

Take a minute to reflect on the memory techniques. You already use some of these techniques without being conscious of them. In the space below, list at least three techniques you have used most in the past and describe how you used them.

_____

GIVE YOUR SECRET BRAIN A CHANCE

Sometimes the way you combine studying with other activities can affect how well you remember information. For example, memory technique #12, "Escape the short-term memory trap," suggested that reviewing or reflecting on material shortly after you learn it allows your brain to store information more effectively in your long-term memory. This kind of learning takes place at a level below your awareness. Consider the following scenarios:

Scenario #1: After accounting class, you go to the student center and put a roll of quarters into Star Invaders from the Monkey Planet. Your score is 26,789,988—not bad, but short of your record—and you quit for dinner. After dinner you watch television for an hour, start feeling guilty, and finally you read your accounting assignment. You complete the assignment and go to bed. You have done well.

Scenario #2: After class you go straight to the library. With the sound of your instructor's voice still echoing in your head, you open your book. The neurons in your brain labeled "accounting" are already warmed up, so you can start reading immediately. You study until dinner, eat, then head to the student center with your roll of quarters. This time, as you blast away at apes from space, your brain is simmering with accounting. Without your accounting assignment hanging over your head, you are able to focus your attention in the here and now, and you wipe out three entire Monkey Planets. You score 36,879,999—a personal best. To end a perfect day, you conduct a five-minute review of your accounting before you go to bed.

It didn't take any more energy to read the assignment earlier instead of later, and your reading session was more powerful with the accounting lecture fresh in your mind. Later, even the galactic gorillas helped you study, by providing a relaxing background for subconscious brain activity. Your quick review before bed further reinforced the day's accounting lesson in your long-term memory. In short, you expended the same amount of energy, had the same amount of fun, and saved yourself hours of review time later in the term. Nice work.

Scenario #3: You've just left your evening Psychology class after a fascinating lecture on Sigmund Freud's theory of dreams. You want to make it home in time to tuck your children in bed, so you hurry out of class. In five minutes you're cruising down the highway. You decide to flip on the radio as you drive. Doesn't matter what station, just something to help you unwind. After all, it's been a long day—nine hours at the office and three in class. You deserve a break. Later, just before going to sleep, you decide to sneak in a few pages of that mystery novel you've wanted to finish. After you find out who poisoned the butler, you settle in for a well-deserved rest.

Scenario #4: Instead of driving yourself home after your session with Sigmund, you have arranged to car pool with a classmate. On the way home, you talk about the lecture. The discussion ignites into a debate as you and your friend take opposite stands on a key point of Freud's theory. After you arrive home, you take some time to check in with your children and talk about the day. Later, just before going to sleep, you mull over the conversation and make a mental note to write down your dreams in the morning. You decide to let the mystery novel wait until tomorrow night.

In the morning, you not only write down your dreams—you remember enough about last night's lecture to explain it to your children at breakfast. While you slept, your brain was not only manufacturing dreams but storing the key points of Freud's theory—something that will come in handy for the mid-term exam. Way to go.

Helen Keller,

author and lecturer, was
left blind, deaf, and mute at
the age of 19 months.

From *The Story of My Life,*
by Helen Keller, 22-24,
1905

The morning after my teacher came she led me into her room and gave me a doll. The little blind children at the Perkins Institution had sent it and Laura Bridgman had dressed it; but I did not know this until afterward. When I had played with it a little while, Miss Sullivan slowly spelled into my hand the word "d-o-l-l." I was at once interested in this finger play and tried to imitate it. When I finally succeeded in making the letters correctly I was flushed with childish pleasure and pride. Running downstairs to my mother I held up my hand and made the letters for doll. I did not know that I was spelling a word or even that words existed; I was simply making my fingers go in monkey-like imitation. In the days that followed I learned to spell in this uncomprehending way a great many words, among them *pin, hat, cup,* and a few verbs like *sit, stand,* and *walk.* But my teacher had been with me several weeks before I understood that everything has a name.

One day, while I was playing with my new doll, Miss Sullivan put my big rag doll into my lap also, spelled "d-o-l-l" and tried to make me understand that "d-o-l-l" applied to both. Earlier in the day we had had a tussle over the words "m-u-g" and "w-a-t-e-r." Miss Sullivan had tried to impress it upon me that "m-u-g" is mug and that "w-a-t-e-r" is water, but I persisted in confounding the two. In despair she had dropped the subject for the time, only to renew it at the first opportunity. I became impatient at her repeated attempts and, seizing the new doll, I dashed it upon the floor. I was keenly delighted when I felt the fragments of the broken doll at my feet. Neither sorrow nor regret followed my passionate outburst. I had not loved the doll. In the still, dark world in which I lived there was no strong sentiment or tenderness. I felt my teacher sweep the fragments to one side of the hearth, and I had a sense of satisfaction that the cause of my discomfort was removed. She brought me my hat, and I knew I was going out into the warm sunshine. This thought, if a wordless sensation may be called a thought, made me hop and skip with pleasure.

We walked down the path to the well house, attracted by the fragrance of the honeysuckle with which it was covered. Someone was drawing water and my teacher placed my hand under the spout. As the cool stream gushed over one hand she spelled into the other the word water, first slowly, then rapidly. I stood still, my whole attention fixed upon the motions of her fingers. Suddenly I felt a misty consciousness as of something forgotten—a thrill of returning thought; and somehow the mystery of language was revealed to me. I knew then that "w-a-t-e-r" meant the wonderful cool something that was flowing over my hand. That living word awakened my soul, gave it light, hope, joy, set it free! There were barriers still, it is true, but barriers that could in time be swept away.

I left the well house eager to learn. Everything had a name, and each name gave birth to a new thought. As we returned to the house every object which I touched seemed to quiver with life. That was because I saw everything with the strange, new sight that had come to me. On entering the door I remembered the doll I had broken. I felt my way to the hearth and picked up the pieces. I tried vainly to put them together. Then my eyes filled with tears; for I realized what I had done, and for the first time I felt repentance and sorrow.

I learned a great many new words that day. I do not remember what they all were; but I did know that *mother, father, sister, teacher* were among them—words that were to make the world blossom for me, "like Aaron's rod, with flowers." It would have been difficult to find a happier child than I was as I lay in my crib at the close of that eventful day and lived over the joys it had brought me, and for the first time longed for a new day to come.

QUIZ

1. Explain how synergy applies to the recite and repeat memory technique.

2. Give a specific example of "setting a trap for your memory."

3. What is a visualization that can help you remember Boyle's Law?

4. Define "acronym" and give an example.

5. Memorization on a deep level can take place if you:

   (A) repeat the idea.
   (B) repeat the idea.
   (C) repeat the idea.
   (D) all of the above.

6. Mnemonic devices are tricks that can increase your ability to:

    (A) distribute your learning.
    (B) manage your time.
    (C) check your tire pressure.
    (D) understand or digest material.
    (E) recall information.

7. Briefly describe at least three memory techniques.

8. There are four general categories for mnemonics given in the text. Explain two of them.

9. Once you unconditionally accept any problem, you will be able to enjoy it. True or false. Explain your answer.

10. Combining studying with other activities allows your brain to store information more effectively in your long-term memory. True or false. Explain your answer.

Journal Entry #22
Discovery Statement

After reading and doing this chapter, write about what you learned about your current memory skills.

_____

_____

_____

Journal Entry #23
Intention Statement

List two things you wanted to get from this chapter and didn't. Then describe the steps you will take to learn these things.

I intend to . . .

_____

_____

_____

Journal Entry #24
Intention Statement

Pick three memory techniques and write a short Intention Statement about how you will use them in the next week.

I intend to . . .

_____

_____

_____

Journal Entry #25
Discovery Statement

Review the Time Monitor/Time Plan exercise on page 42. Describe below something you learned about yourself when doing that exercise.

_____

_____

_____

_____

_____

Chapter 4

Reading

*Reading furnishes our mind only with materials of knowledge;
it is thinking that makes what we read ours.*
JOHN LOCKE

*. . . there would seem to be almost no limit to what people can
and will misunderstand when they are not doing their utmost to
get at a writer's meaning.*
EZRA POUND

Journal Entry #26
Discovery Statement

Think about how reading skills relate to your educational goals. Preview this chapter and review your Discovery Wheel, especially the section on reading. Then list below what you want to learn from this chapter.

I want to learn . . .

In this chapter . . .

This chapter is for students who have the thought, "I can read well," as well as for students who think, "I can't read well." If you apply the techniques in this chapter, you might be able to cut your reading time in half. Even if you don't, you could get more out of the time you do spend.

Muscle reading shows that you have everything you need, right now, to bring a textbook to life. Think of yourself as a master musician. You can do more than reproduce the composer's notes. You could add yourself to the composition. You could create music. The same thing can happen with a textbook.

When your reading slows to the speed of a glacier, use the techniques in *When reading is tough*. They light a path through even the darkest text.

Reading English as a second language reminds us that English has some quirks and suggests how you can navigate through them.

Your mental pictures of the world can sabotage your studies before you begin. *Power Process #4: Notice your pictures and let them go* suggests a solution.

Many students are particularly challenged by reading math and science textbooks. You can meet this challenge with the ideas suggested in *Overcoming math and science anxiety* and *Solving math and science problems*.

Also in this chapter you can learn about *Reading fast*, *Relax with black*, and the dreaded disease, *Mumpsimus*. Each of these articles helps you get past a specific barrier to reading excellence.

Muscle reading

PICTURE YOURSELF SITTING AT A DESK, an open book in your hands. Your eyes are open, too, and it looks like you're reading. Suddenly your head jerks up. You blink. Then you realize your eyes have been scanning the page for ten minutes, and you can't remember a single thing you have read.

Or, picture this: You've had a hard day. You were up at 6 a.m. to get the kids ready for school. A co-worker called in sick and you missed your lunch trying to do your job and his. You picked up the kids, then had to shop for dinner. Dinner was late, of course, and the kids were grumpy. Finally, you got to your books at 8 p.m., and you began plodding through something called "The equity method of accounting for common stock investments." You tell yourself, "I am preparing for the future," as you claw your way through two paragraphs and begin the third.

Suddenly, everything in the room looks different. Your head is resting on your elbow, which is resting on the equity method of accounting. The clock reads 11:30 p.m. Say goodbye to three hours.

Sometimes, the only difference between a sleeping pill and a textbook is that the textbook doesn't have a warning on the label about operating heavy machinery.

"Muscle reading" is a technique you can use to avoid mental mini-vacations and reduce the number of unscheduled naps during study time, even after a hard day. More than that, muscle reading is a way to decrease effort and struggle by increasing energy and skill. Once you learn this technique, you can actually spend less time on your reading and get more out of it.

This is not to say you can avoid all work and still challenge yourself in your education. Muscle reading might even look like more work, at first. Effective textbook reading is an active, energy consuming, sit-on-the-edge-of-your-seat business. That's why this strategy is called muscle reading.

H O W
Muscle reading
W O R K S

The key idea behind muscle reading is that your textbooks have something you want. They have knowledge and valuable information. Sometimes the value is so buried that extracting it requires skill and energy.

Muscle reading is a three-phase technique you can use to accomplish that extraction. Each of the three phases has three steps. To assist your recall of all nine steps, we suggest you memorize three short sentences:

Pry out questions.

Root up answers.

Recite, review, and review again.

Take a moment to invent images for each of those sentences. First, visualize or feel yourself prying questions out of a text. These are questions you want answered based upon your brief survey of the assignment. Make a mental picture of yourself scanning the territory, spotting a question, and reaching into the text to pry it out. Hear yourself saying, "I've got it. Here's my question."

Then root up the answers to your questions. Get your muscles involved. Flex. Feel the ends of your fingers digging into the text to root up the answers to your questions.

Finally, hear your voice reciting what you have learned. Hear yourself making a speech about the material. Hear yourself singing it. Picture yourself on a stage, waving your arms dramatically as you sing what you have learned to an audience. Know that this is your repeat performance.

These sentences form an acrostic. The first letter of each word stands for one muscle reading process. Thus:

Pry out questions.

r	u	u
e	t	e
v	l	s
i	i	t
e	n	i
w	e	o
		n
		s

Root up answers.

e	n	n
a	d	s
d	e	w
r		e
l		r
i		
n		
e		

Recite, review, and review again.

e	e	e
c	v	v
i	i	i
t	e	e
e	w	w

Configured another way, the three phases and nine steps look like this:

Before you read: Pry out questions
Step 1: Preview
Step 2: Outline
Step 3: Question

While you read: Root up answers
Step 4: Read
Step 5: Underline
Step 6: Answer

After you read:
Recite, review, and review again
Step 7: Recite
Step 8: Review
Step 9: Review again

A nine-step reading strategy might seem cumbersome and unnecessary for a two-page reading assignment. It is. Keep in mind that muscle reading is not an all-or-nothing package. Use it appropriately. You can choose what steps to apply as you read.

Muscle reading takes a little time to learn. At first you might feel it's slowing you down. That's natural. Mastery comes with time and practice. If you're still concerned about time, give yourself some options. For example, apply the following techniques to just one article or part of a chapter.

Before you read

Step 1: Preview

Before you begin, survey the entire assignment. (Remember Exercise #1: "Textbook reconnaissance" on page vi) If you are starting a new book, look over the table of contents and flip through the text page by page. Even if your assignment is merely a few pages in a book, you can benefit from a brief preview of the table of contents.

Keep the preview short. If the entire reading assignment will take less than an hour, your preview might take five minutes. Previewing longer assignments can take as much as 15 minutes. Spend even more time previewing books you will use for an entire term. Previewing is also a way to get yourself started when an assignment looks too big to handle. It is an easy way to step into the material.

When previewing, look for familiar concepts, facts, or ideas. These items can help link new information to previously learned material. Look for ideas that spark your imagination or curiosity. Ask yourself how the material can relate to your long-range goals. Inspect drawings, diagrams,

charts, tables, graphs, and photographs. These images register quickly, and they become reference points when you get into actual reading.

Keep an eye out for summary statements. If the assignment is long or complex, read the summary first. Many textbooks have summaries in the introductions or at the end of each chapter.

Read all chapter headlines, section titles, and paragraph headlines. These are often brief summaries in themselves.

If you expect to use a book extensively, read the preface. The author often includes a personal perspective in a preface. A picture of the person behind the words can remove barriers to understanding.

Look for lists of recommended books and articles. If you have difficulty with a concept, sometimes another viewpoint can nail it down for you.

Before you begin reading, take a few moments to reflect upon what you already know about this subject, even if you think you know nothing. This technique prepares your brain to accept the information that follows.

Finally, determine your reading strategy. Skimming might be enough for some assignments. For others, all nine steps of muscle reading might be appropriate. Ask yourself these questions: How will I be tested on this material? How useful will this knowledge be later? How much time can I afford to spend on this assignment?

To clarify your reading strategy, you might write the first letters of the muscle reading acrostic in a margin or at the top of your notes and check off the steps you intend to follow. Or write the muscle reading steps on 3x5 cards and then use them for bookmarks.

You don't have to memorize what you preview to get value from this step. Previewing sets the stage for incoming information by warming up a space in your mental storage area.

THE UNIVERSAL
LAW OF READING

First corollary:
To read effectively, always sit in a canoe and wear a face mask, snorkel, and flippers.

Second corollary:
Don't believe everything you read.

Exercise #12

It's hard to know what's going on . . . until you have the big picture

Read the following paragraph and then summarize it in one sentence.

"With hocked gems financing him, he defied all scornful laughter that tried to prevent his scheme. 'Your eyes deceive,' they said. 'It is like an egg, not a table.' Now three sturdy sisters sought truth. As they forged along, sometimes through calm vastness, yet more often over turbulent peaks and valleys, their days become weeks as many doubters spread fearful rumors about the edge. At last, from nowhere, winged creatures appeared, signifying the journey's end."

Summarize this paragraph now.

Most people have difficulty knowing what in the world the previous paragraph was about. If it was part of a reading assignment you had previewed, and noticed it was about Christopher Columbus, then it would have made more sense. Read it again while thinking about that famous world traveler.

Step 2: Outline

The amount of time you spend on this step will vary. For some assignments, fiction and poetry for example, skip it. For other assignments, a 10-second mental outline is all you need.

With complex material, take time to understand the structure of what you are about to read. If your textbook provides chapter outlines, spend some time studying them.

If a text does not provide an outline, sketch a brief one in the margin of your book or at the beginning of your notes. Then, as you read and take notes, you can fill in your outline.

Section titles and paragraph headlines can serve as major and minor topics for your outline. If assigned reading does not contain section titles or headlines, you can outline the material as you read. In this case, outlining actively organizes your thoughts about the assignment.

Use whatever outline style works best for you. Some readers prefer traditional Roman numeral outlines. Others prefer "mind maps" or notes in the Cornell format. (These formats are explained on page 128.) If your text includes headings in bold or italic print, you can also outline right in the text. Assign numbers or letters to each heading, just as you would for a traditional outline.

Outlining can make complex information easier to understand.

Step 3: Question

Ask yourself what you want from an assignment before you begin reading. Your preview might suggest some questions. Imagine the author is in the room with you. What would you ask him? How can he help

you to get what you want from your education? Create a dialogue. Begin your active participation in the book before you start to read.

Write down a list of questions. Be tough. Demand your money's worth from your textbooks. If you do not understand a concept, write specific questions about it. The more detailed your questions, the more powerful this technique becomes. Knowledge is born of questions.

If a reading assignment seems irrelevant, sit back for a minute and think about what it is you want from your time in school. Check to see if your education will be complete without this piece of the puzzle. Even if a particular assignment doesn't have personal meaning for you in the moment, it may be tied to a broader goal like getting a certain grade in the class.

Another useful technique is to turn chapter headings and section titles into questions. For example, if a subtitle is "Transference and Suggestion" you can ask yourself: What are transference and suggestion? How does transference relate to suggestion? Make up a quiz as if you were teaching this subject to your classmates.

Make the questions playful or creative. Have fun with this technique. You don't need to get an answer to every question you ask. The purpose of making up questions is to get your brain involved in the assignment. Take your unanswered questions to class where they can be springboards for class discussion.

Learning to ask effective questions takes practice, and you can discover rewards for developing this skill. The questions you formulate help you stay alert through complicated reading.

Boredom and fatigue tend to disappear when you're busy finding answers. In fact, when you find one, expect to feel a burst of energy. It might be a small burst, if it was a small question. Or it might bring you right out of your chair, if the question was important to you. If you find a series of answers in a reading assignment, you might finish the assignment feeling more energetic than when you began.

For some assignments, you might spend considerable time previewing, outlining, and asking questions before you start reading. The potential rewards are understanding and remembering more of what you read and saving time.

While you read

Step 4: Read

At last! You have previewed the assignment, organized it in your mind, and formulated questions. Now you are ready to begin reading.

As you read, be conscious of where you are and what you are doing. Practice Power Process #2: "Be here now." When you notice your attention wandering, gently bring it back to the present.

One way to stay in the here and now is to make tick marks on scrap paper whenever you notice your attention flagging.

You might make many tick marks at first. That's OK. The marks signify your attentiveness, so don't be discouraged by lots of them. Most students notice that as they pay attention to their attention, the number of tick marks decreases.

If a personal problem or some other concern is interfering with your concentration, try this idea. Write down the problem along with a commitment to a future course of action. Getting the problem down on paper, with a commitment to take action, can free your mind for the present task.

Another way to stay focused is to avoid marathon reading sessions. Schedule breaks and set a reasonable goal for the entire session. Then reward yourself with an enjoyable activity for five or ten minutes every hour or two. With practice, some students find they can stay focused up to three hours without a break.

For difficult reading, set shorter goals. Read for half an hour, then break. Most students find that shorter periods of reading distributed throughout the day and week can be more effective than long sessions.

You can use the following three techniques to stay focused as you read.

First, visualize the material. Form mental pictures of the concepts as they are presented. If you read that a voucher system can help control cash disbursements, picture a voucher handing out dollar bills. Use the visualization techniques presented in Chapter Three: Memory.

Second, read it out loud—especially complicated material. Some of us remember better and understand more quickly when we hear an idea.

Third, get a feel for the subject, literally. For example, let's say you are reading about a microorganism, a paramecium, in your biology text. Imagine what it would feel like to run your finger around the long, cigar-shaped body of the animal. Imagine feeling the large fold of its gullet on one side, and feel the hairy little cilia as they wiggle in your hand.

A final note: It's easy to fool yourself about reading. Just because you have an open book in your hand and you are moving your eyes across a page doesn't mean you are reading effectively. Reading textbooks takes energy, even if you do it sitting down. One study revealed that corporation presidents usually wear out the front of their chairs first. Approach your reading assignment like the company president. Sit up. Keep your spine straight. Use the edge of your chair.

And avoid reading in bed, except for fun.

HOW
Muscle reading
WORKS

Step 5: Underline

Deface your books. Use them up. Have fun writing and coloring in them. Indulge yourself as you never could with your grade-school texts. Keeping textbooks clean and neat might not help you get what you want from them.

The purpose of underlining and making other marks in a text is to create signals for reviewing. Underlining or highlighting can save lots of time when you study for tests.

A secondary benefit of underlining is that when you read with a pen in your hand, you are involving another mode of perception, your kinesthetic sense—that is, your sense of touch and motion. Being physical with your books can help build strong neural pathways in your memory.

Avoid underlining too soon. Wait until you have completed a section or concept to make sure you know what is important. Then underline. Sometimes stopping after each paragraph works best. For some assignments, you might want to read a larger section before deciding what to underline.

Colored highlighters work better than pens for underlining. Pens can make underlined sections—in other words, the important parts—harder to read than the rest of the book. Use a pen only for making marginal notes and circling important sections.

Underline sparingly, usually less than ten percent. If you underline too much, you defeat the purpose of highlighting, which is to flag the most important material for review.

Write in the margins of your texts. Write summary statements and questions. Mark passages that you don't understand. If you find a list or series of elements in a paragraph, you can circle and number them.

It's true, marking up your textbooks can lower their resale value. The money you lose by doing it is ridiculously small compared to the value of your education. Writing in your textbooks helps you wring every ounce of value out of them.

Step 6: Answer

As you read, get the answers to your questions and write them down. Fill in your outline. Write down new questions and note when you don't get the answers you wanted to find. Use these notes to ask questions in class, or see your instructor personally.

When you read, create an image of yourself as a person in search of the answers. You are a detective, watching for every clue, sitting erect in your straight-back chair, as alert as a Zen master, curious as Sherlock Holmes or Nancy Drew, demanding that your textbook give you what you want—the answers.

After you read

Step 7: Recite

Talk to yourself about what you have read. Or, talk to someone else. When you finish reading an assignment, make a speech about it.

One way to get yourself to recite is to look at each underlined point. Note what you marked, then put the book down and start talking out loud. Explain as much as you can about that particular point.

To make this technique more effective, do it in front of a mirror. It may seem silly, and the benefits can be enormous. You can reap them at exam time.

Friends are even better than mirrors. Form a group and practice teaching each other what you have read. One of the best ways to learn anything is to teach someone else.

There is a secret buried in this suggestion. That secret is: Have someone else do the work. Your instructors might not appreciate this suggestion, but it can be a salvation when you're pressed for time. Find a friend you trust and split up the reading assignment. Each of you can teach half the assignment to the other. (Warning: You might be far better versed in the part you read and taught. And if your friend missed an important point, you could miss it, too.)

Talk about your reading whenever you can.

Step 8: Review

Plan to do your first review within 24 hours of reading the material. Sound the trumpets, this is critical: A review within 24 hours moves information from your short-term memory to your long-term memory. It can save you hours later on. Review within one day. If you read it on Wednesday, review it on Thursday.

During this review, look over your notes and clear up anything you don't understand. Recite some of the main points again.

At first, you might be discouraged by how much you think you forgot from the previous day. Don't worry. Notice how quickly you pick up the material the second time. One of the characteristics of memory is that even when you cannot recall something immediately, you can relearn it sooner if you have already learned it once. And relearning wears a deeper path into your memory.

This review can be short. You might spend as little as 15 minutes reviewing a two-hour reading assignment. Investing that time now can save you hours later when studying for exams.

Step 9: Review again

The final step in muscle reading is the weekly or monthly review. This step can be very short—perhaps only four or five minutes per assignment. Simply go over your notes. Read the highlighted parts of your text. Recite one or two of the more complicated points.

The purpose of these reviews is to keep the neural pathways to the information open and to make them more distinct. That way, the information can be easier to recall. You can accomplish these short reviews anytime, anywhere, if you are prepared. Take your text to the dentist's office, and if you don't have time to read a whole assignment, review last week's assignment or the previous week's assignment. Conduct a five-minute review while you are waiting for a bus, for your socks to dry, or for the water to boil.

Three-by-five cards are a handy review tool. Write ideas, formulas, concepts, and facts on cards and carry them with you. These short review periods can be effortless and fun.

Sometimes longer review periods are appropriate. For example, if you found an assignment difficult, consider rereading it. Start over, as if you had never seen the material. Sometimes a second reading will provide you with surprising insights. Your previous experience acts as a platform from which you can see aspects that didn't appear during the first reading.

Schedule some review periods well in advance. You might set aside one hour on a Saturday or a Sunday to review several subjects. Keep your reviews short and do them often.

Finally, take some time to reflect on what you read. As you walk to and from class, in your discussions with other students, or before you go to bed at night, turn over new ideas in your mind. Take time to play with them. Develop a habit of regular review.

Journal Entry #27
Discovery Statement

Check off the muscle reading techniques you already use.

	Preview	Outline	Question	Read	Underline	Answer	Recite	Review	Review again
Always									
Often									
Sometimes									
Seldom									
Never									

Exercise # 13
Make it a habit

Changing our reading style is as complicated as changing how we tie our shoes. We've been doing both since we started school.
This chapter suggests a significant change in how you read. This exercise can help that change become automatic. During the next week fill out the assignment section of this page, listing pages and book titles that you intend to read within a week or two. As you read each of those assignments, check off the muscle reading techniques as you apply them. By the time you have used this technique ten times, you could have a new habit.

Assignment: Pages ___ to ___ in book ___, actually completed

Preview										
Outline										
Question										
Read										
Underline										
Answer										
Recite										
Review										
Review again										

Journal Entry #28
Discovery Statement

Now that you have read about muscle reading, review your assessment of your reading skills in the Discovery Wheel on page 22. Do you still think that evaluation was accurate? What new insights do you have about the way you read textbooks? Are you a more effective reader than you thought? Less effective? Record observations here.

Exercise # 14
Relax with black

Eye strain can be the result of continuous stress. You can use this exercise to take a break from your reading.

1. Sit on a chair or lie down and take a few moments to breathe deeply.

2. Close your eyes, place your palms over your eyes, and visualize a perfect field of black.

3. Continue to be aware of the blackness for two or three minutes while you breathe deeply.

4. Now remove your hands from your eyes and open your eyes slowly.

5. Relax for a minute more, then continue reading.

Mumpsimus

BEWARE OF THE DREAD CONDITION, MUMPSIMUS. Mumpsimus is dangerous. It has caused the downfall of more than one dictator, more than one nation, and countless individuals. Mumpsimus is as old as mankind.

According to Webster's Dictionary, mumpsimus is an error obstinately clung to. The word comes from the story of an old priest who for 30 years had conducted services using the word mumpsimus as a substitute for the correct Latin word sumpsimus. One day, when his error was finally pointed out to him, he replied, "I will not change my old mumpsimus for your new sumpsimus."

Mumpsimus is blind adherence to a principle or concept. It's a mistake we continue to repeat, even after we know it's a mistake.

In other words, if you have been shown that a drug is harmful, that it can cause pain or illness, and yet you continue to use that drug, then you have a case of mumpsimus.

Another example of mumpsimus is the student who reads the techniques in this chapter, finds the logic behind them solid, recognizes their value, and yet continues to use his old methods. That's the danger of mumpsimus. The afflicted student knows the old concepts haven't worked very well but continues to act as if they did.

Mumpsimus is nothing to feel guilty about; it's just a temporary condition. The cure?

Just say sumpsimus.

Reading fast

THE WAY TO READ FASTER is to read faster. This may sound like double talk, but it is a serious suggestion. The fact is, most people can read faster simply by making a conscious effort to do so. Without any special training or expensive speed-reading courses, you can use your intention to read faster as a powerful tool.

In fact, you probably can read faster without any loss in comprehension. Your comprehension might even improve.

Here are some guidelines from the "Just do it" school of speed reading:

First, get your body ready. Get off the couch. Sit at a desk or table and sit up, on the edge of your chair, with your feet flat on the floor. If you're feeling adventurous, read standing up.

Next, set a time limit. Use a clock or a digital watch with a built-in stopwatch to time yourself. The objective is not to set speed records, so be realistic. For example, set a goal of an hour to read a chapter. If that works, set a goal of 50 minutes to read a similar chapter.

Test your limits. You can even set goals for reading two or three pages. The idea is to give yourself a gentle push, increasing your reading speed *without* sacrificing comprehension.

The final hint from the "Just do it" school is relax. It's not only possible to read fast when you're relaxed, it's easier. Relaxation promotes concentration. (And remember, relaxation is not the same thing as sleep.)

Experiment with the "Just do it" method right now. Read the rest of this article as fast as you can.

After you finish, come back and reread the same paragraphs at your usual rate. Notice how much you remembered from your first sprint through. Many people are surprised to find how well they comprehend material even at dramatically increased speeds.

You also can read faster by moving your eyes faster. When we read, our eyes leap across the page in short bursts called *saccades* (pronounced *sack-AID*). A saccade is also a sharp jerk on the reins of a horse—a violent pull to stop the animal quickly. Our eyes stop like that, too, in pauses called *fixations*.

Although we experience the illusion of continuously scanning each line, our eyes really take in groups of words, usually about three at a time. And more than 90 percent of reading time our eyes are at a dead stop, in those fixations.

Your eyes can move faster if they take in more words with each burst—six instead of three, for example. You can do this by following your finger as you read. The faster your finger moves, the faster your eyes move. You also can use a pen, pencil, or 3x5 card as a guide.

Our eyes also make *regressions*. That is, they back up and reread words. Ineffective readers and beginning readers make many regressions.

You can reduce regressions by paying attention to them. Use the handy 3x5 card to cover words and lines you have read. This can reveal how often you stop and move the card back. Don't be discouraged if you stop often at first. Being aware of it helps you naturally begin to regress less frequently.

You also can reduce regressions by improving your concentration. To do that, use the techniques described in "Muscle reading" in this chapter.

When you're in a hurry, scan the assignment and read the headings, subheadings, lists, charts, graphs, and summary paragraphs. The summaries are especially important. They are usually at the beginning or end of a reading assignment.

Also, pay attention to how an assignment is organized. If you discover that an author is going to make four main points in the reading assignment, look for one- or two-sentence summaries of those points, and read them carefully.

Another way to read faster is to avoid vocalizing. Obviously, you're more likely to read faster if you don't read aloud or move your lips. You can also increase your speed if you don't *subvocalize*—that is, if you don't mentally "hear" the words as you read them. To stop doing it, just be aware of it.

Practice reading faster with simpler material at first. That way you can pay closer attention to technique. Start with a novel, magazine, or comic book then work up to more difficult reading.

A cautionary note about these techniques: Speed isn't everything. Skillful readers vary their reading rate according to what they are reading. An advanced text in analytical geometry, for example, usually calls for a different reading rate than the Sunday comics.

You also can use different reading rates on the same material. For example, you might sprint through an assignment for the key words and ideas, then return to the difficult parts for a more thorough reading.

And finally, remember the first rule of reading fast: Just say, Go!

When reading is tough

SOMETIMES ordinary reading methods are not enough. Every student gets bogged down in a murky reading assignment sooner or later. You can use the following techniques to drain the swamp when you are up to your neck in textbook alligators.

1. Read it again, Sam

Difficult material—such as the technical writing in science courses—is often easier the second time around. If you read an assignment and are completely lost, do not despair. Admit your confusion. Sleep on it, or go to a movie. Your mind can work on those concepts while you rest or play. When you return to the assignment, regard it with fresh eyes.

2. Look for essential words

If you are stuck on a paragraph, mentally cross out all the adjectives and adverbs, and read the sentence without them. Find the important words. These will usually be verbs and nouns.

3. Hold a mini-review

Stop at the end of each paragraph and recite, in your own words, what you have read. Or write a short summary. You can write these in the margin of your text.

4. Read it aloud

Make noise. Read a passage aloud several times, each time using a different inflection, emphasizing a different part of the sentence. Be creative. Imagine that you are the author talking.

5. Use your instructor

Admit when you are absolutely stuck and make an appointment with your instructor. Most teachers welcome the opportunity to work individually with students. Be specific about your confusion. Point out the paragraph that you found toughest to understand.

6. Find a tutor

Many schools provide free tutoring services. Often a tutor is a student who was in your position not long ago. Tutors can give you a new perspective on a problem. If tutoring services are not provided by your school, other students who have completed the course can assist you.

7. Use another text

Find one in the library. Sometimes a concept is easier to understand if it is expressed another way. Children's books, especially children's encyclopedias, can provide useful overviews of baffling subjects.

8. Pretend you understand, then explain it

We often understand more than we think we do. Pretend it's clear as a bell and explain it to another person or even yourself. Write your explanation down. You might be amazed by what you know.

9. Stand up

Changing positions periodically can combat fatigue. Try standing when you read, especially if you get stuck on a tough passage and decide to read it aloud. Sometimes hearing the words makes them more understandable, and pacing back and forth can help to focus concentration. For some people, getting up on their feet works wonders.

Read with a dictionary in your lap

MALCOLM X demonstrated one way to improve vocabulary. While in prison, he read and copied the entire dictionary. Few of us have such a single-minded sense of purpose with regard to vocabulary building. Yet we all share the ability and desire to learn. You can use that natural ability to strengthen your vocabulary by concentrating on words that interest you.

Look up unfamiliar words. Pay special attention to words that arouse your curiosity.

You can regularly use two kinds of dictionaries: the desk dictionary and the unabridged dictionary. A desk dictionary is the one you use several times a day, the one you own. Keep this book within reach (maybe in your lap) so that you can look up unfamiliar words. You can find the large unabridged dictionary in the library. It provides more complete information on words, definitions not included in your desk dictionary, and a history of each word.

Construct a word stack

When you find an unfamiliar word, write it down on a 3x5 card. Copy the sentence in which it occurred below the word. You can look each word up immediately or accumulate a stack of these cards and look them up later. Write the definition on the back of the 3x5 card and add the diacritical marks which tell you how to pronounce it.

To expand your definitions and find the history behind the word, you can take your stack of cards to an unabridged dictionary. As you find related words in the dictionary, add them to your stack.

These cards become another portable study aid which you can review in your spare moments.

Learn—even when your dictionary is across town

When you are listening to a lecture and hear an unfamiliar word, or when you are reading on the bus and run across a word you don't know, you can still build your word stack. Pull out a 3x5 card and write down the word and its sentence. Later you can look up the word and put the definition on the back of the card.

Use more options for learning words

There are other strategies for dealing with new words. One is to guess the meaning of the words from context. To do this, re-read the sentences that surround the new word and see if they point to a logical meaning. Or, simply circle or highlight the word and continue reading. When you're done, you can look up all unfamiliar words at one time.

Another suggestion is to divide the word into syllables and look for familiar parts. This works well if you make it a point to learn common prefixes (beginning syllables) and suffixes (ending syllables). For example, the suffix "tude" usually refers to a condition or state of being. Knowing this makes it easier to conclude that *habitude* refers to a usual way of doing something, or that *similitude* means "being similar or having a quality of resemblance."

Reading English as a second language
En lisant l'anglais comme une deuxieme langue
Englisch lesen als zweite sprache
Читать по-английски как иностранный язык
『第二外国語としての英語講読』
Leer el inglés como segunda lengua

THE ENGLISH LANGUAGE is full of exceptions to the rules. It is probably one of the more difficult languages to learn. Contrary to the rules of phonetics, for example, words are often not spelled the way they sound. Even trying to spell the word "phonetics" using phonetics can get you into trouble.

Sometimes the experts on English disagree. Some think that the word "data" is singular, others think it is plural. Many frown on using the word *ain't* and others accept it, noting that Shakespeare often used it. English is a crazy language.

No matter what your native language is, consider using the following suggestions as you master English.

Give it time. Reading English slowly can aid comprehension. So can reading at different rates by varying your reading speed. Accept how fast you read right now, even as you seek to increase your speed. As you practice, both your reading speed and comprehension can improve. There are no instant pills to take. Learning English takes time.

Your skill in reading English improves as you practice speaking and writing it. That calls for courage and the willingness to look, feel, and sound unskilled. It's OK to move at your own pace and be proud of your emerging bilingual skills.

Use muscle reading. Many of the muscle reading techniques apply to reading English as a second language. For example, it is effective to read some assignments more than once. The first time through, look for major ideas and be aware of the general content. When you read it the second time, fill in more of the details.

Get at word meanings. Have a dictionary handy. Before looking up every unknown word, try to figure out their meanings from the context. If someone says,

"It will probably be cold at the football game so be sure to bring a warm XXXXX," you would probably not show up with a calculator or a fishing pole.

Practice speaking English. Look for times when you can practice speaking English. Asking questions or making comments in class is an effective way to practice. It allows you to be more involved and can increase your understanding of the course content. Another way to practice is to repeat aloud what you have just read.

The more you practice English, the faster you can learn. Relying on translations or spending much of your time speaking your native language could slow your progress.

Practice writing English. Writing in English, which involves spelling and a more precise use of grammar, may be more difficult than either reading or speaking. Grocery lists, to-do lists, notes to friends, appointments in calendars, and personal journal entries are opportunities to practice writing. Even if only parts of what you write are in English, this practice can still be effective.

Think in English. Thinking in English is a variation of speaking it. The next time you want to explore some future project or remember the trip you took last summer, think about it in English. Some students are pleasantly surprised to note that they even start dreaming in English.

Learn academic English. Formal, academic English might vary greatly from your own English dialect. Consider approaching academic English as a foreign language, even if English is your native tongue. The techniques that help you learn French or Spanish can also help you master the English you use in school.

Celebrate your gains. Acknowledge yourself and celebrate when you make small gains. It is probably not possible to improve your English skills 100 percent, all at once. One hundred small gains of one percent each are likely to accomplish the same thing. Lots of little learnings can mount up to major shifts in your English proficiency.

Use school services. Many schools have ESL(English as a Second Language) programs that offer a variety of services. Examples are tutoring services, as well as courses and workshops on learning English. Your advisor or student counseling office can direct you to these programs.

Notice your pictures and let them go

THE BRAIN'S JOB is to manufacture images. We use mental pictures to make predictions about the world, and we base much of our behavior on those predictions. When a cook adds chopped onions, mushrooms, and garlic to the spaghetti sauce, he has a picture of how the sauce will taste and measures each ingredient according to that picture.

Pictures are not strictly visual images. They can involve any of the senses. When you buy a record album, you have a picture of how it will sound. When you buy a sweater, you have a picture of how it will feel.

The pictures we make in our heads are survival mechanisms. Without them, we couldn't get from one end of town to the other. We couldn't feed or clothe ourselves. Without a picture of a socket, we couldn't screw in a lightbulb.

The problem with pictures

Pictures can also get in our way. For example, take the case of a student who plans to attend a college he hasn't visited. He chose this school for its strong curriculum and good academic standing, but his brain didn't stop there. In his mind, the campus has historic buildings with ivory-covered walls and tree-lined avenues. The professors, he imagines, will be combinations of Oprah Winfrey and Phil Donahue. His roommate will be his best friend. The cafeteria will be a cozy nook serving delicate quiche and fragrant teas. He will gather there with fellow students for hours of stimulating, intellectual conversation. The library will have every book, the dorm every luxury.

The school turns out to be four grey buildings downtown, next to the bus station. The first class he attends is taught by an overweight, balding professor wearing a purple and orange bird of paradise tie. He has a bad case of the sniffles. The cafeteria is a nondescript hall with machine food, and the student's dorm room is barely large enough to accommodate his roommate's tuba.

This hypothetical student gets depressed. He begins to think about dropping out of school.

The problem with pictures is that they sometimes prevent us from seeing what is really there. That happened to the student in this story. His pictures prevented him from noticing that the school is at the heart of a culturally vital city—close to theaters, museums, government offices, clubs, and all kinds of stores. The professor with the weird tie is not only an expert in his field, he is a superior teacher. The school cafeteria is skimpy because it can't compete with the variety of inexpensive restaurants in the area. There may even be hope for a tuba-playing roommate.

Anger and disappointment are often the result of our pictures. We set up expectations of events before they occur. These can then lead to disappointment. Sometimes we don't even realize that we had the expectation.

Racism flourishes when people hold inaccurate pictures about each other and refuse to let them go. These pictures can lead to shallow stereotypes. They work against the foreign exchange student in your English class or the visiting lecturer from Mexico.

Next time you discover you are angry, disappointed, or frustrated, look to see which of your pictures aren't being fulfilled.

Often there is disappointment even if the event that you pictured turns out to be better than you imagined. For instance, you might have expected the "Philosophy of Logic" class you're taking as a graduation requirement to be hopelessly boring. You get to class and discover that the professor has a great sense of humor and relates logic processes to practical examples. Disappointment happens when you maintain a position that philosophy is boring. And now there is a conflict between your position about philosophy and your experience in the class.

What to do

Having pictures is unavoidable. Letting these pictures run your life is avoidable. Awareness is the key. The technique for dealing with pictures is so simple, so effortless, that it seems silly.

The way to deal with pictures is to notice them. Be aware of them. Then, in the most gentle manner possible, let them go. Let them drift away as if they were wisps of smoke

picked up by a gentle wind.

Pictures are persistent. They come back over and over again. Notice them again and let them go again. At first, a picture might return repeatedly and insistently. Pictures are like independent beings. They want to live.

If you can see the picture as a thought independent from you, you will likely find it easier to let it go. You are more than your thoughts. Many images and words will pop into your head in the course of a lifetime; you do not have to identify with them all. You can let pictures go without giving up yourself.

If your pictures are interfering with your education, visualize them scurrying around inside your head. See yourself tying them to a brightly colored helium balloon and letting them go. Let them float away again and again.

Overcoming math and science anxiety

When they open books about math or science, some capable students break out in a cold sweat. These are symptoms of two conditions sweeping students across the world—math and science anxiety.

If you want to improve your math or science skills, you're in distinguished company. Albert Einstein felt he needed to learn more math to work out his general theory of relativity. So he asked a friend, mathematician Marcel Grossman, to teach him. It took several years. You won't need that long.

Think of the benefits of overcoming math and science anxiety. Many more courses, majors, jobs, and careers could open up for you. Knowing these subjects can also put you at ease in everyday situations: calculating the tip on a meal, planning your finances, working with a spreadsheet on a computer. Speaking the languages of math and science can also help you feel at home in a world driven by technology.

Many schools offer courses in overcoming math and science anxiety. It pays to check them out. The following suggestions can start you on the road to enjoying science and mathematics.

Notice your pictures about math and science

Sometimes what keeps people from succeeding at math and science is their mental picture of scientists and mathematicians. Often that picture includes a man dressed in a faded plaid shirt, baggy pants, and wing-tip shoes. He's got a calculator on his belt and six pencils jammed in his shirt pocket. This is the guy who has never heard of the Rolling Stones.

Such pictures are far from the truth. Succeeding in math and science won't turn you into a nerd. Not only can you enjoy school more, your friends and family will still like you.

Our mental pictures about math and science can be funny. At the same time, they have serious effects. For many years, science and math were viewed as fields for white males. That excluded women and people of color. Promoting success in these subjects for all students is a key step in overcoming racism and sexism.

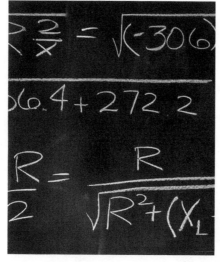

Look out for shaky assumptions

People often make faulty assumptions about how math and science are learned.

They include:

- *Math calls only for logic, not imagination.*
- *If you can't explain how you got the answer, you've failed.*
- *There's only one right way to do a science experiment.*
- *If you don't have a good memory, forget about science.*
- *There is a magic secret to doing well in math or science.*

These ideas can be easily refuted. To begin, mathematicians and scientists regularly talk about the importance of creativity and imagination in their work. At times they find it hard to explain how they arrive at a particular hypothesis or conclusion. Few of them boast about exceptional memories. And as far as we know, the only secret they count on is hard work.

Get your self-talk out in the open and change it

When students fear math and science, their self-talk is often negative. Many times it includes statements such as these:

•*I'll never be fast enough at solving math problems.*
•*I'm one of those people who can't function in a science lab.*
•*I know this law of motion is really simple and I'm just too dumb to get it.*
•*I'm good with words, so I can't be good with numbers.*

Faced with this kind of self-talk, you can take three steps.

1. Get a clear picture of such statements. When they come up, speak them out loud or write them down. When you get the little voice out in the open, it's easier to refute it.

2. Next, do some critical thinking about these statements. Look for the hidden assumptions they contain. Separate what's accurate about them from what's false.

Negative self-statements are usually based on scant evidence. They can often be reduced to two simple ideas: "Everybody else is better at math and science than I am," and "Since I don't understand it right now, I'll never understand it." Both of these are illogical. Many people lack confidence in their math and science skills. To verify this, just ask other students.

Also remember that understanding in math and science comes in small steps over time. These subjects are cumulative—that is, each new concept builds upon previously learned concepts. Learning or reviewing those concepts promotes understanding.

3. Start some new self-talk. Use statements that affirm your ability to succeed in math and science:
•*When learning about math or science, I proceed with patience and confidence.*
•*Any confusion I feel now will be resolved.*
•*I learn math and science without comparing myself to others.*
•*I ask whatever questions are needed to aid my understanding.*
•*I am fundamentally OK as a person, even if I make errors in math and science.*

As with other suggestions in this book, the true test of this one is whether or not it works.

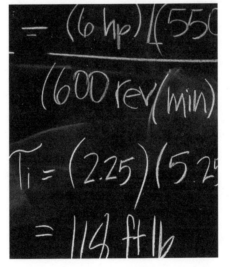

Notice your body sensations

Math and science anxiety are seldom just a "head trip." They register in our bodies, too. Examples are a tight feeling in the chest, sweaty palms, drowsiness, or a mild headache.

Let those sensations come to the surface. Instead of repressing them, open up to them. Doing so often decreases their urgency.

Next, learn and practice relaxation techniques. Many books, tapes, and courses exist on this subject. Also see the techniques for managing stress starting on page 162.

Make your text *A* priority

In a history, English, or economics class, the teacher may refer to some of the required readings only in passing. In contrast, math and science courses are often text-driven. That is, class activities follow the format of the book closely. This makes it doubly important to master your reading assignments. It's crucial to master one concept before going to the next and to stay current with your reading.

Read slowly when appropriate

It's ineffective to breeze through a math or science book as you would the newspaper. To get the most out of your text, be willing to read each sentence slowly and reread it as needed. A single paragraph may merit 15 or 20 minutes of sustained attention.

Read chapters and sections in order, as they're laid out in the text. To strengthen your understanding of the main ideas, study all tables, charts, graphs, case studies, and sample problems. From time to time, stop. Close your book and mentally reconstruct the steps in an experiment or a mathematical proof.

Read actively

Science is not only a body of knowledge but an activity. To get the most out of your math and science texts, read with paper and pencil in hand. Work out examples and copy diagrams, formulas, or equations.

You can also go beyond the text. Invent activities as you read. Construct additional problems similar to those in the book. Devise your own experiment to test the truth of a hypothesis. Relate your current reading to other math and science courses you've taken. Create your own charts and tables.

Consider keeping a running record of your insights and questions, much like a journal. When reading your textbook or taking notes in class, use a two-page format. Summarize the reading or lecture on the right-hand page. Record your guesses, hunches, false starts, questions, and errors on the left. List what you don't know yet and how you intend to find it out. You can use Discovery and Intention Statements like those in this book.

Learn from specific to general

A powerful way to learn many subjects is to get an overview of the main topics before you focus on details. You may want to use the opposite strategy when studying math and science. Learning these subjects often means comprehending one limited concept before going on to the next one. Through this kind of work, you gradually get the big picture. Jumping to general conclusions too soon might be confusing or inaccurate.

Be gentle with yourself

Learning science and math is like mastering any other skill. Some days your work can flow without effort and you'll feel like a candidate for the next Nobel prize. On other days, you may stumble like a baby first learning to walk. That's normal.

Don't be surprised if you feel you're going backwards once in a while—as if something you used to understand so well seems like gibberish now. This can result from the way math and science concepts are presented: The rules and general principles often come first, followed by the exceptions and conflicting evidence.

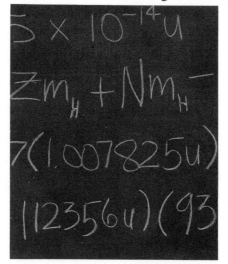

Think critically

Science and math texts are not eternal truth. You're free to ask questions or disagree with the author. If you do so, state your questions precisely and base your disagreements on evidence.

Remind yourself of the big picture

Pause occasionally to get the big picture of the branch of science or math you're studying. What's it all about? What basic problems is the discipline trying to solve? How is this knowledge applied in daily life?

For example, much of calculus has to do with finding the areas of "funny shapes"—shapes other than circles that have curves. Physics studies how matter and energy interact. Physics and calculus are used by many people, including architects, engineers, and space scientists.

Ask questions fearlessly

In any subject, learning comes when we ask questions. And there are no dumb questions. To master math and science, ask whatever questions will aid your understanding. Students come to higher education with widely varying backgrounds in these subjects. What you need to ask may not be the same as the other people in your class. Go ahead and ask.

One barrier to asking questions is the thought, "Will the teacher think I'm stupid or ill-prepared if I ask this? What if he laughs or rolls his eyes?" With competent instructors, this will not happen. If it does, remember your reasons for going to school. The purpose is not to impress the teacher but to learn. And sometimes learning means admitting total ignorance.

Use lab sessions to your advantage

Laboratory work is crucial to many science classes. To get the most out of these sessions, prepare. Know in advance what procedures you'll be doing and what materials you'll need. If possible, visit the lab before your assigned time and get to know the territory. Find out where materials are stored and where to dispose of chemicals or specimens. Bring your lab notebook and worksheets to record and summarize your findings.

If you're collecting data during an experiment, keep in mind that there's no such thing as a perfect measurement. Two people following the same instructions may come up with different results. When you chart or graph your results, your data points may not follow a straight line or smooth curve. Mathematical formulas are precise, while our measurements are approximations.

If you're not planning to become a scientist, the main point is to understand the process of science—how scientists observe, collect data, and arrive at conclusions. This is more important than the result of any one experiment.

Journal Entry #29
Discovery Statement

Most of us can recall a time when learning became associated with anxiety. For many people, this happened early with math and science.

One step to getting past this anxiety is to write a math or science autobiography. Recall specific experiences when you first felt stress over these subjects. Where were you? How old were you? What were you thinking and feeling? Who else was with you? What did those people say or do?

Describe one of these experiences in the space below.

_____
_____
_____
_____
_____
_____

Now recall any incidents in your life that gave you positive feelings about math or science. Describe one of these incidents in the space below.

_____
_____
_____
_____
_____
_____
_____
_____

Now sum up the significant discoveries you made while describing these two sets of experiences.

I discovered that my biggest barrier to success in math or science is . . .

_____
_____

I discovered that the most satisfying part of doing math and science is . . .

_____
_____
_____

Journal Entry #30
Intention Statement

List three actions you will take to overcome any anxiety you feel about math or science. Then schedule a specific time for taking each action.

1. _____

2. _____

3. _____

Solving math and science problems

Solving word problems is a key part of reading textbooks about math and science. Approach math and science problems the way rock climbers approach mountains. The first part is devoted to preparations you make before you get to the rock. The second part is devoted to techniques used on the rock (problem) itself.

To the uninitiated, rock climbing looks dangerous. For the unprepared, it is. A novice might come to a difficult place in a climb and panic. When a climber freezes, he is truly stuck. Experienced climbers figure out strategies in advance for as many situations as possible. With preparation and training, the sport takes on a different cast.

Sometimes students get stuck, panic, and freeze with academic problems. Use the following techniques to avoid that. Experiment with these techniques as you work through textbooks in math and science. You can also use them on tests.

Before you get to the rock

1. Practice

Work lots of problems. Do assigned problems and more. Make up your own. Work with a classmate and make up problems for each other to solve. The more problems you do, the more comfortable you're likely to feel solving new ones. Set clear goals for practice and write Intention Statements about meeting those goals.

Some students memorize the problems and answers discussed in class—without learning the formulas or general principles behind the problem. This kind of rote learning doesn't allow them to practice applying the principles or formulas to new problems. The solution is to understand *how* to arrive at those answers.

2. Divide problems by type

Make a list of the different kinds of problems and note the elements of each. By dividing problems into type or category, you can isolate the kinds of problems you have that are difficult for you. Practice those more and get help if you need it.

3. Know your terminology

Mathematicians and scientists often borrow words from plain English and assign new meanings to them. For example, for most of the world, "work" means a job. For the physicist, "work" is force multiplied by distance. To ensure that you understand the terminology, see if you can restate the problem in your own words. Translate equations into English sentences. Use 3x5 flashcards to study special terms.

4. Understand formulas

You might be asked to memorize some formulas for convenience. If you understand the basic concepts behind these formulas, it is easier to recall them accurately. More importantly, you will probably be able to recreate the formulas if your recall falters. Understanding is always preferable to memorization.

5. Use summary sheets

Groups of terms and formulas can be easier to memorize if you list them on a sheet of paper or put them on 3x5 cards. Mind map summary sheets allow you to see how various kinds of problems relate to one another. You create a structure on which you can hang data, and that helps your recall.

6. Play with possibilities

There's usually not one "right" way to solve a problem. Several approaches or formulas may work, though one may be more efficient than another. Be willing to think about the problem from several angles or proceed by trial and error.

7. Notice when you're in deep water

It's tempting to shy away from difficult problems. Unfortunately, the more you do this, the more difficult the problems become. Math and science courses present wonderful opportunities to use the First Step technique explained in Chapter One. When you feel that you're beginning to get in trouble, write a precise Discovery Statement about the problem. Then write an Intention Statement about what you will do to solve the problem.

8. When practicing, time yourself

Sometimes speed counts. Notice how fast you can work problems. This gives you an idea of how much time to allot for different types of problems.

9. Use creative visualizations

Before you begin a problem-solving session, take a minute to relax, breathe deeply, and prepare yourself for the task ahead. Then use the techniques described on page 314 to see yourself solving problems successfully.

On the rock

1. Survey the territory thoroughly

Read the problem at least twice before you begin. Read slowly. Be certain you understand what is being asked.

Let go of the expectation that you'll find the solution right away. You may make several attempts at solving the problem before you find one that works.

2. Sort the facts

Survey the problem for all of the givens. Determine the principles and relationships involved. Look for what is to be proven or what is to be discovered. Write these down.

3. Set up the problem

Before you begin to compute, determine the strategy you will use to arrive at the solution. When solving equations, carry out the algebra as far as you can before plugging in the actual numbers.

Remember that solving a math or science problem is like putting together a puzzle. You may work around the edges for a while and try many pieces before finding one that fits.

4. Cancel and combine

When you set up a problem logically, you can take shortcuts. For example, if the same term appears in both dividend and divisor, they will cancel each other.

5. Draw a picture

Make a diagram. Pictures help keep the facts straight. They show relationships more effectively than words.

To keep on track, record your facts in tables. Consider using three columns titled "what I already know," "what I want to find out," and "what relates the two." This last column is the place to record a formula that can help you solve the problem.

6. Read the problem aloud

Sometimes the sound of your voice will jar loose the solution to a problem. Talk yourself through the solution. Read equations out loud.

7. Check results

Work problems backwards, then forwards. Start at both ends and work towards the middle to check your work.

Take a minute to make sure you kept the units of measurement clear. Say that you're calculating the velocity of an object. If you're measuring distance in meters and time in seconds, then the final velocity should be in meters per second.

Another way to check your work is to estimate the answer before you compute it. Then ask if the answer you actually got seems in the ballpark.

8. Savor the solution

Savor the times when you're getting correct answers to most of the problems in your textbook. Relish the times you feel relaxed and confident as you work, or when you look over the last few pages and they seem easy. Then remember these times whenever you feel math or science anxiety.

Barbara Jordan,

Black congresswoman and lawyer, was named one of the ten most influential women in Texas.

Excerpt from Barbara Jordan, a Self-Portrait, *by Barbara Jordan. Copyright 1979 by Barbara Jordan and Shelby Hearon. Reprinted by permission of The Wendy Weil Agency, Inc.*

So I was at Boston University in this new and strange and different world, and it occurred to me that if I was going to succeed at this strange new adventure, I would have to read longer and more thoroughly than my colleagues at law school had to read. I felt that in order to compensate for what I had missed in earlier years, I would have to work harder, and study longer, than anybody else. I still had this feeling that I did not want my colleagues to know what a tough time I was having understanding the concepts, the words, the ideas, the process. I didn't want them to know that. So I did my reading not in the law library, but in a library at the graduate dorm, upstairs where it was very quiet, because apparently nobody else there studied. So I would go there at night after dinner. I would load my books under my arm and go to the library, and I would read until the wee hours of the morning and then go to bed. I didn't get much sleep during those years. I was lucky if I got three or four hours a night, because I had to stay up. I had to. The professors would assign cases for the next day, and these cases had to be read and understood or I would be behind, further behind than I was.

I was always delighted when I would get called upon to recite in class. But the professors did not call on the "ladies" very much. There were certain favored people who always got called on, and then on some rare occasions a professor would come in and would announce: "We're going to have Ladies Day today." And he would call on the ladies. We were just tolerated. We weren't considered really top drawer when it came to the study of law.

At some time in the spring, Bill Gibson, who was dating my new roommate, Norma Walker, organized a black study group, as we blacks had to form our own. This was because we were not invited into any of the other study groups. There were six or seven in our group—Bill, and Issie, and I think Maynard Jackson—and we would just gather and talk it out and hear ourselves do that. One thing I learned was that you had to talk out the issues, the facts, the cases, the decisions, the process. You couldn't just read the cases and study alone in your library as I had been doing; and you couldn't get it all in the classroom. But once you had talked it out in the study group, it flowed more easily and made a lot more sense . . .

Finally I felt I was really learning things, really going to school. I felt that I was getting educated, whatever that was. I became familiar with the process of thinking. I learned to think things out and reach conclusions and defend what I had said.

In the past I had got along by spouting off. Whether you talked about debates or oratory, you dealt with speechifying. Even in debate it was pretty much canned because you had, in your little three-by-five box, a response for whatever issue might be raised by the opposition. The format was structured so that there was no opportunity for independent thinking. (I really had not had my ideas challenged ever.) But I could no longer orate and let that pass for reasoning because there was not any demand for an orator in Boston University Law School. You had to think and read and understand and reason. I had learned at twenty-one that you couldn't just say a thing is so because it might not be so, and somebody brighter, smarter, and more thoughtful would come out and tell you it wasn't so. Then, if you still thought it was, you had to prove it. Well, that was a new thing for me. I cannot, I really cannot describe what that did to my insides and to my head. I thought: I'm being educated finally.

QUIZ

1. What is an acrostic that can help you remember the nine steps of muscle reading?

2. You must complete all nine steps of muscle reading to get the most out of any reading assignment. True or False. Explain your answer.

3. Describe at least four strategies you can use to preview a reading assignment.

4. What is a benefit of outlining a reading assignment?

5. Beware of the dread condition, mumpsimus. This condition is dangerous because it involves

   (A) doing what you're doing when you're doing it.
   (B) being similar or having the quality of resemblance.
   (C) eyes leaping across the page in short bursts.
   (D) blind adherence to a principle or concept.
   (E) not believing everything you read.

6. Pens and colored highlighters work equally well to underline reading material. True or false. Explain your answer.

7. Discuss at least three techniques you can use when reading is tough.

8. Explain how reading math or science texts can differ from reading a text for history or English.

9. After talking with her classmates about issues, facts, cases, decision, and process, Barbara Jordan:

   (A) learned that others were brighter, smarter, and more thoughtful than she was.
   (B) discovered that the material flowed more easily and made a lot more sense.
   (C) realized that she could work by herself, challenging her own ideas and thinking independently.
   (D) decided to work harder and study longer than anybody else.
   (E) all of the above.

10. Discuss at least three hints for increasing your reading speed.

Journal Entry #31
Discovery Statement

Review what you learned in this chapter and complete the following sentence:

In reading and doing this chapter, I discovered that I . . .

_____

_____

_____

_____

Journal Entry #32
Intention Statement

Describe one thing you wanted to get from this chapter and didn't. Then describe what you will do to learn it.

I learned that I . . .

_____

_____

_____

_____

Journal Entry #33
Intention Statement

Quickly review this chapter and choose three techniques that you will put into practice.

I intend to . . .

_____

_____

_____

_____

_____

Journal Entry #34
Discovery Statement

Consider your attitude about memory. Have your ideas changed since reading Chapter Three?

Concerning my memory attitudes, I learned that I . . .

_____

_____

_____

_____

_____

_____

_____

Chapter  5

Notes

Rather than try to gauge your note-taking skill by quantity, think in this way: am I simply doing clerk's work or am I assimilating new knowledge and putting down my own thoughts? To put down your own thoughts you must put down your own words . . . .
If the note taken shows signs of having passed through a mind, it is a good test of its relevance and adequacy.
JACQUES BARZUN AND HENRY GRAFF

This is what learning is. You suddenly understand something you've understood all your life, but in a new way.
DORIS LESSING

 **Journal Entry #35**
Discovery Statement

How do you want to improve your note-taking skills? Do you want to be able to write faster? More clearly? Do you want notes that are easier to review? Write here what you want to get from this chapter.

In this chapter . . .

Many students complain that their notes are confusing, incomplete, or useless at exam time. Learn how to take powerful notes by following three essential steps. It's all in *The note-taking process flows.* You can apply the same ideas to *Taking notes on reading.*

Improving your handwriting is for people who say: "I can't help it. My writing is just hard to read." There's no need to resign yourself to chicken scratching when you follow the suggestions in this article.

In this chapter you'll learn how to take notes even *When instructors talk fast.* Experiment with these techniques in the exercise *Television note-taking practice.*

Take responsibility for boring classes, tests, and irritating people by applying *Power Process #5: I Create it all.* You can turn such frustrations into experiences that promote your academic success.

The note-taking process flows

ONE WAY TO UNDERSTAND NOTE-TAKING is to realize that taking notes is the least important part of the process.

Effective note-taking consists of three parts: observing, recording, and reviewing. First, you observe an event—most often a statement by the instructor. Then you record your observations of that event— that is, you "take notes." Finally, you review what you have recorded.

Each part of the process is essential, and each depends on the others. Your observations determine what you record. What you record determines what you review. Less obviously, how well you review can determine how effective your next observations will be. For example, if you review your notes on the Sino-Japanese War of 1894, the next day's lecture on the Boxer Rebellion of 1900 will make more sense.

Certainly, legible and speedy handwriting is also useful in taking notes. A knowledge of outlining is handy, too. A nifty pen, a new notebook, even a fancy tape recorder are all great note-taking devices.

And they're all worthless, unless you participate as an energetic observer in class and regularly review your notes after class. If you take those two steps, you can turn even the most disorganized chicken scratches into a powerful tool.

Observe

The note-taking process flows

Sherlock Holmes, a fictional master student, could track down a villain by observing the wrinkles in his hat and the mud on his shoes. In real life, a doctor can save a life by observing a suspicious mole. An accountant can save a client thousands of dollars by observing the details of a spreadsheet. A student can save hours of study time by observing that she gets twice as much done at a particular time of day.

The best scientists are good observers. The best writers are good observers. The best counselors, cooks, policemen, engineers, painters, mechanics, and accountants are good observers. Keen observers see facts and relationships. They know how to focus their attention on the details, then tap their creative energy to discover patterns.

To sharpen your classroom observation skills, experiment with the following techniques and continue to use those that you find most valuable.

Set the stage

1. Complete outside assignments. Nothing is more discouraging (or boring) than sitting through a lecture on the relationship of the Le Chatelier principle to the principle of kinetics if you have never heard of Le Chatelier or kinetics.

Instructors usually assume that students complete assignments, and they construct their lectures accordingly. The more familiar you are with a subject, the better you can observe what happens in class. For example, a knowledgeable football fan often sees more during a football game than a person who knows nothing of the game. A seasoned bird watcher sees more birds than someone who knows nothing about birds.

To get the most out of a lecture, open your mind to the subject before you get to class. Complete the reading assignments and work the assigned problems. Generate questions as you prepare and be ready to ask them.

2. Bring the right materials. A good pen does not make you a good observer, but the lack of a pen or a notebook can be distracting enough to take the fine edge off your concentration. Make sure you have a pen, pencil, notebook, and any other materials you will need. Consider bringing your textbook to class, especially if the lectures relate closely to the text.

If you are consistently unprepared for class, that might be a message about your intentions concerning the course. Find out if it is. The next time you're in a frantic scramble to borrow pen and paper 37 seconds before class begins, notice the cost. Use the borrowed pen and paper to write yourself a Discovery Statement about your lack of preparation. Consider whether you intend to be successful in the class.

3. Sit front and center. Students who get as close as possible to the front and center of the classroom do better on tests, for several reasons.

The closer you sit to the lecturer, the harder it is to fall asleep.

The closer you sit to the front, the fewer interesting—or distracting—heads there are to watch between you and the instructor.

Material on the board is easier to read from up front.

The instructor can see you more easily when you have a question.

Instructors are usually not trained as actors or performers. Some instructors can project their energy to a large audience; many cannot. A professor who sounds boring from the back of the room might sound more interesting if you're closer. Get close to the energy.

And finally, sitting up front is a way to commit yourself to getting what you want out of your education. One reason students gravitate to the back of the classroom is that they think the instructor is less likely to call on them. Most instructors are wise to this ploy, yet some students assume it works. Sitting in back can signal a lack of commitment.

When you sit in front you are declaring your willingness to take a risk and participate.

4. Conduct a short pre-class review. Arrive early, then put your brain in gear by reviewing your notes from the previous class. Scan your reading assignment. Look at the sections you have underlined. Review assigned problems and exercises. Note questions you intend to ask. Depending on the type of material, the mind can take from two to ten minutes to warm up to a subject. Give yourself a head start.

5. Clarify your intentions. Write a short Intention Statement about what you plan to get from the class. Describe your intended level of participation, or the quality of attention you will bring to the subject. Be specific. If you found previous class notes to be inadequate, write down things you

intend to do to make your notes from this class session more useful.

"Be here now" in class

6. Accept your wandering mind. The techniques in Power Process #2: "Be here now" can be especially useful when your head soars into the clouds.

Don't fight daydreaming. When you notice your mind wandering, look at it as an opportunity to refocus your attention. Whenever you notice that your attention is wandering from thermodynamics to beach parties, let go of the beach. Every time you bring your mind back to the here and now, you strengthen your observer consciousness. Eventually you will increase your ability to stay on task.

Be gentle with yourself about daydreaming. Let each daydreaming episode become an opportunity to return to the task. Trust the process.

7. Notice your writing. When you discover yourself slipping into a fantasy land, notice how your pen feels in your hand. Notice how your notes look. Paying attention to the act of writing can bring you back to the here and now.

Taking notes connects your hands and eyes to your ears, and it connects all three to your brain. Think of writing as a multichannel process that improves your

 **Journal Entry #36**
Discovery Statement

Think about the way you have conducted reviews of your notes in the past. Answer the following questions by checking "always," "often," "sometimes," "seldom," or "never" after the question.

I review my notes immediately after class.	___ALWAYS	___OFTEN	___SOMETIMES	___SELDOM	___NEVER
I conduct weekly reviews of my notes.	___ALWAYS	___OFTEN	___SOMETIMES	___SELDOM	___NEVER
I make summary sheets of my notes.	___ALWAYS	___OFTEN	___SOMETIMES	___SELDOM	___NEVER
I edit my notes within 24 hours.	___ALWAYS	___OFTEN	___SOMETIMES	___SELDOM	___NEVER
Before class, I conduct a brief review of the notes I took in the previous class.	___ALWAYS	___OFTEN	___SOMETIMES	___SELDOM	___NEVER

The note-taking process flows

concentration and your ability to remember the information later.

You also can use writing more directly to clear your mind of distracting thoughts. Pause for a few seconds and write those thoughts down. If you're distracted by thoughts of errands you want to run after class, list them on a 3x5 card and stick it in your pocket. Or, simply put a symbol in your notes, such as an arrow or asterisk, to mark the places your mind started to wander. Once your distractions are out of your mind and safely stored on paper, you can gently return your attention to taking notes.

8. Be with the instructor. In your mind, put yourself right up front with the instructor. Imagine that you and the instructor are the only ones in the room and the lecture is a personal talk with you. Pay attention to the instructor's body language and facial expressions. Look the instructor in the eye. (This is a good reason to sit as close to the front and center of the classroom as you can get.)

9. Notice your environment. When you become aware of yourself daydreaming, bring yourself back to class by paying attention to the temperature in the room, the feel of your chair, or the quality of light in the room. Run your hand along the surface of your desk. Listen to the fan running or the sound of the teacher's voice. Be in that environment.

10. Postpone debate. When you hear something you disagree with, note your disagreement and let it go. Don't allow your internal dialogue to drown out subsequent material. If your disagreement is persistent and strong, write down the point and move on. Internal debate can prevent you from absorbing new information. It is OK to absorb information you don't agree with. Just absorb it with the mental tag, "I

don't agree with this and my instructor says . . . ."

11. Let go of judgments about lecture styles. Human beings are judgment machines. We evaluate everything, especially other people, automatically. If another person's eyebrows are too close together (or too far apart), if she walks a certain way or combs her hair a certain way, we instantly make up a story about her. We do this so quickly that the process is usually not a conscious one.

Instructors have idiosyncrasies. They use the same phrases over and over, such as "You know.", "OK. OK.", "Six of one, half a dozen of the other.", "Well, my Aunt Clara . . ." They wear strange clothes, they talk too loudly, they talk too softly—the list is long.

The problem is, these judgments filter our perceptions and screen out information that doesn't fit with our pictures. This process can be damaging during a lecture. It can prevent you from getting what you want from your education.

Don't let your attitude about an instructor's lecture style, habits, or appearance get in the way of your education. You can decrease the power of your judgments if you pay attention to them and let them go.

You can even let go of judgments about rambling, unorganized lectures. Turn them to your advantage. Take the initiative and organize the material yourself. While taking notes, separate the key points from the examples and supporting evidence. Note the places you got confused and make a list of questions to ask.

You can discuss lecture style problems with your instructors. Perhaps they will make adjustments to suit you. You can also look for ways to adjust to their styles. Remember that you are not there to love or hate your instructors but to learn from them. Developing the ability to learn from a variety of lecture styles will help insure your success in school.

12. Participate in class activities. Ask questions. Volunteer for demonstrations. Join in class discussions. Be willing to take a risk or look foolish if that's what it takes for you to learn.

It's OK to feel self-conscious about saying the wrong thing or asking a dumb question. Ask anyway. Chances are the question you think is "dumb" also is on the minds of several of your classmates.

13. Relate the class to your goals. If you have trouble staying awake in a particular class, write at the top of your notes how that class relates to a specific goal. Note the reward or payoff for reaching that goal.

14. Think critically about what you hear. This might seem contrary to #10: "Postpone debate." It's not.

Sometimes taking notes involves transferring words from the instructor's mouth to the student's notebook—without any ideas entering the student's mind. However, the purpose of attending class is not to passively record the instructor's words, like a robot, but to grapple with the ideas and make them your own.

You may choose not to think critically about the instructor's ideas during the lecture. That's fine. Do it later, as you review and edit your notes. This is a time to list questions or write your agreements and disagreements. These thoughts can become the seed for a term paper.

Critical thinking means that you're actively involved in the process of learning. That increases your chances of remembering the material. In addition, you're enlisting the help of the greatest teacher you know—yourself.

Watch for clues

15. Be alert to repetition. When an instructor repeats a phrase or idea, make a note of it. Repetition is a signal that the instructor thinks the information is important.

16. Listen for introductory, concluding, and transition words and phrases. These include phrases like "the following three factors . . .," "in conclusion . . .," "the most important consideration . . .," "in addition to . . .," and "on the other hand . . . ." These phrases and others signal relationships, definitions, new subjects, conclusions, cause and effect, and examples. In other words, they reveal the structure of the lecture. You can use these phrases to organize your notes.

17. Watch the board or overhead projector. If an instructor takes time to write something down, consider that another signal that the material is important. Copy all diagrams and drawings, equations, names, places, dates, statistics, and definitions.

18. Watch the instructor's eyes. If an instructor glances at her notes and then makes a point, it is probably a signal that the information is especially important. Anything she reads from her notes is a potential test question.

19. Highlight the obvious clues. Instructors will often tell students point-blank that certain information is likely to appear on an exam. Make stars in your notes beside this kind of information. Instructors are not trying to hide what's important.

20. Notice the instructor's interest level. If the instructor is excited about something, it is more likely to appear on an exam. Pay attention if she seems more animated than usual.

Record
The note-taking process flows

The format and structure of your notes are more important than how fast you write or how pretty your handwriting is. The following techniques can improve the effectiveness of your notes.

1. Use the Cornell format of note-taking. **On each page of your notes, draw a vertical line, top to bottom, 1 1/2 inches from the left edge of the paper. Write your notes to the right of the line. Reserve the area to the left of the line for key word clues and sample questions. Fill in the left-hand column when you review your notes.**

Metal Conductive	Hard, shiny, malleable (roll into sheets), ductile (pulled into wires). Conducts electric current & heat. 3 or fewer electrons in outer level so good conductors because electrons can move thru.
Metallic Bond	Outer electrons distributed as common electric cloud. Electrons shared equally by all ions which explains properties (conductive, malleable, ductile) → ions slide by each other & can be displaced w/o shattering.
Alkali Metals	Soft metals. Most reactive – kept under oil so won't react directly w/oxygen or H₂0. Forms compound by ionic bonding.

2. Create mind maps. This system, developed by Tony Buzan, can be used in conjunction with the Cornell system, although in some circumstances you might want to use mind maps exclusively. The benefit of mind maps is that they show the relationships between ideas in a visual way—quickly, vividly, and accurately.

Mind maps can start anywhere on the page. If you begin in the middle of the page, you will have more room to expand.

Write the main point on a line or in a box, circle, or any other shape. (See the illustration on page 135.) This might be the general subject of the lecture, a single sentence, or a key word relating to the subject of the lecture.

Record subordinate points on lines branching out from the central subject. In turn, each subordinate point can have its own branches. Mind maps spread out over the page, and each mind map takes on its own shape as it develops.

Be creative. Use different pencils or pens. Include illustrations, diagrams, and drawings—any image that will aid your memory.

Use different size sheets of paper. Mind maps can be done on anything from a 3x5 card to a wall-sized piece of newsprint. Another option is to find software that allows you to draw flow charts or diagrams. Then you can generate mind maps on a computer.

One mind map does not have to include all the ideas in a book or article. Instead, you can link mind maps. For example, draw a mind map that sums up the five key points in a chapter; then make a separate, more detailed mind map for each of those key points. Within each mind map, include references to the other mind maps. This helps in seeing the relationships among many ideas.

Some students pin several mind maps next to each other on a bulletin board or tape them to a wall. That gives them a dramatic and effective look at the big picture.

Mind maps can be used along with Cornell-format notes in a number of ways. You can divide your note paper in half, reserving one half for mind maps and the other for information more suited to the traditional paragraph method: equations, long explanations, and word-for-word definitions. You also can incorporate a mind map into your paragraph-style notes wherever you feel one is appropriate. Mind maps are also useful for summarizing notes taken in Cornell format.

Another way to use mind maps is to abandon the Cornell format, draw a line down the center of the page, and use the left-hand side for mind mapping and the right-hand side for more linear information, such as lists, graphs, and paragraphs.

3. Write notes in outline form. You can use a standard Roman numeral outline or a more free-form, indented outline to organize the information in a lecture.

The outline form illustrates major points and supporting ideas. The main advantage to taking notes in outline form is that it can totally occupy your attention. You are not only recording ideas but organizing them. That can be an advantage if material is presented in a disorganized way.

4. Write notes in paragraphs. When it is difficult to follow the organization of a lecture or to put information into outline form, create a series of informal paragraphs. These paragraphs will contain few complete sentences. Reserve complete sentences for precise definitions, direct quotes, and important points that the instructor emphasizes by repetition or other signals, like the phrase "This is an important point." For other material, apply the suggestions in technique #5, "Use key words."

Write related thoughts in a paragraph and leave a space when the lecturer moves to another point. That way, you can go back and add information the instructor offers later. When you review your notes, you can reorganize them and create an outline.

5. Use key words. An easy way to sort the extraneous material from the important points is to take notes using key words.

Key words or phrases contain the essence of communication. They include technical terms, names, numbers, equations, and words of degree: *most, least, faster, etc.*

Key words are laden with associations. They evoke images and associations with other words and ideas. They trigger your memory. That makes them powerful review tools.

One key word can initiate the recall of a whole cluster of ideas. A few key words can form a chain from which you can reconstruct an entire lecture.

In order to see how key words work, take yourself to an imaginary classroom. You are now in the middle of an anatomy lecture. Picture what the room looks like, what it feels like, how it smells. You hear the instructor say:

OK, what happens when we look directly over our heads and see a piano falling out of the sky? How do we take that signal and translate it into the action of getting out of the way? The first thing that happens is that a stimulus

Bio I
9/27

Bones - living organs, 206 in body, 18% of weight
A. Marrow - in center of bones. Contains nerves + blood vessels
  1. Red
    a. in flat bones (ribs) + ends of long bones
    b. produces red blood cells in adults
  2. Yellow - mostly flat tissue
    a. in center of long bones
    b. might make red blood cells if great blood loss or w/ certain blood diseases
B. Haversian canals - carry blood thru bones (for oxygen, food + waste)
C. Periostium - protective membrane covers bone
D. Composed of:
  1. Minerals, organic matter, H₂0
    a. Calcium + phosphorus present as calcium phosphate (Ca₃(PO₄)₂) +

Exercise #15
Television note-taking practice

You can use evening news broadcasts to practice listening for key words, writing quickly, focusing your attention, and reviewing.

Next time you watch the news, do it with pen and paper. During the commercials, review and revise your notes. At the end of the broadcast, spend five minutes reviewing your notes. Create a mind map of a few news stories, then recreate the news of the day for a friend.

This exercise will help you develop an ear for key words. Since you can't ask questions or ask the speaker to slow down, you train yourself to stay totally in the moment. If you get behind, you learn not to panic, but to leave a space and return to the broadcast.

Don't be discouraged if you miss a lot the first time around. Do this exercise several times and observe how your mind works.

You can also ask a friend to do the same exercise and then compare notes the next day.

is generated in the neurons—receptor neurons—of the eye. Light reflected from the piano reaches our eyes. In other words, we see the piano. The receptor neurons in the eye transmit that sensory signal, the sight of the piano, to the body's nervous system. That's all they can do, pass on information. So, we've got a sensory signal coming into the nervous system. But the neurons that initiate movement in our legs are effector neurons. The information from the sensory neurons must be transmitted to effector neurons or we will get squashed by the piano. There must be some kind of interconnection between receptor and effector neurons. What happens between the two? What is the connection?

Key words you might note in this example include *stimulus*, *generated*, *receptor neurons*, *transmit*, *sensory signals*, *nervous system*, *effector neurons*, and *connection*. You could reduce the instructor's 148 words to these 12 key words. With a few transitional words, your notes might look like this:

> Stimulus (piano) generated in receptor neurons (eye). Sensory signals transmitted by nervous system to effector neurons (legs). What connects receptor to effector?

Note the last key word, *connection*. This word is part of the instructor's question, which leads to the next point in the lecture. Be alert for questions like this. They can help you organize your notes, and they are often clues for test questions.

6. *Use pictures and diagrams.* Make relationships visual. Copy all diagrams from the board and invent your own. This technique can be used anytime, with or without mind mapping.

A drawing of a piano falling on someone who is looking up, for example, might be used to demonstrate the relationship of receptor neurons to effector neurons. Label the eyes *receptor* and the feet *effector*. That picture implies that the sight of the piano must be translated into a motor response. By connecting the explanation of the process with the unusual picture of the piano falling, you can link the elements of the process together.

7. *Copy material from the board.* Record all formulas, diagrams, and problems. Copy dates, numbers, names, places, and other facts. If it's on the board, put it in your notes. You can even use your own signal or code to flag that material. If it appears on the board, it can appear on a test.

8. *Use a three-ring binder.* Three-ring binders have several advantages over other kinds of notebooks.

First, pages can be removed and spread out when you review. This way you can get the whole picture of a lecture.

Second, the three-ring binder format will easily allow you to insert handouts right into your notes.

Third, you can insert your own out-of-class notes in the correct order. You can make additions, corrections, and revisions easily.

9. *Use only one side of a piece of paper.* When you use one side of a page,

you can review and organize all your notes by spreading them out side by side. Most students find the benefit well worth the cost of paper.

10. *Use 3x5 cards.* As an alternative to notebook paper, use 3x5 cards to take lecture notes. Copy each new concept on a separate 3x5 card. Later these cards can be organized in an outline form, and they can be used as pocket flash cards.

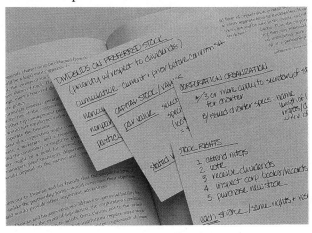

11. *Keep your own thoughts separate.* For the most part, avoid making editorial comments in your lecture notes. The danger is that when you return to your notes, you may mistake your own idea for that of the instructor. If you want to make a comment—either a question to be asked later or a strong disagreement—clearly label it as your own. Pick a symbol or code and use it for every class. Another option is to record your own thoughts on separate 3x5 cards or sheets of paper.

12. *Use a "lost" signal.* No matter how attentive and alert you are, you might get lost and confused in a lecture. If it is inappropriate to ask a question, record in your notes that you were lost. Invent your own signal—for example, a circled question mark. When you write down your code for "lost," leave space for the explanation or clarification that you will get later. The space also will be a signal that you missed something. Then, you can call your instructor or ask to see a fellow student's

notes. As long as you are honest with yourself when you don't understand, you can stay on top of the course.

13. *Label, number, and date all notes.* Develop the habit of labeling and dating your notes at the beginning of each class. Number the pages, too. Sometimes the sequence of material in a lecture is important. Write your name and phone number in each notebook. Class notes become more and more valuable as a term proceeds.

14. *Use standard abbreviations.* Be consistent with your abbreviations. If you make up your own abbreviations or symbols, write a key explaining them in your notes.

Avoid vague abbreviations. When you use an abbreviation like *comm.* for, say, *committee*, you run the risk of not being able to remember whether you meant committee, commission, common, commit, community, communicate, or communist.

One way to abbreviate is to leave out vowels. For example, *talk* becomes *tlk*, *said* becomes *sd*, *American* becomes *Amcn*.

WARNING: Abbreviations can be hazardous to your academic health. If you are inconsistent or if you use vague abbreviations, there will be a price to pay in confusion later on. One way to avoid that is to write out abbreviated terms during pauses in a lecture, when the meaning of your shorthand is still fresh in your short-term memory.

Abbreviations also make your notes difficult to read for other students—students who are willing to trade notes with you.

15. *Use blank space.* Notes tightly crammed into every corner of the page are hard to read and difficult to use for review. Give your eyes a break by leaving plenty of space.

Later, when you review, you can use the blank space in your notes to clarify points, write questions, or add other material. Often, instructors return to material covered earlier in the lecture. If you have left adequate space, you can add information.

Advertising designers have a special term for blank space. They call it "white space," and they know it can be a powerful communication tool. White space makes it easier to get information off the page and into the brain, which is their business. The next time you read a magazine, notice how white space is used in advertisements. See which ones are easiest to read. Chances are those ads use plenty of blank space.

16. Use tape recorders effectively. There are persuasive arguments for not using a tape recorder. Here are the main ones:

When you tape a lecture, there is a strong temptation to daydream. After all, you can always listen to the lecture again. Unfortunately, if you let the recorder do all the work, you are skipping a valuable part of the learning process. Your active participation in class can turn a lecture into a valuable study session.

Second, listening to tape recorded lectures takes a lot of time—much more time than reviewing written notes.

Third, tape recorders can't answer the questions you didn't ask in class.

Fourth, tape recorders malfunction. In fact, the unscientific Hypothesis of Recording Glitches states that the tendency of tape recorders to malfunction is directly proportional to the importance of the material.

With those warnings in mind, some students can use a tape recorder effectively.

For example, you can use recordings as back-ups to written notes. Turn the recorder on, then take notes as if it weren't there. Recordings can be especially useful if an instructor speaks fast. (Check with your instructor first. Some prefer not to be taped.)

You also could record yourself after class, reading your written notes. Teaching

the class to yourself is a powerful review tool. Instead of taping all your notes, for example, you might just record the key facts or concepts.

You can have fun, too. As you tape, speak in funny voices. Do imitations of your teacher or favorite actors. Add background music. Make these tapes enjoyable for listening.

You can use the recordings you make, or back-up recordings from class, to review while you drive, wash dishes, or exercise.

Some tape recorders have a feature called compressed speech. This speeds up the voice on the tape, which can save you listening time.

Knowing the pitfalls of tape recorders, experiment for yourself. Then adopt a strategy what works for you.

17. Use graphic signals. The following ideas can be used with any note-taking format, including mind maps.

Brackets, parentheses, circles, and squares can be used to group information that belongs together.

Use stars, arrows, and underlining to indicate important points. Flag the most important points with double stars, double arrows, or double underlines.

Use arrows and connecting lines to link related groups, to show causation, and to replace words like *leads to*, *becomes*, and *produces*.

Use equal signs and greater- and less-than signs to indicate compared quantities.

Use question marks for their obvious purpose. Use double question marks to signal tough questions or especially confusing points.

To avoid creating confusion with graphic symbols, use them carefully and consistently. Write a "dictionary" of the symbols you use in the front of your notebooks, like the one shown here.

[ ], ( ), ◯, ▢ = *info that belongs together*

←, ↘, = = *important*

←*, ↘↘, ≡, !!! = *extra important*

\> = *greater than*   < = *less than*

= *equal to*

→ = *leads to, becomes*
Ex: *school → job → money*

= *huh?, lost*

? = *big trouble, clear up immediately*

18. Use complete sentences when material is important. Sometimes key words aren't enough. When an instructor repeats a sentence using exactly the same words, she might be sending you a signal. Technical definitions are often worded precisely because even a slightly different wording will render the definition useless or incorrect.

19. Take notes in different colors. You can use colors as highly visible organizers. For example, you can signal important points with red. Or use one color ink for notes on the text and another color for lecture notes. Notes that are visually pleasing can be easier to review.

Review
The note-taking process flows

Think of reviewing as an integral part of note-taking rather than an added task. In order for information to be useful, it needs to be available to your recall.

1. Review within 24 hours. In the last chapter, when you read the suggestion to review what you've read within 24 hours, you were asked to sound the trumpet. Well, if you have one, get it out and sound it again. This might be the most powerful note-taking technique you can use. It can save you hours of review time later in the term.

Many students are surprised by how much they can remember of a lecture in the minutes and hours after class. They are even more surprised by how well they can read even the sloppiest notes.

Unfortunately, short-term memory deteriorates quickly. The good news: If you get back to your notes for a quick review soon enough, you can move that information from short-term to long-term memory. And you can do it in just a few minutes—often, ten minutes or less.

The sooner you review your notes the better, especially if the class was difficult. In fact, you can start reviewing *during* class. When your instructor pauses to set up the overhead projector or erase the board, scan your notes. Dot the i's, cross the t's, and write out unclear abbreviations. Another way to use this technique is to get to your next class as quickly as you can. Then use the four or five minutes before the lecture to review the notes you just took in the previous class.

If you do not get to your notes immediately after class, you can still benefit by reviewing later in the day. A review right before you go to sleep can also be valuable.

Think of the day's unreviewed notes as leaky faucets, constantly dripping, losing precious information until you shut them off with a quick review. Remember, it's possible to forget up to 80 percent of the material within 24 hours--unless you review..

2. Edit notes. During your first review, fix words that are illegible. Write out abbreviated words that might be unclear to

The note-taking process flows

you later. Make sure you can read everything. If you can't read something or don't understand something you can read, mark it and make a note to ask your instructor or another student. Check to see that your notes are labeled with the date and class and that the pages are numbered. You can edit with a different colored pen or pencil if you want to distinguish between what you wrote in class and what you filled in later.

3. Fill in key words in left-hand column. This task is important if you are to get the full benefit of using the Cornell format explained on page 128. Using the key word principles described earlier in this chapter, go through your notes and write key words or phrases in the left-hand column.

These key words will speed the review process later. As you read your notes and focus on extracting key concepts, your understanding of the lecture is further reinforced.

4. Organize your notes with graphic signals. While taking notes in class, you may have included graphic signals. During your immediate review, you can change them or add more. Use arrows, brackets, and other signals that aid the organization of your notes. Circle related concepts. Fill out diagrams. Illustrate important points.

5. Conduct short weekly review periods. Once a week, review all your notes again. The review sessions don't need to take a lot of time. Even a 20-minute weekly review period is valuable. Some students find that a weekend review, say on Sunday afternoon, helps them stay in continuous touch with the material. Scheduling regular review sessions in your calendar helps develop the habit.

As you review, step back for the larger picture. In addition to reciting or repeating the material to yourself, ask questions about it: Does this relate to my goals? How does this relate to information I already know, in this field or another? Will I be tested on this material? What will I do with this material? How can I relate it to something that deeply interests me? Am I unclear on any points? If so, what exactly is the question I want to ask?

6. Use your key words as cues to recite. With a blank sheet of paper, cover your notes, leaving only the key words in the left-hand margin showing. Take each key word in order and recite as much as you can about the point. Then, uncover your notes and look for important points you missed.

7. Create mind map summaries. Mind mapping is an excellent way to make summary sheets.

Start with the main subject to be reviewed. Write the topic in the center of a page; then, on lines branching out from the starting point, write everything you can think of concerning that subject. Use key words. Write each word on a line and write related words on lines branching out from the original. Continue this process until you can't think of anything else to write.

When you are sure you have exhausted your ability to recall, look at your original notes and fill in anything you missed. This system is fun to use. It's quick, and it gives your brain a hook on which to fasten the material.

8. Consider typing up your notes. Some students type clean copies of their handwritten notes, either on a typewriter or computer. The argument for doing it is twofold. First, typed notes are easier to read and take up less space. In addition, the process of typing them forces you to review the material.

Yet another alternative is to bypass handwriting altogether and take notes on a small laptop computer. Some newspaper reporters do this. The drawbacks: Laptops are expensive. You can't draw diagrams. You must be an efficient typist. Computer errors can wipe out your notes.

In any case, you can experiment with typing notes and see what works for you. For example, you might type up portions of notes or summaries or outlines. Some computer software can "collapse" and "expand" outlines so that you see all the subheadings or just the major headings. That can help you get an overview of an entire subject.

9. Conduct pre-class reviews. Reviewing your notes and assignments can help you set the stage for clear observation. Link information from each lecture to the preceding lecture.

Journal Entry #37
Discovery Statement

For this journal entry, you will need a few pages of your old notes—the older, the better. If possible, use notes from last year. If you have some notes you took several years ago, they will work perfectly.

Look over those notes as if you were to be tested on them tomorrow. Then, in the space provided here, write down a one-paragraph summary of what those notes tell you today.

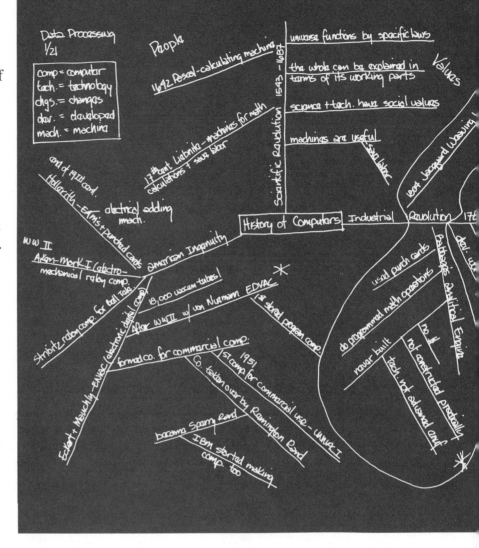

Next, put on your critic's hat and evaluate your notes. And remember, critics look for the positive as well as the negative. Write down what works in your notes and what doesn't. Be specific about strengths and weaknesses of your old note-taking techniques.

Improving your handwriting

Many people are resigned to writing illegibly for the rest of their lives. They feel they have no control over penmanship.

Yet everyone's handwriting does change. Your signature, when you're on top of the world, is not the same as when you are down in the dumps. Handwriting also changes as we mature.

If handwriting changes unconsciously, you can change it consciously. The prerequisite for improving your handwriting is simply a desire to do so.

Many people live productive, fulfilling, happy lives and never write legibly. And as long as they don't care about how they write, their writing might never change. For these people, none of the following techniques will work. If you want to write more legibly, however, here are some possibilities.

1. Use the First Step technique. Take a First Step by telling the truth about the problem. Admit it and acknowledge your desire to improve.

The problem, by the way, is not bad handwriting; it's the impact of the writing. The problem is, "I can't read my notes and therefore I have difficulty studying," or, "The people I work with are always getting upset because they can't read what I write."

2. Intend to improve. Use the power of your intentions. Write an Intention Statement about your handwriting. Be specific about the results you intend to achieve.

3. Use creative visualizations. Find a quiet spot to sit, relax your whole body, close your eyes, and see yourself writing clearly. Feel the pen as it moves over the page and picture neat, legible letters as you write them. Practice visualizations for a few minutes every day. Results will come.

4. Keep your eye on the ballpoint. Watch the way you write. Don't "try" to change. Focus all your attention on the tip of the pen, right where it meets the paper. When you do this, let go of judgments or evaluations about how you write. By focusing your attention on the tip of your pen, you are giving your brain something to do, thereby letting your body do the writing.

5. Demonstrate your excellence. At least once a day, write something as clearly as you can. Write it as if it were going to appear on the front page of the *New York Times*. You will program your body to write clearly.

6. Revise sloppy writing immediately. Use an erasable pen or pencil. When you write something sloppy, fix it immediately. At first, you might find yourself rewriting almost everything. Using this technique helps you naturally learn to write it legibly the first time.

7. Practice with the best materials. When you put a quality pen to fancy paper, there is incentive to produce clean, crisp, pleasing lines. Practice with these fine materials by writing letters to people you care about.

8. Take a calligraphy course. Improve your eye-hand coordination with calligraphy. Of course, you can't take notes in Gothic script, but the practice you get working with a calligraphy pen may improve your overall writing.

9. Dot all i's and cross all t's. The time you spend dotting and crossing will eliminate time spent scratching your head.

10. Insure that holes exist. Leave holes in your a's, e's, and o's. If you don't, they can easily be mistaken for i's.

11. Notice problem letters. Go through your notes and circle letters you have difficulty deciphering. Practice writing these letters. Simply knowing that your n's look like r's can improve your note-taking ability.

12. When understanding is critical, print. When an important idea must be letter-perfect, print it. Doing so prevents misunderstanding. Printing will stand out from your other notes. And you can read printing faster when you review.

13. Appreciate the value of legible writing. Notice how you feel when your own handwriting works well for you. Give yourself a pat on the back. Write a Discovery Statement when you become aware that you have improved your handwriting, and list the benefits of the improvement.

WHEN INSTRUCTORS TALK FAST

1. Take more time to prepare for class. Familiarity with a subject increases your ability to pick out key points. If an instructor lectures quickly or is difficult to understand, then conduct a thorough preview of material to be covered. Set the stage for the lecture.

2. Be willing to make choices. When an instructor talks fast, focus your attention on key points. Instead of trying to write everything down, choose what you think is important. Sometimes students paralyze themselves with fear that they are missing something important. Occasionally you will make a wrong choice and neglect an important point. Worse things could happen. Stay with the lecture, write down key words, and revise your notes immediately after class.

3. Exchange photocopies of notes with classmates. Your fellow students might write down something you missed. At the same time, your notes might help them. If this is true, then exchange notes regularly.

4. Leave large empty spaces in your notes. Leave plenty of room for filling in information you missed. Use a symbol that signals you've missed something so you can remember to come back to it.

5. See the instructor after class. Take your class notes with you and show the instructor what you missed. You can also ask questions you didn't get to ask in class.

6. Use a tape recorder. Taping a lecture gives you a chance to hear it again, whenever you choose. You may not need to listen to the whole tape again; chances are that only certain parts of the lecture are unclear to you. Some tape recorders will allow you to vary the speed of the tape. With this feature, you can perform magic and actually slow down the instructor's speech

7. Before class, take notes on your reading. This suggestion works well when the instructor's lecture closely follows the format of the text. You can take detailed notes on the text before class. Take these notes with you to class and simply add your lecture notes to them.

You can use at least two different formats for these notes. One is to just leave more space than usual in your notes on the text. Then add class notes in these blank places. Another format is to divide your page in half. Write text notes on one side of the paper and lecture notes on the other.

8. Go to the lecture again. Many classes are taught in multiple sections. That gives you the chance to hear a lecture at least twice—once at your regular class time and again in another section of the class.

9. Learn shorthand. Some note-taking systems, known as shorthand, are specifically designed for getting ideas down

E=mc2, numeric filing ... soid, Henry VII, database ... emi-quavers, GAAP, capital st ... Wars, ge ... arnings, tricuspid, transitive ver ...

When you become sleepy in class, the problem might be lack of oxygen. You can run through the following process in 30 seconds.

1. Straighten your spine. Put both feet on the floor, uncross your arms and legs, sit up straight, and hold your head up straight.

2. Take a deep breath and while you're holding it, tense the muscles in your body. Start with the muscles in your feet, then the legs, thighs, stomach, chest, shoulders, neck, jaw, forehead, arms, and hands. Hold these muscles tense for the count of five and then relax and exhale.

3. Breathe deeply three times. Inhale slowly and deeply, breathing into your belly as well as your chest. Pause momentarily at the top of the breath and then exhale completely. When you have exhaled as much as you can, force out more air by contracting the muscles of your stomach. Do this breathing three times.

4. Repeat step #2. You've now activated all of your muscles and filled your body with oxygen. You are ready to return your attention to the task at hand.

Practice this exercise now by completing it twice. Then make a mental note so that next time you're sleepy in class, or when you're studying, you can use this exercise. With a little practice, you can make it subtle. Your instructor and classmates won't even notice you're doing it.

fast. Books and courses are available to help you learn these systems. You can also devise your own shorthand. Invent one- or two-letter symbols for common words and phrases.

10. Ask questions—even if you're totally lost. Most instructors allow time for questions. This is a time to ask about the points you missed.

There may be times when you feel so lost that you can't formulate a question. That's OK. One option is to just report this fact to the instructor. The instructor can often guide you to a clear question. Chances are that other people in the room will breathe a sigh of relief: "Whew! I'm not the only person in the room who is confused."

Another option is to just ask *any* question. Often this will lead you to the question you really wanted to ask.

Before stating what you don't understand, state what you *do* understand. This gives positive feedback to the teacher and provides a context for your question.

11. Ask the instructor to slow down. This is the most obvious suggestion. If asking her to slow down doesn't work, ask her to repeat what you missed.

TAKING NOTES ON READING

Taking notes on reading requires the same skills that apply to class notes: observation, recording, and review. Almost all techniques in this chapter can be applied to notes on reading. Reading also requires some special considerations.

There are two kinds of notes on reading: review notes and research notes.

Review notes

Review notes will look like the notes you take in class. Sometimes you will want more extensive notes than you can write in a margin of your text. You can't underline or make marginal notes in library books, so make separate notes when you use these sources.

Mind map summaries of textbook material are particularly useful for review. You can also outline the material in the text or take notes in paragraph form. Single out a particularly difficult section of a text and make separate notes. Or make mind map summaries of overlapping lecture and text material.

Use the left-hand column for key words and questions, just as you do in your class notes.

Research notes

Research notes—those you make for papers and speeches—follow a different format. Creating papers and speeches is a special challenge, and the way you take notes can help you face those challenges.

Use the mighty 3x5 card. There are two kinds of research cards: source cards and information cards. Source cards identify where information is found. For example, a source card on a book will show the title, author, publisher, date, and place of publication. Source cards are written for magazine articles, interviews, tapes, or any other research material.

When you write source cards, give each one a code—either the initials of the author, a number, or a combination of numbers and letters.

The beauty of using source cards is that you are creating your bibliography as you do the research. When you are done, simply alphabetize the cards by author and voila!—instant bibliography.

Write the actual notes on information cards. At the top of each information card, write the code for the source from which you got the information. Also include the page number your notes are based on.

The most important point to remember about information cards: Write only one piece of information on each card. You can use your information cards to construct an outline of the paper by sorting the cards.

Placing more than one fact on each card creates a barrier to organizing your outline.

Thinking about notes

Whether you are making review notes or research notes, use your own words as much as possible. When you do so, you are thinking about what you are reading. If you do quote your source word for word, put that material in quotation marks.

Many students like to close the book after reading an assignment and quickly write down their first impressions of the material. This writing can be loose, without following any structure or format.

The important thing is to do it right away, while the material is fresh in your mind. You might choose to summarize what you've just read, list the questions you have about it, relate the ideas to events in your life, or all of these. Just write freely, without stopping—much as you would write in a personal journal. Even if you forget to review this writing, it can help you remember what you've read.

Special cases

The style of your notes can vary according to the material.

If you are assigned a short story or poem, read the entire work once without taking any notes. On your first reading, enjoy the piece. When you finish, write down your immediate impressions. Then go over the piece and make brief notes on characters, images, symbols, settings, plot, point of view, or other aspects of the work.

Normally, you would ask yourself questions before you read an assignment. When you read fiction or poetry, however, ask yourself questions after you have read the piece. Then reread (or skim if it's long) to get answers. Your notes can reflect this question-and-answer process.

When you read scientific or other technical material, copy important formulas. Write down data that might appear on an exam. Recreate important diagrams and draw your own visual representations of concepts.

I create it all

THIS IS A POWERFUL TOOL in times of trouble. When things go wrong, Power Process #5 can lead the way to solutions. "I create it all" means treating all the experiences, events, and circumstances in your life as if you create them.

For example, when your dog tracks fresh tar on the white shag carpet, when your political science teacher is a crushing bore, when your spouse dents the car, when your test on Latin American literature focuses on an author you've never read— that's when it's time for Power Process #5. Tell yourself: "I created it all."

"Baloney!" you shout. "I didn't let the dog in, that guy *really is* a bore, I wasn't even in the car, and nobody told me to read Gabriel Garcia Marquez. I didn't create these disasters."

Good points.

Obviously, "I create it all" is one of the most unusual and bizarre suggestions in this book. It certainly is not an idea to be believed. In fact, believing it can get you in trouble. "I create it all" is strictly a practical idea. When it works, use it. When it doesn't, don't. Whenever you operate Power Process #5, keep Power Process #1: "Ideas are tools" by your side.

Keeping that caution in mind, consider how powerful Power Process #5 can be. This is really about the difference between two distinct positions in life: being a victim or being self-responsible (self-generating— a victor).

A victim of circumstances is controlled by outside forces. We've all felt like victims, at one time or another. When tar-footed dogs tromped on the white shag carpets of our lives, we felt helpless.

In contrast, we can take responsibility. "Responsibility" is the important word. It does *not* mean "blame." Far from it. Responsibility is "response-ability." It is *the ability to choose a response*, rather than reacting automatically.

How this process works

Many students approach grades from the position of being victims. The student who sees the world this way gets an F and reacts something like this:

"Oh, no!" (Slaps forehead.)

"Rats!" (Slaps forehead again.)

(Students who get lots of F's often have flat foreheads.)

"Another F! That teacher couldn't teach her way out of a wet paper bag. She can't teach English for nothing. And that textbook—what a bore! How could I read that with a houseful of kids making noise all the time? And then the gang came over and wanted to party and . . ."

The problem with this viewpoint is that while the student is justifying herself, she's robbing herself of the power to get anything but an F. She's giving all her power to a "boring teacher," a "bad textbook," "noisy children," and "the gang."

There is another way, called "choosing your response." You can say that you choose your grades by choosing your actions. Then you are the source, rather than the result, of the grades you get. The student who got an F could react like this:

"Oh, no!" (Slaps forehead.)

"Rats!" (Slaps forehead again.)

(Let's face it. We've all done a little forehead flattening in our time.)

"Another F. Oh, shoot, well, hmmm . . . . How did I choose to get this F? What did I do to create it?"

Now, that's power. By asking, "How did I choose it?" you give yourself a measure of control. You are no longer the victim.

This student might continue by saying, "Well, let's see. I didn't review my notes after class. That might have done it." Or, "I studied in the same room with my children while they watched TV. Then I went out with my friends right before the test. Well, that probably helped me fulfill some of the requirements for getting an F."

The point is this: When the F is the result of your kids, your roommate, the book, or the teacher, then you probably can't do anything about it. However, if you chose the F, you can choose differently next time. You are in charge.

Choosing our thoughts

There are times when you don't create it all. You do not "create" earthquakes, floods, avalanches, or monsoons. If we look closely, we discover that we do create a larger part of our circumstances than most of us are willing to admit.

For example, we can choose our thoughts. And thoughts can control our perceptions by screening information from our senses.

We know something exists only because of our ability to see it, smell it, feel it, taste it, or hear it. You experience the chair you are sitting in only because you can feel it under you, touch it with your hands, hear it scrape against the floor, or see it. Yet until this moment, you might not have been aware of your chair at all.

We are never conscious of everything in our environment. If we were, we'd go crazy from sensory overload. Instead, our brains filter out most sensory inputs, and this filtering colors the way we think about the world.

Imagine for a moment that the universe is whole and complete. It is filled with everything you would ever want, including happiness, love, and material wealth. When you adopt this position, your brain will look for sensory input that supports this idea.

Now take the opposite view. Imagine that happiness, love, and wealth are scarce. Now your brain has a different mission. You will tend to see the stories about poverty, hate, suicide, drug addiction, or unemployment. You could easily miss the stories of people who recovered from addiction, rose out of poverty, or resolved conflict.

Many people have no experience of abundance or happiness. Maybe it is because their thoughts limit what they see. By choosing new thoughts, we can see the same circumstances in new ways.

Choosing our behaviors

Moment by moment we make choices about what we will do and where we will go. The result of these choices is where we are in life.

All those choices help create our current circumstances—even those circumstances that are not "our fault." After a car accident we tell ourselves: "It just happened. That car came out of nowhere and hit me." We forget that driving five miles per hour slower and paying closer attention might have allowed us to miss the driver who was "to blame."

Some cautions

The presence of blame is a warning that "I create it all" is being misused. Power Process #5 is not about blaming yourself or others.

And it is not to be applied to other people. For example, if someone confronts you about an aspect of your behavior that she finds annoying, this is not the time to reply, "Get off my back. *You* create it all." Rather, this is the time to examine how you created her creating you irritating. Remember, the power in this idea is seeing how *you* create it, not how she did.

Similarly, "guilt" is another warning signal. Power Process #5 is not about guilt.

Nor is Power Process #5 a religion. Acting as if you "create it all" does not mean denying God. It is simply a way to expand the choices you already have.

Power Process #5 is easy to deny. Tell your friends about it, and they're likely to say, "What about world hunger? I didn't cause that. What if I'm locked up in prison? I wouldn't have the power to create anything. What about people that get cancer? Did they create that?"

These are good arguments, and they miss the point. Some people approach world hunger, imprisonment, and even cancer with the attitude: "Pretend for a moment that

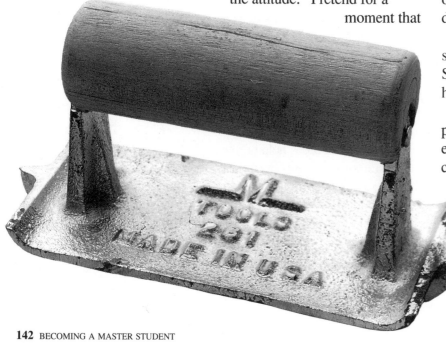

I am responsible for this. What will I do about it?" These people see problems in a new way, and they find choices that other people miss.

Power Process #5 is not always about disaster. It also works when life is going great. Often we give credit to others for our good fortune when, in fact, it's time to pat ourselves on the back. By choosing our behavior and thoughts, we can create A's, interesting classes, enjoyable relationships, material wealth, and contributions to a better world.

How people use this process

Throughout history, people have used Power Process #5, even if they didn't call it by the same name.

Viktor Frankl, a famous psychiatrist and a survivor of Nazi concentration camps, created courage and dignity out of horror and humiliation. Reflecting on his experiences at Auschwitz and other camps, he wrote, ". . . everything can be taken from a man but one thing: the last of the human freedoms—to choose one's own attitude in any given set of circumstances, to choose one's own way."

Malcolm X turned prison into a school, and writer William E.B. DuBois created an enduring book—*The Souls of Black Folk*—out of the experience of racial discrimination in America.

Helen Keller shows light and hope in spite of dwelling in darkness and silence. She went on to inspire millions through her writing.

Thousands of people are living productive lives and creating positive experiences out of a circumstance called cancer.

Whenever tar-footed dogs are getting in the way of your education, remember Power Process #5. By choosing to "create it all," you take yourself out of the role of victim and into the role of victor. You instantly open yourself to a world of choices. You give yourself power.

Journal Entry #38
Discovery/Intention Statement

Of the classes in which you are presently enrolled, pick the one you find least interesting. In this space, write all the ways you make the class uninteresting (or less interesting than other classes).

_____

_____

_____

_____

Now write down three ways you can re-create this class as interesting.

_____

_____

_____

_____

Exercise #17
They made me do it

Write down some of the activities you have completed in the last 24 hours, from making the bed to going to class. List these activities in one of the following columns: the activities you chose to do or the activities that other people required you to do. If there was a particular person requiring you to do something, write that person's name after the activity.

Activities I chose	*Activities others chose for me*

Of the activities others chose for you, which ones were truly consistent with your values and purposes? If you discover you did some things that you didn't want to do, consider not doing them in the future. On a separate sheet of paper, write how you feel about the activity and why you don't want to do it. Consider sending this communication to the person who "made" you do the activity.

Rudolfo Anaya,

Chicano novelist, short story writer, playwright, and scriptwriter, uses religion, dreams, and Spanish-American legends and folklore in his critically acclaimed trilogy of novels about growing up in New Mexico.

From Chicano Authors: Inquiry by Interview *by Juan D. Bruce-Novoa. Copyright 1980. Reprinted by permission of University of Texas Press.*

I read a great deal when I was a child, in grade school. I not only ran in a gang and did everything that normal, red-blooded Chicano boys do as they grow up, but I also used to spend a lot of time reading. I was the only one in the gang that used to go to the library on Saturday mornings. It was a decrepit, old building, run by one of the teachers, who volunteered to open it on Saturdays. Many Saturday mornings she and I were the only ones at the library. I sat there and read and leafed through books, and took some home. I read a lot of comic books and saw a lot of movies. I think all of that was important, in some respect, to the question of what influenced me when I was young. I also heard stories. Any time that people gathered, family or friends, they told stories, *cuentos* (tales), *anecdotes*, *dichos* (sayings), *adivinanzas* (riddles). So I was always in a milieu of words, whether they were printed or in the oral tradition.

Later, I read a great deal in American literature when I was at the university, and it was as formative a period for me as my childhood, because both were very full and alive with the mystery of discovery in literature. Through formal education, I was exposed to many writers, not only to American literature and contemporary writers, but world literature. I think it's very important for Chicano students, whether or not they're going to be writers, to engage in some kind of educational process. There are those who say that education will change who you are, how you think, destroy your culture, assimilate you—I think that's nonsense. Those are people who are afraid of change. We cannot hide our heads in the sand and pretend that everything that is important and good and of value will come only out of our culture. We live in a small world where many other cultures have a great deal to offer us. This is very important for the writer—to read as much as he possibly can, to learn a bit of the analytical study of literature. That's important.

Both my father and my mother spoke Spanish, and I was raised speaking Spanish in an almost completely Spanish background. I did not learn English until I started first grade. Now I speak more fluently in English. The thrust of my education has been in English literature and I wrote in English when I began to write, so I am more fluent and more comfortable with English.

There are some of us who have had, at one time, a great disadvantage. We came from poor families, poor in the sense that we had no money, but we were rich with love and culture and a sense of sharing and imagination. We had to face a school system that very often told us we couldn't write. It did not teach us our own works, and we had nothing to emulate, to read of our own. So of course we were very disadvantaged in that way. For example, when I began to write I had a hard time to find those models that would click, that had a relevance to my internal being. But I kept at it, I kept at it. You can call it what you want; it's something you know you have to do, and eventually you find the rhythm and you keep practicing the skills and the elements. I don't think they become any easier, to tell you the truth. After ten or fifteen years now, I'm still in the process of learning about writing; a process that never finishes. That's exciting!

Even today Chicano children are being told they are at a disadvantage because they don't have command of the English language. The sooner you begin to tell children that, the more they begin to believe it; you build in a self-fulfilling prophecy. That is not right! We have, as I have stated before, a rich culture, rich tradition, a rich oral tradition, and we have, through part of our roots, a rich literary tradition. So we have to change that around *y en vez de decir que no tenemos el talento* [and instead of saying that we don't have the talent], say, "You can write! You do have talent! You can produce literature that is valuable!" We have to go out and tell the kids in high school and grade school, *cuando estan chiquitos* (when they are little), "You can write, you can write about what you know, your experience is valuable, who you are is valuable, and how you view the world and society and the cosmos is valuable. Put it down on paper, paint a picture, make a drawing, write music!"

1. What are the three essential steps of effective note taking?

2. Techniques you can use to "set the stage" for note-taking do *not* include:

    (A) Completing outside assignments.
    (B) Bringing the right materials.
    (C) Setting aside questions in order to concentrate.
    (D) Conducting a short pre-class review.
    (E) Sitting front and center.

3. What is the advantage of sitting front and center in a classroom?

4. You can observe when instructors behave in ways that indicate the material they are presenting is important. Describe at least three ways to watch for these clues.

5. An effective way to postpone debate during a lecture is to passively record the instructor's words. True or false. Explain your answer.

6. When using the Cornell Method of note taking:

(A) Write the main point on a line or in a box, circle, or any other shape.
(B) Use a Roman numeral outline or a more free-form, indented outline to organize the information.
(C) Copy each new concept on a separate 3X5 card.
(D) Know that it doesn't work when used along with a mind map format.
(E) Draw a vertical line 1 1/2 inches from the left edge of the paper.

7. Explain how key words can be used. Then select and write down at least five key words from this chapter.

8. Reviewing within 24 hours assists short-term memory only. Long-term memory requires reviews over a longer period of time. True or false. Explain your answer.

9. Compare and contrast source cards and information cards. (How are they alike and how are they different?)

10. Briefly discuss one of the cautions given regarding the use of Power Process # 5: "I create it all."

Journal Entry #39
Discovery Statement

Quickly review this chapter and then describe what you discovered about your note-taking skills:

    I discovered that I . . .

Journal Entry #40
Intention Statement

Did you get what you wanted from this chapter? List one thing you wanted to learn and didn't. Then describe how you intend to learn it.

    I intend to . . .

Journal Entry #41
Write an Intention Statement declaring how you will use two techniques from this chapter.

    I intend to . . .

Exercise #18
Apply a process

"Love your problems" was the Power Process presented in Chapter Three: Memory. Below, write how you can apply the idea of loving your problem to the task of note-taking.

Chapter 6

Tests

When we begin to take our failures non-seriously, it means we are ceasing to be afraid of them. It is of immense importance to learn to laugh at ourselves.
KATHERINE MANSFIELD

Learn from the mistakes of others—you can never live long enough to make them all yourself.
JOHN LUTHER

Journal Entry #42
Discovery Statement

What I want to get from this chapter is ...

In this chapter . . .

See how to make study sessions (rehearsals) more effective. Energy is focused. A skilled director knows exactly what is to be accomplished every minute. You can teach yourself to be your director, working toward a successful exam (opening night).

Prepare for a test the way a performer prepares for a concert. Tests are performances—opportunities to demonstrate your mastery. What it takes is learning the skills in: *Disarm tests*, *What to do before the test*, *What to do during the test*, *Develop a master review schedule*, *Rehearse for success*, and *How to predict test questions*.

Special techniques for math and science tests suggests how to solve the mysteries that sometimes arise in these subjects.

Release yourself from negative emotions during tests with *Power Process #6: Detach, Have some fun during exam week*, and *Let go of test anxiety*.

You don't have to go it alone. Use the support of others to help you prepare for tests, as explained in *Study with people*.

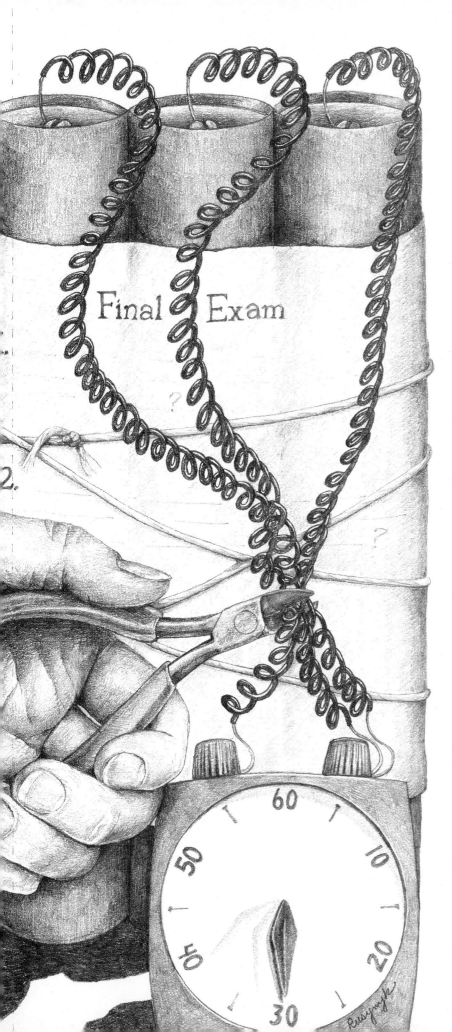

Disarm tests

O N THE SURFACE, tests don't look dangerous, but we treat them like they're land mines.

Suppose a man walks up to you on the street and asks, "Does a finite abelian P-group have a basis?" Will you break out in a cold sweat? Will your muscles tense up? Will your breathing become shallow?

Probably not. Even if you have never heard of a finite abelian P-group, you are likely to remain coolly detached. However, if you find that same question on a test, and if you have never heard of a finite abelian P-group, then your hands might get clammy.

Grades (A to F) are what we use to give power to tests. And there are lots of misconceptions about what grades are.

Grades are not a measure of intelligence. Grades don't measure creativity. They are not an indication of your ability to contribute to society. Grades are simply a measure of how well you do on tests.

Some people think that a test score measures what a student accomplished in a course. This is false. A test score is a measure of what a student scored on a test. If you are anxious about a test and blank out, then the grade cannot measure what you learned. The reverse is also true: If you are good at taking tests and a lucky guesser, the score won't be an accurate reflection of what you've learned.

Grades are not a measure of self-worth. Yet we tend to give test scores the power to determine how we feel about ourselves. Common thoughts are, "If I fail the test, I'm a failure," or, "If I do badly on a test, I'm a bad person." The truth is that if you do badly on a test you are a person who did badly on a test. That's all.

Carrying around misconceptions about tests and grades can put undue pressure on your performance. It's like balancing on a railroad track. Many people can walk along the rail and stay balanced for several seconds. Yet the task seems entirely different if the rail is placed between two buildings, ten stories up.

It is easier to do well on exams if you don't exaggerate the pressure on yourself. Don't give the test some magical power over your worth as a human being. Academic tests are usually not a matter of life or death. Even scoring low on important tests—entrance tests for college or medical school, law boards, CPA exams—usually only means a delay.

Whether a risk is real or imaginary, it can reach the point where it is paralyzing. The way to deal with tests is to keep the risk in perspective. Keep the railroad track on the ground.

What to do before the test

MANAGE REVIEW TIME

A key to successful test preparation is managing review time.

The biggest benefit of early review is that facts have time to roam around in your head. A lot of learning takes place when you are not "studying." Your brain has time to create relationships that can show up when you need them—like during a test. Use short daily review sessions to prepare the way for major review sessions. Reviewing with a group often generates new insights and questions. Also, be specific about your intention to review from the beginning of the term.

Daily reviews

Daily reviews include the short pre- and post-class reviews of lecture notes. You can also conduct brief daily reviews when you read. Before you begin a new reading assignment, scan your notes and the sections you underlined in the previous assignment. Use the time you spend waiting for the bus or doing the laundry to conduct short reviews.

Concentrate daily reviews on two kinds of material: material you have just learned, either in class or in your reading, and material that involves simple memorization (equations, formulas, dates, definitions).

Conduct short daily reviews several times throughout the day. To make sure you do, include them on your daily to-do list. Write down, "5 min. review of biology," or "10 min. review of economics," and give yourself the satisfaction of crossing them off. Regular daily reviews often pay off during exam week.

Begin to review the first day of class. The first day, in fact, is important for review. Most instructors outline the whole course at that time.

You can start reviewing within seconds after learning. During a lull in class, go over the notes you just took. And immediately after class, review your notes again.

Weekly reviews

Weekly reviews are longer—about an hour per subject. These review periods are also more structured than short daily reviews. When a subject is complex, the brain requires time to dig into the material. Avoid skipping from subject to subject too quickly. Review each subject at least once a week.

These weekly sessions include reviews of assigned reading and lecture notes. Look over any mind map summaries or flashcards you have created. You can also practice answering questions.

Major reviews

Major reviews are usually conducted the week before finals or other major exams. They integrate concepts and deepen understanding of the material presented throughout the term. These are longer review periods, two to five hours at a stretch, punctuated by sufficient breaks. Remember that the effectiveness of your review begins to drop after an hour or so unless you give yourself a short rest.

After a certain point, short breaks every hour might not be enough to refresh you. That's when it's time to quit. Each of us has our own limit. In a marathon 10-hour review session, a student might accomplish only a half hour's worth of review in the last two or three hours. In other words, he might as well be at the movies. Learn what your limits are by being conscious of the quality of your concentration. During long sessions, study the most difficult subjects when you are the most alert: at the beginning of the session.

Your commitment to review is your most powerful ally. Create a system of rewards for time spent reviewing. Clarify your intentions about reviewing. Use the Intention Statements in this chapter or invent your own to draw detailed plans for review time.

Reviewing is easy to postpone. For ideas on dealing with procrastination, see "The seven-day anti-procrastination plan" on page 63 and "Motivation—Or 'I'm just not in the mood'" on page 18.

CREATE REVIEW TOOLS

Study checklists, mind map summaries, and flashcards take the guesswork and much of the worry out of studying. When you use these tools, you divide a big job into smaller parts. Your

confidence could increase and you will probably sleep better at night.

Study checklists

Study checklists are used the way a pilot uses a pre-flight checklist. Pilots go through a standard routine before they take off. They physically mark off each item: test flaps, check magnetos, check fuel tanks, adjust instruments, check rudder. They use a written list to be absolutely certain they don't miss anything. Once they are in the air, it's too late, and the consequences of failing to check the fuel tanks could be drastic.

Taking an exam is like flying a plane. Once the test begins, it's too late to memorize that one equation you forgot. And the consequences could be unpleasant.

Make a list for each subject. List reading assignments by chapters or page numbers. List dates of lecture notes. Write down various types of problems you will need to solve. Write down other skills you must master. Include major ideas, definitions, theories, formulas, and equations. For math and science tests, choose some problems and do them over again as a way to review for the test.

A study checklist is not a review sheet; it is a kind of to-do list. Checklists contain the briefest possible description of each item to study.

Keep a study checklist beginning the very first day of class. Add to it as the term progresses. Then, when you conduct your final review sessions, check items off the list as you review them.

A study checklist for a history course might look like the example on the left.

Study Checklist—Amer. History

Materials:
   Text pages: 190-323
   Lecture notes: 9/14-10/29
   The Federalist: 1, 3, 14, 18, 26, 41
   C.A. Beard, Ec. Interpr. Const.
     pgs. 56-81, 114-117
   Rossiter: pgs. 314-336
   Hill: pgs. 175-183, 214-226

Subjects:
   Hamilton + bank
   Frontier crisis
   Jay's treaty + foreign policy
   Election 1796
   Alien & Sedition Acts
   Pinckney's Treaty
   John Adams' presidency:

Mind map summary sheets

Traditional, Roman numeral/capital letter outlines contain main topics which are followed by minor topics which, in turn, are subdivided further. They organize a subject in a sequential, linear way.

This kind of organization, however, doesn't reflect some other aspects of brain function.

This point has been made in the discussions about "left brain" and "right brain" activities. Some people use "right brain" when referring to creative, pattern-making, visual, intuitive brain activity. They speak of the "left brain" when talking about the orderly, logical, step-by-step characteristics of thought.

A mind map uses both kinds of brain functions. Mind maps can contain lists and sequences and show causes. They also provide a picture of a subject. Mind maps are visual patterns that can provide a framework for recall. They work on both verbal and nonverbal levels.

Further, mind mapping helps you think from general to specific. By choosing a main topic, you focus first on the big picture, then zero in on subordinate ideas.

By using key words, you can condense a large subject into a small area on a mind map. You review more quickly by looking at the key words on a mind map than by reading notes word for word.

Making a mind map is simple. Write the main subject in the center of a sheet of paper. Write related subjects on lines branching out from the main subject. Indicate relationships between elements of a subject by drawing arrows between them, enclosing related ideas in circles, boxes, or other shapes, or by color coding them. Use symbols, graphic signals, and pictures for emphasis.

There are several ways to make a mind map as you study for tests. You can start by creating a map totally from memory. When you use this technique, you might be surprised by how much you already know. Mind maps release floods of information from the brain because the mind works by association. Each idea is linked to many other ideas. When you think of one, other associations come to mind. An advantage of mind mapping is that you don't have to stifle any of these associations just because they don't come next in a sequential outline.

Everything fits in a mind map. Let the associations flow, and if one seems to go some place else, simply start another branch on your map. After you have gone as far as you can using recall alone, go over your notes and text and fill in the rest of the map.

Another way to create a mind map summary is to go through your notes and pick out key words. Then, without looking at your notes, create a mind map of everything you can recall about each key word. Finally, go back to your notes and fill in material you left out. You can also start a mind map with underlined sections from your text.

Make mind maps for small, detailed subjects, as well as for large ones. You can mind map a whole course, or a single lecture, or a single point from a lecture.

As you build a mind map on paper, you are also constructing a map in your mind. When you are finished, the picture of the map enters your memory. You could throw away your paper mind map and still retain most of the benefit of making it.

Flashcards

Three-by-five flashcards are like portable test questions. You can take them with you anywhere and use them anytime. On one side of the card, write the questions. On the other, write the answer. It's that simple.

Use flashcards for formulas, definitions, theories, key words from your notes, axioms, dates, foreign language phrases, hypotheses, and sample problems.

Create flashcards regularly as the term progresses. You can buy an inexpensive card file to keep your flashcards arranged by subject.

Carry a pack of flashcards with you whenever you think you might have a spare minute to review them. Keep a few blank cards with you, too. That way you can make new flashcards whenever you recall new information to study.

PLAN A STRATEGY

Knowing what is going to be on your test does not require using highly sophisticated technology or breaking intricate coded messages. Before a test, some instructors hand out lists of questions to be used as study guides. Even if they don't, the following strategies can help you predict most of the test questions.

Do a dry run

One of the most effective ways to prepare for a test is to practice the tasks you'll actually do on the test. Say that the test will include mainly true/false or short answer questions. Brainstorm a list of such questions—a mock test—and do a dry run. Do the same with other kinds of questions, such as essay questions.

Also, predict the level of questions. Some are likely to call for rote memory, others might require application or analysis.

You might even type up this "test" so it looks like the real thing. You could write out your answers in the room where the test will actually take place. When you walk in for the real test, you'll be in familiar territory.

Ask the instructor what to expect

One great source of information about the test is the person who will create it— your instructor. Ask him what to expect. What topics will be emphasized? What kinds of questions will it contain? How can you best allocate your review time? The

instructor may decline to give you any of this information. Even so, you've lost nothing by asking. More often, though, instructors will answer some or all of your questions about the test. Also ask about the general rules of the exam room, such as the procedure for asking questions, materials allowed in the room, etc.

Get copies of old exams

Copies of previous exams for the class may be available from the instructor, other students, the instructor's department, the library, or the counseling office. Old tests can help you plan a review strategy.

One caution: If you rely on old tests exclusively, you may gloss over material the instructor has added since the last test. Ask your instructor about this. Also check your school's policy on making past tests available to students. Some may not allow it, or allow it only on a limited basis.

What to do during the test

AS YOU BEGIN

Prepare yourself for the test by arriving early. That often leaves time to do a relaxation exercise.

While you're waiting for the test to begin and talking with classmates, avoid the question "How much did you study for this test?" This question doesn't get at any important information. In fact, it may only fuel the anxiety that you didn't study enough.

Pay particular attention to verbal directions given as the test is distributed. Then scan the whole test immediately. Evaluate the importance of each section. Notice how many points each part of the test is worth and estimate how much time you will need for each section; use its point value as your guide. For example, don't budget 20 percent of your time for a section that is worth only 10 percent of the

Disarm tests

points. Jot down a short time plan to keep you on track during the test.

Read the directions *slowly*. Then reread them. Nothing is more agonizing than to discover that you lost points on a test only because you failed to follow the directions. If the directions call for short answers, give short answers. Sometimes you will be asked to answer two out of three questions. Oh, the frustration of finding that out as you finish your third answer! When the directions are confusing, ask about them.

Jot down memory aids, formulas, equations, facts, or other material you know you'll need and might forget. Do this in the margins. If you use a separate sheet of paper, you may appear to be cheating.

Now you are ready to begin.

IN GENERAL

It's time to begin. If necessary, allow yourself a minute or two of "panic" time. This is time to notice any tension you feel and apply one of the techniques explained in "Let go of test anxiety" on page 161.

Answer the easiest, shortest questions first. This gives you the experience of success. It also stimulates associations and prepares you for more difficult questions.

Next answer multiple choice, true/false, and fill-in-the-blank questions.

Then proceed to short-answer and essay questions.

Use memory techniques when you're stuck. If your recall on a certain point is blocked, remember something else that's related. Start from the general and go to the specific. Use a small mind map in the test margin to stimulate your memory.

Pace yourself. Watch the time; if you are stuck, move on. Follow your time plan.

Leave plenty of space between answers. The space makes it easier on the person who grades your test. You can use the extra space, if there's time, to add information.

Look for answers in other test questions. A term, name, date, or other fact that escapes you might appear in the test itself. You can also use other questions to stimulate your memory.

In quick-answer questions (multiple choice, true/false), your first instinct is usually best. Avoid changing your answer unless you are sure the second choice is correct. If you think your first answer is wrong because you misread the questions, do change your answer.

Multiple choice questions

Check the directions to see if the questions call for more than one answer.

Answer each question in your head before you look at the possible answers. If you can come up with the answer before you look at the choices, you eliminate the possibility of being confused by those choices.

Mark questions you can't answer immediately and come back to them if you have time.

Be sure to read all answers to multiple choice questions before selecting one. Sometimes two answers will be similar and only one will be correct.

If you have no clue as to what the answer is, and if incorrect answers are not deducted from your score, use the following guidelines to guess:

1. If two answers are similar, except for one or two words, choose one of these answers.

2. If two answers have similar sounding or looking words (intermediate-intermittent), choose one of these answers.

3. If the answer calls for a sentence completion, eliminate the answers that would not form grammatically correct sentences.

4. If two quantities are almost the same, choose one.

5. If answers cover a wide range (4.5, 66.7, 88.7, 90.1, 5000.11), choose one in the middle.

6. If there is no penalty for guessing and none of the above techniques work, close your eyes and go for it.

Note: None of these suggestions for guessing are meant to take the place of studying for the test.

True/false questions

Answer true/false questions quickly. Often these questions are not worth many points individually. Don't invest a lot of time to get two points on a 100-point exam.

Read carefully. Sometimes one word can make a statement inaccurate. If any part of the true/false statement is false, the statement is false.

Look for qualifiers like *all*, *most*, *sometimes*, *never*, or *rarely*. These are the key words upon which the question depends. Absolute qualifiers such as *always* or *never* generally indicate a false statement.

Machine-graded tests

To do well on these tests, make sure the answer you mark corresponds to the question you are answering. Check the test booklet against the answer sheet whenever you switch sections and again at the top of each column. Watch for stray marks. These can look like answers.

Open-book tests

When studying for the test, write down any formulas you will need on a separate sheet. Tape tabs onto important pages of the book (tables, for instance) so you don't have to waste time flipping through the pages. You could also use paper clips.

If you plan to use your notes, number

them and write a short table of contents.

Prepare thoroughly for open-book exams. They are almost always the most difficult tests.

Short-answer/fill-in-the-blank questions

These questions often ask for definitions or short descriptions. Concentrate on key words and facts. Be brief.

Here's where overlearning the material really pays off. When you know a subject backwards and forwards, you can answer this type of question almost as fast as you can write.

Essay questions

When you set out to answer an essay question, your first task is to find out what the question is asking—*precisely*. If a question asks that you *compare* Gestalt and Reichian therapies, no matter how eloquently you *explain* them, you are on a one-way trip to No Credit City.

Standard essay question words are defined in this chapter on page 156. Knowing them can make all the difference on an essay test.

Before you write, make a quick outline. There are three reasons for doing this. First, you might be able to write faster. Second, you're less likely to leave out important facts. Third, if you don't have time to finish your answer, your outline could win you some points.

When you start to write, get to the point. Forget introductions. Sentences such as, "There are many interesting facets to this difficult question" cause acute pain for teachers grading tests.

One way to get to the point is to include part of the question in your answer. Suppose the question asks, "Discuss how increasing the city police budget may or may not contribute to a decrease in street crime." Your first sentence might read, "An increase in police expenditures will not have a significant effect on street crime

for the following reasons." Your position is clear. You are on your way to the answer.

When you expand your answer with supporting ideas and facts, start out with the most solid points. Don't try for drama by saving the best for last.

Some final points in regard to style:

1. Write legibly. Grading essay questions is in large part a subjective process. Sloppy, difficult-to-read handwriting might actually lower your grade.

2. Be brief. Avoid filler sentences that say nothing. ("The question certainly bears careful deliberation in order to take into account all the many interesting facts pertaining to this important period in the history of our great nation.") Write as if you expect the person grading your test to be tired, bored, and overworked. Even a well-rested instructor doesn't like to wade through a swamp of murky writing in order to spot an occasional lonely insight.

3. Use a pen. Many instructors will require this because pencil is difficult to read.

4. Write on one side of the page only. Writing will show through and obscure writing on the other side. If necessary, use the blank side to add points you missed. Leave a generous left-hand margin with plenty of space between your answers, in case you need to add to them later.

Finally, if you have time, review your answers for grammar and spelling errors, clarity, and legibility.

Words to watch for in essay questions

The following words are commonly found in essay test questions. Understanding them is essential to success on such questions. If you want to do well on essay tests, then study this page thoroughly. Know these words backwards and forwards. To heighten your awareness of them, underline the words when you see them in a test question.

Analyze
Break into separate parts and discuss, examine, or interpret each part.
Compare
Examine two or more things. Identify similarities and differences. Comparisons generally ask for similarities more than differences
Contrast
Show differences. Set in opposition.
Criticize
Make judgments. Evaluate comparative worth. Criticism often involves analysis.

Define
Give the meaning; usually a meaning specific to the course or subject. Determine the precise limits of the term to be defined. Explain the exact meaning. Definitions are usually short.
Describe
Give a detailed account. Make a picture with words. List characteristics, qualities, and parts.
Discuss
Consider and debate or argue the pros and cons of an issue. Write about any conflict. Compare and contrast.

Enumerate
List several ideas, aspects, events, things, qualities, reasons, etc.
Explain
Make an idea clear. Show logically how a concept is developed. Give the reasons for an event.
Evaluate
Give your opinion or cite the opinion of an expert. Include evidence to support the evaluation.
Illustrate
Give concrete examples. Explain clearly by using comparisons or examples.

Interpret
Comment upon, give examples, describe relationships. Explain the meaning. Describe, then evaluate.
Outline
Describe main ideas, characteristics, or events. (Does not necessarily mean "write a Roman numeral/letter outline.")
Prove
Support with facts (especially facts presented in class or in the text).
Relate
Show the connections between ideas or events. Provide a larger context.

State
Explain precisely.
Summarize
Give a brief, condensed account. Include conclusions. Avoid unnecessary details.
Trace
Show the order of events or progress of a subject or event.

If any of these terms are still unclear to you, go to your unabridged dictionary. Thorough knowledge of these words helps you give the teacher what he is requesting.

NOTABLE FAILURES—
PART TWO

People often fail, or at least are told they are failures, many times before they reach their goals. The list started on page 83 continues below.

Einstein's parents thought he was retarded. He spoke haltingly until age 9, and after that he answered questions only after laboring in thought about them. He was advised by a teacher to drop out of high school: "You'll never amount to anything, Einstein."

Charles Darwin's father said to his son, "You will be a disgrace to yourself and all your family." (Darwin did poorly in school.)

Thomas Edison's father called his son a "dunce." His headmaster told Edison he would never make a success of anything.

Henry Ford barely made it through high school.

Sir Isaac Newton did poorly in school and was allowed to continue only because he failed at running the family farm.

Pablo Picasso was pulled out of school at 10 because he was doing so poorly. A tutor hired by Pablo's father gave up on Pablo.

Giacomo Puccini's first music teacher said that Puccini had no talent for music. Later Puccini composed some the world's best-known operas.

The machines of the world's greatest inventor, *Leonardo Da Vinci*, were never built, and many wouldn't have worked anyway.

Clarence Darrow became a legend in the courtroom as he lost case after case.

Edwin Land's attempts at instant movies (Polarvision) absolutely failed. He described his attempts as trying to use an impossible chemistry and a nonexistent technology to make an unmanufacturable product for which there was no discernable demand. This created the optimum working conditions, he felt.

After the success of the show *South Pacific*, composer *Oscar Hammerstein* put an ad in *Variety* that listed a dozen or so of his failures, in case anyone had forgotten them. At the bottom of the ad, he repeated the credo of show business, "I did it before, and I can do it again."

Asked once about how he felt when his team lost a game, *Joe Paterno*, coach of the Penn State University football team, replied that losing was probably good for the team since that was how the players learned what they were doing wrong.

Testifying before a House subcommittee, violinist *Isaac Stern* said, "The most important thing the National Council on the Arts can do is to give the creative mind the right to fail. It is only through failure and through experiment that we learn and grow."

R. Buckminister Fuller built his geodesic domes by starting with a deliberately failed dome and making it "a little stronger and a little stronger. . . a little piece of wood here and a little piece of wood there, and suddenly it stood up."

Jonas Salk, who developed the polio vaccine, spent 98 percent of his time documenting the things that didn't work until he found the thing that did.

Igor Stravinsky said, "I have learned throughout my life as a composer chiefly through my mistakes and pursuits of false assumptions, not by my exposure to the founts of wisdom and knowledge."

Charles Goodyear bungled an experiment and discovered vulcanized rubber.

Before gaining an international reputation as a painter, *Paul Gauguin* was a failed stockbroker.

Alfred Butts invented the game of SCRABBLE® after he lost his job as an architect during the Depression.

The game MONOPOLY® was developed by Charles Darrow, an unemployed heating engineer. Darrow brought his first version of the game to a toy company in 1935. That company originally rejected the game for containing 52 "fundamental errors." Today the game is so successful that its publisher, Parker Brothers, prints more than $40 billion of MONOPOLY® money each year. That's twice the amount of real money printed annually by the U.S. mint.

At one point in his life, *Malcolm X* was imprisoned. He used the time to copy a dictionary word-for-word into his journals and sharpen his writing and reading skills.

Sources for this list of notable failures include *Diet For A New America* by John Robbins, Walpole, NH: Stillpoint Publishing, 1987 and *Information Anxiety* by Richard Saul Wurman, copyright 1989 used by permission of Doubleday a division of Bantam Doubleday, Dell Publishing Group, Inc.

How to predict test questions

Predicting test questions can do more than get you a better grade on a test. It can keep you focused on the purpose of the course and help you design your learning strategy. It can be fun, too.

First, get organized. Have a separate section in your notebook labeled "Test Questions." Add several questions to this section after every lecture and assignment.

You also can create your own code or graphic signal—maybe a "T!" in a circle—to flag possible test questions in your notes.

The format of a test can help you predict questions. Ask your instructor to describe the test—how long it will be and what kind of questions to expect (essay, multiple choice, problems). Do this early in the term so you can be alert for possible test questions from the very beginning.

During lectures you can watch for test questions by observing not only *what* the instructor says but *how* he says it. Instructors give clues. For example:

They might repeat important points several times, write them on the board, or return to them in subsequent classes.

They might use certain gestures when making crucial points. They might pause, look at notes or read passages word-for-word.

Also pay attention to questions the instructor poses to students, and note questions other students ask.

When material from reading assignments also is covered extensively in class, it is likely to be on the test.

Use the essay question words on page 156 as a guide to turn the key words in your notes into questions.

Put yourself in your instructor's head. What kind of question would you ask? Make practice test questions.

Save all quizzes, papers, lab sheets, and graded material of any kind. Quiz questions have a way of appearing, in slightly altered form, on final exams. If copies of previous exams are available, use those to predict questions.

For science courses and other courses involving problem solving, practice working problems using different variables.

You can also brainstorm test questions with other students. This is a great activity for study groups.

Finally, be on the lookout for these words: "This material will be on the test."

Exercise #19

Master review schedule

Schedule review time on this one-month calendar. Mark the appropriate dates of the month in the upper left-hand corner of every square, then schedule weekly review periods for each subject. Write down the name of the subject and block out time to review it. If you already use a monthly or weekly planner, use it to schedule your review time.

Also schedule at least two major review periods. The length of these review periods could range from two to five hours, depending on your needs.

The more difficult it is for you to find time for review, the greater the benefit of this exercise. Use your imagination and skill to create extra time to review.

This exercise will give you an opportunity to step back and look at your overall review habits. For a longer view, photocopy this calendar and make a review plan for two or three monthss.

Monday	Tuesday	Wednesday	Thursday	Friday	Saturday	Sunday

Month ____

Monday	Tuesday	Wednesday	Thursday	Friday	Saturday	Sunday

Month _____

Let go of test anxiety

Exercise #20
Twenty things I like to do

One way to relieve tension is to mentally yell "Stop!" and substitute a pleasant image (daydream) for the stressful thoughts and emotions you are experiencing.

In order to create a supply of pleasant images to recall during times of stress, conduct an eight-minute brainstorm about things you like to do. Your goal is to generate at least 20 ideas. Time yourself and write as fast as you can. Use the space below.

When you have completed your list, study it. Pick out two activities that seem especially pleasant, and elaborate on them by creating a mind map of each one. Write the activity in the center of a piece of paper. Then, using the mind mapping technique, write down all the memories you have about that activity.

You can use these images to calm yourself in stressful situations.

If you freeze during tests and flub questions when you know the answers, you might be suffering from test anxiety.

A little tension before a test is good. That tingly, butterflies-in-the-stomach feeling you get from extra adrenalin can sharpen your awareness and keep you alert. Sometimes, however, tension is persistent and extreme. It causes loss of sleep, appetite, and maybe even hair. That kind of tension is damaging. It is a symptom of test anxiety, and it can prevent you from doing your best on exams.

Other symptoms include nervousness, fear, dread, irritability, and a sense of hopelessness.

Boredom also can be a symptom of test anxiety. Frequent yawning immediately before a test is a common reaction. Yawning looks like boredom, and it is often a sign of tension. It means oxygen is not getting to the brain because the body is tense. A yawn is one way the body increases its supply of oxygen.

You might experience headaches, an inability to concentrate, or a craving for food. For some people, test anxiety makes asthma or high blood pressure worse.

During an exam, symptoms can include confusion, panic, mental blocks, fainting, sweaty palms, or nausea.

Symptoms after a test include:

Mock indifference: "I answered all the multiple choice questions as 'none of the above' because I was bored."

Guilt: "Why didn't I study more?"

Anger: "The teacher never wanted me to pass this stupid course anyway."

Blame: "If only the textbook weren't so dull."

Depression: "After that test, I don't see any point in staying in school."

Test anxiety can be serious. Students have committed suicide over test scores.

It can also be managed.

Test anxiety has two components, mental and physical. The mental component of stress includes all your thoughts and worries about tests. The physical component includes feelings, sensations, and tension.

The following techniques deal with the mental and physical components of stress in any situation, whether it be test anxiety or stage fright.

Dealing with thoughts

1. Yell stop! When you notice that your thoughts are racing, that your mind is cluttered with worries and fears, that your thoughts are spinning out of control, mentally yell "Stop!"

If you're in a situation that allows it, yell it out loud.

This action is likely to momentarily break the cycle of worry. Once you've stopped it for a moment, you can use any one of the following techniques:

2. Daydream. When you fill your mind with pleasant thoughts, there is no room left for anxiety. When you notice yourself worrying about an upcoming test, substitute your thoughts of doom with visions of something you like to do. Daydream about being with a special friend or walking alone in a special place.

3. Visualize success. Most of us live up to our own expectations, good or bad. If you spend a lot of time mentally rehearsing how it will be to fail, you increase your chances for failure.

Once you've stopped the cycle of worry, take time to rehearse what it will be like when you succeed. Be specific. Create detailed pictures, actions, and even sounds as part of your visualization.

4. Focus. Focus your attention on a specific object. Examine details of a painting, study the branches on a tree, observe the face of your watch, right down to the tiny scratches in the glass.

During an exam, take a few seconds to listen to the sound of the lights in the room. Touch the surface of your desk and notice the texture.

Concentrate all your attention on one point. Don't leave room in your mind for anxiety-related thoughts.

This focusing is very similar to meditation techniques. The idea is to calm your mind by occupying it with a particular sensation—sight, sound, or touch.

5. Praise yourself. Talk to yourself in a positive way. Many of us take the first opportunity to say, "Way to go, dummy, you don't even know the answer to the first question on the test." Most of us wouldn't dream of treating a friend that way, yet we do this to ourselves.

An alternative is to give yourself some encouragement. Treat yourself as well as you would treat your best friend. Consider phrases like, "I am very relaxed," "I am doing a great job on this test," "I'm answering these questions very well," "I'm writing very neatly," "I never forget anything, and I have lots of tools that will help me recall."

6. Consider the worst. Rather than trying to stop worrying, consider the very worst thing that could happen. Expand on your fear. Take the fear to the limit of absurdity.

For example, if you're sitting in a test worrying about whether or not you're going to be successful, stop for a moment. Imagine the catastrophic problems that might occur if you fail the test. You might say to yourself: "Well, if I fail this test, I

PEANUTS

might fail the course, lose my financial aid and get kicked out of school. Then I won't be able to get a job, so the bank would repossess my car, and I'd start drinking. Pretty soon I'd be a bum on skid row. I'd be so ashamed I'd have to move to another city, where I wouldn't have any friends and I'd lose my health and . . . ."

Keep going until you see the absurdity of your predictions. After you stop chuckling, you can backtrack to discover a reasonable level of concern.

Your worry about failing the entire class if you fail the test might be justified. At that point ask yourself, "Can I live with that?" Unless you are taking a test in parachute packing and the final question involves demonstrating jumping out of a plane, the answer will almost always be yes. (If the answer is no, use another technique. In fact, use several other techniques.)

The cold facts are hardly ever as bad as our worst fears. Shine a light on your fears and they become more manageable.

Dealing with feelings

1. Breathe. You can calm physical sensations within your body by focusing your attention on your breathing. Concentrate on the air going in and out of your lungs. Experience it as it passes through your nose and mouth.

Do this for two to five minutes. If you notice that you are taking short, shallow breaths, begin to take longer and deeper breaths. Fill your lungs and abdomen, then release all the air. Imagine yourself standing on the tip of your nose. Watch the breath pass in and out as if your nose were a huge ventilation shaft for an underground mine.

2. Scan your body. Simple awareness is an effective technique to reduce the tension in your body.

Sit comfortably and close your eyes. Start at your feet. Focus your attention on the muscles in your feet and notice if they are relaxed. Tell the muscles in your feet that they can relax.

Move up to your ankles and repeat the procedure. Next go to your calves and thighs and buttocks, telling each group of muscles to relax.

Do the same for your lower back, diaphragm, chest, upper back, neck, shoulders, jaw, face, upper arms, lower arms, fingers, and scalp.

3. Tense and relax. If you are aware of a particularly tense part of your body, or if you discover tension when you're scanning your body, you can release this with the tense-relax method.

To do this, find a muscle that is tense and make it even more tense. If your shoulders are tense, pull them back, arch your back, and tense your shoulder muscles even more tightly, then relax. The net result is that you can be aware of the relaxation and allow yourself to relax more.

You can use the same process with your legs, arms, abdomen, chest, face, and neck. Clench your fists, tighten your jaw, straighten your legs, and tense your abdomen all at once. Then relax.

By Schulz

4. Use guided imagery. Relax completely and take a quick fantasy trip. Close your eyes, relax your body, and imagine yourself in a beautiful, peaceful, natural setting. Create as much of the scene as you can. Be specific. Use all your senses.

For example, you might imagine yourself at a beach. Hear the surf rolling in and the sea gulls calling to each other. Feel the sun on your face and the cool sand between your toes. Smell the sea breeze. Feel the mist from the surf on your face. Notice the ships on the horizon and the rolling sand dunes.

Some people find that a mountain scene or a lush meadow scene works well. You can take yourself to a place you've never been or re-create an experience out of your past. Find a place that works for you and practice getting there. When you become proficient you can return to it quickly for trips that may only last a few seconds.

With practice you can even use this technique while you are taking a test.

5. Describe it. Focus your attention on your anxiety. If you are feeling nauseated or if you have a headache, then concentrate on that feeling. Describe it to yourself. Tell yourself how large it is, where it is located in your body, what color it is, what shape it is, what texture it is, how much water it might hold if it had volume, and how heavy it is.

Be with it. Describe it in detail and don't resist it.

If you can completely experience a physical sensation, it will often disappear. People suffering from severe and untreatable pain have used this technique successfully.

6. Exercise aerobically. This is one technique that won't work in the classroom or while you're taking a test. But it is an excellent way to reduce body tension.

Do some kind of exercise that will get your heart beating at twice your normal rate

and keep it beating at that rate for 15 or 20 minutes. Aerobic exercises include rapid walking, jogging, swimming, bicycling, basketball, or anything that elevates your heart rate and keeps it elevated.

7. Get help. When these techniques don't work, when anxiety is serious, get help. If you become withdrawn, have frequent thoughts about death, get depressed and stay depressed for more than a few days, or have prolonged feelings of hopelessness, see a counselor.

Depression and anxiety are common among students. Suicide is the second leading cause of death among young adults between the ages of 15 and 25. This is tragic and unnecessary. Many schools have counselors available. If not, the student health service or another office can refer you to community agencies where inexpensive counseling is available.

Journal Entry #43
Discovery Statement

On a separate sheet of paper, do a timed, four-minute brainstorm of all the reasons, rationalizations, justifications, and excuses you have used to avoid studying. Be creative. Then review your list, pick the three you use most, and write them in the space below.

_____

_____

Journal Entry #44
Intention Statement

Pick one of the reasons for avoiding studying that you listed in Journal Entry #43. Write an Intention Statement about what you will do to begin eliminating that excuse. Make this Intention Statement keepable with a timeline and a reward.

I intend to . . .

_____

_____

Journal Entry #45
Discovery Statement

Explore your feelings about tests. Complete the following sentences.

As exam time gets closer, one thing I notice I do is . . .

When it comes to taking tests, I have trouble . . .

The night before a test I usually feel . . .

The morning of a test I usually feel . . .

During a test I usually feel . . .

After the test I usually feel . . .

When I get my score I usually feel . .

Exercise #21
Rehearse for success

Sit up in a chair, legs and arms uncrossed. Close your eyes, let go of all thoughts, and focus on your breathing for a minute or two.

Then relax various parts of your body, beginning with your feet. Relax your toes, your ankles. Move up to your calves and thighs. Relax your buttocks. Relax the muscles of your lower back, abdomen, and chest. Relax your hands, arms, and shoulders. Relax your neck, jaw, eyelids, and scalp.

When you are completely relaxed, imagine yourself in an exam room. It's the day of the test. Visualize taking the test successfully. The key is detail. See the test being handed out. Notice your surroundings. Hear the other students shuffle in their seats. Feel the desk, the pencil in your hand and the exam in front of you. See yourself looking over the exam calmly and confidently. You discover that you know all the answers.

Stay with this image for a few minutes. Next, imagine yourself writing quickly. Watch yourself turn in the test with confidence. Finally, imagine receiving the test grade. It is an A. Savor the feeling.

As soon as you realize you are feeling anxious about an upcoming test, begin using this technique. The more you do this visualization, the better it can work.

SPECIAL TECHNIQUES FOR MATH AND SCIENCE TESTS

1. Translate problems into English.

Putting problems into words aids your understanding. When you study equations and formulas, put those into words, too. The words help you see a variety of applications for each formula.

For example, the Pythagorean Theorem, $C^2 = A^2 + B^2$, can be translated as "The square of the hypotenuse of a right triangle is equal to the sum of the squares of the other two sides."

2. Perform opposite operations.

If a problem involves multiplication, check your work by dividing; add, then subtract; factor, multiply; square root, square; differentiate, integrate.

3. Use time drills.

Practice working problems fast.

Time yourself. Exchange problems with a friend and time each other. You can also do this in a study group.

4. Analyze before you compute.

Set up the problem before you begin to solve it. When a problem is worth a lot of points, read it twice, slowly. Analyze it carefully. When you take time to analyze a problem you can often see ways to take computational short-cuts.

5. Make a picture.

Draw a picture or a diagram if you are stuck. Sometimes a visual representation will clear a blocked mind.

6. Estimate first.

Estimation is a good way to double-check your work. Doing this first can help you notice if your computations go awry, and then you can correct the error quickly.

7. Check your work systematically.

When you check your work, ask yourself: Did I read the problem correctly? Did I use the correct formula or equation? Is my arithmetic correct? Is my answer in the proper form?

Avoid the temptation to change an answer in the last few minutes—unless you're sure the answer is wrong. In a last minute rush to finish the test, it's easier to choose the wrong answer.

8. Review formulas.

Right before the test, review any formulas you'll need to use. Then write them out on scratch paper as soon as possible during the test.

How to cram
(even though you shouldn't)

*F*IRST, KNOW THE LIMITATIONS OF CRAMMING *and be aware of the costs. Cramming won't work if you haven't cracked a book all semester and skipped all the lectures except the ones you daydreamed through.*

The more courses you have to cram for, the less effective cramming will be.

Cramming is not the same as learning. When you rely on cramming, you cheat yourself of true education. You won't remember what you cram.

This point is especially important to recognize if you cram for mid-term exams. Some students think they are actually learning the material they cram into their heads during mid-term tests. They will be unpleasantly surprised during finals. Without substantial review and practice, material learned in cramming sessions is generally unavailable to recall after one or two days.

Cramming is also more work. It takes longer to learn material when you do it under pressure. You can't save time by cramming.

The purpose of cramming, therefore, is only to make the best of the situation. Cram to get by in a course so that you can do better next time. It might help raise a grade, if you have been reasonably attentive in class, taken fair notes, and have read or skimmed most of the material for the course.

Those are the limitations and costs of cramming. Here is a six-step cramming process:

1. Make choices. Don't try to learn it all when you cram. You can't. Instead, pick out a few of the most important elements of the course and learn those backwards, forwards, and upside down.

Sometimes these choices will be difficult. You might be tempted to go over everything lightly. Resist this temptation. If you cover a lot of material lightly, chances are you will recall none of it during the exam. Be courageous and choose a few important items.

For example, you can devote most of your attention to the topic sentences, tables, and charts in a long reading assignment instead of reading the whole assignment. A useful guideline is to spend 25 percent of cramming time learning new material and 75 percent of cramming time drilling yourself on that material.

2. Make a plan. Cramming is always done when time is short. That is all the more reason to take a few minutes to create a plan. Choose what you want to study (suggestion #1), determine how much time you have, and set deadlines for yourself. It's easy to panic and jump right in. Making a plan can save you time and allow you to work faster.

3. Use mind map review sheets and flashcards. Condense the material you have chosen to learn into mind maps. Choose several elements of the mind maps to put on 3x5 flashcards. Practice recreating the mind maps, complete with illustrations. Drill yourself with the flashcards.

4. Recite ad nauseam. The key to cramming is repetitive recitation. Recitation can burn facts into your brain like no other study method. Go over your material again and again and again. One option is to tape record yourself while you recite. Then play the tape as you fall asleep and as you wake up in the morning.

Repeat out loud what you have chosen to study until you are confident that you will be able to recall it.

5. Relax. Because you do not learn material well when you cram, you are more likely to freeze and forget it under the pressure of an exam. Relaxation techniques can be used to reduce test anxiety, both before and during the test.

6. Don't "should" on yourself. The title of this article uses a word you should avoid: "Should." For example, you could start your cramming session by telling yourself you *should* have studied earlier, you *should* have read the assignments, and you *should* have been more conscientious. By the time you open your book you might feel too guilty and depressed to continue.

Consider this approach. Tell yourself it would have been more *effective* to study earlier and more often. Remind yourself you will have an opportunity to do that next time. Give yourself permission to be the fallible human being you are.

In short, lighten up. Our brains work better when we aren't criticizing ourselves.

And one more thing. Don't say "don't," either.

HAVE SOME
FUN

CONTRARY TO POPULAR BELIEF, FINALS WEEK DOES NOT HAVE TO BE A DRAG.
In fact, if you have used techniques in this chapter, exam week can be fun. By planning ahead, you will have done most of your studying long before finals arrive. You will feel confident and relaxed.

When you are well prepared for tests, you can even use fun as a technique to enhance your performance. The day before a final, go for a run or play a game of basketball. Take in a movie or a concert. Watch television. A relaxed brain is a more effective brain. If you have studied for a test, your mind will continue to prepare itself even while you're at the movies.

Get plenty of rest, too. There's no need to stay up until 3 a.m. cramming if you have used the techniques in this chapter.

On the day of the big test you can wake up refreshed, have a good breakfast, and walk into the exam room with a smile on your face.

You can leave with a smile on your face, too, knowing that you are going to have a fun week. It's your reward for studying regularly throughout the term.

If this kind of exam week sounds inviting, you can begin preparing for it right now.

STUDY WITH PEOPLE

EDUCATION OFTEN LOOKS LIKE COMPETITION. We compete for entrance to school, for grades when we're in school, and for jobs when we leave school. In that climate, it's easy to overlook the power of cooperation. Consider the idea that competition is not necessary for success in school. In some cases, competition actually works *against* your success. It is often stressful. It can strain relationships. What's more, competition can be inefficient. People can get more done by sharing their skills and resources than by working alone.

We are social animals, and we draw strength from groups. Study groups feed you energy. Aside from the camaraderie, the fellowship, and the fun, study groups elevate your spirit on days when you just don't want to work at your education. You are more likely to keep an appointment to study with a group than to study by yourself. If you skip the solo study session, no one may know. If you declare your intention to study to others and know they are depending on you, your intention gains strength.

In addition to drawing strength from the group when you're down, you can support others. There is power in contribution. A study support group is a place to build rewarding relationships.

Almost every job is accomplished by the combined efforts of many people. For example, manufacturing a single car calls for the contributions of designers, marketing executives, electricians, welders, painters, office workers, computer programmers, and many others. Jobs in today's economy call for teamwork—the ability to function well in groups. That's a skill you can start developing by studying with others.

Study groups are especially important if going to school has thrown you into a new culture. Being from a different country or a different racial group than most other students on campus can feel uncomfortable and isolating. Joining a study group with people you already know, as well as with people from other cultures, can ease the transition. Promote your success in school by refusing to go it alone.

HOW TO FORM A GROUP

When you form a support group, look for dedicated students. Find people you are comfortable with and who share some of your academic goals.

You can include people who face academic or personal challenges similar to your own. For example, if you are divorced and have two toddlers at home, you might look for other single parents who have returned to school.

Also include people who face challenges different from yours, to get the benefit of other perspectives.

Studying with friends is fine, but if your common interest is beer and jokes, beware of getting together to work.

The challenge of forming a study group is in making the first contacts and asking others to participate. You can recruit members by approaching people directly or by advertising.

Look for people who stay conscious, ask questions, and take notes during class. Ask them to join your group. Choose people with similar educational goals but different backgrounds and methods of learning. You can gain from seeing the material from a new perspective.

Suggest to two or three others that you meet for a snack and talk about group goals, meeting times, and other logistics. You don't have to make an immediate commitment.

Limit groups to five or six people. Larger groups are unwieldy.

Test the group first by planning a one-time-only session. If that session works, plan another. After several successful sessions, you can schedule regular meetings.

Another way to get into a group is to post a note on a bulletin board asking interested students to contact you. Or pass around a sign-up sheet before class. The advantage of these methods is you don't have to face rejection. The disadvantage is that this method takes more time and you don't get to choose who applies.

HOW TO CONDUCT A STUDY GROUP

There are many ways to conduct a study group. Begin with the following suggestions and see what works.

Test each other by asking questions. Each group member can agree to bring four or five test questions to each meeting, then you can all take the test made from these questions.

Practice teaching each other. Teaching is a great way to learn something. Turn the material you're studying into a list of topics. Then assign specific topics for each person to teach the group. When you teach something you naturally assume a teacher's attitude—"I know this"—as opposed to a student's attitude—"I still have to learn this." Also, the vocalization involved in teaching further reinforces your memory.

Compare notes. Make sure you all heard the same thing in class and that you all recorded the important information. Ask other students about material in your notes that is confusing to you.

Brainstorm test questions. Set aside five or ten minutes each study session, and use the brainstorming techniques described on page 179. You can add these to the "Test Questions" section of your notebook.

Conduct open-ended discussions and debates designed to produce understanding.

Take advantage of group support in personal areas. Other people might have insight into your problems involving transportation, child care, finances, time scheduling, or other barriers to getting what you want from school.

Set an agenda for each meeting. Select activities from this article, or create other activities to do as a group. Set approximate time limits for each agenda item and determine a quitting time. Finally, end each meeting with assignments for each member.

Journal Entry #46
Intention Statement

I intend to form a study group. I intend to take the following steps to get the group organized:

_____

_____

_____

I will set up the first group meeting by: (date)

_____

My reward for successfully fulfilling this intention will be

_____

_____

POWER PROCESS #6:
Detach

POWER PROCESS #6 ALLOWS YOU TO RELEASE THE POWERFUL, natural student within you. It is especially useful whenever negative emotions are getting in the way of your education. Attachments are addictions. When we are attached to something, we think we cannot live without it, just as a drug addict feels he cannot live without drugs. We believe our well-being depends on fulfilling our attachments.

We can be attached to just about anything . . . expectations, ideas, objects, self-perceptions, people, results, rewards. The list is endless.

One person, for example, may be so attached to his car that he takes an accident as a personal attack. Pity the poor unfortunate who backs into this person's car. He might as well back into the owner himself.

Another person may be attached to his job. His identity and sense of well-being depend on it. He could become suicidally depressed if he gets fired.

We can be addicted to our emotions as well as to our thoughts. We can identify with our anger so strongly that we are unwilling to let it go. We can also be addicted to our depression and reluctant to give it up. Rather than perceive these emotions as liabilities, we can see them as indications that it's time to practice detachment.

Most of us are addicted, to some extent, to our identities. We are Americans, veterans, high achievers, Elks, bowlers, loyal friends, Episcopalians, business owners, humanitarians, devoted parents, dancers, hockey fans, or birdwatchers. If we are attached, these are not just roles. Instead, they dictate who we are.

When these identities are threatened, we might fight for them as if we were defending our lives. The more addicted we are to the identity, the harder we fight. It's like a drowning man—the more he resists drowning, the more he literally becomes "attached" to his would-be rescuer, grasping and grabbing, until they both sink.

How to recognize an attachment

When we are attached and things don't go our way, we might feel irritated, angry, jealous, confused, fatigued, bored, frightened, or resentful.

Suppose you are attached to getting an A on your physics test. Your success in life depends on getting an A. It's not just that you want an A. You need an A.

During the exam the thought "I must get an A" is in the back of your mind as you begin to work a problem. And the problem is difficult. The first time you read it you have no idea how to solve it. The second time you aren't even sure what it's asking. The more you read it, the more confused you get. To top it all off, this problem is worth 40 percent of your score.

The harder you work, the more stuck you get and the louder the thought in the back of your head: "I must get an A; I Must Get An A; I MUST GET AN A!"

At this point your hands begin to sweat and shake. Your knees feel weak. You feel nauseated. You can't concentrate. You flail about for the answer as if you're drowning. You look up at the clock, sickened by the inexorable sweep of the second hand. You are doomed.

Now is a time to reach for Power Process #6: Detach.

How to use this process

Practice a variety of strategies to move toward detachment.

Practice observer consciousness. This is the quiet state above and beyond your usual thoughts, the place where you can be aware of being aware. It's a tranquil place, apart from your emotions. From here, you observe yourself objectively, as if you were someone else. Pay attention to your emotions and physical sensations. If you are confused and feeling stuck, tell yourself, "Here I am, confused and stuck." If your palms are sweaty and your stomach is one big knot, admit it.

Watch yourself and detach.

Practice perspective. Put current circumstances into a larger perspective. View your personal issues within the larger context of your community, your nation, or your planet. You will likely see them from a different point of view. Imagine the impact your current problems will have 20 or even 100 years from now.

Take a moment to consider the worst that could happen. During that physics exam, notice your attachment to getting an A. Even flunking the test will not ruin your life. Seeing this helps you put the test in perspective.

Practice breathing. Calm your mind and body with a breathing or relaxation technique.

It might be easier to practice these techniques when you're not feeling strong emotions. Notice your thoughts, behaviors, and feelings while watching television or discussing ideas. The skill you gain at these times can make it easier to detach in more difficult circumstances.

Practice detaching. The key is to let go of automatic emotional reactions whenever you don't get what you want.

Some cautions

Giving up an addiction to being an A student does not mean giving up being an A student. And giving up an addiction to a car doesn't mean getting rid of the car. Rather, it means not investing your well-being in the grade or the car. Keep your desires and goals alive and healthy while detaching from the need to reach them.

Notice also that detachment is different from denial. Denial implies running from whatever you find unpleasant. In contrast, detachment includes accepting your emotions and knowing the details of them— down to the very thoughts and physical sensations involved. It's OK to be angry or sad. Once you accept and fully experience your emotions, you can more easily move beyond them. The more you deny them, the more they persist.

Being detached is not the same as being apathethic. We can be 100 percent detached and 100 percent involved at the same time. In fact, our commitment to achieving a particular result is usually enhanced by being detached from it.

Detach and succeed.

When we are detached, we perform better. When we think we have a great deal at stake, results might suffer. Without anxiety and the *need* to get an A on the physics test, we are more likely to recognize the problem and remember the solution.

Power Process #6 is useful when you notice that attachments are keeping you from getting what you want. Behind your attachments is a master student. By detaching, you release that master student. Detach.

Golda Meir,

a pioneer in the creation of Israel, was elected its fourth Prime Minister.

Reprinted by permission of George Weidenfeld & Nicolson Limited from My Life *by Golda Meir, Copyright 1975 by Golda Meir.*

I started school in a huge, fortresslike building on Fourth Street near Milwaukee's famous Schlitz beer factory, and I loved it. I can't remember how long it took me to learn English (at home, of course, we spoke Yiddish, and luckily, so did almost everyone else on Walnut Street), but I have no recollection of the language ever being a real problem for me, so I must have picked it up quickly. I made friends quickly, too. Two of those early first- or second-grade friends remained friends all my life, and both live in Israel now. One was Regina Hamburger (today Medzini), who lived on our street and who was to leave America when I did; the other was Sarah Feder, who became one of the leaders of Labor Zionism in the United States. Anyhow, coming late to class almost every day was awful, and I used to cry all the way to school. Once a policeman even came to the shop to explain to my mother about truancy. She listened attentively but barely understood anything he said, so I went on being late for school and sometimes never got there at all—an even greater disgrace. My mother—not that she had much alternative—didn't seem to be moved by my bitter resentment of the shop. "We have to live, don't we?" she claimed, and if my father and Sheyna—each for his and her own reasons—would not help, that didn't mean I was absolved of the task. "So it will take you a little longer to become a rebbetzin [a bluestocking]," she added. I never became a bluestocking, of course, but I learned a lot at that school.

More than fifty years later—when I was seventy-one and a prime minister—I went back to that school for a few hours. It had not changed very much in all those years except that the vast majority of its pupils were now black, not Jewish, as in 1906. They welcomed me as though I were a queen. Standing in rows on the creaky old stage I remembered so well, freshly scrubbed and neat as pins, they serenaded me with Yiddish and Hebrew songs and raised their voices to peal out the Israeli anthem "Hatikvah" which made my eyes fill with tears. Each one of the classrooms had been beautifully decorated with posters about Israel and signs reading SHALOM (one

of the children thought it was my family name), and when I entered the school, two little girls wearing headbands with Stars of David on them solemnly presented me with an enormous white rose made of tissue paper and pipe cleaners, which I wore all day and carefully carried back to Israel with me.

Another of the gifts I got that day in 1971 from the Fourth Street School was a record of my grades for one of the years I had spent there: 95 in reading, 90 in spelling, 95 in arithmetic, 85 in music, and a mysterious 90 in something called manual arts, which I cannot remember at all. But when the children asked me to talk to them for a few minutes, it was not about book learning that I chose to speak. I had learned a lot more than fractions or how to spell at Fourth Street, and I decided to tell those eager, attentive children—born, as I myself had been, into a minority and living, as I myself had lived, without much extravagance (to put it mildly)—what the gist of that learning had been. "It isn't really important to decide when you are very young just exactly what you want to become when you grow up," I told them. "It is much more important to decide on the way you want to live. If you are going to be honest with yourself and honest with your friends, if you are going to get involved with causes which are good for others, not only for yourselves, then it seems to me that that is sufficient, and maybe what you will be is only a matter of chance." I had a feeling that they understood me.

1. Preparing for tests can include creating review tools. What are at least two of these tools?

2. For multiple choice questions, it is effective to read all the possible answers before answering the question in your head. True or false.

3. The presence of absolute qualifiers such as "always" or "never" generally indicates a false statement. True or False.

4. When answering essay questions, which of the following techniques is *least* effective?

   (A) Before you write, make a quick outline.
   (B) Try for drama by saving the best points for last.
   (C) Find out precisely what the question is asking by knowing standard essay question words.
   (D) Include part of the question in your answer.
   (E) Avoid filler sentences that say nothing.

5. Grades are:

   (A) a measure of creativity
   (B) an indication of your ability to contribute to society
   (C) a measure of intelligence
   (D) a measure of test performance
   (E) C and D

6. How is detachment different from denial?

7. Choose one technique for taking math and science tests and explain how it, or some variation of it, could apply to taking a test in another subject.

8. What are at least three benefits of participating in a study group?

9. Describe at least three techniques for dealing with the thoughts connected to test anxiety.

10. Describe at least three techniques for dealing with the physical feelings connected to test anxiety.

Journal Entry #47
Discovery Statement

Review what you learned in this chapter and complete the following sentence:
    In reading and doing this chapter, I discovered that I . . .

_____

Journal Entry #48
Intention Statement

List what you wanted to learn from this chapter and didn't. Then describe what you will do to get what you wanted.

_____
_____
_____
_____

Journal Entry #49
Intention Statement

Write a statement about your intention to practice one of the relaxation techniques and one of the test-taking hints from this chapter.
    I intend to . . .

_____
_____
_____

Journal Entry #50
Discovery Statement

Describe a time in your life when you blamed someone else for something that happened to you. Switch your perception and write about how you can apply the Power Process "I Create it all" to this event.

_____
_____
_____
_____
_____

Chapter 7

Creating

*You do not know what is in you—
an inexhaustible fountain of ideas.*
BRENDA UELAND

*Creativity was in each one of us as a small child. In children it
is universal. Among adults it is almost nonexistent. The great
question is: What has happened to this enormous and universal
human capacity? That is the question of the age.*
TILLIE OLSEN

*In most lives insight has been accidental. We wait for it as
primitive man awaited lightning for a fire. But making mental
connections is our most crucial learning tool; the essence of
human intelligence is to forge links; to go beyond the given; to
see pattern, relationships, context.*
MARILYN FERGUSON

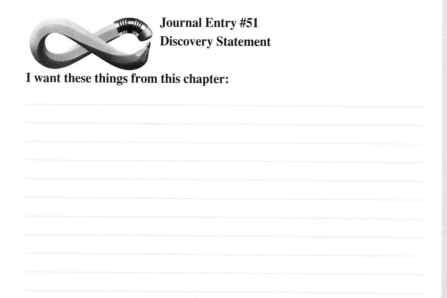

Journal Entry #51
Discovery Statement

I want these things from this chapter:

_____

_____

_____

_____

_____

_____

_____

_____

_____

In this chapter . . .

Becoming creative means knowing how to set the stage for it. This chapter includes some strategies for doing so in *Finding "Aha!" and following through* and *Creativity techniques*. Knowing them can pay off when you're assigned a paper or speech.

Writing papers and speeches is a task almost every student faces. When approached with a plan, these tasks could become rewarding and fun. Find out how in *Writing and refining papers* and *Preparing and delivering speeches*.

Choosing your point of view on an issue is a creative act that is part of writing papers and preparing speeches. *Critical thinking fuels creativity* can help you ignite your mental engines prior to writing or speaking.

Today some people prefer to write the old-fashioned way, with typewriter or pencil. Others use computers to create and revise papers. The process is essentially the same, no matter which method you use. *The cheapest word processor* explains the advantages of cutting and pasting.

You can promote creativity by experimenting with ideas, even if they seem outlandish at first. *Power Process #7: Be a fool* presents the advantages of doing so.

Exercises in this chapter are designed to unleash your creativity.

Finding "Aha!" and following through

THE FIRST SIX CHAPTERS of this book are about the nuts and bolts of education. They offer suggestions for how to tell the truth about your skills as a student and how to set goals to improve them. Also included are guidelines for managing your time, making your memory more effective, improving your reading skills, taking useful notes, and prospering during exams. Those techniques are about the business of acquiring knowledge.

The point of knowledge is not to *have* knowledge. The point is to *use* knowledge—not in a mechanical way, like a computer, but in imaginative and innovative ways. Knowledge can be used to expand our awareness and open the door to new possibilities. All of this can be energizing and fun.

The fun stuff is the "Aha!" And you can use the techniques in this chapter to find it.

Skeptics might be suspecting a scam by now. After all, they may reason, the only thing less fun than writing term papers is giving speeches, and that's in here, too.

Nineteenth-century poet Emily Dickinson described the aha! this way: "If

Tangram

A tangram is an ancient Chinese game that stimulates the "play instinct" so critical to creative thinking. The cat figure on the left was created by rearranging the seven sections of a square. Hundreds of images can be created in this manner. Playing with tangrams allows you to see relationships you didn't see before. Rules to the game are simple: Use these seven pieces to create something that wasn't there before. Be sure to use all seven.

Make your own tangram by cutting pieces like these out of poster board .(See pattern on the following page.) When you make a pattern you like, trace around the outside edges of it and see if a friend can discover how you did it.

I feel physically as if the top of my head were taken off, I know that is poetry." Aha! is the burst of creative energy heralded by the arrival of a new, original idea. It is the sudden emergence of a new pattern, a previously undetected relationship, or an unusual combination of familiar elements. It is an exhilarating experience.

Aha! does not always result in a timeless poem or a Nobel Prize. It can be inspired by anything from playing a new riff on a guitar to discovering why your car's fuel pump doesn't work. A nurse might notice that one of his patients has a symptom everyone else missed. That's an aha! An accountant might discover a tax break for a client. That's an aha! A teacher might invent a way to reach a difficult student. Aha!

School is a natural breeding ground for aha's! Term papers, speeches, math problems, science projects, even tests—all of these can inspire aha!, especially in the hands of skilled students. These students can be joyful, alive, energetic, and spontaneous. All of these qualities attract aha!

The flip side of aha! is following through. The creative process is both fun *and* work. It is effortless and uncomfortable. It's the result of luck and persistence. It involves spontaneity and step-by-step procedures.

Most people overlook the other side of creativity, the molding and shaping of a rough-cut idea into a polished creation. Employers in all fields are desperately seeking those rare people who can find aha! and do something with it.

Doing something often involves effective communication. Creative communicators rise to the challenge of making themselves heard over the howl of today's information blizzard. That's why the articles in this chapter on writing and speaking are so important.

Effective writers express ideas powerfully and persuasively. They can organize information and adapt it to different audiences. They can put plans on paper, create clear instructions, and clarify goals.

Writing also is a powerful way to learn. When you write, you not only gather information, you analyze it. You sift through the data, play with it, and sort it out. You look for relationships and patterns. You get a clear picture of what you know, what you don't know, and where to look for the missing pieces. You turn data into insight. In short, you create.

As the poet C. Day Lewis said, "We do not write in order to be understood; we write in order to understand."

Effective speakers can inspire, persuade and coach—in any field. They make ideas live and breathe, for small groups at the office or large groups at the arena. However, the fear of public speaking might be the most common of all phobias. That makes people who are willing and able to speak publicly even more valuable to almost any organization.

The fact is, effective writing and speaking are marketable skills. To verify this, flip through the help-wanted section of a large Sunday newspaper and note how many job descriptions call for both.

Writing and speaking depend upon critical thinking—the ability to spot assumptions, weigh evidence, separate fact from opinion, organize thoughts, and avoid errors in logic. These activities are creative, too, even though they call for a different kind of creativity than painting pictures or playing music.

This chapter is about having fun. It's about the joy of aha! and the deeper satisfaction of following through.

Make your own tangram symbols by cutting pieces like these out of poster board.

Creativity techniques

You can use these techniques to generate ideas on everything from term papers and math problems to remodeling a house or rewriting the Constitution. With practice, you can set the stage for creative leaps, jump with style, and land on your feet with brand new ideas in your hands.

CONDUCT A BRAINSTORM

Brainstorming is a technique for finding solutions, creating plans, and discovering new ideas. When you are stuck on a problem, brainstorming can break the logjam.

For example, if you run out of money two days before payday every week, you could brainstorm ways to make your money last longer. You can brainstorm ways to get home during spring break. You can brainstorm ways to pay for your education. You can brainstorm ways to find a job.

The purpose of brainstorming is to generate as many solutions as possible. Sometimes the craziest, most outlandish solutions, while unworkable in themselves, lead to new ways to solve problems.

The brainstorming process works like this:

First, formulate the issue or problem precisely by writing it down. For example, you might write: "Methods and techniques I can use to get more information on multinational trade organizations in Central Africa."

Next, set a time limit for your brainstorming session. Use a clock to time it to the minute. Digital sports watches with built-in stopwatches work well. Experiment with various lengths of time. Both short and long brainstorms can be powerful.

Before you begin, sit quietly for a few seconds to collect your thoughts. Then start timing and write as fast as you can.

Write down everything. Accept every idea. If it pops into your head, put it down on paper. Quantity, not quality, is the goal. Avoid making judgments and evaluations during the brainstorming session.

After the session, review, evaluate, and edit. Toss out the truly nutty ideas, but not before you give them a chance.

For example, during your brainstorm on Central African trade organizations you might have written: "Go to Central Africa and ask someone about them." Impossible? Are you certain your school wouldn't give you a semester of independent study to research the subject? Are you positive a trade organization wouldn't offer a scholarship to pay for the trip?

Brainstorms often produce surprising solutions that look whacky at first and that later produce life-changing results. Stay open to possibilities.

Here are some other tips for brainstorming sessions:

Let go of the need for a particular solution. Brainstorming sessions can reveal new ways of thinking about old problems.

Relax. Creativity is enhanced by a state of relaxed alertness. If you are tense or anxious, use one of the relaxation techniques on page 163 before you begin.

Set a quota or goal for the number of solutions you want to generate. Goals give your subconscious mind something to aim for.

Use 3x5 cards for each solution. When you review your session you can lay the cards out on a table and arrange them in patterns to look for relationships. Or you can arrange them in order of priority.

Brainstorm with others. This is a powerful technique. Group brainstorms take on lives of their own. Assign one member of the group to write down solutions. Feed off the ideas of others, and remember to avoid evaluating or judging anyone's ideas during the brainstorm.

Multiply brainstorms. Pick one item from your first brainstorm and conduct another brainstorm about that idea.

Be wild and crazy. If you get stuck, think of an outlandish idea and write it down. One well-placed crazy idea can unleash a flood of other, more workable solutions.

FOCUS AND LET GO

Focusing and letting go are alternating parts of the same process. Intense focus taps the resources of your conscious mind. Letting go gives your subconscious mind time to work. When you focus for intense periods and then let go for awhile, the conscious and subconscious parts of your brain work in harmony. Each brings its own strengths and talents to produce the highest quality result.

Focusing attention means being in the here and now. In order to focus your attention on a project, notice when you pay attention and notice when it wanders. And involve all your senses.

For example, if you are having difficulty composing at a typewriter or word processor, practice focusing by listening to the sounds as you type. Notice the feel of the keys as you strike them. When you know the sights, sounds, and sensations you associate with being truly in focus, you'll be able to repeat the experience and focus on your composing more easily.

You can use your body to focus your concentration. Some people concentrate better lying down. Others focus more easily if they stand or pace back and forth. Still others need to have something in their hands. Notice what works for you and use it.

Be willing to accept conflict, tension, and discomfort. Notice them and allow them to be, rather than fighting against them. Look for the specific thoughts and body sensations that make up the discomfort. Allow them to come fully into your awareness and let them pass.

You might not be focused all the time. Periods of inspiration may last only seconds. Be gentle with yourself when you notice your concentration has flagged.

In fact, that might be a time to let go. "Letting go" means not forcing yourself to be creative.

Practice focusing for short periods, at first, then give yourself a break. Phone a friend. Get up and take a walk around your desk or around your block. Take a few minutes to look out your window. Listen to a couple tunes on the stereo or, better yet, sing a couple of songs to yourself.

You also can break up periods of focused concentration with stretches, sit-ups, or push-ups. Use relaxation and breathing exercises. Muscle tension and the lack of oxygen can inhibit self-expression.

Movies, music, walks in the park, and other pleasant activities stir the creative soup that's simmering in your brain.

Take a nap when you are tired. Thomas Edison took frequent naps. Then the lightbulb clicked on.

CULTIVATE CREATIVE SERENDIPITY

The word *serendipity* comes from an 18th century story by Horace Walpole, "The Three Princes of Serendip." The princes had a knack for making lucky discoveries. Serendipity is that knack.

It is more than luck. It is the ability to see something valuable that you weren't looking for. History is full of serendipitous people.

Edward Jenner noticed "by accident" that milkmaids seldom got smallpox. The result was his discovery that mild cases of cowpox immunized them.

Penicillin also was discovered "by accident." Alexander Fleming was growing bacteria in a laboratory petri dish. A spore of Penicillium notatum, a kind of mold, apparently blew in the window and landed in the dish. It killed the bacteria. Fleming isolated the active ingredient. A few years later, during World War II, it saved thousands of lives. Had Fleming not been alert to the possibility, the discovery might never have been made.

You can train yourself in the art of serendipity.

First, keep your eyes open. You might find a solution to an accounting problem in a Saturday morning cartoon. You might discover a term paper subject at the corner convenience store.

Multiply your contacts with the world. Resolve to meet new people. Join a study or discussion group. Read. Go to plays, concerts, art shows, lectures, and movies. Watch television programs you normally wouldn't watch. Use idea files and play with data, as described below.

Finally, expect discoveries. One secret of "luck" is being prepared to recognize it when you see it.

KEEP IDEA FILES

We all have ideas. People labeled "creative" are those who treat their ideas with care. That means recognizing, recording, and following up on them.

One way to keep track of ideas is to write them on 3x5 cards. Invent your own categories and number the cards so you can cross-reference them. For example, if you have an idea about making a new kind of bookshelf, you might file it under "Remodeling." The card might also be filed under "Marketable ideas." On one card, you can write your idea, and on the other you can write, "see card #132— Remodeling."

Include in your files powerful quotes, random insights, notes on your reading, and useful ideas you encounter in class. Collect jokes, too.

Keep a journal. Journals don't have to be exclusively about your thoughts and feelings. You can include your observations of the world around you, quotes from friends, important or off-beat ideas—anything.

To fuel your creativity, read voraciously, including newspapers and magazines. Keep a clip file of interesting articles. Explore beyond mainstream journalism. There are hundreds of small-circulation specialty magazines. They cover almost any subject you can imagine.

At a seminar on creativity a few years ago, one of Johnny Carson's writers was asked how he could create so many new jokes day after day for years at a stretch.

"Stuff your brain," he replied. "Keep pumping information into it. Read anything you can get your hands on. Read anything that interests you. Don't worry about whether you can use it or how you will use it, just pump it in there. Give your brain lots of raw material. Then give it a chance to 'cook.'"

Keep letter-size files of important correspondence, magazine and newspaper articles, and other material. You can also create idea files on a personal computer using word processing, outlining, or database software.

Safeguard your ideas even if you're pressed for time. Jotting down four or five words is enough to capture the essence of an idea. You can write down one quote in a minute or two. And if you carry 3x5 cards in a pocket or purse, you can record ideas while standing in line or waiting for appointments to begin.

Review your files regularly. Something that was an amusing thought in

Exercise #22
Fix the world brainstorm

This exercise works best with four to six people. Pick a major world problem like hunger, nuclear proliferation, poverty, totalitarianism, or pollution. Then conduct a 10-minute brainstorm on all the steps an individual could take to contribute to solving the problem. Use the brainstorming techniques described on page 179. Remember not to evaluate or judge the solutions during the process. The purpose of a brainstorm is to generate a flow of ideas.

After the brainstorming session, discuss the process and the solutions that it generated. Did you feel any energy from the group? Were any new or exciting ideas created? Are any of the ideas worth pursuing? Write Discovery and Intention Statements about them.

November might be the perfect solution to a problem the following March.

COLLECT AND PLAY WITH DATA

Look at the data you collect from all sides. Switch your attention from one aspect to another. Examine each fact, and avoid getting stuck on one particular part of a problem.

Turn a problem upside down by picking a solution first, before you know it will work, and working backwards.

Ask other people to look at the data. Solicit opinions.

Living with the problem invites a solution. Write down data, possible solutions, or a formulation of the problem on 3x5 cards and carry them with you. Look at them before you go to bed at night. Review them when you are waiting for the bus. Make them part of your life and think about them frequently.

Look for the obvious solution or the obvious "truths" about the problem, then dump them. Ask yourself, "Well, I know X is true, but if X were not true, then what would happen?" Or, ask the reverse: "If that were true, then what would follow next?"

Put unrelated facts next to each other and invent a relationship, even if it seems absurd at first.

Make imaginary pictures with the data. Condense it. Categorize it. Put it in chronological order. Put it in alphabetical order. Put it in random order. Order it from most to least complex. Reverse all those orders. Look for opposites.

It has been said that there are no new ideas, only new ways to combine old ideas. Creativity is the ability to discover those new combinations.

CREATE WHILE YOU SLEEP

There's a part of our minds that works as we sleep. You've experienced this directly if you've ever fallen asleep with a problem on your mind and awakened the next morning with a solution. For some people, the solution appears in a dream or in the twilight consciousness just before falling asleep or waking.

You can experiment with this process. Ask yourself a question as you fall asleep. Keep pencil and paper or a tape recorder near your bed. The moment you wake up, begin writing or speaking and see if an answer to your question emerges.

To capture your ideas, keep a notebook by your bed at all times. Many people have awakened from a dream with a great idea, only to fall asleep and lose it. Put the notebook where you can find it easily.

REFINE IDEAS AND FOLLOW THROUGH

Most people ignore this part of the process. How many great money-making schemes have we had that we never pursued? How many good ideas for short stories have we had that we never wrote? How many times have we said to ourselves, "You know, what they ought to do is attach two handles to one of those things, paint it orange, and sell it to police departments. They'd make a fortune."

And we never realize that we are "they."

True genius resides in the follow-through—the application of perspiration to inspiration. One powerful tool you can use to follow through is the Discovery and Intention Journal System.

Write your idea in a Discovery Statement and what you intend to do about it in an Intention Statement. Use the guidelines on pages 14-15.

You also can use the writing techniques on pages 186-191 as a guide for refining your ideas.

Another way to refine an idea is to simplify it. And if that doesn't work, mess it up. Make it more complex.

Finally, keep a separate file in your idea file for your own inspirations. Return to it regularly to see if there is anything you can use. Today's defunct term paper idea could be next year's A in speech class.

TRUST THE PROCESS

Learn to trust your creative process—even when no answers are in sight.

Often people are reluctant to look at problems if no immediate solution is in sight. They are impatient. If the answer isn't quickly apparent, they avoid frustration by giving up. Most of us do this to some degree with personal problems. If we are having difficulty with a relationship and don't see an immediate solution, we deny the problem's existence rather than face it.

Trust that a solution will show up. Frustration and a feeling of being stuck are often signals that a solution is imminent.

Sometimes solutions break through in a giant AHA! More often they come in a series of little aha!'s. Be aware of what your aha!'s look, feel, and sound like.

Create on your feet

The latest thing around executive offices these days are "stand-up" desks. These desks are raised; you stand at them instead of sitting.

Standing has advantages over sitting for long periods. You stay more alert and creative when you're on your feet. Standing is great for lower back pains, too. Sitting aggravates the spine and supporting muscles.

You can join the ranks of some influential people who spend their days standing rather than sitting on the job. Roger Birk, chairman of Merrill Lynch & Co.; George Shinn, chairman and chief executive officer of First Boston Corp.; C. Peter McColough, chairman of Xerox, along with Xerox's president and at least one vice president, all have switched to standing-style desks. They get more done and are more comfortable doing it.

Thomas Jefferson used a stand-up desk upon which he wrote the Declaration of Independence. Donald Rumsfeld, former Secretary of Defense, used one at the White House and continues to use one in private business. Winston Churchill, Ernest Hemingway, and Virginia Woolf were fond of standing while working.

Experiment with this idea. Consider setting your desk up on blocks or putting a box on top of your desk so you can stand while writing, preparing speeches, or studying.

Critical thinking fuels creativity

Society depends on persuasion. Advertisers want you to spend money. Political candidates want you to "buy" their stands on the issues. Teachers want you to agree that their classes are vital to your success. Parents want you to accept their values. Authors want you to read their books. Broadcasters want you to spend your time in front of the radio or television, consuming their programs and not those from the competition. The business of persuasion embraces all of us.

All this leaves us with hundreds of choices about what to buy, what to do, and who to be. It's easy to lose our heads in the cross currents of competing ideas—unless we develop skills in critical thinking. This kind of thinking means sorting out the conflicting claims, weighing the evidence for them, letting go of personal biases, and arriving at reasonable views. When we think critically, we make choices with open eyes.

Critical thinking underlies reading, writing, speaking, and listening. These are the basic elements of communication—a process that occupies most of our waking hours. Though there are dozens of approaches to critical thinking, the process can be boiled down to a four-step strategy. This strategy works for evaluting your own views as well as the views of others.

Step 1: Understand the point of view

Strictly speaking, none of us live in the same world. Our habits, preferences, outlooks, and values are as individual as our fingerprints. Each of them is shaped by our culture, our upbringing, our experiences, and our choices. Speeches, books, articles, works of art, television programs, views expressed in conversation—all of them come from people who inhabit a different world than yours.

Understanding precedes criticizing. In critical thinking, until we've lived in another person's world for a while, it's ineffective to dismiss her point of view. This basic principle is central to many professions. Physicians diagnose before they prescribe. Lawyers brief themselves on the opponent's case. Effective teachers find out what a student already knows before they guide her to new ideas. Skilled salespeople find out what a customer's needs are before they present a product.

Effective understanding calls for listening without judgment. To enter another person's world, sum up her viewpoint in your own words. If you're conversing with that person, keep revising your summary until she agrees you've stated her position accurately. If you're reading an article, write a short summary of it. Then scan the article again, checking to see if your summary is on track. Once you understand, then you're prepared for the remaining steps in critical thinking.

Step 2: Seek other views

Imagine Karl Marx, Che´ Guevara, and Donald Trump gathered in one room to choose the most desirable economic system. Picture Ghandi, Winnie Mandela, and General George Patton in a seminar on conflict resolution. Or, visualize Jesse Jackson, George Bush, and Mother Theresa in a discussion about how to balance the national budget. When you seek out alternate points of view, such events can take place in your mind's arena.

Dozens of viewpoints exist on every critical issue—how to reduce crime, end world hunger, prevent war, educate our children, and countless others. In fact, few problems allow for any permanent solution. Each generation produces new answers, based on current conditions. In effect, our search for answers is a conversation that spans centuries. On each question, there are many voices waiting to be heard. You can take advantage of this diversity by seeking out alternative viewpoints on an issue.

Step 3: Evaluate the various views

It's easier to compare and evaluate viewpoints when you look for assumptions, the starting points in our thinking. These are the key assertions on which the speaker's or writer's argument rests. Spotting assumptions can be tricky, since they are usually unstated and offered without evidence.

As an example, take this claim from an advertisement: "Successful students have large vocabularies, so sign up today for our seminar on word power!" Embedded in this sentence are several assumptions. One is that a cause-effect relationship exists between a large vocabulary and success in school. Another is that a large vocabulary is the single or most important factor in that success. This claim also assumes that the advertiser's seminar is a good way to develop your vocabulary.

In reality, none of the assumptions may be true. A large vocabulary is only one factor in student success. It's also doubtful that large vocabularies cause student success. Instead, both may be related to other factors, such as the ability to read well. Finally, other methods of developing your vocabulary might be just as effective as the advertiser's seminar.

You can follow a three-step method for testing the truth of any viewpoint. First, look for the assumptions or implied assertions. Second, state the assumptions or assertions directly. Finally, see if you can find any exceptions to them. This technique helps to detect many errors in critical thinking.

You can also look specifically for selective perception, either/or thinking, personal attacks, oversimplification, and other gaps in logic. For more details, refer to the *Critical Thinking Supplement to Becoming a Master Student*. Also see the materials on reading and writing listed in the Bibliography.

Step 4: Construct a reasonable view

One humorist compared finding the truth to painting a barn door by throwing open cans of paint at it. Few people who throw at the door miss it entirely. Yet no one can really cover the whole door in one toss.

People who express their viewpoints are seeking truth. Yet almost no reasonable person claims to have covered the whole barn door—to have the Whole Truth about anything. Instead, each viewpoint is one approach among many possible approaches. If you don't think that any one viewpoint is complete, then it's up to you to combine the perspectives on the issue. In doing so, you choose an original viewpoint. This, like composing a song or painting a picture, is a creative act and an exhilarating exercise in critical thinking.

Writing and refining papers

It's easy to put off writing until the last minute, when anxiety forces you to commit words to paper. There are easier ways to get a writing project done.

This article outlines a three-phase process for writing any paper or speech:

1. Creating something from nothing—Getting ready to write
2. Getting down to it—Writing the first draft
3. Polishing your gems—Revising your draft

Every writer has an individual style. Even though this article lays out the process step-by-step, remember that writing is highly personal. You might go through the steps in a different order or find yourself working on several at once.

Phase 1: Creating something from nothing—Getting ready to write

Step 1:
List and schedule writing tasks

Now you can break the goal—a finished paper—into smaller steps that you can tackle right way. Estimate how long it will take to complete each step. Start with the date your paper is due and work *backwards* to the present. Say that the due date is December 1, and you have about three months to do the paper. List November 20 as your target completion date; plan what you want to get done by November 1; then list what you want to get done by October 1.

Step 2:
Generate ideas
Speak it
To get ideas flowing, start talking. Admit your confusion or lack of clear idea. Then just speak. By putting your thoughts into words, you'll start thinking more clearly. Novelist E. M. Forster said, "Speak before you think is creation's motto."

Use free writing
Free writing sends a depth probe into your creative mind. This is one way to bypass your internal censors, those little voices in your head that constantly say, "That sentence wasn't very good. Why don't you stop this before you get hurt?"

There's only one rule in free writing: Write without stopping. Set a time limit—say, 10 minutes—and keep your pencil in motion or your fingers dancing across the keyboard the whole time. Give yourself permission to keep writing, even if you don't think it's very good, even if you want to stop and rewrite. There's no need to worry about spelling, punctuation, or grammar. It's OK if you stray from the initial subject. Just keep writing. Now you're starting to get ideas down on paper.

Step 3:
Refine your initial ideas
Select a topic and working title
It's easy to put off writing if you have

a hard time choosing a topic. However, it is almost impossible to make a wrong choice at this stage. The best way to choose is to just do it.

Using your instructor's guidelines for the paper or speech, sit down and make a list of topics that interest you. Write as many of these as you can think of in two minutes. Then choose one. If you can't decide, use scissors to cut your list into single items, put them in a box, and pull one out. To avoid getting stuck on this first step, set a precise deadline for yourself: "I will choose a topic by 4 p.m. on Wednesday."

The most common pitfall is selecting a topic that's too broad. "Harriet Tubman" is not a useful topic for your American history paper. Instead, consider "Harriet Tubman's activities as a Union spy during the Civil War."

Write a thesis statement

Clarify what you want to say by summarizing it in one concise sentence. This sentence is called a thesis statement, and it refines your working title. It also helps in making a preliminary outline.

You might write a thesis statement such as: "Harriet Tubman's activities with the Underground Railroad led to a relationship with the Union army during the Civil War." A statement that's clear and to the point can make your paper easier to write.

Remember that it's OK to rewrite your thesis statement as you learn more about your topic.

Step 4:
Consider your audience, purpose, and content

Writing flows from a purpose. This means your writing is more effective when you know exactly what your purpose is.

Clarify the purpose of your assignment with your instructor. Think about how you'd like your reader or listener to change after considering your

ideas. Do you want her to think differently, to feel differently, or to take a certain action? Your writing strategy is greatly affected by how you answer these questions.

If you want someone to think differently, make your writing clear and logical. Support your assertions with evidence. If you want someone to feel differently, consider crafting a story. Write about a character your audience can sympathize with, and tell how she resolves a basic problem. And if your purpose is to move the reader into action, explain exactly what steps to take and offer a solid benefit for doing so.

Your writing can be more powerful if you work with a specific audience in mind. Audience analysis is complex. However, these questions help writers stay on track: Who is my primary audience? What does my audience already know about this subject? What is their attitude toward this subject? How will they use this information?

Step 5:
Do initial research

At this stage, your research is not about uncovering specific facts about your topic. That comes later. Now you want to get an overview of the subject. Find out the structure of your topic—its major divisions, issues, or branches. Say you want to persuade the reader to vote for a certain candidate. Then learn enough about this person to state her stands on key issues and sum up her background.

Step 6:
Outline

Many people shun outlining. They forget that the primary purpose of an outline is to save time. It's much like plotting a route when you travel to a new place. When you follow a map, you avoid getting lost. Likewise, an outline keeps you from wandering off the topic.

To start an outline, gather a stack of

Exercise #23
Free writing

Think about a paper or other writing project you've been assigned. Pick a limited topic related to that project. Or pick any topic you'd like to write about.

With your topic in mind, write for 10 minutes. Follow the guidelines for free writing: Jot down phrases, sentences, single words, pictures— anything that comes to mind, in any order. Imagine yourself talking about this topic to a friend over a cup of coffee. Write down what you would say. Just keep your hand moving.

Remember that this writing sample is not for keeps, and you won't show it to anybody. Anything that comes out is OK for now.

Set a timer and go for it. Write for a full 10 minutes.

After you're done, go back and circle any passages you like. Consider filing these for use in future writing projects.

Using mind maps, 3x5 cards, or other materials you feel comfortable with, create specific, narrowed working titles for the following subjects:

Fashion models
World hunger
Garbage
American cars
Space travel
Loud music
Television

For example:

Subject: Sports
Working Title: The effect of the increased popularity of jogging on the health of the population of Little Rock, Arkansas."

3x5 cards and brainstorm ideas you want to include in your paper. Write one idea per card.

Then experiment with the cards. Group them into separate stacks, each stack representing one major category. After that, arrange the stacks in order. Finally, arrange the 3x5s *within* each stack in a logical order. Rearrange cards until you discover an organization you like.

If you write on a computer, consider using outlining software. These programs allow you to record and rearrange ideas on the screen, much like you'd create and shuffle 3x5 cards.

Step 7:
Research

You can find information about research skills in Chapters Five and Eleven of this book. Following are added suggestions.

Handling 3x5 cards

If 3x5 cards haven't found their way into your home by now, joy awaits you. These cards work wonders in researching. Just write down one idea per card. This makes it easy to organize—and reorganize—your ideas.

Organizing research cards as you create them saves time. Use rubber bands to keep source cards separate from information cards, and to maintain general categories. (For a description of these two types of cards, see page 139.)

You can also save time in two other ways. First, copy all information correctly. Always include the source code and page number on information cards. Second, write legibly and use the same format for all your cards.

In addition to source cards and information cards, generate idea cards. If you have a thought as you are researching, write it down on a card. Label these cards clearly as your own ideas.

An alternative to 3x5 cards is a computer outlining or database program.

Some word processing packages also include features that can be used for note-taking.

Sense the time to begin writing

A common mistake of beginning writers is to hold their noses, close their eyes, and jump into the writing process with both feet and few facts. Avoid this temptation by gathering more information than you can use.

On the other hand, you can begin writing even before your research is complete. The act of writing creates ideas and reveals holes in research.

Finding a natural place to begin is one signal to begin writing. This is not to say that the skies will suddenly open and your whole paper will appear before your eyes, flanked by trumpeting angels. You might just get a strong sense of how to write one small section of your paper. When this happens, write.

Phase 2: Getting down to it— Writing the first draft

If you're adequately prepared to write, you've already done much of the hard work. Now you can relax into writing your first draft.

Just gather your notes, arranged to follow your outline. Now, write about the ideas in your notes. As you do, experiment with the following ideas.

Remember the first draft "ain't no piano"

Give yourself permission to turn out a first draft that doesn't meet your standards. Your goal at this point is simply to generate lots of material.

So don't worry about grammar, punctuation, or spelling. Write as if you were explaining the subject to a friend. Let words flow. The act of writing releases creative energy.

Write freely

Many writers prefer to get their first draft down quickly. They suggest that you keep writing, with occasional pauses to glance at your notes and outline.

There's no obligation to write straight through, following your outline from beginning to the end. You may feel more comfortable with certain aspects of your topic than others. Dive in where you want. That warms you up for the other sections of your paper.

Be yourself

As you write, let go of the urge to sound "official" or "scholarly." Write to an intelligent friend. Visualize this person and choose the most important things you'd say to her about the topic.

Let your inner writer take over

There may be times during a first draft when it feels like the ideas are just running through you, flowing from head to hand without conscious effort on your part. This is a natural "high" similar to states that accomplished athletes, musicians, and artists report. Often those moments come just after a period of feeling stuck. Welcome getting stuck. A breakthrough is on its way.

Ease into it

Some people find it works well to forget the word "writing." Instead, they ease into the task with activities that help generate ideas. You can free associate, cluster, daydream, doodle, draw, visualize, talk into a tape recorder—anything that gets you started.

Make writing a habit

"Inspiration" is not part of the working vocabulary for many professional writers. Instead of waiting for inspiration to strike, they simply make a habit of writing at a certain time each day. You can use the same strategy. Simply schedule a block of time to write your first draft. The very act of writing can breed inspiration.

Hide it in your drawer for a while

Give yourself time to step back from the first draft. A few minutes, a few hours, or a few days worth of perspective usually makes it easier to get on to the next step: Polishing your creation.

Phase 3: Polishing your creation—Revising your draft

When you wrote your first draft, you turned off your internal critic. Now that you've moved into revising, you can put on your critic's hat. You're shifting roles.

The purpose here is not to beat yourself up or bruise your paper. Rather, you revise to let the fire of your ideas glow through the haze of creation.

There's a difference in pace between writing a first draft and revising it. Keep in mind the saying, "Write in haste, revise at leisure." When you edit and revise, slow down and take a microscope to your work. One guideline is to allow 50 percent of writing time for planning, research, and writing the first draft. Then give the remaining 50 percent to revising.

One of the best ways to revise your paper is to read it out loud. Another technique is to have a friend revise your

LE₀RN T% t✦pE
LEaRN T✪ tYP#
LEaRN TO tYPE
LEARN TO TYPE!

Computers—micro, mini, and monster— are run by keyboard. Many executives who have relied on others to handle the typing are discovering that keyboard skills are valuable for everyone.

The biggest sales pitch for learning to type is that most themes and papers must be typewritten. If you know how to type effectively and accurately, you can save hours of misery— and money.

Typing is not difficult. It can be self-taught or learned in a class. Tutorial typing programs are also available for computers. Using program drills and performing under time limits will help you learn to type accurately and with speed.

Writing and refining papers

paper. Though this is not a substitute for your own revision, a friend can often see mistakes you miss.

These techniques can help you in each step of rewriting: cut, paste, fix, prepare, and proof.

Step 1: Cut

To save time, decide now which words you want to keep and which you want to cut. That leaves you with fewer words to edit.

Look for excess baggage. Approach your rough draft as if it were a chunk of granite from which you plan to chisel the final product. In the end, much of your first draft could be lying on the floor. What's left is the clean, clear, polished product.

Sometimes the revisions are painful. Sooner or later, every writer invents a phrase that is truly clever but makes no contribution. These phrases look at us with big, watery doe eyes and beg for life. "I'm cute," they say. "I show everyone how smart you are. Please let me stay in your paper." Grit your teeth and throw them out.

For maximum efficiency, make the larger cuts first—sections, chapters, pages. Then go for the smaller cuts—paragraphs, sentences, phrases, words.

Step 2: Paste

In deleting passages, you might remove some of the original transitions and connecting ideas. The next task is to rearrange what's left of your paper so it flows logically.

Now that you've cut words, look at what remains. Are the concepts presented in a logical order? Does one point flow into the next? Will it hang together for the reader? Or will the reader feel that points are being made in a random order?

If your draft doesn't hang together, then reorder your ideas. Imagine yourself with a scissors and glue. You're going to cut the paper into scraps—one scrap for each point. Then you can paste these points down in a new, more logical order.

Step 3: Fix

Now it's time to look at individual words and phrases.

In general, write with nouns and verbs. Relying too much on adjectives and adverbs weakens your message and adds unnecessary bulk to your writing. Write about the details, and be specific. Also, use the active rather than the passive voice. Some examples follow:

1. Instead of writing in the passive voice:
A project was initiated.
You can make it active by writing:
The research team began a project.

2. Instead of writing verbosely:
After making a timely arrival and perspicaciously observing the unfolding events, I emerged totally and gloriously victorious.
You can write, as Julius Caesar did:
I came, I saw, I conquered.

3. Instead of writing vaguely:
The speaker made effective use of the television medium, asking in no uncertain terms that we change our belief systems.
You can write specifically:
The reformed criminal stared straight into the television camera and shouted: "Take a good look at what you're doing. Will it get you what you really want?"

Next, go through the paper again, paying attention to grammar and spelling. Also define any terms the reader may not know and put them into plain English whenever you can. These are touches that polish your writing.

Step 4: Prepare

In a sense, any paper is a sales effort. If you hand in a paper with its shirt tail hanging out, its hair tangled and unwashed, and its face unshaven, your instructor is less likely to buy.

To avoid this situation, type your

paper following an acceptable format for margin width, footnotes, title pages, and other details. Use quality paper for your final version. For an even more professional appearance, bind your paper with a paper or plastic cover. This shows that you take care with your work.

Step 5: Proof

Reading your paper out loud is one way to spot awkward sentences. Another option is to ask a friend to proof your paper. Be sure and ask someone who is competent and will give you candid feedback.

When you're done proofreading and have your final copy in hand, take a minute to savor the experience. You've just witnessed something of a miracle—the mind attaining clarity and resolution. That's the Aha! in writing.

Journal Entry #52
Discovery Statement

This Journal Entry is for people who avoid writing.

As with any anxiety, approach writing anxiety by accepting it fully. Realize that it's OK to feel anxious about writing. That feeling is shared by others, and many people have worked with it successfully.

Begin by telling the truth. Describe exactly what happens when you start to write. What thoughts or images run through your mind? Do you feel any tension or discomfort in your body? Where? Let them come to the surface without resistance. Write your description of them in the space below.

When I begin to write, I discover that I . . .

_____

_____

_____

_____

_____

_____

_____

_____

_____

Journal Entry #53
Intention Statement

Choose three of the suggestions explained in the article "Writing and refining papers." Describe how and when you will use these suggestions to complete a writing assignment.

I intend to . . .

_____

_____

_____

_____

_____

The cheapest word processor

Writing usually is not a matter of finding a clever phrase. It is more often a matter of presenting material in a logical, effective order.

Computers with word processing programs are great tools for moving ideas around quickly. You can do much the same thing with a pair of scissors and a jar of rubber cement.

First, write a rough draft. For the best results, type it double- or triple-spaced. Then cut the whole thing into pieces, paragraph by paragraph, and spread the paragraphs out on a large desk or table. Or use the floor.

Now you can practice rearranging the paragraphs, until you find the most logical, effective way to organize your paper. One way to make sure your plan works is to read the paper through, as if you were giving a speech. If the elements don't follow each other logically, if the transitions are weak, your ears will pick it up. When you hear a clinker, move the paragraphs around until it sounds right.

Then paste the paragraphs, in their new order, onto new sheets of paper. You are ready to write a refined second draft.

Preparing and delivering speeches

Polishing your speaking skills can help you think on your feet and communicate clearly. These are skills you will use during school and in any career you choose.

Organizing your speech

Some people tune out during a speech. Just think of all the times you have listened to instructors, lecturers, politicians, and others. Think of all the wonderful daydreams you had during their speeches.

Your audiences are like you. The way you organize your speech can determine the number of people in your audience who stay with you until the end.

Speeches are usually organized in three main parts: the introduction, the main body, and the conclusion.

Introduction

The introduction sets the stage for your audience. This is the time to make clear to the audience where you are taking them (to "tell them what you're going to tell them"). Unless you are a brilliant presenter such as Jesse Jackson or Mario Cuomo, avoid rambling speeches with no clear organization. They put audiences to sleep.

The following introduction, for example, tells exactly what is coming. The speech has three distinct parts, each in logical order.

Cock fighting is a cruel sport. I intend to describe exactly what happens to the birds, tell you who is doing this, and show you how you can stop this inhumane practice.

To make an effective speech, be precise about your purpose. Speeches can inform, persuade, motivate, or entertain. Choose what you want to do, and let your audience know what you intend.

When the choice is yours, talk about things that hold your interest. Include your personal experiences. Your enthusiasm will reach the audience.

Start with a bang! Compare the following two introductions to speeches on the subject of world hunger. Example number one:

I'm very honored to be here with you today. I intend to talk about malnutrition and starvation. First, I want to outline the extent of these problems, then I will discuss some basic assumptions concerning world hunger, and finally, I will propose some solutions.

You can almost hear the snores from the audience.

Example number two:

More people have died from hunger in the past five years than have been killed in all the wars, revolutions, and murders in the past 150 years. Yet there is enough food to go around. I'm honored to be with you today to discuss the problem . . .

Most people pay attention to the first few seconds of a speech, so this is a good time to highlight your best points.

One practical note: Before you begin,

be sure you have the audience's attention. If people are still filing into the room or adjusting seats, they're not ready to listen.

Main body

The main body of the speech is the content—70 to 90 percent of most speeches. In the main body, you will develop your ideas much the way you develop a written paper. This is where you "tell them."

In speeches, transitions are especially important. Give your audience a signal when you change points. ("On the other hand, until the public realizes what is happening to children in these countries . . .", "The second reason hunger persists is . . .".)

In long speeches, recap from time to time and preview what's to come. Using facts, descriptions, expert opinions, statistics, and other concrete details will help you hold audience attention.

Conclusion

At the end of the speech, sum up your points and draw your conclusion ("tell them what you've told them"). You started with a bang, so finish with drama.

The first and last parts of the speech are most important. Make it clear to your audience when you've reached the end. Avoid endings such as, "This is the end of my speech," or "Well, I guess that's it." A simple standby is, "So, in conclusion I want to reiterate three points: First . . . ." When you are finished, stop talking.

Using notes

Some professional speakers recommend keeping notes on 3x5 cards. They make it easy to keep your speech in order. Number the cards so that if you drop them, you can quickly put them in order again. As you finish the information on each card, move it to the back of the pile. Write information clearly and in letters large enough to be seen from a distance.

The disadvantage of the 3x5 card system is that it involves a lot of card shuffling. Some speakers prefer to use standard outlined notes. Another option is mind mapping. Even an hour-long speech can be mapped on one sheet of paper. You can also use memory techniques to memorize the outline of your speech.

How to practice

The key to successful public speaking is practice. When you practice, do so in a loud voice. Your voice sounds different when you talk loudly, and this can be unnerving. Get used to it before the big day.

If possible, practice in the room where you will deliver your speech. Hear what your voice sounds like over a sound system. If you can't practice your speech in the actual room, at least visit the site ahead of time. Also list materials you will need for your speech, including audiovisual aids.

To get the most out of your practice, record your speech and listen to it. Better yet, videotape your presentation. Many schools have video equipment available for student use. Check the library.

When practicing, listen for repeated phrases: "you know," "kind of," "really," plus any little "uh's," "umm's," and "ah's." To get rid of these mannerisms, simply tell yourself that you intend to notice every time they pop up in your daily speech. When you hear them, tell yourself that you

Preparing and delivering speeches

don't use those words anymore. Eventually, they will disappear.

Practice your speech in front of friends or while looking in a mirror. Speaking before one or two friends builds confidence; it can be more demanding than talking in front of a large group. You can also practice by speaking up often in class.

Use stress reduction techniques before and during your speech. Practice them ahead of time. Then before you speak, visualize yourself in the room successfully giving the speech.

When you practice your speech, avoid delivering it word for word, as if you're reading a script. Know your material and present the information in a way that is most natural for you. Diligent practice relieves you of having to rely heavily on your notes.

One more note on getting ready: If you want to get your message across, dress appropriately. Dress up to speak before the Association of University Presidents— unless they're having a picnic.

Delivering the speech

For some beginners, the biggest problem in delivering a speech is nervousness. If this is your concern, give yourself a hand by knowing your material inside out.

Nervousness is common. You can deal with it by noticing it. Tell yourself, "Yes, my hands are clammy. I notice that my stomach is slightly upset. My face feels numb." Allow these symptoms to exist. Experience them fully. When you do, those symptoms often become less persistent. Use Power Process #3: "Love your problems."

Also use Power Process #2: "Be here now." Be totally in the present moment. Notice how the room feels. Notice the temperature and lighting. See the audience. Look at them. Make eye contact. Notice all your thoughts about how you feel and gently release them.

Another technique is to look at your audience and imagine them all dressed as clowns. Chances are that if you lighten up and enjoy your presentation, so will the audience.

When you speak, talk loudly enough to be heard. To help yourself project, avoid leaning over your notes or the podium.

Also maintain eye contact. When you look at people, they become less frightening. Remember that it is easier to listen to someone who looks at you. Find a few friendly faces around the room and imagine that you are talking to them individually. If you notice a side conversation in the room, continue speaking and look directly at the people who are visiting.

You can increase the impact of words by keeping track of the time during your speech. Better to end early than run late. The conclusion of your speech is what is likely to be remembered, and you might lose this opportunity if people are looking at the clock.

Use audiovisual aids, flip charts, and other props whenever possible.

Only a fraction of our communication is verbal. Be aware of what your body is telling your audience. Contrived or staged gestures will look dishonest. Be natural. If you don't know what to do with your hands, notice that. Then don't do anything with them.

Pause where appropriate. Beginners sometimes feel they have to fill every moment with the sound of their voice. Let your audience take a mental deep breath from time to time.

And lighten up. Friendliness and humor are usually appropriate. There are few reasons to take yourself too seriously.

After you speak

Review and reflect upon your performance. Did you finish on time? Did you cover all the points you intended to cover? Was the audience attentive? Did you handle any nervousness effectively? What can you do to improve your performance and delivery next time?

Welcome evaluation from others. Most of us find it difficult to hear criticism about our speaking. Be aware if you resist such criticism, then let go of your resistance. Listening to feedback will increase your skill.

Journal Entry #54
Intention Statement

Participating in class is an excellent way to practice speaking in public. Write an Intention Statement concerning how you intend to participate in class in order to experience talking to a group of people. Be specific about which class you intend to speak in, how you will set up the opportunity to speak (i.e having questions ready, sitting in front, asking to give a presentation, etc.), and how you intend to record your observations of the experience.

I intend to . . .

Journal Entry #55
Discovery Statement

Think back to a time when you were called upon to answer a question in class or speak before a group. Write down what you remember about that situation. Describe your physical sensations, the effectiveness of your presentation, feedback from the audience, etc.

Be a fool

A POWERFUL PERSON HAS THE COURAGE TO BE A FOOL. This idea can work for you because you already are a fool. Don't be upset. All of us are fools, at one time or another. There are no exceptions. If you doubt it, think back to that stupid thing you did just a few days ago. You know the one. Yes, that one. It was embarrassing and you tried to hide it. You pretended you weren't a fool. This happens to everyone.

People who insist they have never been fools are perhaps the biggest fools of all. We are all fallible human beings. Most of us, however, spend too much time and energy trying to hide our fool-hood. No one is really fooled by this—not even ourselves. What's more, whenever we pretend to be something we're not, we miss part of life.

For example, many people never dance because they don't want to look ridiculous. They're not wrong. They probably *will* look ridiculous. That's the secret of being a fool. It's OK to look ridiculous dancing. It's all right to sound silly singing to your kids. Sometimes it's OK to be absurd.

And sometimes it's not. Power Process #7 comes with a warning label: Being a fool does not mean we get to escape responsibility for our actions. "Be a fool" is not a suggestion to get drunk at a party and make a fool of yourself. It is not a suggestion to act the fool by disrupting class. It is not a suggestion to be foolhardy or to "fool around."

"Be a fool" means recognizing that foolishness, along with dignity, courage, cowardice, grace, clumsiness, and other qualities, is a human characteristic. We all share it. You might as well risk being a fool because you already *are* one, and nothing in the world can change that. Why not enjoy it once in a while?

Consider the case of the person who won't dance because she's afraid she'll look foolish. This same person will spend an afternoon tripping over her feet on a basketball court. If you say that her jump shot from the top of the key looks like a circus accident, she might even agree.

"So what?" she might say. "I'm no Michael Jordan." She's right. On the basketball court, she is willing to be a fool in order to enjoy the game.

She is no Ginger Rogers, either. For some reason, *that* bothers her. The result is that she misses the fun of dancing. (Dancing badly is as much fun as shooting baskets badly—and maybe a lot more fun.) Many potential writers quit when they are embarrassed by their first products. Potentially great public speakers have gone undiscovered because they were unwilling to practice and make public mistakes.

Again, remember the warning label. Power Process #7 does not suggest that the way to be happy in life is to do things badly. Mediocrity is not the goal. On the contrary, the prerequisite for mastery in most activities is the willingness to try something new, fail, make corrections, fail again, and so on. On the way to becoming a good writer, be willing to be a bad writer.

Consider these revised cliches: Anything worth doing is worth doing badly at first. Practice makes improvement. If at first you don't fail, try again.

Most artists and athletes have learned the secret of being foolish. Comedians are especially well versed in this art. All of us know how it feels to tell a joke and get complete silence. Our faces get flushed and hot. It feels as though we've been punched in the stomach. We truly look and feel like fools.

Professional comedians risk feeling that way for a living. Being funny is not enough for success in the comedy business. A comedian must have the courage to face failure.

For a student, the willingness to be a fool means the willingness to take risks, to experiment with new skills, to grow. The rewards are expanded creativity, more satisfying self-expression, and more joy.

Here's an experiment you can conduct to experience the joys of fool-hood. The next time you do something silly or stupid, *experience* the feeling. Don't deny it. Don't cover it up. Notice everything about it, including the physical sensations and your inner thoughts. Acknowledge your foolishness. Be exactly who you are. Explore all the emotions, thoughts, images, and sensations surrounding your experience.

And forgive yourself. Know that, at this moment, you are the best that you can be. (At this exact moment, what else can you be but what you are?)

When fully experienced, the fear of being foolish loses its power. Then you have the freedom to expand and grow.

Be willing to be a fool.

William A. Nolen,

surgeon and author, practiced medicine for years. He wrote several popular books and his articles have appeared in many leading magazines.

From A Surgeon's World *by William A. Nolen, M.D. Copyright 1970, 1972 by William A. Nolen, M.D. Reprinted by permission of Random House, Inc.*

In contrast to my four relatively miserable years at Holy Cross, I enjoyed, for the most part, the four years at Tufts Medical School . . .

For almost the first time in my academic career I was studying material that I knew was going to be of value to me the rest of my life. Anatomy was a course that required mostly brute memory. It wasn't easy to remember where the deltoid muscle began, where it ended, what muscles were next to it, and what blood vessels and nerves nourished it and made it work, but I could see the practicality of having all that information tucked away in my mind. So I studied, not only because I wanted a decent grade but because I wanted to be a knowledgeable doctor.

Like most pre-med students I had resented the time I spent in college on subjects which seemed unrelated to my future as a doctor. I know now that my attitude was based in immaturity. College is a place where a student ought to learn not so much how to make a living, but how to live. In the 1970's we're trying to reduce the time a man has to spend becoming a doctor. Some medical schools will accept students after three years of college—others are combining the fourth year of medical school with the internship. It's possible in some programs to acquire an M.D. degree six years after high school graduation, rather than the usual eight.

The purpose in shortening medical education is to produce more doctors. Personally, I don't think it will work. With every year that passes there is more and more knowledge that a doctor should have. How in the world can we expect students to learn more in less time?

What will happen, I'm afraid, is that we'll start producing pure technicians. If anything is to be eliminated from the would-be doctor's education, it won't be biochemistry, anatomy or pharmacology; it will be the course in Shakespeare, the year of philosophy, the semesters of French. One of the major problems in medicine now is that doctors tend to have depth but not breadth to their knowledge. There is a saying, well known to all medical students, that the General Practitioner is a doctor who learns less and less about more and more, until he eventually knows nothing about everything; the specialist is the man who learns more and more about less and less, until he eventually knows everything about nothing. This is the age of the specialist, and because their interests are so narrow, the specialists tend to see patients as faceless carriers of disease, technical problems to be solved, rather than as human beings. What we need in medicine are doctors who are more the artist and less the scientist. I don't think that shortening medical education will produce them.

1. Explain what is meant in this chapter by "Aha!"

2. It is important to list and schedule all writing tasks before you do any initial research when writing a paper. True or false. Explain your answer.

3. What are at least three methods that can assist you to write the first draft of a paper?

4. "Free writing" refers to catalogues that are available in most libraries. True or false. Explain your answer.

5. An "Aha!" happens:

   A) through luck.
   B) through persistence.
   C) spontaneously.
   D) through a step-by-step process.
   E) all of the above.

6. Guidelines for brainstorming do *not* include:

    (A) formulating the issue or problem precisely.
    (B) setting a time limit for your brainstorm.
    (C) Write down only those ideas that make sense.
    (D) Before you begin, sit quietly for a few seconds to collect your thoughts.
    (E) Allow wild and crazy ideas.

7. Define serendipity and give an example.

8. What are the four recommended steps for evaluating your own views as well as the views of others?

9. How does the text recommend using the "cheap word processor?"

10. Describe at least three techniques for practicing and delivering a speech.

Journal Entry #56
Discovery Statement

Review this chapter and then list the creativity techniques you already use.

    I discovered that I . . .

_____

_____

_____

Journal Entry #57
Intention Statement

Think about a specific problem you have in creating papers or speeches and write about what you will do to solve that problem.

    I intend to . . .

_____

_____

_____

Journal Entry #58
Intention Statement

Choose two techniques from this chapter and descibe when and where you will use them.

    I intend to . . .

_____

_____

_____

Exercise #25
Master mind map

    On a separate sheet of paper, create a mind map of the first six chapters of this book. Do this without reviewing. (Don't even look up chapter titles.) This exercise is for you to demonstrate to yourself how much material you retain. You might be surprised by the results.

Chapter

8

Relationships

You have two ears and one mouth.
Remember to use them in more or less that proportion.
PAULA BERN

Candor is a compliment; it implies equality.
It's how true friends talk.
PEGGY NOONAN

Journal Entry #59
Discovery Statement

After previewing this chapter, complete the following sentence.
What I want from this chapter is . . .

In this chapter . . .

Our success in school and on the job hinges on skill in relating to other people. Chapter Eight explores the subject of relationships in detail.

Communication is a circular, give-and-take process. *The communication loop* suggests how misunderstandings can begin in the process of creating messages. Both *Listening* and *Sending your message* suggest how you can prevent and resolve misunderstanding.

Making promises and keeping agreements is one of the most powerful ways to keep relationships working well. We can also use our speaking to transform our lives. *Power Process #8: Employ your word* explains how to begin this process.

Relationships have cycles and seasons of their own. Understanding this in advance can help you enjoy the highs and cope with the heartaches. *Relationships can work* and *Relationships change* suggest how.

Developing effective relationships with instructors is one of the most powerful strategies for success in school. Learn practical suggestions for doing so in *Create your instructor*.

The number of people from diverse races and cultures continues to increase in our classrooms and workplaces. *Communicating across cultures* can promote your success. So can *Dealing with sexism and sexual harassment*.

There's a line between *Assertion and aggression*. Knowing the difference can help you get your ideas across without stepping on others.

What to do with the four C's suggests how you can respond effectively to conflict, complaints, criticism—and compliments.

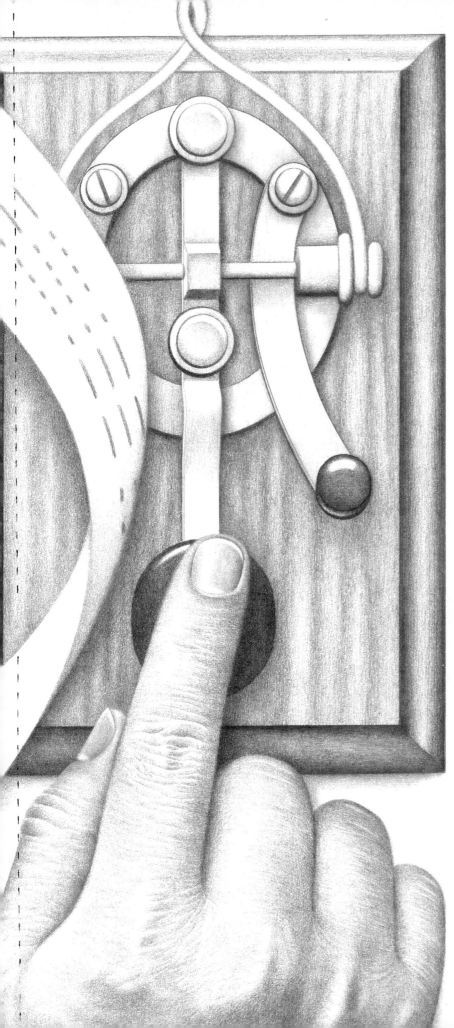

The communication loop

COMMUNICATION IS OFTEN GARBLED when we try to send and receive messages at the same time. One effective way to improve your ability to communicate is to be aware of when you are the receiver and when you are the sender. If you are receiving (listening), then just receive. Avoid switching into the sending mode. When you are sending (talking), then stick with it until you are done.

If the other person is trying to send a message when you want to be the sender, you have at least three choices: Stop sending and be the receiver, stop sending and leave, or ask the other person to stop sending so you can send. It is ineffective to try to send and receive at the same time.

This becomes clear when we look at what happens in a conversation. When we talk, we put thoughts into words. Words are a code for what we experience. This is called encoding. The person who receives the message takes our words and translates them into his own experience. This is called decoding.

A conversation between two people is like communication between two telegraph operators. One encodes a message and sends it over the wire. The operator at the other end receives the coded signal, decodes it, evaluates it, and sends back another coded message. The first operator decodes this message and sends another. The cycle continues. The messages look like this:

..--..--.-.-   --.--..---   OPERATOR 1

--.-..-..   -..- --...-. OPERATOR 2

In this encoding-decoding loop you continually switch roles. One minute you send; the next, you receive. It's a problem when both operators send at the same time. Neither operator knows what the other one sent. Neither can reply. Communication works best when each of us has a complete chance to send, sufficient time to comprehend, and plenty of time to respond.

There are other problems in communication. Only a small percentage of communication is verbal. All of us send messages with our bodies and with the tone of our voices. Throw in a few other factors, like a hot room or background noise, and it's a wonder we communicate at all.

Another problem is that the message sent is often not the message received. This process of continually encoding and decoding words can result in the simplest message being muddled. For some, "chair" conjures up the image of an overstuffed, rocking recliner. Others visualize a metal folding chair. And some people think of the person who "chairs" a meeting. If simple things like this can be misunderstood, it's easy to see how more complex ideas can wreak havoc on communication. For example, a "good teacher" can mean someone who is smart, entertaining, easy, challenging, attractive—or a hundred other things.

Communicating effectively means getting on the same wave length. Even then, it helps to keep checking with each other to make sure we are talking about the same thing.

These difficulties are never fully overcome. They can be partially alleviated by using effective communication techniques and by having a sincere intention to understand one another.

Listening

The communication loop

You observe a person in a conversation who is not talking. Is he listening? Maybe. Maybe not. He may be preparing his response or daydreaming.

Listening is not easy. Doing it effectively requires concentration and energy

It's worth it. Listening well promotes success in school—more powerful notes, more productive study groups, better relationships with students and instructors. A skilled listener is appreciated by friends, family, and business associates. The best salespeople and managers are the best listeners. People love a good listener. Through skilled listening, you gain more than respect. You gain insight into other people. You learn about the world and about yourself.

To be a good listener, decide to listen. Once you've made this choice, you can use the following techniques to be a more effective listener. These ideas are especially useful in times of high emotional tension.

NONVERBAL LISTENING
Much of listening is nonverbal. Here are five guidelines for effective nonverbal listening.

1. Be quiet. Silence is more than staying quiet while someone is speaking. Allowing several seconds to pass before you begin to talk gives the speaker time to catch his breath or gather his thoughts. He may want to continue. Someone who talks non-stop might fear he will lose the floor if he pauses.

If the message being sent is complete, this short break gives you time to form your response and helps you avoid the biggest barrier to listening—listening with your answer running. If you make up a response before the person is finished, you miss the end of the message—which is often the main point.

Pausing for several seconds might be inappropriate. Ignore this suggestion completely when someone asks in a panic where to find the nearest phone to call the fire department.

2. Maintain eye contact. Look at the other person while he speaks. It demonstrates your attention and it helps keep your mind from wandering. Your eyes also let you "listen" to body language and behavior. When some of us remove our glasses, we not only can't see—we can't hear.

Avoid staring too long. The speaker might think he is talking to a zombie. Act appropriately.

This idea is not an absolute. People from some cultures are uncomfortable with sustained eye contact. Others learn primarily by hearing; they can listen more effectively by turning off the visual input once in a while. Keep in mind the differences between people.

3. Display openness. You can communicate openness by your facial expression and body position. Uncross your arms and legs. Sit up straight. Face the other person and remove any physical barriers between you, such as a pile of books.

4. Listen without response. This doesn't mean you should never respond. It means wait.

When listening to another person, we often interrupt with our stories, opinions, suggestions, and inappropriate comments:

"Oh, I'm so excited. I just found out that I am nominated to be in *Who's Who in American Musicians.*"

"Yeah, that's neat. My uncle Elmer got into *Who's Who in American Veterinarians.* He sure has an interesting job. One time I went along when he was

treating a cow and . . . ."

Watch your nonverbal response, too. A look of "Good grief!" from you can keep the other person from finishing his message.

5. Send acknowledgments. Periodically it is important to let the speaker know you are still there. Your words or nonverbal gestures of acknowledgment let the speaker know you are interested and that you are with him and his message. These include "Umhum," "OK," "yes," and head nods.

These acknowledgments do not imply your agreement. If people tell you what they don't like about you, your head nod doesn't mean you agree. It just indicates that you are listening.

VERBAL LISTENING

Sometimes speaking promotes listening.

1. Feed back meaning. Paraphrase the communication. This does not mean parroting what another person says. Instead, briefly summarize. Feed back what you see as the essence of that person's message. "Let me see if I understood what you said . . ." or, "What I'm hearing you say is . . ."

Often the other person will say, "No, that's not what I meant. What I said was . . ."

There will be no doubt when you get it right. The sender will say, "Yeah, that's it," and either continues with another message or stops sending when he knows you understand.

If you don't understand the message, be persistent. Ask the person to please repeat what he said; then paraphrase it again. Effective communication involves a feedback loop.

Be concise. This is not a time to stop the other person by talking on and on about what you think you heard.

2. Listen beyond words. Be aware of nonverbal messages and behavior. You may point out that the speaker's body language seems to be the exact opposite of his words. For example, "I noticed you said you are excited, but you look very bored."

Keep in mind that the same nonverbal behavior can have different meanings, depending on the listener's cultural background. Someone who looks bored may simply be listening in a different way.

The idea is to listen not only to the words, but to the emotion behind the words. Sometimes that emotional message is more important than the verbal content.

3. Take care of yourself. People seek out good listeners, and there are times when you don't want to listen. You may be busy or distracted with your own concerns. Be honest. Don't pretend to listen. You can say, "What you're saying is important, and I'm pressed for time right now. Can we set aside another time to talk about this?" It's OK not to listen.

4. Listen for requests and intentions. "This class is a waste of time." "Our instructor talks too fast." An effective way to listen to complaints is to look for the request hidden in them.

"This class is a waste of my time" can be heard as, "Please tell me what I'll gain if I participate actively in class?" "The instructor talks too fast" can become, "What strategies can I use for taking notes when the instructor covers the material rapidly?"

We can even transform complaints into intentions. Take the complaint, "The parking lot by the dorms is so dark at night that I'm afraid to go to my car." This complaint can result in a project—installing a light in the parking lot.

Viewing complaints this way gives us more choices. When the complaint becomes a request or an intention, we can decide whether to grant the request or take on the project. That's more powerful than responding to complaint with defensiveness ("What does he know anyway?"), resignation ("It's always been this way and always will"), or indifference ("It's not my job").

Sending

The communication loop

We have been talking for years, and we usually manage to get our message across. There are times, though, when we don't. Often these times are emotionally charged. Sometimes we feel wonderful or rotten or sad or scared and we want to express it. Emotions can get in the way of the message. Described below are four techniques for delivering a message through tears, laughter, fist-pounding, or hugging. They are: Replacing "You" messages with "I" messages, avoiding questions that aren't really questions, noticing nonverbal messages, and noticing barriers to communication.

The "I's" have it!

It can be difficult to disagree with someone without his becoming angry or your becoming upset. When conflict occurs, we often make statements about the other person, or "You" messages:

"You are rude."

"You make me mad."

"You must be crazy."

"You don't love me anymore."

This kind of communication results in defensiveness. The response might be:

"I am not rude."

"I don't care."

"No, *you* are crazy."

"No, *you* don't love *me!*"

"You" messages are hard to listen to. They label, judge, blame, and assume things that may or may not be true. They demand rebuttal. Sometimes even praise can be an ineffective "You" message. "You" messages don't work.

When communication is emotionally charged, consider limiting your statements to descriptions about yourself. Replace "You" messages with "I" messages.

For example:

"You are rude" might become "I feel upset."

"You make me mad" could be "I feel angry."

"You must be crazy" can be "I don't understand."

"You don't love me anymore" could become "I'm afraid we're drifting apart."

Suppose a friend asks you to pick him up at the airport. You drive 20 miles and wait for the plane. No friend. You decide your friend missed his plane, so you wait three hours for the next flight. No friend. Perplexed and worried, you drive home. The next day, you see your friend downtown.

"What happened?" you ask.

"Oh, I caught an earlier flight."

"You are a rude person," you reply.

Look for the facts, the observable behavior. Everyone will agree that your friend asked you to pick him up; he did take an earlier flight; you did not receive a call from him. But the idea that he is "rude" is not a fact, it's a judgment.

He may go on to say, "I called your home and no one answered. My mom had a stroke and was rushed to Valley View. I caught the earliest flight I could get." Your judgment no longer fits.

When you saw your friend, you might have said, "I waited and waited at the airport. I was worried about you. I didn't get a call. I feel angry and hurt. I don't want to waste my time. Next time, you can call me when your flight arrives and I'll be happy to come get you."

"I" messages don't judge, blame, criticize, or insult. They don't invite the other person to counterattack with more of the same. "I" messages are also more accurate. They report our own thoughts and feelings.

"I" messages may feel uncomfortable or forced at first. That's OK. Use the "Five ways to say 'I'" on the next page. With practice, you'll feel more at home with this technique.

Questions are not always questions

You've heard these "questions" before. A parent asks, "Don't you want to look nice?" Translation: "I wish you'd cut your hair, lose the blue jeans, and put on a tie." Or how about this question from a spouse: "Honey, wouldn't you love to go to an exciting hockey game tonight?" Translation: "I already bought the tickets."

We use questions that aren't questions to sneak our opinions and requests into conversations, without owning up to them publicly.

"Doesn't it upset you?" means "It upsets me," and "Shouldn't we hang the picture over here?" means "I want to hang the picture over here."

Communication improves when we say, "I'm upset," "Let's hang the picture up here," and "The game begins at eight."

Noticing nonverbal messages

How you say something can be more important than what you say.

Your tone of voice and your gestures can support, modify, or contradict your words. Your posture, the way you dress, how often you shower, and even the poster hanging on your wall can negate your words before you say them.

Most nonverbal behavior is unconscious. We can learn to be aware of it. Then we can choose our nonverbal messages. The key is to be clear about our intention and purpose. When we know what we want to say and are committed to getting it across, our inflections, gestures, and words work together and send a unified message.

Notice barriers to sending your message

Sometimes fear stops us from sending messages. We are afraid of other people's reactions, sometimes justifiably. Being truthful doesn't mean being insensitive to others' reactions. Tact is a virtue; letting fear prevent communication is not.

Assumptions also can be used as excuses for not sending messages. "He already knows this," we tell ourselves. "I told him last week." You may have sent the message last week, but sometimes people don't receive messages and sometimes they don't remember. Reminders can be useful.

Predictions of failure also can be barriers to sending. "He won't listen," we tell ourselves. That statement may be inaccurate. Perhaps the other person senses that we're angry and listens in a guarded way. Or perhaps the other person *is* listening and sending nonverbal messages we don't understand.

Or we might predict, "He'll never do anything about it if I tell him." Again, assuming can kill your message before you send it.

It's easy to make excuses for not communicating. If you have fear or some other concern about sending a message, be aware of it. Don't expect the concern to go away. Realize that you can communicate even with your concerns. You can choose to make them a part of the message. "I am going to tell you how I feel, and I'm afraid you will think it's stupid."

Talking to someone when you don't want to could be a matter of educational survival. A short talk with an advisor, teacher, friend, or family member may solve a problem that jeopardizes your education.

Notice your barriers and make choices that promote your success.

Five ways to say "I"

An "I" message can include any or all of the following five parts. The more you include, the more effective your message.

1. Observations

Describe the facts—the indisputable, observable realities. Talk about what you—or anyone else—can see, hear, smell, taste, or touch. Avoid judgments, interpretations, or opinions. Instead of saying, "You're a slob," say, "Last night's lasagna pan was still on the stove this morning."

2. Feelings

Describe your own feelings. It is easier to listen to, "I feel frustrated" than "You never help me." Talking about how you feel about another's actions can be valuable feedback for that person.

3. Thoughts

Communicate your thoughts, and use caution. Just because your statement begins with an "I" doesn't qualify it as an "I" message. "I think you are a slob" is a "You" judgment in disguise. Instead, say, "I'd have more time to study if I didn't have to clean up so often."

4. Wants

You are far more likely to get what you want if you say what you want. If someone doesn't know what you want, he doesn't have a choice about helping you get it. Ask clearly. Avoid demanding or using the word "need." Most people like to feel helpful, not obligated. Instead of, "Do the dishes when it's your turn, or else!" say, "I want to divide the housework fairly."

5. Intentions

The last part of an "I" message is a statement about what you intend to do. Have a plan that doesn't depend on the other person. For example, instead of, "From now on we're going to split the dishwashing evenly," you could say, "I intend to do my share of the housework and leave the rest undone."

Exercise #26
Write an "I" message

Pick something about school that irritates you. Pretend you are talking to the person who is associated with this irritation.

First, write what you would say as a "You" message.

_____

_____

_____

_____

_____

Now, write the same complaint as an "I" message. Include all of the elements suggested in "Five ways to say 'I'."

_____

_____

_____

_____

_____

_____

Journal Entry #60
Discovery/Intention Statement

Think about one of your relationships for a few minutes. It might be with a parent, sibling, spouse, child, friend, hairdresser, etc.

Next, write about some things that are not working in the relationship. What bugs you? What do you find irritating or unsatisfying?

_____

_____

_____

Now, think for a moment, about what you want from this relationship? More attention? Less nagging? More openness, trust, security, money, or freedom?

After deciding what you want from the relationship, describe a suggestion from this chapter you could use to make the relationship work.

_____

_____

_____

Employ your word

WHEN YOU SPEAK and give your word, you are creating—literally. Your speaking brings life to your values and purpose. In large part, others know who you are by the words you speak and the agreements you make. You can learn who you are by observing which commitments you choose to make and which ones you avoid.

Giving your word makes things happen. Circumstances, events, and attitudes fall into place. The resources needed to accomplish whatever was promised become available. What makes it happen is promising a result.

The person you are right now is, for the most part, a result of the choices and agreements you've made in your life. Your future is largely determined by the choices and agreements you make from now on. Giving your word is a big step in creating your future.

The world works by agreement

There are over five billion people on planet Earth. We live on different continents, in different nations, and communicate in different languages. We have diverse political ideologies and subscribe to various social and moral codes.

This complex planetary network is held together by people keeping their word. Agreements minimize confusion, prevent social turmoil, and keep order. Projects are finished, goods are exchanged, and treaties are made. People, organizations, and nations know what to expect when agreements are kept. When people keep their word, the world works.

Agreements are the foundation of many things that are often taken for granted. Words, our basic tool of communication, work only because we agree about their meanings. A pencil is a pencil only because everyone agrees to call a thin wood-covered column of graphite a pencil. We could just as easily call them ziddles. Then you might hear someone say, "Do you have an extra ziddle? I forgot mine."

Money exists only by agreement. If we leave a $100 MONOPOLY bill (play money) on a park bench next to a real $100 bill (backed by the U.S. Treasury), one is more likely to disappear than the other. The only important difference between the two pieces of paper is that everyone agrees that one can be exchanged for goods and services and the other cannot. Shopkeepers will sell merchandise for the "real" $100 bill because they trust a continuing agreement.

Relationships work by agreement

Relationships are built on agreements. They begin with our most intimate personal contacts and move through all levels of families, organizations, communities, and nations.

When we break a promise to be faithful to a spouse, to help a friend move to a new apartment, or to pay a bill on time, relationships are strained and the consequences can be painful. When we keep our word, relationships are more likely to be satisfying and harmonious. Expectations of trust and accountability develop. Others are more likely to keep their promises to us.

Perhaps our most important relationship is the one we have with ourselves. Trusting ourselves to keep our word is enlivening. As we experience success, our self-confidence increases.

When we commit to complete an assignment, and then keep our word, our understanding of the subject improves. So does our grade. We experience satisfaction and success. If we break our word, we create a gap in our learning, a lower grade, and possibly a self-degrading feeling.

How to make and keep agreements

Being cautious about making promises can improve the quality of our lives. Making only those promises that we fully intend to keep improves the likelihood of reaching our goals. It helps to ask ourselves what level of commitment we have to a particular promise.

At the same time, if we are willing to risk, we can open new doors and increase our possibilities for success. The only way to be certain we keep all of our agreements is either to make none, or to make only those that are absolutely guaranteed. In either case, we are cheating ourselves. Some of the most powerful promises we can make are those that we have no idea how to keep. We can stretch ourselves and set goals that are both high and realistic.

If we break an agreement, we can choose to be gentle with ourselves. We can be courageous, quickly admit our mistake to the people involved, and consider ways to deal with the consequences.

Examining our agreements can improve our effectiveness. Perhaps we took on too much—or too little. Perhaps we did not use all the resources that were available to us— or we used too many. Perhaps we did not fully understand what we were promising. When we learn from both our mistakes and

successes, we become more effective at employing our word.

Move up the ladder of powerful speaking

The words used to talk about whether or not something will happen fall into several different levels. We can think of each level as one rung on a ladder—the ladder of powerful speaking. As we move up the ladder, our speaking becomes more effective.

The lowest rung on the ladder is obligation. Words used at this level include "I should", "He ought to", "Someone better", "They should", "I must", and "I had to." Speaking this way implies that people and circumstances other than ourselves are in control of our lives. When people live at the level of obligation, they often feel passive and helpless to change anything.

When we move to the next rung, we leave behind the world of obligation and step into the world of self-generation. All of the rungs to come can build on and reinforce each other. Rather than leaving them behind, we can rely on them as we move up the ladder of powerful speaking.

The next rung up is possibility. At this level, we examine new options. We play with new ideas, possible solutions, and alternate courses of action. As we do so, we learn that we can make choices that dramatically affect the quality of our lives. We are not the victims of circumstance. Phrases that signal this level include "I might," "I could," "I'll consider," "I hope to," and "maybe."

Above possibility is a rung called passion. Again, certain words signal this level: "I want to," "I'm really excited to do that," "I can't wait." Possibility and passion are both exciting places to be. Even at these levels, though, we're still far from action. Many people want things and have no specific plan to get them.

Action comes with the next rung: planning. When people use phrases such as "I intend to," "My goal is to," and "I'll try like mad to," they're at the level of planning. The Intention Statements you write in this book are examples of planning.

The highest rung on the ladder is promising. This is where the power of your word really comes into play. At this level, it's common to use phrases such as these: "I will", "I promise to", "I am committed", "You can count on it." This is where we bridge from possibility and planning to action. Promising brings with it all the risks—and all the benefits—of keeping your word.

ASSERTION AND AGGRESSION

To get what we want, we communicate. Whether we want to order a chicken salad sandwich, convince someone of the merits of a democratic form of government, or request a reevaluation of a test grade, we want to express it in a way that will get results. To do this, we use either assertive or aggressive behavior.

Aggressive behavior is not generally effective in relationships. People who act aggressively are domineering. They get what they want by putting other people down. When they win, other people lose.

Assertive behavior is a sign of a healthy, strong personality. Assertive people are confident and respectful of others as well as themselves. They ask directly for what they want without feeling embarrassed or inadequate. When they don't get what they want, their self-esteem does not suffer.

Here are five guidelines for acting assertively:

1. Ask specifically for what you want. Be willing to do this more than once, with more than one person.
2. Know that you are worthy, and so are your opinions and desires.
3. Be open-minded and tolerant. Others' opinions and desires are also worthy.
4. Use effective communication techniques. ("I" messages are explained in this chapter.)
5. Expect to get what you want. If you feel apologetic about asking for it, notice that feeling and let it go.

Many people don't act assertively for fear they will appear aggressive. However, passive behavior—neither assertive nor aggressive—can get us nowhere. By remaining quiet and submissive, we allow others to infringe on our rights. When others run our lives, we fail to have the lives we want. The alternative is to ask for what we want, appropriately and assertively.

Exercise #27
V.I.P.'s (Very Important Persons)

Step 1

Under the column below titled "Name," write the names of at least five people who have influenced your life. They may be relatives, friends, teachers, or perhaps someone you have never met. (Complete each step before moving on.)

Step 2

In the next column, rate your gratitude for this person's influence. (From 1 to 5: 1-a little grateful, 5-extremely grateful.)

Step 3

In the third column, rate how fully you have communicated your appreciation to this person. (Again, 1 to 5: 1-not communicated, 5-fully communicated.)

Step 4

In the final column, put a "U" beside the persons with whom you have unfinished business (important communication that you have not taken an opportunity to send).

Name	Grateful (1-5)	Communicated (1-5)	U?
1.			
2.			
3.			
4.			
5.			
6.			
7.			
8.			

Step 5

Now, select two persons with U's beside their names and write them a letter. Express the love, tenderness, and joy you feel towards them. Tell them exactly how they have helped change your life and how you are glad they did.

Step 6

You also have an impact on others. Make a list of people whose lives you have influenced. Consider sharing with these people why you enjoy being part of their lives.

Communicating across cultures

*T*hose of us who can study, work, and live with people from other cultures and races can enjoy more success in school, on the job, and in our neighborhoods. This means learning new ways to think, speak, and act. Communicating across cultures opens up a myriad of possibilities and an education in itself. It can be frightening, frustrating, or even painful at first. It can also be exciting, enriching, and affirming.

No longer will our classrooms, offices, and factories be dominated by white male faces. Each of them will become a "rainbow coalition" of people from many different cultures and races. By the year 2056, the "average" U.S. resident will list his or her ancestry as African, Asian, Hispanic, or Arabic—not white European. In many city school systems, white students are already a minority in numbers. This is not resulting from government policy or pressure from social action groups. It simply is a fact—one for which many people feel ill-prepared.

The cultures of the world meet daily. Several forces are shrinking our globe. One is the growth of a world economy. Another is the "electronic village"—the links across nations forged by newspapers, radios, televisions, telephones, fax machines, and computers.

We have an opportunity to prepare for and benefit from this change instead of merely reacting to it. At one time, only sociologists and futurists talked about the meeting of cultures. Now all of us can enter this conversation. We can value cultural diversity and learn how to thrive with it.

We have always been diverse

We have always lived with people of different races and cultures. Many of us come from families who immigrated to the United States or Canada just two or three generations ago. What's more, the things we eat, the tools we use, and the words we speak are a cultural tapestry woven by many different peoples.

Think about a common daily routine. An American citizen awakens in a bed (an invention from the Near East). After dressing in clothes (from Italy), he eats breakfast on plates (made in China), eats a banana (grown in Honduras), and brews coffee (shipped from Nicaragua). And after breakfast he reads the morning newspaper (printed by a process invented in Germany upon paper, originally made in China). Then he flips on a tape player (made in Japan) and listens to music (performed by a band from Cuba).

Diversity is valuable

Today we are waking up not only to the fact of diversity but to the *value* of diversity. This is a central value of education: learning alternative viewpoints; seeing a question from different angles;

watching people come up with different strategies for solving the same problem.

When we look at the world through the eyes of another culture, we "walk a mile in the other's moccasins." This is something that art, literature, and music can inspire us to do. In the process, our own view of the world becomes broader, more complete, and more inclusive. We can learn much about ourselves when we take the time and energy to learn about others. The goal is to see that we are part of a complex world—that our culture is different from, not better than, others. Knowing this, we can stop saying "This is *the* way to work, learn, relate to others, and view the world." Instead, we can say, "Here is my way. Now what is yours?"

Awareness of other cultures is a habit

According to management consultant Stephen R. Covey, a *habit* is the point where desire, knowledge, and skill meet. Desire is about *wanting* to do something. Knowledge is seeing *what* to do. And skill is understanding *how* to do it. These three factors are equally important.

Communicating with people of other cultures is a habit, fusing desire, knowledge, and skill. What follows are suggestions in each of these three areas. Many of them apply equally to overcoming others' barriers of bias, including sexism, ageism, and discrimination against people with disabilities.

Desire to communicate across cultures

When our actions are truly grounded in the *intention* to understand others, we can be much more effective. Knowing techniques for communicating across cultures is valuable. Yet these cannot take the place of the sincere desire and commitment to create understanding. Without this desire, techniques will ring false.

Consider a politician who seeks your vote in the next election. You meet him, and he shakes your hand firmly. He makes eye contact with you and uses your name several times while you converse about the issues.

Even though he's using all the "right" listening skills, you still might not feel you've truly been heard. You may feel he's listening because he feels obligated to, or merely because he wants your vote. The techniques may be present; the desire to understand you may not.

A close friend can be a more effective listener than the politician, even though he's not taken any workshops in communication. The difference is that your friend's listening is rooted in the intention to understand you.

Prescriptions for communicating across cultures—generic "do's" and "don'ts"—may not work without the intention to understand. If you see the value of cultural diversity, you will discover and create ways to build bridges to other people.

Know about other cultures

People from different cultures read differently, write differently, think differently, love differently, and learn differently than you. Knowing this, you can be more effective with your classmates, co-workers, and neighbors.

Cultures differ in many dimensions. One of the most important dimensions is *style*. For example, there are real differences in the way people perceive and learn information. An African tribesman may look at a photograph and see only a pattern of black and white dots, not a picture of himself. This is one example of a cognitive style. We can also speak of learning styles, communication styles, relationship styles, and other styles.

James Anderson, a professor at Indiana University of Pennsylvania, speaks of the relationship between *analytic* and *relational* styles. Most of our schools favor students with an analytical style. These students learn abstract concepts easily and are adept at reading, writing, and discussing ideas. They can learn parts of a subject even if they don't have a view of the whole. Often these students are self-directed, and their performance is not affected by the opinions of others.

A bias toward the analytical style tends to exclude students with a relational style. Students with relational styles learn by getting the big picture of a subject before the details. They learn better initially by speaking, listening, and doing, rather than by reading or writing. These students prefer to learn about subjects that relate to their

concerns or about subjects presented in a lively, humorous way. In addition, they are influenced by the opinions of people they value and respect. All these things point to a unique learning style.

Differing styles exist in every aspect of life—family structure, religion, relationships with authority, and more. Native Americans might avoid confrontation and seek mediators to resolve conflict. People from certain Asian cultures might feel it's rude to ask questions. Knowing about such differences can help you avoid misunderstanding.

Today there is a wealth of material about cultural diversity. Begin with an intention to increase your sensitivity to other cultures. Be willing to ask questions and share ideas with all kinds of people. You can learn something valuable from anyone if you are willing to reach out.

Remember, too, that general stereotypes are not always useful. Members of the same culture or race vary greatly from each other. Not all African Americans

will learn in the same way, nor will all Native Americans, white Americans, or Asian Americans. People within the same ethnic or racial group are still individuals.

Gain skill in communicating across cultures

With the desire to communicate and some knowledge of other cultures, you can work on specific skills. Some possibilities follow.

Be active

Learning implies activity. Learning how to communicate across cultures is no exception. It's ineffective to assume that this skill will come to you merely by being in the same classrooms with people from other races and ethnic groups. It's not their responsibility to raise your cultural awareness. That job is yours, and it calls for effort. The other suggestions listed here will get you started.

Look for common ground

Some goals cross culture lines. Many students, for example, want to succeed in school and prepare for a career. They share the same teachers. They have access to many of the same resources at school. They meet in the classroom, on the athletic field, and at cultural events. To promote cultural understanding, we can become aware of and celebrate our differences. We can also return to our common ground.

A related strategy is to cultivate friends from other cultures. Do this through volunteer work, serving on committees, or joining study groups—any activity where people from other cultures are also involved. In this way, your understanding of other people unfolds in a natural, spontaneous way.

Assume differences in meaning

Each day, we can make an intention to act and speak with the awareness that cultures differ. To do so, look for other possible meanings of your words and actions. Assume such meanings exist, even if you don't know what they are. After speaking to anyone, avoid the assumption that you've been understood—or that you fully understand the other person.

This extends to actions as well as words. The same action can have different meanings at different times, even for members of the same culture.

Look for individuals, not group representatives

Sometimes the way we speak glosses over differences among individuals and reinforces stereotypes. For example, a student worried about his grade in math expresses concern over "all those Asian students who are skewing the class curve." Or, a white music major assumes that his African American classmate knows a lot about jazz. We can avoid such errors by seeing people as individuals—not spokespersons for an entire group.

Get inside another culture

You may find yourself fascinated by one particular culture. Consider learning as much about it as possible. Immerse yourself in that culture. Read novels, see plays, go to concerts, listen to music, look at art, take courses. Seek out opportunities to speak with members of that culture. Your knowledge will be an opening to conversation.

Find a culture "broker"

Diane de Anda, a professor at the University of California, Los Angeles, speaks of three kinds of people who can communicate across cultures. She calls them *translators*, *mediators*, and *models*.

A translator is someone who is truly bicultural—a person who relates skillfully to people in a mainstream culture and people from a contrasting culture. This person can share his own experiences in overcoming discrimination, learning another language or dialect, and coping with stress. He can point out differences in

meaning between cultures and help resolve conflict.

Mediators are people who belong to the dominant or mainstream culture. Unlike translators, they may not be bicultural. However, mediators value diversity and are committed to cultural understanding. Often they are teachers, counselors, tutors, mentors, or social workers.

Models are members of a culture who set a positive example. They are students from any racial or cultural group who participate in class and demonstrate effective study habits. Models can also include entertainers, athletes, and community leaders.

Your school may have people that serve these functions, even if they're not labeled translators, mediators, or models. Some schools have mentor or "bridge" programs that pair new students with teachers of the same race or culture. Students in these programs get coaching in study skills and life skills; they also develop friendships with a possible role model. Ask your student counseling service about such programs.

Celebrate your own culture

Learning about other cultures does not mean abandoning your own. You could gain new appreciation for it. You might see how your culture's assumptions and customs have shaped your world view. You might become aware of shortcomings in your own culture. And you can gain new appreciation for another culture.

Ask for help

If you're unsure about how well you're communicating, ask questions. "I don't know how to make this idea clear for you. How do you learn best?" "When you look away from me during our conversation, I feel uneasy. Is there something else we need to talk about?" "None of you are asking questions. Does this mean the idea is clear to everybody, or do you want more explanation?" Questions like these can get cultural differences out in the open in a constructive way.

Point out discrimination in institutions

You might see people from another culture ignored in class, passed over in job hiring, under-represented in school organizations, or ridiculed by other students. The only way to stop these actions is to point them out. Federal civil rights laws, as well as the written policies of most schools, ban discrimination on racial and ethnic grounds. If your school receives federal aid, it must set up procedures that protect students against such discrimination. Find out what those procedures are, and use them if necessary.

Be sensitive to organizations you belong to and notice if they support

cultural diversity. Encourage your organization to sponsor a diversity day or create a diversity theme for the year. Find out where and when a multicultural retreat will be sponsored and send leaders of your organization to it.

The price we pay for failure to understand other cultures is racism, prejudice, and bigotry. Each presumes that one person has the right to define all other people. These attitudes cannot withstand the light of knowledge, compassion, and common values—the long-term rewards of learning to communicate across cultures.

Students with disabilities— Ask for what you want

Journal Entry #61
Discovery/Intention Statement

Even the most well-intentioned instructors can forget how to promote learning for people with disabilities (chronic illnesses, physical challenges, and learning disabilities.) That's when it pays for you to speak up. Articles in this chapter present techniques for being assertive, using "I" messages, listening, and other communication skills. All of them can help you succeed in school, and so can the following suggestions.

Use available resources

A wealth of resources already exists to help you find materials, money, and people. To start, check into services offered by your state. Departments of rehabilitation often provide funds for education or can help you find that money. State commissions on disabilities act as clearinghouses that can guide you to services. Many provide assistive equipment and transportation as well.

Also find out about services at your school. Libraries might furnish books in braille or audio tapes for the visually impaired. Many counseling and student health centers offer services for people with disabilities. Some schools offer disability resource centers. Typically these provide interpreters, student assistants, tutors, or alternative educational materials. They may also help resolve conflicts between instructors and students with disabilities.

Speak assertively

Tell instructors when it's appropriate to consider your disability. If you use a wheelchair, for example, ask for appropriate transportation on field trips. If you have a visual disability, ask instructors to speak as they write on the chalkboard. Also ask them to use high-contrast colors and write legibly.

Choose instructors carefully

Meet with your counselor or advisor to design an educational plan—one that takes your disability into account. A key part of this plan is choosing instructors. Ask for recommendations. In addition, interview prospective instructors and sit in on their classes. Express an interest in the class, ask to see a course outline, and discuss any adjustments that could help you successfully complete the course.

Use empowering words

Changing just a few words can make the difference between asking for what you want and apologizing for it. When people refer to disabilities, you might hear words like *special treatment.* Experiment with using *adjustment* and *alternative* instead. The difference between these terms is equality. Asking for an adjustment in an assignment is asking for the right to produce equal work—not for special treatment that changes the assignment.

Ask for appropriate treatment

Many instructors are eager to help you. At times they might go overboard and offer an adjustment you really don't want.

For example, a student who has trouble writing by hand might ask to complete in-class writing assignments on a computer. "OK," the teacher replies, "and take a little extra time. For you there's no rush."

For some students, this is a welcome response. However, for others there is no need for an extended timeline. They can say, "Thank you for thinking of me. I'd prefer to finish the assignment in the time frame alloted for the rest of the class." Such a response acknowledges the instructor's assistance. It also communicates what treatment is appropriate.

Take care of yourself

Many students with chronic illnesses or disabilities find that rest breaks are essential. If this is true for you, write such breaks into your daily or weekly plan.

A related suggestion is to treat yourself with respect. If your health changes in a way that you don't like, avoid berating yourself. Even when you do not choose the conditions in your life, you can choose your attitude toward those conditions. The Power Processes in this book present tools for doing so. Also useful are the First Step, Discovery Wheel, and goal-setting exercises.

It's important to accept compliments and periodically review your accomplishments in school. Fill yourself with affirmation. As you educate yourself, you are attaining mastery.

There are things we think about telling people, but don't. Examine your relationships and complete the following statements.

I realize that I am not communicating about _____ with_____

I realize that I am not communicating about _____ with_____

I realize that I am not communicating about _____ with_____

Now choose one idea from this chapter that can open communication with these people in these areas. Describe how you will use this idea.

Create your instructor

There are "poor" instructors, and there are as many definitions of "poor instructor" as there are students.

For some students, "poor" means boring, rude or insensitive. Or maybe it's an instructor who blows his nose every five minutes, stuffs the dirty Kleenex in his pockets, and wears an aftershave that could halt a hamster at thirty paces.

Maybe it's a teacher who laughs at your questions, sneers at incorrect answers, or writes test questions that could only be answered by someone with a Ph.D.

"Poor" might mean an instructor who refuses to make eye contact with the class, mumbles for two hours straight, and squeaks chalk across the board.

Faced with such facts, you have some choices. One is to label the instructor a "dud," "dweeb," "geek," or "airhead" and let it go at that. When you choose this solution you get to endure class, complain to other students, and wait for a miracle. This choice puts you at the mercy of circumstance. It gives your instructor responsibility for the quality of your education, not to mention responsibility for giving you value for your money.

You do not have to give away your power. Instead, you can take responsibility for your education. Use any of the following techniques to change the way you experience your instructors. In effect, you can "create your instructors." Here's how:

1. Research the instructor. There are formal and informal sources of information you can turn to, before you register for class. One is the school catalog. Alumni magazines or newsletters or the school newspaper may have run articles on teachers. In some schools, students circulate informal evaluations of instructors. Also talk to students who have taken courses from the instructor.

Or introduce yourself to the instructor. Visit him during office hours and ask about the course. He may be willing to give you a course syllabus, sample handouts, or a list of assignments. Doing so can help you get the flavor of the class and clues to his teaching style.

2. Show interest in class. Students give teachers moment-by-moment feedback in class. That feedback comes through posture, eye contact, responses to questions, and participation in class discussions.

If you find a class boring, recreate the instructor through a massive display of interest. Ask lots of questions. Show enthusiasm through nonverbal language—sitting up straight, making eye contact, taking detailed notes. Participate.

Ask classmates to do the same. After class, compliment the teacher on his strengths and share your excitement about the class.

Studies suggest that when teachers expect students to do well, students do better. Use the same theory in reverse, on your instructor. You might be surprised by the results.

3. Take responsibility for your attitudes. Maybe your instructor reminds you of someone you don't like—your annoying uncle Fred, a rude store clerk, or the fifth grade teacher who kept you after school. Your attitudes are in your own head and beyond the instructor's control.

An instructor's beliefs about politics, religion, or feminism are not related to teaching ability. Likewise, using a formal or informal lecture style does not indicate knowledge of subject matter. Knowing such things will help you let go of negative judgments.

4. Get to know the instructor better. You might be missing the strong points of an instructor you don't like. Meet with your instructor during office hours. Ask questions you didn't get answered in class.

Teachers who seem boring in class can be fascinating in person. Prepare to notice your pictures and let them go.

5. Separate liking from learning. You don't have to like an instructor to learn from one. Focus on content instead of form.

Form is the way something is organized or how it's presented. If you sit through a three-hour class irritated at the sound of an instructor's voice, you're focusing on the form of his presentation. When you put aside your concern about his voice and rivet your attention to the points he's making, then you're focusing on content.

Personal preferences can get in the way, too. That happens when you don't like the instructor's clothes, hair style, political views, or taste in music. If you see this happening, note your response without judgment. Then gently return your attention to the class content.

6. Form your own opinion about each instructor. Students talk about teachers, and you may hear conflicting reports. Decide for yourself.

7. Seek alternatives. You may feel more comfortable with another teacher's style or way of organizing the same subject. Consider changing teachers, asking another teacher for help outside of class, or attending an additional section taught by another instructor.

You can also learn from other students, other courses, tutors, study groups, books, and tapes. You can be a master student, even when you have teachers you don't like. Your education is your creation.

8. Avoid excuses. Instructors know them all. Most teachers can see a snow job coming before the first flake hits the ground. Accept responsibility for your own mistakes, and avoid thinking you can fool the professor. When you treat instructors honestly, you are more likely to get the same treatment in return.

9. Submit professional work. Prepare papers and projects as if you were submitting them to an employer. Pay attention to form. Imagine that a promotion and raise will be determined by your work. Instructors often grade hundreds of papers during a term. Your neat, orderly, well-organized paper can lift an instructor's spirits after a long night of deciphering gibberish. And if you make it easy to read your work, your instructor can concentrate on its content.

10. Arrive early for class. You can visit with your instructor and get to know him better. You can review notes and prepare for class. Being on time demonstrates your commitment and interest.

11. Sit up front. This is a simple solution to the problem of instructors who speak softly. Make a conscious effort to keep your eyes either on the instructor's face or on your notes.

When you can hear everything the instructor says, you might discover it is interesting after all. You also might discover that the instructor does look at the class and even ventures a smile once in a while. Voila! You've created a new instructor.

12. Accept criticism. Learn from your teacher's comments about your work. It is a teacher's job to correct. Don't take it personally.

13. Use conference time effectively. Know your instructors' office hours. Some instructors have additional or special hours around exam time.

Instructors are usually happy to answer questions about class content. To get the most out of conference time, be prepared to ask those questions. Bring your notes, text, and other materials you need.

During this session you also can address more difficult subjects, such as grades, attendance policies, lecture styles, term papers, or personality conflicts.

Instead of trying to solve a serious problem in the few minutes before or after class, set up a separate meeting. The instructor might feel uncomfortable discussing the problem in front of the other students.

Using the communication techniques suggested in this chapter can make your conference more effective. For example, imagine how you would react if a student marched into your office and said: "Are you crazy? You gave me a C! Do you hate me?" Judgments like those limit the possibility for effective and open communication. Instead, use "I" messages. Consider saying: "I worked hard on this paper and feel disappointed about my grade. I expected a higher grade. I want to know how I could have improved this paper to get a better grade." It is easier to listen to a complaint about a specific problem than to a personal attack.

Listen without judgment to your instructor's comments. Discuss the issue openly, and be assertive. Ask for what you want.

14. Use course evaluations. Most instructors want to promote student success. Many welcome feedback on their effectiveness from students and will adjust or change teaching strategies that are not working.

In many classes you'll have an opportunity to evaluate the instructor. When you're asked to do so, respond honestly. Write about the aspects of the class that did not work well for you. Offer specific ideas for improvement. Also note what *did* work well.

You also can use conferences during office hours to give your instructor informal feedback. Again, use "I" messages, as described in suggestion #13.

Formal evaluations often come late in the course, after final tests and assignments. This may lead students to gloss over evaluations or give only vague feedback. If you want your feedback to make a difference, treat this evaluation as you would an assignment.

15. Take further steps, if appropriate. Sometimes severe conflicts develop between students and instructors. Feedback from students may not be enough to resolve it. In such cases, you might decide to file a complaint or ask for help from a third party, such as an administrator.

If you do, be prepared to document your case in writing. When talking about the instructor, offer details. Describe specific actions that created problems for the class. Stick to the facts—that is, to events that other class members can verify.

Your school may have specific grievance procedures to use in these cases. Before you act, understand what the policies are.

For example, if you can't resolve a problem after meeting with your instructor, you can talk to the department head or the next level of administration. If you are still unsatisfied and feel your cause is just, go higher. Go to the president of the school if necessary.

You are a consumer of education. You have a right and a responsibility to complain if you think you have been treated unfairly.

COMPLAINTS

Whining, blaming, pouting, kicking, and spitting usually don't get results. Here are some guidelines for complaining effectively.

1. Go to the source. Start with the person who is most directly involved with the problem.

2. Present the facts without blaming anyone. Your complaint will carry more weight if you document those facts. Keep track of names and dates. Note what actions were promised and what results actually occurred.

3. Go up the ladder to people with more responsibility. If you don't get satisfaction at the first level, go to that person's direct supervisor. Requesting a supervisor's name will often get results. Write a letter to the company president.

4. Ask for commitments. When you find someone who is willing to solve your problem, get him to say exactly what he is going to do and when.

5. Use available support. There are dozens of groups, as well as government agencies, willing to get involved in resolving complaints. Contact consumer groups or the Better Business Bureau. Trade associations can sometimes help. Ask city council members, county commissioners, state legislators, and senators and representatives. All of them want your vote, so they usually are eager to help.

6. Take legal action if necessary. Small claims court is relatively inexpensive, and you don't have to hire a lawyer. These courts can handle cases involving small amounts of money (up to $1000 or $2000 usually). Legal aid offices can sometimes answer questions.

7. Don't give up.

CRITICISM

Although receiving criticism is rarely fun, it is often educational. Here are some ways to get the most value from it.

1. Avoid finding fault. When your mind is occupied with finding fault in others, you aren't open to hearing constructive comments about yourself.

2. Take it seriously. Some people laugh or joke to cover their anger or embarrassment at being criticized. Humor can be mistaken for a lack of concern.

3. React to criticism with acceptance. Most people don't enjoy pointing out another's faults. Denial, argument, or joking make it more difficult for them to give honest feedback. You don't have to agree with criticism to accept it calmly.

4. Keep it in perspective. Avoid blowing the criticism out of proportion. The purpose of criticism is to generate positive change and self-improvement. There's no need to beat yourself with it.

5. Listen without defensiveness. You can't hear the criticism if you're busy building your case.

WHAT TO DO WITH THE FOUR C'S

CONFLICT

Conflict can lead to anger, hostility, and further conflict. Or, it can be used as a powerful opportunity for solving problems.

For example, you can handle conflict by denying the problem exists, smoothing it over, or trying to overpower the other person. These lead to win/lose situations. When you resolve conflict through collaboration and compromise, you can achieve win/win solutions. Here are seven steps to transform a conflict into a solution in which both parties win.

1. State the problem. Using "I" messages (page 208), explain the problem. Allow the other person to do the same. You may have different problems. This is the time to clearly define the conflict. It's hard to fix something before everyone agrees on what's broken.

2. Understand all points of view. If you want to defuse tension or defensiveness, set aside your opinions for a moment. Take the time to understand the other points of view. Sum up those points of view in words that the other parties can accept. When people feel they've been heard, they're often more willing to listen.

3. Brainstorm solutions. Dream up as many solutions as you can. Be outrageous. Don't evaluate them. Quantity, not quality, is the key. If you get stuck, restate the problem and continue brainstorming.

4. Evaluate the solutions. Discard the unacceptable ones. This step will require time and honesty. Talk about which solutions will work and how difficult they will be to implement. You may hit upon a totally new solution.

5. Choose the solution. Choose one most acceptable to all. Be honest.

6. Implement. Decide who is going to do what by when. Then keep your agreements.

7. Re-evaluate. Review the effectiveness of your solution. If it works, pat yourselves on the back. If not, be open to making changes or implementing a new solution.

COMPLIMENTS

For some people, compliments are more difficult to accept than criticisms. Here are some hints for handling compliments.

1. Accept the compliment. We sometimes respond to praise with, "Oh, it's really nothing," or, "This old thing? I've had it for years." This response undermines both you and the person who sent the compliment.

2. Choose another time to deliver your own compliments. Automatically returning a compliment can appear suspiciously polite and insincere.

3. Let the compliment stand. "Do you really think so?" questions the integrity of the message. It can also sound like we're fishing for more compliments. Accepting compliments is not the same as being conceited. You are worthy and capable. Allow people to acknowledge that.

DEALING WITH SEXISM

Sexism and sexual harassment are real. They are terms for events that happen at schools, colleges, and universities across the world. And nearly all of these incidents are illegal or against school policies.

In the United States alone, women make up over half of all students in higher education. Yet they can still encounter a bias based on gender.

This bias can take many forms. For example, instructors might gloss over the contributions of women. Students in philosophy classes may never hear of Hypatia, the ancient Greek philosopher. Those majoring in computer science may never learn about Grace Hopkins, the computer pioneer and developer of compilers. (Compilers are programs that translate other programs from one computer language into another). And your art history textbook may not mention the Mexican painter Frida Kahlo or the American artist Georgia O'Keeffe.

Even the most well-intentioned students and teachers may behave in ways that hurt or discount women. One way is simply using masculine pronouns—"he," "his," and "him"—to refer to both men and women. Sexism also takes place when:

•Career counselors hint that certain fields are not appropriate for women.

•Students pay more attention to feedback from a male teacher than from a female teacher.

•Women are not called on in class, their comments are ignored, or they are overly praised for answering the simplest questions.

•Examples given in a textbook or lecture assign women only to traditionally "female" roles—wife, mother, day care provider, elementary school teacher, nurse, and the like.

•People assume that middle-aged women who return to school have too many family commitments to study adequately or do well in their classes.

SEVERAL KINDS OF SEXIST BEHAVIOR fall under the title of sexual harassment. This occurs, for example, when women or men are told they must have sex in order to get a certain grade or job. Sexual harassment can be verbal as well as physical. Examples are comments that point to the "sexiness" of a woman's or a man's body or imply an interest in having sex.

The feminist movement has raised our awareness about discrimination against women, both in schools and in the work force. In addition to learning about this movement, we can look out for sexism and sexual harassment in the places we live, work, and go to school. Specific strategies are listed on the facing page.

AND SEXUAL HARASSMENT

POINT OUT SEXIST LANGUAGE AND BEHAVIOR

When you see examples of sexism, point them out. Your message will be more effective if you use "I" messages instead of personal attacks. Point out the specific statements and actions that you consider sexist.

OBSERVE YOUR LANGUAGE AND BEHAVIOR

Looking for sexist behavior in others is effective; detecting it in yourself can be even more powerful. Write a Discovery Statement about specific statements that could be seen as sexist. Then notice if you say these things. Also ask people you know to point out such statements.

ENCOURAGE NETWORKS FOR WOMEN

Through networks, women can work to overcome the effects of sexism. Sample strategies include study groups for women, women's job networks, professional organizations (such as Women in Communications), counseling services and health centers for women, family planning agencies, and rape prevention centers. Check your school catalog and library to see if such options are available at your school.

CREATE AN ALTERNATIVE

If your school does not have the womens' networks you want, form them. Sponsor a one-day or one-week conference on women's issues. Create a discussion or reading group for the women in your class, department, residence hall, union, or neighborhood.

IF YOU ARE SEXUALLY HARASSED, TAKE ACTION

Some key federal legislation protect the rights of women. This includes Title VII of the Civil Rights Act of 1964 and Title IX of the Education Amendments of 1972. Learn your school's procedures for complying with these laws and use them when appropriate. The nearest federal government agencies, such as the Office for Civil Rights and the Equal Employment Opportunity Commission, can also help.

Your community and school may also offer resources to protect women against discrimination. Examples are unions that employ lawyers to represent students, public interest law firms, and legal aid societies.

Relationships can work

Sometimes relationships work exceptionally well; sometimes they don't. Of all the factors that affect relationships, the biggest is communication (which is discussed in this chapter). Here's a list of other factors that can benefit or damage your relationships.

Do tell the truth. Life is complicated when you don't. For example, if you think a friend is addicted to drugs, telling him so in a supportive, nonjudgmental way is a sign of friendship.

Do support others. Encourage fellow students to reach their goals and be successful. Respect their study time. Helping them to stay on purpose can help you as well.

Don't pry. Being a good listener is invitation enough for fellow students to share their problems, feelings, and personal goals.

Don't borrow . . . too much. Borrowing a book or a tennis racket may seem like a small thing. Yet these requests can become a sore point in a relationship. Some people have difficulty saying no and resent lending things. Consider keeping borrowing to a minimum.

Do divide chores. Whether it's a class project or a household chore, do your part. Frustrations result when people fail to agree upon a fair division of work.

Don't gripe. There is a difference between griping and sharing problems. Gripers usually don't seek solutions. They just want everyone to know how unhappy they are. Sharing a problem is an appropriate way of starting the search for a solution.

Do get involved. Extracurricular activities are a great way to meet people with common interests. If you commute and have little time for these activities, study at the library, eat at the cafeteria, or relax at the student union. You may be surprised at how many friends you make. It is easy to feel left out. It is also easy to get involved.

Don't brag. Other students are turned off by constant references to how much money you have, how great your boyfriend is, your social successes, or your family's accomplishments. There is a difference between sharing excitement and being obnoxious.

Do detach. Allow others to accept responsibility for their problems. Pitying them, getting upset along with them, or assuming responsibility for solving the problem is not helpful.

Do write a letter. Sometimes it's not easy to express ourselves face-to-face with another person. If you have something to say and haven't found the right time or the right words, write a letter. Writing can help you sort out your thoughts.

Do allow people to be upset. Trying to joke people out of their anger, discounting their frustration, or minimizing their disappointment invalidates their feelings. You can best support them by allowing them to experience their emotions.

Do ask for help. One of the central messages of this book is that you are not alone. You can draw on the talent, strength, and wisdom of other people. People often respond to a genuine request for help.

Do share yourself. When we brood on negative thoughts and refuse to speak them out loud, we lose perspective. And when we keep joys to ourselves, we diminish our satisfaction. A solution is to regularly share what we think and feel. Doing so opens the door to new relationships and deepens existing friendships. Imagine a community where people freely and lovingly speak their minds—without fear or defensiveness. That can be your community.

Don't preach. This piece of advice must sound funny at the end of a sermon of do's and don'ts. Sometimes people ask for advice. It's OK to share your values and opinions. It's not OK to pretend you know what's best for someone else. Don't try to reform the world.

Relationships change

Relationships change, and the changes can be painful. Be prepared. Forget about buying broken heart insurance. You are too high a risk. In fact, anytime you choose to care about another person you risk a painful, but rarely fatal, broken heart.

Relationships grow and die. Lovers and spouses leave. Children grow up and move away. Parents die. We may even surpass the people we once looked to as models; that's a kind of loss, too. All these events can lead to pain.

Pain is part of living and can be dealt with in ways that help us learn. When an important relationship ends and you feel badly, allow yourself to experience that feeling. It is appropriate to be miserable when you are. It's normal to cry and express your feelings. It is also possible to go to class, study, work, eat, sleep, get your laundry done, and feel miserable at the same time.

Sometimes emotional pain is intense. If you feel absolutely rotten, useless, ugly, and unlovable, look in the mirror and tell yourself over and over again how rotten, useless, ugly, and unlovable you are. It might be hard to berate yourself for very long and keep a straight face. (Apply this suggestion with care.)

One option is to throw a pity party and talk about how rotten things have been going for you. Be prepared for your depressed mood to change quickly.

If you are determined to feel sorry for yourself, go all the way. Increase your misery by studying a few extra hours. This method works especially well on a Saturday night. You can get the most out of being depressed and deprived while everyone else is out having fun.

It could go like this: You get some extra studying done and start feeling like a good student. Maybe you are more worthwhile than you thought. You fight it, but you can't help feeling pleased with yourself. The pain subsides. Feeling good about yourself has an interesting side effect. Usually others start feeling good about you, too.

Another way to work through this kind of pain is to do something. Do anything. Exercise. Mop the kitchen floor, clean out your dresser drawers, iron your shirts.

This sounds ridiculous, but it works. Remember that your purpose is not to avoid pain, but to face it from a more balanced viewpoint. Staying active can restore the balance.

Do things with other people. Include old friends. Make new friends. It's rarely effective to become a hermit. Talking to people is a way of healing.

You can also use the Power Processes when you feel pain. Tell the truth about your feelings and fully experience them. Embrace this barrier and "be here now" with it. Surrender to your negative feelings. Yes, it can be difficult to practice the Power Processes at times like this. And when your practice becomes this intense, it can yield the most learning.

Writing about your feelings and what you're learning through the pain can also bring perspective. Your journal is one friend who is on call, 24 hours each day, every day of the year. You can approach this friend in any mood and say anything at all. Now that's unconditional acceptance.

Emotional pain doesn't last forever. Often it ends in a matter of weeks. One case disappeared in four hours and 12 minutes.

If you feel severely depressed and stay that way, talk to someone. If friends and family can't help, most colleges and communities have counselors available. Take action. Depression can affect your health, and it can be alleviated. There's no need to let a broken heart stop your life. Though you can find buckets full of advice on the subject, a powerful idea to remember is, "This, too, shall pass."

MASTER STUDENT

Fran Worden Henry,

businesswoman, enrolled at Harvard Business School at the age of 32.

Reprinted by permission of Charlotte Sheedy Literary Agency, Inc., from **Toughing It Out At Harvard,** *by Fran Worden Henry, Copyright 1983 by Fran Worden Henry.*

. . . I went to my desk and wrote out a few pages of notes to remind me of why I wanted to get an MBA. I needed some special support and validation that wasn't to be found in my professors or my classmates or the things I was learning.

I review the whys again. Why did I want an MBA? Why from Harvard? I recalled knowing years before that I wanted a useful graduate degree, one which gave me practical tools I didn't already have. I remembered hearing about how MBA's could telescope years of business experience into a few months of learning. I remembered, too, that when I had called the Harvard admissions office for the application, I was scared that they would reject my voice over the phone, knowing as they must that I wasn't qualified, that I hadn't taken math since high school.

Then I remembered an event that was a kind of turning point in my decision to apply. It had occurred during a business trip in 1979. I was on a plane, flying from London to Bangkok. I flew First Class as there were no coach seats left by the time I booked my flight. While I liked the comfortable seats in First Class, I was dismayed to find the only other women in the cabin were waiting on the men. I had thought I would have my row to myself on the flight, but just before the door closed a stout, balding man in a dark blue pinstriped suit eased himself into the seat next to me.

After we had been flying for a while, he asked about my T-shirt. It was dark blue with a sun and it said NO NUKES. I explained that I had bought it at a demonstration in Washington, D.C. a few weeks before. And I went on to say the demonstration was to support solar and other alternative energies so that we wouldn't put ourselves and our children at risk with nuclear power. He looked at me with his head tilting one way and his eyes slanting another. I know he thought I was, at the very least, strange.

"And what about you, where are you going?" I asked.

"I'm flying from London to Dubai," he said. "I'm an executive for an oil firm and I've just come from my annual holiday."

Dubai is the capital of the United Arab Emirates. It was at least eight hours away, so I decided to talk. We chatted about the oil situation and about living abroad. He asked where I was going and whether I was on vacation.

"No, I'm traveling to Bangkok for my company. It's a firm in Washington, D.C. that supports the efforts of developing countries to use appropriate technologies. That usually means, for poor countries, labor-intensive rather than capital-intensive projects. You know, like building many small village hand pumps with community workers instead of building huge dams which benefit only a few."

Well, no, it was clear that he didn't understand. But we discussed these concepts for a good two hours. Basically, he saw things in a way that was diametrically opposite from mine. After a while he gave me a smug grin and stopped talking. A few hours later he spoke to me again, when we were flying over Turkey, and he asked about our meal, which was outstanding. It was clear that he was no longer interested in my opinion of serious topics.

More to be pleasant, I believe, than anything else, he said, "And what will you do with your career?"

I told him just exactly what was on my mind. In the coming year I planned to apply to Harvard and Stanford business schools and get my MBA.

From that moment on he never stopped talking. He asked me at least a dozen questions about politics, about Carter, about the U.S. dollar, about personnel problems. He and I talked for the rest of the trip, and when he got off at Dubai, I was greatly relieved not to have to bend my neck in that direction anymore. I thought and thought about his reaction. How could an English oil executive who worked in the Mideast value an American MBA so much that it overshadowed his distaste for my point of view?

Back in my dorm room with my thoughts, I was exhausted from the strength of my emotions. But I wasn't finished writing or finished with the subject of why I was at Harvard Business School, struggling to fit in against what seemed like impossible odds. I remembered one aspect of the incident on the airplane that was so important to all of my feelings about being in graduate school. It was the power to influence people, the power to be listened to and taken seriously.

I would try to stay at Harvard. I didn't want to be better than anybody else and I knew that earning the degree wouldn't make me better. But it certainly did feel good to be equal, and that was worth some pain.

QUIZ

1. Diversity is valuable because:

   (A) We can learn more about ourselves.
   (B) We may learn different strategies for solving problems.
   (C) We can learn about alternative viewpoints.
   (D) We can gain a broader, more complete, and more inclusive view of the world.
   (E) All of the above

2. How is encoding different from decoding?

3. One suggested guideline for nonverbal listening is to respond frequently to the speaker.
   True or false. Explain your answer.

4. What characteristic differentiates the top four rungs of the ladder of powerful speaking
   from the bottom rung?

5. The suggested techniques for verbal listening include:

   (A) parroting exactly what another person says.
   (B) pay attention to the speaker's words and not to the emotions behind the words.
   (C) Put your own wants aside in order to listen attentively.
   (D) Look for the requests hidden in complaints.
   (E) Use facial gestures to show your reactions.

6. Describing your feelings is an effective part of an "I" message. True or false. Explain your answer.

7. List the five parts of an "I" message (the five ways to say "I").

8. Briefly discuss how you can change the way you experience your instructors.

9. What is the difference between assertive and aggressive behavior?

10. Discuss at least three strategies that can make your complaints more effective.

Journal Entry #62
Discovery Statement

Review what you learned in this chapter about listening and complete the following sentence:

After reading and doing this chapter, write down the strategies for effective listening that you already practice. I discovered that I . . .

_____

_____

_____

_____

_____

_____

Journal Entry #63
Intention Statement

Describe a specific issue in one of your current relationships that was not addressed in this chapter. Then write an Intention Statement about what you will do to resolve this issue.

I intend to . . .

_____

_____

_____

_____

_____

Exercise #28
Observing behavior: A spectator sport

Brainstorm behaviors you have observed in others in stressful situations. List them below.

_____

_____

_____

_____

_____

_____

Look back at your list and decide if some of the behaviors you noted are actually judgments. For example: *anger, rudeness, jealousy,* or *meanness* are judgments—not behaviors.

A behavior is something factual, observable. For instance, yelling, arriving 10 minutes after the movie starts, or pulling a dog's tail are all observable behaviors.

Chapter 9

Health

Emotion, which is suffering, ceases to be suffering as soon as we have a clear picture of it.
BARUCH SPINOZA

Disease is not only suffering, but also the body fighting to restore itself to normal—a sort of healing source within.
HIPPOCRATES

To be somebody you must last.
RUTH GORDON

Journal Entry #64
Discovery Statement

What I want to get out of this chapter is . . .

In this chapter . . .

Our bodies are a gift. Yet some people give their physical health less attention than they give their cars. This chapter explores how you can ***Take care of your machine*** so that it keeps providing the fuel for learning.

Addiction in its many forms puts up a huge barrier to success in school. You can learn how to recognize addiction, ask for help, and promote healing in the addictive family by reading ***Addiction— The truth, Addiction is a family affair*** and ***Where to turn for more information on recovery.***

Advertisers do not always have a stake in promoting your health. Learn more about weighing their claims for products in ***Advertising can be dangerous to your health.***

Emotional pain is not a sickness reminds us that emotional ups and downs are part of a healthy life. This article also suggests what you can do to cope with emotional stress.

Power Process #9: Surrender suggests a way to handle even the most overwhelming problems, physical or emotional.

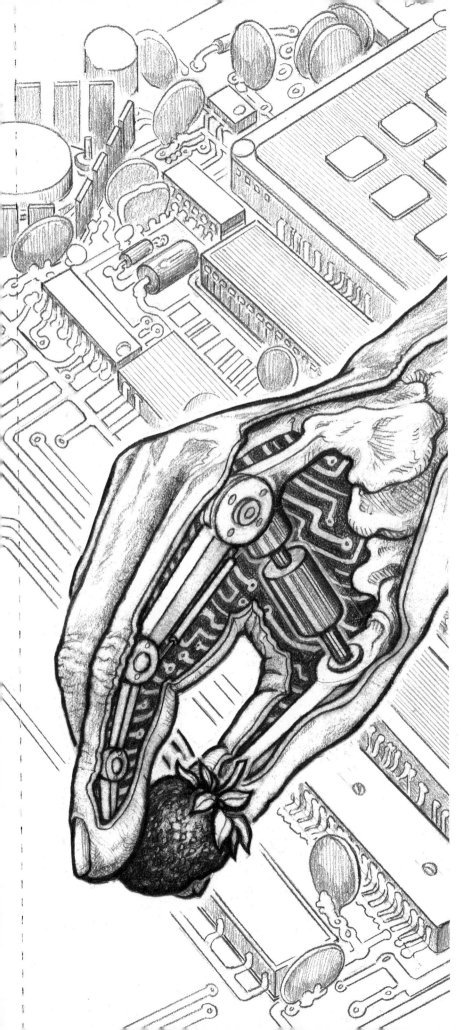

Take care of your machine

SOME PEOPLE ARE OFFENDED by the notion that a body is a machine. This analogy is made with great respect for our bodies and with the understanding that we are more than our bodies. We have a mind and a soul that are certainly separate from our bodies even though they are connected. And, in order to house the mind and soul, we have a body—a fantastic machine.

Our machines are truly incredible. They often continue to operate despite abuse. We pollute them, dent them, run them too hard, let them sit idle for years, even wreck them, and still they continue to run—most of the time. Ironically, we can also take excellent care of our machines, only to have them quit on us just when we need them.

To an extent greater than most of us imagine, we choose our level of health. You can promote your health by taking definite steps.

When we buy a car or a new appliance, we generally look at the owner's manual. We study it to find out just how this new machine works. We make sure we understand all the features and what is needed to properly maintain the equipment.

The following suggestions are accepted by almost all experts on health. Study them as if they made up an owner's manual for a priceless machine, one that can't be replaced, one that your life depends on. That machine is your body.

Your machine: Fuel it

It is a cliche', but it's true: You are what you eat. The brain needs nutrients to function properly. What you eat can have immediate and long-term effects on your performance as a student. That giant jelly donut can make you drowsy within minutes, and a steady diet of them can affect the amount of energy you have to meet and juggle the demands of classes, jobs, extracurricular activities, family, and other activities.

There have been hundreds of books written about nutrition. One says don't drink milk. Another says buy a cow. Some say load up on 5,000 milligrams of Vitamin C a day. Others say avoid oranges. This debate can be confusing. There is, however, some agreement among nutritional scientists.

A list of guidelines was developed by a committee of experts and published by the U.S. Senate. You'll find it on page 243. Though you might find a healthier diet, you can do well by following these guidelines.

Weight control is a problem for millions, and self-starvation can be as dangerous as obesity. Both conditions can be controlled. Working with others who have similar problems is often effective and brings lasting results. Look for support groups.

If you are overweight, avoid people, groups, diets, or chemicals that claim a quick fix. Even if that "Lose 20 pounds in 20 days!" diet works, you're likely to gain the weight back in a few weeks—plus a few extra pounds.

The formula for weight loss is simple: Eat better food, eat less food, and exercise. And to maintain your health, avoid losing more than two pounds per week.

Local newspapers and the Yellow Pages list classes and support groups that can help you to reduce and to maintain your ideal weight.

There are two eating disorders that affect many students. Bulimia is a serious illness that runs in cycles of excessive eating and forced purges. A person with this disorder might gorge on a large pizza, 14 donuts, or a gallon of ice cream, then force herself to vomit. Or, she might compensate for the overeating by using excessive laxatives, enemas, or diuretics. Anorexia nervosa is an illness characterized by starvation, either through extended fasts or by eating only one food for weeks at a time. Both these conditions can be addictive disorders that call for treatment. Contact any of the organizations shown in the box below for further information and help. Support groups also exist for these conditions.

National Association of Anorexia
Nervosa and Associated Disorders
Box 7
Highland Park, IL 60035
708-831-3438

Bulimia Anorexia Self-Help
P.O. Box 39903
Saint Louis, MO 63139
800-762-3334

Anorexia Nervosa and Related
Eating Disorders, Inc.
P.O. Box 5102
Eugene, OR 97405
503-344-1144

American Anorexia/Bulimia
Association, Inc.
418 East 76th Street
New York, NY 10021
212-734-1114

Your machine: Move it

Regular exercise can improve your performance in school. Your brain usually functions better if the rest of your body is in shape, and the right kind of exercise is an effective way to dissipate the tension that you build up hunched over a keyboard hammering out that term paper.

Our bodies were meant to exercise. The world ran on muscle back in the days when we had to track down a woolly mammoth every few days, kill it, and drag it back to the cave by hand. Now we can grab a burger at the drive-up window. It's convenient, but it doesn't do much for our deltoids, quadriceps, and other muscles. The heart is a muscle that can get fat, too. A fat belly may be unattractive. A fat heart can be lethal.

Lean muscles absorb nutrients more efficiently than muscles marbled with fat. The best reason to get in shape isn't to improve how you will look in designer jeans. With lean muscles, you function better at whatever you do, whether it's mammoth hunting or boning up on math.

Sometimes people who are out of shape or overweight think they cannot change. The human body *can* change. Inside even the most dilapidated body there is a trim, healthy, energized body that wants to escape.

Begin by taking a First Step. Tell the truth about the problem and declare your desire to change. You can make real progress in a matter of weeks. Sticking to an exercise schedule for just three weeks can bring rewards. Remember, dieting alone doesn't create lean muscles and a strong heart. The only way to get lean is by moving.

You don't have to train for the Boston Marathon, however. It's not even smart, unless you're in great shape. Do something you enjoy. Start by walking briskly 15 minutes every day. Increase that time gradually and add a little running.

Once you're in reasonable shape, you can stay there by doing three 20- to 30-minute sessions a week of aerobic activity—the kind that elevates your heart

Before beginning any vigorous exercise program, consult a doctor. This is critical if you are overweight, over 60, in poor condition, a heavy smoker, or have a history of health problems.

rate to a faster and steady pace.

School can be a great place to get in shape. Classes may be offered in aerobics, swimming, volleyball, basketball, golf, tennis, and other sports.

Your machine: Rest it

Human bodies also need to rest. It is possible to drive a person crazy or even to kill her by depriving her of sleep.

You might be tempted to drastically cut back on your sleep once in a while. All-nighters are common for some students. If you find you are indulging in them often, read Chapter Two for some time management ideas. Depriving yourself of sleep is a choice you can avoid.

Sometimes getting to sleep isn't easy, even when you feel tired. If you have trouble falling asleep, experiment with these suggestions:

Exercise daily. For many people, this promotes sounder sleep.

Keep your sleeping room cool.

Take a warm bath, not a shower, just before bed.

While lying in bed, practice relaxation techniques.

If you can't fall asleep after 30 minutes, get up and study or do something else until you're tired.

If sleeplessness persists, see a doctor.

Avoid naps during the daytime.

Sleep in the same place each night. When you're there, your body gets the message: "It's time to go to sleep."

How much sleep is enough? Your body knows when it's tired. Also look for signs of depression, irritability, and other emotional problems. Lack of sleep can interfere with your memory, your concentration, and your ability to stay awake in class. The solution is a good night's sleep.

You can sleep 12 hours a day and still not get enough rest if you are not managing stress effectively. School can be an especially stressful environment, so it is important that students know how to relax.

Stress is not always harmful. It can result from pleasant experiences as well as unpleasant ones. The excitement of a new term—new classes, new instructors, new classmates—can be fun and stressful at the same time.

Oddly enough, your body perceives excitement almost the same way it perceives fear. Both emotions produce rapid heart rates, increased adrenaline flow, and muscle contractions. Both emotions produce stress.

Stress, at appropriate times and at manageable levels, is normal and useful. It can sharpen our awareness and boost our energy just when we need it the most. When stress persists or becomes excessive, then it is harmful.

Chances are your stress level is too high if you consistently experience any of the following symptoms: irritability; depression; low productivity; strained relationships at work or home; health problems such as upset stomach, frequent colds, and low energy level; a pattern of avoiding tasks; difficulty falling asleep or staying asleep; feeling burned out at home or at work; feeling tense, nervous, or fearful.

Stress has both mental and physical components. The mental components include thoughts and worries; the physical components include illness and tension. The fact that stress has these two elements points to two broad strategies for managing it.

One of the best ways to deal with stressful thoughts is to manage our self-talk. We can notice and regulate the little voice in the back of our minds that is constantly giving us messages. Exercises that help us mentally rehearse success and visualize positive events increase the odds for positive results.

Methods of dealing with the physical element of stress include breathing exercises, relaxation techniques such as body scans and guided imageries, massage, and aerobic exercise.

Some schools offer training in these techniques. Free or reasonably-priced classes also are available through community education programs, churches or synagogues, the YMCA, and local libraries.

Or read this book. See the index for a listing of relaxation and breathing exercises. Many of the Power Processes and techniques for letting go of test anxiety can help you manage stress.

If these techniques don't work within a few weeks, get help. There are trained relaxation therapists in most cities. Ask a doctor, counselor, or school dean for a referral. Also check with the student health service or counseling center at your school.

Stress management is a well-researched field. There is no need to continue to have a pain in your neck, a knot in your stomach, cold feet, or a dozen other symptoms of tension. Relax.

Your machine: Observe it

You are an expert on your body. Wherever you go, there it is. You are more likely to notice changes first. Pay attention to them. They often are your first clue about the need for repairs.

Watch for these signs:

1. Weight loss of more than 10 pounds in 10 weeks with no apparent cause.

2. A sore, scab, or ulcer in the mouth or on the body which does not heal in three weeks.

3. A skin blemish or mole that bleeds, itches, or changes size, shape, or color.

4. Persistent or severe headaches.

5. Sudden vomiting that is not preceded by nausea.

6. Fainting spells.

7. Double vision.

8. Difficulty swallowing.

9. Persistent hoarseness or nagging cough.

10. Blood that is coughed up or vomited.

11. Shortness of breath for no apparent reason.

12. Persistent indigestion or abdominal pain.

13. A big change in normal bowel habits, such as alternating diarrhea and constipation.

14. Black and tarry bowel movements.

15. Rectal bleeding.

16. Pink, red, or unusually cloudy urinating.

17. Discomfort or difficulty in urinating.

18. Lumps or thickening in a breast.

19. Vaginal bleeding between menstrual periods or after menopause.

If you are sick, get help. Even if you think it might not be serious, check it out. Without prompt treatment, illness or injury can lead to serious problems.

Your machine: Protect it

PROTECT AGAINST SEXUALLY TRANSMITTED DISEASES

Choices about sex can be life-altering. Sex is a basic human drive, and it can be wonderful. Sex can also be hazardous to your physical and psychological health.

It pays to be clear about the pitfalls. These dangers include sexually transmitted diseases, unwanted pregnancies, and rape.

Discussing these dangers indicates maturity and leads to well-informed, responsible choices. Our sexuality flourishes when we make choices after contemplating all possible consequences.

Technically, anyone who has sex is at risk of getting a sexually transmitted disease (STD).

STDs are usually spread through sexual contact with an infected person. Some diseases, like Acquired Immune Deficiency Syndrome (AIDS), can also be spread in other ways.

There are more than 25 kinds of STDs. They are the most common contagious diseases in the United States, and they affect about one in every six adults. Surprisingly, there is still widespread ignorance about how these diseases develop and how to prevent them. Here are some facts:

Without treatment, some of these diseases can lead to blindness, infertility, cancer, heart disease, or even death.

STDs can be harder to diagnose in women, and they can cause long-term damage to female reproductive organs. The risks are tubal pregnancies, miscarriages, and infertility. STDs can also be passed from an infected, pregnant mother to her fetus.

STDs are often spread through body fluids that are exchanged during sex, including semen, vaginal secretions, and blood. Some STDs such as herpes and genital warts are spread by direct contact with infected skin.

The more common STDs include chlamydia, gonorrhea ("clap"), syphillis, genital warts, genital herpes, and trichomoniasis. Sometimes there are no signs or symptoms of an STD, and the only way to tell if you're infected is to get a test from a doctor.

AIDS is one of the most serious STDs, and it is different from the others in several respects. AIDS is the last stage of a viral infection caused by the Human Immunodeficiency Virus (HIV). A person with AIDS is unable to fight off many kinds of infections and cancers.

HIV is transmitted in ways other than through sex. These include sharing needles used to inject drugs. The virus can also be passed from an infected pregnant mother to her fetus. Before 1985, HIV was sometimes spread through contaminated blood transfusions. Since March 1985, blood supplies have been screened for HIV, and the chances of acquiring the virus this way are remote.

Someone infected with HIV may feel no symptoms for months—sometimes years. Many times, the people who are spreading HIV don't even know they have it.

Public hysteria and misinformation still flourish about AIDS. You cannot get AIDS from touching, kissing, hugging, food, coughs, mosquitoes, toilet seats, or swimming pools. HIV is actually a weak virus and hard to catch.

AIDS is not exclusive to male homosexuals, either. It is increasingly common among heterosexuals. AIDS cases among women have been increasing steadily, and it is predicted to become one of the five leading causes of death among women by the early 1990s. According to the U.S. Center for Disease Control, one in 500 college students is infected with HIV.

Being infected with HIV is not a death sentence. Some people live with HIV for years without developing AIDS.

STDs other than AIDS and herpes can be cured if treated early. Prevention is better.

The only ways to be absolutely safe from STDs is to abstain from sex or have sex exclusively with one person who is free of infection and has no other sex partners.

The more people you have sex with, the greater your risk. You are at risk even if you have sex only with one person who is infected. If you have sex with several different people, get checked for STDs twice each year. Do so even if you have no symptoms.

Protect yourself and others from STDs by using latex condoms. Both women and men can carry them and insist they be used. If you use a lubricant, make sure it is water-based, not oil-based. Oil-based lubricants such as Vaseline damage latex condoms.

For added protection, use a birth control foam, jelly, or cream along with condoms. Make sure these include a spermicide, preferably Nonoxynol-9. Condoms used with Nonoxynol-9 provide some protection against AIDS.

If you think you have an STD, call your doctor, student health service, or local STD clinic. You can also call the National STD Hotline (1-800-227-8922) or the National AIDS Hotline (1-800-342-AIDS). These sources can give you the latest information on STDs.

PROTECT AGAINST UNWANTED PREGNANCY

There are more ways to avoid pregnancy now than ever before, and new methods are being developed for both men and women. Following is some information that can help you avoid unwanted pregnancy. Supplement it with information from your doctor.

Abstinence is choosing not to have intercourse, and it is 100 percent effective in preventing pregnancy. Contrary to popular belief, many people exist happily without sexual intercourse. You may feel pressured to change your mind about this choice. If so, remember that abstinence, as birth control, is guaranteed only when it is practiced without exception.

The "pill" is a synthetic hormone that tells a woman's body not to produce eggs. To be effective, it must be taken every day for 21 days a month. Birth control pills must be prescribed by a doctor because the type of pill and the dose varies from one woman to the next. Side effects sometimes include slight nausea, breast tenderness, weight gain from water retention, and moodiness.

Though the pill is about 97 percent effective in preventing pregnancy, its long-term effects are still not known. Some women should not take the pill because it poses too many health risks. Consult your doctor.

An intrauterine device (IUD), is a

Exercise #29
Setting your bio-alarm

Sometimes, after only a few hours of sleep, we wake up feeling miserable. Other times, we bounce out of bed feeling terrific. How we feel in the morning often depends on how we program our bio-alarm clock the night before.

After a long night of studying, you may go to bed with the thought, "I shouldn't have stayed up so late. I'll be exhausted tomorrow. I hope I hear the alarm in the morning." The next morning, you oversleep and miss class.

To wake up refreshed, experiment with this exercise:

Before going to bed, decide what time you want to get up in the morning. Now say aloud, "I am going to get up at 7 a.m." (or whatever time you choose).

Next, lie in bed and allow your body to relax. Imagine feeling heavy and sinking into the bed. Now softly say (out loud if possible), "I will wake naturally at 7 a.m. feeling refreshed, rested, and ready to start my day."

Then relax each part of your body starting with your feet, then ankles, legs, lower back, and so forth until you are completely relaxed and asleep.

You will probably wake up feeling great, at exactly the time you chose. Set your alarm clock for five minutes later than usual and experiment with this exercise a few times. After a while, you may never have to wake up to the buzz again.

small metal or plastic device that is inserted in the uterus and left there for months at a time. It is 94 percent effective in preventing fertilized eggs from developing. Side effects may include heavier menstrual flow, anemia, pelvic infection, perforation of the cervix or uterus, or septic abortion.

Many IUDs were removed from the market after lawsuits against their manufacturers. The people who took this legal action claimed the IUDs caused complications that resulted in permanent injury or death. However, some clinics may still recommend an IUD. Work closely with a doctor if you consider using an IUD.

A diaphragm is a shallow rubber dome that is covered with sperm-killing cream and inserted in the vagina. It fits over the cervix, which is the opening of the uterus, and prevents sperm from getting to the egg. A doctor must measure and fit the diaphragm. It must be inserted before intercourse and left in place for six to eight hours. It is more than 80 percent effective.

A contraceptive sponge works something like a diaphragm. It is effective for 24 hours, and you can buy it over the counter at drug stores. Side effects might include odor, difficult removal, or allergic reactions. Sponges are more than 80 percent effective.

Foams, creams, tablets, suppositories, and jellies are chemicals that are placed in the vagina before intercourse and prevent sperm from getting to the egg. They are about 85 percent effective when used consistently.

Condoms are thin membranes stretched over the penis prior to intercourse. They prevent semen from entering the vagina. When used properly and consistently, condoms are over 95 percent effective.

Another method, natural family planning, is based on looking for specific signs of fertility in a woman. (This is not to be confused with the rhythm method.)

These signs include secretion of a certain kind of mucus from the cervix and a change in body temperature. There are no side effects with natural family planning, and this method is gaining acceptance. Before you consider this method, however, talk to a qualified instructor.

The rhythm method involves avoiding intercourse during ovulation. It is about 80 percent effective. The problem with this method is that it is difficult to know for sure when a woman ovulates.

Douching is flushing the vagina with water or other liquid after intercourse. Do not use it for birth control. Even if you douche immediately, this method is ineffective. Sperm are quicker than you are.

Withdrawal is the act of removing the penis before ejaculation occurs. This is also ineffective, since sperm can be present in pre-ejaculation fluid.

Sterilization is a permanent form of birth control, and one to avoid if you still want to have children. It is almost 100 percent effective.

PROTECT YOURSELF AGAINST RAPE

Rape and other forms of sexual assault are all too common at schools, colleges, and universities. Women and men can take steps to protect themselves. For example:

Get together with a group of people and take a tour of the campus. Make a special note of danger spots, such as dark paths and unguarded buildings.

Ask if your school has escort services for people taking evening classes. These may include personal escorts, car escorts, or both. If you do take an evening class, ask if there are security officers on duty before and after class.

Take a course or seminar on self-defense and rape prevention. To find out where they are being held, check with your student counseling service, community education center, or local library. Hospitals, schools, police departments, and YWCAs often sponsor rape prevention programs and sexual assault hotlines.

If you are raped, get to the nearest rape crisis center, hospital, student health service, or police station as soon as you can. It's wise to report the crime even if you don't want to press charges. Also arrange for follow-up counseling.

Date rape—the act of forcing sex on a date—is the most common form of rape on college campuses. According to a study conducted for the National Institute of Mental Health in 1984 and 1985, one in nine college women had been raped. A more recent study estimated that one in six had been raped, and 90 percent of those rapes were committed by men the women knew.

Date rape is rape. It is a crime. It is particularly dangerous when neither the victim nor perpetrator realize a crime has taken place. A person who has been raped by a date might become depressed, feel guilty, have difficulty in school, lose a sense of trust, have sexual problems, or experience self-blame.

You can take steps to protect yourself by communicating clearly what you want and don't want. That means being assertive. It also pays to be cautious about using alcohol or other drugs and be wary of dates who get drunk or high. You might also provide your own transportation on dates and avoid going to secluded places with people you don't know well.

It is never all right to force someone to have sex—on a date or anywhere else. We have the right to refuse to have sex with anyone, including dates. We also have the right to refuse sex with our partner, fiance, or spouse.

PROTECT YOURSELF AGAINST ACCIDENTS

More than four million disabling injuries occur every year in the haven called the home. Each year over 27,000 people die of accidents in their homes. Almost twice that many die in their cars. You can greatly reduce the odds of this happening to you.

1. Don't drive after drinking alcohol or using psychoactive drugs.
2. Drive with the realization that other drivers are possibly preoccupied, intoxicated, or careless.
3. Put poisons out of reach of children and, for adults, label them clearly. Poisoning takes a larger toll on people ages 15 to 45 than on children.
4. Keep stairs, halls, doorways, and other pathways clear of shoes, toys, newspapers, or other debris.
5. Don't smoke in bed.
6. Don't leave burning candles.
7. Keep children away from hot stoves and turn pot handles inward.
8. Check electrical cords for fraying, loose connections, or breaks in insulation. Don't overload extension cords.
9. Keep a fire extinguisher handy.
10. Watch for ways that an infant or toddler could suffocate or choke—small objects that can be swallowed, old refrigerators or freezers that can act as air-tight prisons, unattended or unfenced swimming pools, kerosene heaters in tightly-closed rooms, and plastic kitchen or clothing bags.

Journal Entry #65
Intention Statement

Brainstorm for three minutes things you can do during the next month to improve your health. Use a separate sheet of paper for your brainstorm.

Next, pick three of your ideas that you can begin to use or practice this week. Finally, write an Intention Statement about how and when you intend to use them.

Journal Entry #66
Intention Statement

Choose one habit related to your health that you would like to begin changing today. Write an intention statement about changing this habit so that your body can begin experiencing greater health.

Journal Entry #67
Discovery Statement

If you look and feel healthy, a greater awareness of your body can let you know what you're doing right. If you are not content with your present physical or emotional health, you may discover some ways to improve.

This exercise is a structured Discovery Statement that allows you to look closely at your health. As with the Discovery Wheel exercise in Chapter One: First Step, the usefulness of this exercise is determined by your honesty and courage.

1. On a separate sheet of paper, draw a simple outline of yourself. You might have positive and negative feelings about various internal and external parts of your body. Label the parts, and include a short description of the attributes you like or dislike. For example: straight teeth, fat thighs, clear lungs, double chin, straight posture, etc.

2. The body you drew substantially reflects your past health practices. To discover how well you take care of your body, complete the following sentences.

EATING

1. The truth about what I eat is. . .

2. What I know about the way I eat is. . .

3. What I would like to change most about my diet is. . .

4. My eating habits lead me to be. . .

EXERCISE

1. The way I usually exercise is. . .

2. The last time I did 20 minutes or more of heart/lung (aerobic) exercise was. . .

3. As a result of my physical conditioning I feel. . .

4. And I look. . .

5. It would be easier for me to work out regularly if I . . .

6. The most important benefit for me in exercising more is..

HARMFUL SUBSTANCES

1. My history of cigarette smoking is. . .

2. An objective observer would say my use of alcohol is. . .

3. In the last 10 days the number of alcoholic drinks I have had is . . .

4. I would describe my use of coffee, colas, and other caffeine drinks as. . .

5. I have used the following illegal drugs in the past week. . .

6. When it comes to drugs, what I am sometimes concerned about is. . .

7. I take the following prescription drugs. . .

RELATIONSHIPS

1. Someone who knows me fairly well would say I am emotionally. . .

2. The way I look and feel has affected my relationships by. . .

3. My use of drugs or alcohol has been an issue with. . .

4. The best thing I could do for myself and my relationships would be. . .

SLEEP

1. The number of hours I sleep each night is. . .

2. On weekends I normally sleep. . .

3. I have trouble sleeping when. . .

4. Last night I. . .

5. The night before last I. . .

6. The quality of my sleep is usually. . .

What concerns me more than anything about my health is. . .

The experts recommend
SEVEN DIETARY GUIDELINES

1. *Eat a variety of foods.* Include fruits, vegetables, whole grains, breads, cereals, milk, cheese, yogurt, meats, poultry, fish, and eggs in your diet.

2. *Maintain healthy weight.* Overweight people tend to have high blood pressure, heart disease, strokes, common diabetes, and certain cancers. To lose weight, eat less sugar and fat. Avoid alcohol. Eat slowly. Avoid second helpings. Eat smaller portions.

3. *Choose a diet low in fat, saturated fat, and cholesterol.* This is a good idea even if you are not overweight. High blood cholesterol is a health risk. Lean meat, fish, poultry, dry beans, and peas are low cholesterol sources of protein. Limit your intake of eggs, organ meats, butter, cream, shortening, and oil. Broil, bake, or boil rather than fry. Cut off excessive fat before cooking meat.

4. *Choose a diet with plenty of vegetables, fruits, and grain products.* Include at least three servings of vegetables, two servings of fruit, and six servings of grain (preferably whole grain) products daily.

5. *Use sugars only in moderation.* Obesity, impaired circulation, tooth decay, and other problems relate to excessive sugar in the diet. Many prepared foods contain excessive sugar. Do not select foods if sugar is listed as the first, second, or third ingredient on the label. Sometimes sugar is called corn syrup, dextrose, fructose, glucose, maltose, sucrose, honey, or molasses.

6. *Use salt and sodium only in moderation.* Your body does need sodium chloride (salt). However, you need much less than most people eat and reduction will benefit those people whose blood pressure rises with salt intake. Use salt sparingly, if at all, in food preparation or at the table. Limit your intake of salty foods like pretzels, potato chips, cheese, salted nuts, pickles, and popcorn.

7. *If you drink alcoholic beverages, do so in moderation.* Moderate drinking is no more than one drink in one day for women, two for men. Some people should not drink at all. Too much alcohol may cause cirrhosis of the liver, inflammation of the pancreas, damage to the heart and brain, high blood pressure, hemorrhagic stroke, and increased risk for many cancers. Do not drink and drive.

Crazed glazed donut runs amok

By Bill Harlan

PANCREAS CITY, IOWA—A glazed donut, apparently out of control, caused a multisugar pileup here early yesterday.

The entire state is reeling in lethargy, and the governor has called in extra fatty tissue.

The pileup occurred shortly after 9 a.m., when assistant brain cells in Hypothalamusville noticed an energy shortage. They telephoned the state procurement office in Right Hand with a request for a glazed donut.

Procurement officers delivered the donut to Mouth, two miles north of Throat, at 9:04 a.m. "We were only following orders," one said.

When the donut reached Stomach, the town was nearly deserted. "No one had been here since dinner the night before," a witness said. The donut raced straight through Duodenum Gap and into Intestine County.

Records indicate the energy level throughout the state did rise for more than a half hour. However, about 45 minutes after the donut was delivered, residents in Eyelid noticed what one witness described as "a sort of a drooping effect." Within 90 minutes the whole state was in a frenzy. Energy levels dropped. Tremors were reported in Hand. A suspicious "growl" was heard near Stomach.

By that time, confusion reigned in Pancreas. Officials there later claimed the donut was pure glucose, the kind of sugar that causes an immediate but short-lived energy boost. The glazed perpetrator apparently burned itself out in a metabolic rampage. Soon, only the smoking traces of burned glucose remained.

Minutes later, terror-stricken cells near Stomach began screaming, "Send down a candy bar." The cry was taken up throughout the state, as cells everywhere begged for more sugar.

For the rest of the day, the state reeled under an assault of caffeine and sugar. Three candy bars. Four soft drinks. Pie and coffee.

By evening, the governor's office had called up alcohol reserves.

"We've been recommending complex carbohydrates and small amounts of protein since Tuesday," said a highly placed source, who was reached on vacation at the Isle of Langerhans in Lake Pancreas. "Carbohydrates and proteins burn energy gradually, all day. An egg, some cereal, a piece of fruit, and this tragedy could have been avoided. Heck, a burger would have been better. This donut thing has got to stop."

This morning, a saddened state lies under a layer of fat.

"I'm guessing it will take a hard 10-mile run to get this mess cleaned up," an administrative assistant in Cerebellum said.

Officials in Legs could not be reached.

The facts

Male alcoholics take their own lives 11 times more frequently than other men. Women alcoholics kill themselves 16 times more often than women who are not alcoholics.

Drug users consume three times the medical benefits and are five times as likely to file workers compensation claims than their nonaddicted counterparts.

The misuse of alcohol, cigarettes, and both illegal and legal drugs is by far the predominant cause of premature and preventable illness, disability, and death in our society.

Alcohol and drug abuse afflict an estimated 25.5 million Americans.

The cost of alcohol related car accidents, fires, and health care has been estimated at $136.3 billion for 1990 and is predicted to grow to $150 billion in 1995.

Drug abuse accounts for $46.9 billion a year in direct and indirect costs to business and the economy.

Nearly 450,000 people die each year from smoking-related illnesses.

It takes five to 15 years for an adult to become an alcoholic; an adolescent can become an alcoholic in six to 18 months of heavy drinking.

Experience with illegal drugs rose from two percent or less of the population in the early 1960's to more than a third of the population— 70.4 million Americans—in 1985.

At commonly used doses, marijuana impairs short-term memory, concentration, judgment, information processing, perception, and fine motor skills. Even when marijuana use is discontinued, memory loss may continue for three to six months.

One out of eight adults grew up with at least one alcoholic parent.

Mixing alcohol and pregnancy contributes to Fetal Alcohol Syndrome leading to physical and mental abnormalities in the developing child. Prenatal alcohol exposure is now one of the leading causes of mental retardation.

Alcohol, tobacco, and drugs—The truth

The truth is, getting high can be fun. In our culture, and especially our media, getting high has become synonymous with having a good time. Even if you don't smoke, drink, or take drugs, you are certain to come in contact with people who do.

We are a drug-using society. Drugs (legal and illegal), alcohol, tobacco, and caffeine are accepted and sought-after answers to practically any problem anyone has. Do you have a headache? Take a drug. Is it hard for you to fall asleep? Take a drug. Is it hard to stay awake? Take a drug. Are you depressed? Are you hyperactive? Are you nervous? Are you too skinny? Too fat? The often-heard answer is "Take something." There is a brand of alcohol, a certain cigarette, or a faster acting drug that can help.

There is a big payoff in using alcohol, tobacco, caffeine, prescription drugs, cocaine, heroin . . . or people wouldn't do it. The payoff is sometimes direct—relaxation, self-confidence, comfort, excitement, pleasure. At times, the payoff is not so obvious—avoiding rejection, masking emotional pain, peer group acceptance, rejecting authority.

Some people enjoy using drugs and alcohol so much they try to push these substances on to others. "Here, have another drink. Loosen up. Enjoy yourself." "I can't believe this stuff. Here, try some." "Come on, try it. Are you some kind of a lightweight?"

In addition to the payoff, there is a cost. For most people, the cost is much greater than the payoff. Yet they continue to abuse.

That cost goes beyond money. If cocaine, heroin, and other drugs don't make you broke, they can make you crazy. This is not necessarily the kind of crazy where you dress up like Napoleon, but the kind where you care about little else except finding more drugs— friends, school, work, and family be damned.

Lectures about why to avoid alcohol and drug abuse can be pointless. Ultimately, we don't take care of our bodies because we "should." We might take care of ourselves when we see that using a substance is costing us more than we're getting for our trouble. You choose. It's your body. On the left side of this page are some facts—the truth— that can help you make choices about what to put into your body.

Exercise #30
Addiction, how do I know. . .

People who have problems with drugs and alcohol are great at hiding the problem from themselves and others. It is also hard to admit that a friend or loved one might have a problem.

The purpose of this exercise is to give you an objective way to look at your relationship to drugs or alcohol. This exercise is also useful in looking to see if a friend might be addicted. Addiction can be emotional and not physical. These are signals that let us know when drug or alcohol use has become abusive. Answer the following questions quickly and honestly with "yes" or "no." If you are concerned about someone else, replace each "you" in the following questions with that person's first name.

_____ *Are you uncomfortable discussing drug abuse or alcoholism?*

_____ *Are you worried about your drug or alcohol use?*

_____ *Are any of your friends worried about your drug or alcohol use?*

_____ *Have you ever hidden from a friend, spouse, employer, or co-worker the fact that you were drinking? (Pretended you were sober? Covered up alcohol breath?)*

_____ *Do you sometimes use alcohol or drugs to escape lows rather than produce highs?*

_____ *Have you ever gotten angry when confronted about your use?*

_____ *Do you brag about how much you consume? ("I drank her under the table.")*

_____ *Do you think about or do drugs when you are alone?*

_____ *Do you store up alcohol, drugs, cigarettes, or caffeine (in coffee or soft drinks) so you are sure you won't run out?*

_____ *Does having a party almost always include alcohol or drugs?*

_____ *Do you try to control your drinking so that it won't be a problem ("I only drink on weekends now," "I never drink before 5 p.m.," "I only drink beer.")*

_____ *Do you often explain to other people why you are drinking? ("It's my birthday," "It's my friend's birthday," "It's Veteran's Day," "It sure is a hot day.")*

_____ *Have you changed your friends to accommodate your drinking? ("She OK, but she isn't excited about getting high.")*

_____ *Has your behavior changed in the last several months? (Grades down? Lack of interest in a hobby? Change of values or what you think is moral?)*

_____ *Do you drink to relieve tension? ("What a day! I need a drink.")*

_____ *Do you have medical problems that could be related to drinking (stomach trouble, malnutrition, liver problems, anemia)?*

_____ *Have you ever decided to quit drugs or alcohol and then changed your mind?*

_____ *Have you had any fights, accidents, or similar incidents related to drinking or drugs in the last year?*

_____ *Has your drinking or drug use ever caused a problem at home?*

_____ *Do you envy people who go overboard with alcohol or drugs?*

_____ *Have you ever told yourself you can quit at any time?*

_____ *Have you ever been in trouble with the police after or while you were drinking?*

_____ *Have you ever missed school or work because of alcohol or drugs?*

_____ *Do you feel uncomfortable at a party if you don't drink or get high?*

_____ *Have you ever done badly on a test because you had a hangover?*

_____ *Have you ever had a blackout (a period you can't remember) after drinking?*

_____ *Do you wish that people would mind their own business when it comes to your use of alcohol or drugs?*

Now count the number of questions you answered "yes." If you answered "yes" more than five times, talk with a professional. Five "yes" answers do not mean that you are an alcoholic or that you have a serious problem. They do point out that drugs or alcohol are adversely affecting your life. It is very important that you talk to someone with alcohol and drug abuse training. Do not rely on the opinion of anyone without such training.

If you answered this questionnaire about another person, and you answered "yes" more than five times, your friend may need help. You probably can't provide that help alone. Seek out a counselor or a support group such as Al-Anon. (Call the local Alcoholics Anonymous Chapter for an Al-Anon meeting near you.)

Seeing the full scope of addiction

Substance abuse—that is, addiction to a chemical in alcohol or drugs—is only part of the picture. People can also be addicted to food, gambling, sugar, spending money, sex, unhealthy relationships, and even work.

Here are some guidelines that can help you decide if addiction is a barrier for you right now. Most addictions share some key features:

•**Compulsive use of the substance or indulgence in the activity.**

•**Continued use or activity in spite of adverse consequences.**

•**Preoccupation with getting and keeping the substance or doing the activity.**

•**A loss of control over the substance or activity.**

•**A pattern of relapse—vowing to quit or limit the activity or substance and continually failing to do so.**

The same basic features can be present in anything from cocaine use to compulsive gambling. All this can add up to a continuous cycle of abuse.

It's these common features that prompt many people to call some forms of addiction a disease. The American Medical Association formally recognized alcoholism as a disease in 1956.

Some people do not agree that alcoholism is a disease, or that all addictions can be labeled with that term. You do not have to wait until this question is settled before examining your own life.

What to do

If you have a problem with addiction, consider getting help. Your problem may be your own addiction or perhaps the behavior of someone you love. In any case, consider acting on several of these suggestions.

1. Admit the problem. People with active addictions are a varied group—rich and poor, young and old, successful and unsuccessful. Often these people do have one thing in common: They are masters of denial. They deny they are unhappy. They deny that they have hurt anyone. They are convinced they can quit anytime they want. They sometimes become so adept at hiding the problem from themselves that they die.

2. When you use, pay attention. If you do use a substance compulsively or behave in compulsive ways, do it with awareness. Then pay attention to the consequences. Act with deliberate decision rather than out of habit or pressure from others. Use of addictive substances is so acceptable that we often do it automatically. When you consciously *choose* to indulge in addiction, you may discover that you can also choose *not* to do so.

3. Look at the costs. There is always a trade-off. You may feel great after ten beers, and you will probably remember that feeling. No one feels great the morning after ten beers, but it seems easier to forget pain. Often people don't notice how badly alcoholism, drug addiction, or other forms of addiction make them feel.

4. Instead of blaming yourself, take responsibility for recovery. Nobody plans to be an addict. If you have pneumonia, you can recover without guilt or shame. Approach an addiction in yourself or others in the same way. You can take responsibility for your recovery without blame, shame, or guilt.

5. Get help. Many people find that addiction is not a condition they can treat alone. Addictive behaviors are often symptoms of an illness that needs treatment.

Two broad options exist for getting help with addiction. One is the growing self-help movement. The other is formal treatment. People recovering from addiction often combine the two.

Many self-help groups are modeled after Alcoholics Anonymous. AA is made up of recovering alcoholics and addicts. These people understand the problems of abuse first-hand, and they have a systematic, 12-step approach to living without it. With over a million members, this is one of the oldest and most successful self-help programs in the world. Every chapter of AA welcomes people from all walks of life, and you don't have to be an alcoholic to attend most meetings.

Programs based on AA principles exist for many forms of addiction. These range from Narcotics Anonymous, Overeaters Anonymous, and Gamblers Anonymous to groups for sex addicts and adult children of alcoholics.

Some people feel uncomfortable with the AA approach. Other resources exist for these people, including private therapy, group therapy, and organizations such as the Secular Organization for Sobriety.

Treatment programs are available in almost every community. They may be residential (you live there for weeks or months at a time) or outpatient (you visit several hours a day). Find out where these treatment centers are located by calling a doctor, mental health professional, or a local hospital.

Alcohol and drug treatment are now covered by many health insurance programs. If you don't have insurance, it is usually possible to arrange some other payment program. Cost is no reason to avoid treatment.

It pays to evaluate a treatment program before using it. The questions listed below will give you a start:

•Is this program accredited? By whom?

•Do you regularly treat people for this kind of addiction?

•What is your treatment philosophy? Do you offer a Twelve-Step program (based on Alcoholics Anonymous) or some other kind of program?

•How much will I need to pay out-of-pocket for treatment? How much will be covered by insurance?

•What kinds of services do you offer for family members?

•What kind of training do your counselors have?

•What is a typical case load for one of your counselors?

•Have any of your counselors left during the past year?

•How do you help people plan for continued recovery after treatment ends?

•What can this program do for women, the elderly, adolescents, and different ethnic or racial groups?

Where to turn for more information on recovery

You can begin with your doctor, school health care center, or local chapter of Alcoholics Anonymous. Other resources are these:

PRIDE Drug Information Line
1-800-677-7433

National Institute on
Drug Abuse Hotline
1-800-662-4357

National Clearinghouse for
Alcohol and Drug Information
1-800-729-6686

National Council on Alcoholism
and Drug Dependence, Inc.
12 West 21st Street
New York, NY 10010
212-206-6770

Alcoholics Anonymous
World Services
PO Box 459
Grand Central Station
New York, NY 10163
1-212-686-1100

Institute on Black Chemical Abuse
2614 Nicollet Avenue South
Minneapolis, MN 55408
1-612-871-7878

National Black Alcoholism Council
1629 K Street NW
Suite 802
Washington, DC 20006
1-202-296-2696

National Coalition of Hispanic Health
& Human Services Organizations
1030 15th Street NW
Suite 1053
Washington, DC 20005
1-202-371-2100

National Hispanic Leadership and
Policy Development Institute
1500 Farragut Street NW
Washington, D.C. 20011
1-202-723-7227

National Association of Native
American Children of Alcoholics
PO Box 18736
Seattle, WA 98118
1-206-322-5601

National Asian Pacific Families Against
Substance Abuse
6303 Friendship Court
Bethesda, MD 20817
1-301-530-0945

Addiction is a family affair

It's been said that addicts don't have relationships—they take hostages. Such blanket statements are seldom fair, but they point to a fact: Addiction is more than an individual condition. It affects almost anyone who cares about a person with an addiction.

Families and friends of alcoholics and drug addicts often have their own serious problems. Those problems are discussed with two common terms: codependence and adult children of alcoholics.

Codependence

Not everyone agrees on the meaning of codependence. However, the suffering of those who love an addict is real—no matter what words we use to describe that suffering.

For over thirty years, treatment professionals have recognized this. Early on, they used the words *coalcoholic, co-addict,* and *enabler* to describe behaviors now called codependence.

One of those behaviors is *denial*. This happens when the addict's loved ones pretend that there's really no problem. The addict can "quit any time she wants to," they might say. "There's no way she can be alcoholic. She's not a street bum; she comes from a good family."

Compulsive caretaking is another action we can call codependent. It happens when people refuse to let the addict experience the consequences of addictive behavior. For example:

Joanne, a college student, spends so much on cocaine that she has no money left for tuition. She lies to her parents about where the money is going and asks her roommate Cheryl to join in the deception. Cheryl agrees to say the "right things" in case Joanne's parents question her.

Michael gets drunk several nights during the week before a term paper is due. His brother Tom decides to cancel his plans for Friday night so he can re-type Michael's rough draft, polish it up a little, and turn it in Monday.

Henry was out drinking all day Sunday and into the night. He is passed out and his wife knows when he gets up he'll have a hangover. She calls work and tells his boss that Henry has the flu and will not come to work today.

Family and friends may also feel *enmeshed* with the addicted person. Their sense of well being depends almost wholly on that person. If their addicted loved one is feeling happy, so are they; if the addicted person is worried, they are, too. Sometimes it's hard to draw emotional boundaries between the people involved.

People who care about an addict can also report a *decreased quality of life in general.* They feel depressed and experience illnesses related to stress. In their efforts to deny or cover up addictive behavior, they can become perfectionists or develop their own addictions. Some may even feel suicidal.

These feelings are similar to those reported by many who grew up in alcoholic families.

Adult children of alcoholics

In recent years, children of alcoholics have shared their stories more openly. They talk about incest, beatings, and other forms of sexual and physical abuse at the hands of their parents. They also talk about an inability to get close to people, tendencies to marry alcoholics or drug addicts, and their own addictions to alcohol, drugs, sex, gambling, or food.

The first Adult Children of Alcoholics support group met in 1977. One of its members, Tony A., compiled a "laundry list" describing his own experience in an alcoholic family. Some of the items on that list are:

We live life from the viewpoint of victims and are attracted by that weakness in our love and friendship relationships.

We confuse love and pity and tend to "love" people we can "pity" and "rescue."

We have "stuffed" our feelings from our traumatic childhoods and have lost the ability to feel

or express our feelings because it hurts so much.

We judge ourselves harshly and have a very low sense of self-esteem.

We are dependent personalities who are terrified of abandonment, and we will do anything to hold on to a relationship in order not *to experience the painful abandonment feelings that we received from living with people who were never emotionally there for us.*

No list is definitive, and not all adult children of alcoholics show these characteristics. Yet such lists have helped adult children of alcoholics begin talking about their lives.

Recovery

Today many treatment centers open their doors to the spouses, partners, parents, children, and friends of people with addictions. Counselors and support groups focus on the problems of codependence and adult children of alcoholics.

If you feel that certain problems in your life spring from codependence or growing up in an alcoholic family, take action. Places you can turn include school health care centers and counseling services. Even if they don't offer counseling for conditions related to addiction, they can refer you to someone who does. So can your local United Way or county social service agency.

Also ask at your nearest chapter of Alcoholics Anonymous. A number of support groups based on AA principles focus on codependence and adult children of alcoholics. Examples are Al-Anon, Ala-teen, Adult Children of Alcoholics, and Co-Dependents Anonymous. For a list of such meetings in your area, contact:

Adult Children of Alcoholics
PO Box 3216
2522 W. Sepulveda Boulevard
Suite 200
Torrance, CA, 90505
1-213-534-1815.

Co-Dependents Anonymous
PO Box 33577
Phoenix, AZ 85067-3577
1-602-277-7991.

Advertising... CAN BE DANGEROUS TO YOUR HEALTH

The average American is exposed to thousands of advertising messages per day. The United States, with six percent of the world's population, receives 57 percent of theworld's advertising. Unless you are stranded on a desert island, you are affected by commercial messages. Advertisers spend tens of billions of dollars a year to convince you to buy, buy, buy.

Advertising pervades television and television pervades our culture. Upon graduation from high school, a typical student has spent about 11,000 hours in classes and 25,000 hours watching television.

Advertising serves a useful function. It helps us make choices about spending money. We decide among cars, kitchen appliances, health clubs, books, plants, groceries, home builders, dog groomers, piano tuners, vacation spots, locksmiths, movies, amusement parks, and the list is endless.

Advertising space is also expensive and the messages are carefully crafted. They can play on our emotions and be dangerously manipulative. Be aware of what the advertiser wants to accomplish and be critical about how you allow advertising to affect you.

Advertising alcohol, tobacco, and pain relievers is big business. Newspapers, magazines, radio, and television depend on these products for much of their revenue.

Ads for alcohol glorify drinking. One of their aims is to convince heavy drinkers that the amount they drink is normal. Twenty-seven percent of all people who drink consume 93 percent of the alcohol sold. Advertisers imply that daily drinking is the norm, pleasant experiences are enhanced by drinking, holidays naturally include alcohol, parties are a flop without it, relationships are more romantic over cocktails, and everybody drinks. Each of these implications is questionable.

Advertising can affect our self images. A typical advertising message is, "You are not OK. But if you buy our product, you will be OK." These messages are painstakingly programmed to get you to buy clothes, makeup, and hair products to make you look OK;

drugs, alcohol, and food to make you feel OK; perfumes, toothpaste, and deodorant to make you smell OK. Advertising also promotes the idea that buying the right product is essential to having valuable relationships in your life.

Advertising affects what we eat. Multi-media advertisers portray the primary staples of our diets as breakfast cereals, candy bars, and soft drinks. A U.S. Department of Agriculture study revealed that the least nutritious foods receive the most advertising money.

Another problem with advertising is the image it has commonly portrayed of women. The basic message has been that women are inferior to men, lack intelligence, and are sex objects. The woman presented in many ads either spends her day discussing floor wax and laundry detergent, or sits around looking sexy. Other women handle everything from kitchen to bedroom to board room—Superwoman.

These images are demeaning to women and damaging to men. Women lose when they allow their self images to be influenced by ads. Men lose when they expect real-life women to be as shallow or as beautiful as portrayed. Many men pointlessly search for a woman who looks like the ones they see on television and in magazines. Advertising photography creates illusions. Next time you're in a crowd, notice how few people look like those in the media.

Advertising frequently excludes people of color. If our perceptions were based solely on advertising, we would be hard pressed to know that our society is racially and ethnically diverse.

To avoid brainwashing, be an informed, self-determining observer. Know how a multi-billion dollar industry threatens your health and well-being. Consider the claims made by advertisers, and look for the logic and evidence that support them.

Journal Entry #68
Discovery Statement

Think of a time that you craved a certain food or drink, or that you really wanted to buy something, after seeing an advertisement or commercial. On a separate piece of paper, describe in detail which part of the advertising influenced you.

Emotional pain is not a sickness

Emotional pain has gotten a bad name. This type of slander is undeserved. There is nothing wrong with feeling bad. It's OK to feel miserable, depressed, sad, upset, angry, dejected, gloomy, or unhappy.

It may not be pleasant to feel bad, but it can be good for you. Often, the appropriate way to feel is bad. When you leave a place you love, sadness is natural. When you lose a friend or lover, misery might be in order. When someone treats you badly, it probably is appropriate to feel angry.

Some people will try almost anything to avoid feeling bad, even if the cure is worse than the sadness. That kind of behavior is promoted by messages we get every day.

It started when we were children and adults told us, "Poor thing, don't cry," or, "Stop that crying right now!" "Oh, cheer up!" Later in life, we get similar advice. "Sleep on it. You'll feel better in the morning." "Have a drink. It's a great way to perk up." "Take two of these pills and you'll feel great."

These messages usually come from well-meaning people who don't want you to feel too bad.

Unless you are suicidally depressed, it is almost impossible to feel too bad. Feeling bad for too long can be a problem. If depression, sadness, or anger persist, get help. Otherwise, allow the feelings. They are usually appropriate and necessary for personal growth.

When a loved one dies, it is necessary to grieve. The grief might appear in the form of depression, sadness, or anger. That is OK. The sadness might feel out of control. That is OK. There is nothing wrong with extreme emotional pain. It is natural, and it doesn't have to be fixed.

When feeling bad becomes a problem, it is usually because you didn't allow yourself to feel bad. So, next time you feel rotten, go ahead and feel rotten. It will pass; and it will probably pass more quickly if you don't fight it or pretend it doesn't exist.

Here are some good ways to feel bad:

1. Give yourself permission. Most of us have been taught from the time we were little not to feel bad. Send yourself a reverse message. Say to yourself, out loud if you can, "It's all right for me to feel the way I do," or "I feel bad and that is good."

2. Don't worry about reasons. Sometimes we allow ourselves to feel bad if we have a good reason. "Well, I feel very sad, but that is because I just found out my best friend is moving to Madagascar." It's all right to know the reason that you are sad, and it is fine not to know. You can feel bad for no apparent reason. And, the reason doesn't matter.

3. Set a time limit. If you are concerned about feeling bad, if you are worried that you need to "fix it," give yourself a little time. Before you force yourself not to feel the way you feel, set a time limit. Say to yourself, "I am going to give myself until Monday at noon, and if I don't feel better by then, I am going to try to fix

myself." Sometimes, it is appropriate to fix a bad feeling. There might be a problem that needs a solution. You can use feeling bad as your motivation to solve the problem. And, sometimes it helps to just feel bad for a while.

4. Tell others. Sometimes other people—friends or family, for example—have a hard time letting you feel bad. They might be worried that they did something wrong and want to make it better. They want you to quit feeling bad. Tell them you will. Assure them that you will feel good again but that, for now, you just want to feel bad.

5. This is no joke. Sometimes students think this whole idea of allowing yourself to feel bad is a joke, reverse psychology, or something. It isn't. This suggestion is based on the notion that good mental health is only possible if you allow yourself to feel bad as well as good. So, have a rotten day.

POWER PROCESS #9:

Surrender

LIFE CAN BE MAGNIFICENT and satisfying. It can also be devastating. Sometimes there is too much pain or confusion. Problems can be too big and too numerous. Life can bring us to our knees in a pitiful, helpless, and hopeless state. A broken relationship with a loved one, a diagnosis of cancer, total frustration with a child's behavior problem, or even the prospect of four long years of school are situations that can leave us feeling overwhelmed and powerless.

In these troubling situations, the first thing we can do is admit that we don't have the resources to handle the problem. We can humble ourselves. No matter how hard we try and no matter what skills we bring to bear, some problems remain out of our control. When this is the case, we can tell the truth. "It's too big and too mean. I can't handle it."

Desperately struggling to control a problem can easily result in the problem controlling you. Surrender is letting go of being the master in order to avoid becoming the slave.

Once you have acknowledged your lack of control, all that remains is to surrender. Many traditions make note of this. Western religions speak of surrendering to God. Buddhists say surrender to the Self. Members of Alcoholics Anonymous talk about turning their lives over to a Higher Power. Agnostics might suggest surrendering to the ultimate source of power.

Surrender works for life's major barriers as well as for its insignificant hassles.

You might say, as you struggle to remember someone's name, "It's on the tip of my tongue." Then you surrender. You give up trying and say, "Oh well, it will come to me later." Then the name pops into your mind.

After trying unsuccessfully for years to have a baby, a couple finally surrenders and considers adoption. She then conceives in a few months.

After finding out she has terminal cancer, a woman shifts between panic and depression. Nothing seems to console her. Finally, she accepts the truth and stops fighting her tragedy. She surrenders. Now at peace, she invests her remaining time in meaningful participation and communication with the people she loves.

Surrender is not resignation. It is not a suggestion to simply quit and do nothing about your problems. You have many skills and resources. Use them. You can apply all your energy to handling a situation and surrender at the same time. Surrender includes doing whatever you can in a positive, trusting spirit. Giving up is fatalistic and accomplishes nothing. So let go, keep going, and know that the true source of control lies beyond you.

Watching yourself with detachment can help your ability to surrender. Pretend that you are floating away from your body, and then watch what's going on from a distance. Witness the drama of your life unfolding objectively, as if you were watching a play. When you see yourself as part of a much broader perspective, surrender seems obvious and natural. "Surrender" might seem inconsistent with Power Process #5: "I Create it all." An old parable says the Garden of Truth, the grand place everyone wants to enter, is guarded by two monsters—Fear and Paradox. Most of us can see how fear keeps us from getting what we want. The role of paradox may not be as clear.

The word *paradox* refers to two ideas that seem contradictory or absurd but may actually be true. Suspend the sovereignty of logic for now. However paradoxical, both "Surrender" and "I Create it all" are valuable tools.

Master Student

May Lemke,

four and one-half feet tall and weighing 90 pounds, married an American serviceman in World War II. She raised five children previous to taking on Leslie when she was 52 years old.

Excerpts from "The Miracle of May Lemke's Love" by Joseph P. Blank. Reprinted with permission from the October 1982 Reader's Digest. Copyright 1982 by The Reader's Digest Assn., Inc.

The Milwaukee County General Hospital had a serious problem: a six-month-old infant named Leslie. Mentally retarded and without eyes, the baby also had cerebral palsy. He was a limp vegetable, totally unresponsive to sound or touch. His parents had abandoned him.

The hospital staff didn't know what to do—until a pediatrician mentioned May Lemke, a nurse-governess living nearby. A nurse telephoned May and explained that in all likelihood Leslie would die in a short time. "Would you help us by taking care of him while he lives?" the nurse asked.

"If I take him he certainly will not die, and I will take him," May replied. . .

When May accepted the baby, she accepted him as just that, a baby—no different from the others—to be taught and loved. . .

She bathed him, cuddled him for hours, talked to him, sang to him. He never moved or uttered a sound.

Year after year she cared for him, but there was no movement. No smile. No tears. No sound. . .

The Lemkes then had a chain-link fence erected along the side of their property, and May stood Leslie next to it, thrusting his fingers through the openings. After several weeks he finally got the idea of letting the fence support him. He stood. He was 16. . .

One day she noticed Leslie's index finger moving against a taut piece of string around a package, as if plucking it. Was this a sign? she wondered. What did it mean?

Music! she exclaimed to herself. That's it. Music. From then on the Lemke house was filled with music from the record player, the radio and the TV. Hour after hour the music played. Leslie gave no indication that he was listening.

May and Joe bought an old upright piano for $250.00 and placed it in Leslie's bedroom. Repeatedly, May pushed his fingers against the keys to show him that his fingers could make sounds. He remained totally indifferent.

It happened in the winter of 1971. May was awakened by the sound of music. It was 3 a.m. Someone was playing Tchaikovsky's *Piano Concerto No. 1*. She shook Joe. "Did you leave the radio on?" she asked.

"No," he said.

"Then where's the music coming from?" She swung out of bed and turned on a living room light. It dimly illuminated Leslie's room. Leslie was at the piano. May saw a smile glowing on his face.

He had never before gotten out of bed on his own. He had never seated himself at the piano. He had never voluntarily or deliberately struck the keys with his fingers. Now he was actually playing a concerto—and with deftness and confidence.

May fell to her knees. *Thank you, dear God. You didn't forget Leslie. . .*

. . ."Coming out" musically opened the door for all kinds of emotions and developments. Occasionally a single word popped from his mouth. Then one afternoon some children were playing on the other side of the chain-link fence, and May asked them what they were doing. One of them answered, "We're having fun." Leslie took a few steps along the fence. "I'm having fun," he said in a thick but understandable voice. It was his first complete sentence, and May grabbed him and hugged him. . .

. . .Two years ago, at the age of 28, Leslie began talking in earnest. Although he cannot hold a give-and-take conversation, he makes statements and can ask and answer questions. Sometimes he expresses an opinion. While listening to TV one night Leslie got fed up with the dialogue in a situation comedy. "Better get that off," he said. "They're all crazy."

As news of Leslie's talent traveled, groups requested him for concerts. May pondered the invitations; then she decided that public appearances would be valuable to Leslie. The music would give him a sense of participating in society. "And those people sitting out there, watching and listening, might get a sense of wonderment and a feeling of hope that they might never have had. They would see what can happen to a human being thought to be absolutely hopeless and helpless. . ."

. . .There are still many things that Leslie cannot do. Those fingers that perform so brilliantly at the keyboard cannot use a knife or fork. Conversation does not flow easily. But ask what music means to him and he replies with a voice that is firm. "Music," says Leslie, "is love."

QUIZ

1. The strategies suggested for dealing with stress do *not* include:

   (A) Manage self-talk.
   (B) Practice relaxation techniques.
   (C) Cut back on exercising.
   (D) Mentally rehearse success and visualize positive events.
   (E) Check with the student health service.

2. How is surrender, as discussed in Power Process #9, different from giving up?

3. A person infected with HIV may feel no symptoms for months—sometimes years.
   True or False.

4. Define date rape and describe at least two ways that can help prevent it from happening.

5. List at least three dietary guidelines that can contribute to your health.

6. HIV is:

    (A) a strong virus and hard to catch.
    (B) a weak virus and easy to catch.
    (C) a weak virus and hard to catch.
    (D) a strong virus and easy to catch.

7. Name at least three ways that can help prevent unwanted pregnancy.

8. The *only* way to be absolutely safe from STD's is to abstain from sex. True or false. Explain your answer.

9. Describe codependent behavior.

10. What are at least two ways that advertising can be dangerous to your health?

Journal Entry #69
Discovery Statement

Review what you learned in this chapter about the way you take care of your "machine." Then complete the following sentence:

     I discovered that I . . .

Journal Entry #70
Intention Statement

List one concern about your health that was not addressed in this chapter. Then describe what you will do to alleviate that concern.

     I intend to . . .

Journal Entry #71
Intention Statement

Choose one health-related activity you can increase or do for the first time. Describe when and where you will do this activity today so that your healthy body can begin to emerge.

     I intend to . . .

Journal Entry #72
Discovery Statement

After reading "Employ your word" in Chapter Eight, take a few minutes to list one problem in your life and how it could be related to broken agreements.

     I discovered that I . . .

10 Money

So much is a man worth as he esteems himself.
FRANCOIS RABELAIS

Develop a plan of control over your spending. Then you will make progress toward the kind of living which means the most to you.
SYLVIA PORTER

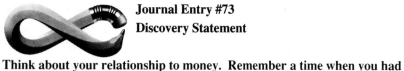

Journal Entry #73
Discovery Statement

Think about your relationship to money. Remember a time when you had money problems. Write about what you would like to get from this chapter that can help you deal with money.

_____

_____

_____

_____

_____

_____

_____

_____

_____

In this chapter . . .

There are no secrets to managing personal finances. If you can add and subtract, you have all the skill you need to manage your money. Learn simple techniques that can create financial peace of mind in *Money in-money out*, *Increase money in*, *Decrease money out*, and *Planning for the future*.

"I can't afford it" is the most common reason students give for dropping out of school. It's often more accurate to say "I don't know how to pay for it" or "I don't think it's worth it." Get past both dilemmas by reading *You can pay for it* and *It's worth it*.

You already are wealthy. Learn what this means in *We live like royalty*.

You can have lots of fun without spending money. Find out how in *Free fun*.

The way we relate to money says a lot about the way we manage the rest of our lives. Positive change in just one area can transform others. Learn a basic technique for this in *Power Process #10: The process is always the same*.

Money in-money out

THE MOST FREQUENT REASON students give for dropping out of school is, "I can't afford it." For most students, that statement is inaccurate. Money produces more unnecessary conflict and worry than almost anything else.

It doesn't seem to matter how much money a person has. People who earn $5,000 a year never have enough. That is understandable. People who earn $15,000 a year never seem to have enough, either. Let's say they earned $150,000 a year. Then they'd have enough, right? Wrong. Money worries seem to upset people no matter how much they have.

"I don't have enough," can have several meanings. One is, "I don't have enough money to meet my obligations." Another is, "I want to have the same things that people with more money have." Both kinds of upset are usually unnecessary.

Money problems result from spending more than is available. It's that simple. We do everything we can to make the problem complicated.

The solution is also simple: Don't spend more than you have. If you are spending more than you have, increase your income, decrease your spending, or do both. This idea has never won a Nobel Prize in economics, but you can't go broke applying it.

There is a big payoff in making money management seem more complicated than it really is. If we don't understand money, we don't have to be responsible for it. After all, if you don't know how to change a flat tire, you don't have to be the one responsible for fixing it. If you never learn to cook, then someone else can take responsibility for making dinner.

It works the same way with money. If you never learned how to manage money, you have an excuse for not facing the truth about it. The responsibility belongs to someone or something else. That no longer works when you admit the truth about money: It doesn't work to spend more than you have.

Telling the truth about money is a First Step to an even bigger payoff—the end of your money worries. Here's how it works. First, tell the truth about how much money you have and how much you spend. Then commit to following this simple suggestion: Spend no more than you have. Doing these two things can put an end to many money worries.

That is what this chapter is about. You can use a Money Monitor to tell the truth about your money. Then you can use the Money Plan to apply that non-Nobel Prize winning suggestion: Spend no more than you have.

This principle does not require that you live like a miser, pinching pennies, and saving used dental floss. On the contrary, mastering money is more likely to bring prosperity. The basics of this system can be mastered by anyone.

Start with a budget. Budgeting is really a type of planning. And, like other forms of planning, it creates freedom. When you have a budget and stick to it, you can relax. You are confident. You don't have to worry about whether you can pay your bills. When you plan, you're more assured of having money in the future for major purchases, trips, tuition, or unexpected emergencies. Budgeting allows you to make choices about money that are consistent with how you want to live.

Budgeting is easy because it is mechanical once you get started. The idea is to project how much money is coming in and how much is going out.

Budgets are most useful when you have one for the next month and one for the long-range—a year or more.

A monthly budget usually includes the recurring income and expense items—such as paychecks, food costs, and housing—that vary little from one month to the next. It also lists unusual income and expenses, such as loans for school, tuition, and trips.

The long-range budget shows the big picture. It helps you make realistic choices about how to make or spend money now so you have what you need in the future.

The budget system in this chapter is set up on a cash basis. That means you consider only the money you are actually getting or spending each month.

Businesses often use a different system, the accrual method. Under income, they include money that hasn't actually been received but that has been billed ("accrued" on their books). Under expenses, they include money that has not actually been spent (bills received but not paid). This form of accounting is unnecessary for most individuals, as long as bills are kept up-to-date.

After you complete Exercise #32 and Exercise #33 you will have a budget system in place. Monitor your money each month and set up a cycle of budget-monitor-budget-monitor. This cycle allows you to continually refine your money management process. When you discover that the money coming in is less than the money going out, you have three options. You can increase money in, decrease money out, or both. Generally, it is easier to do both.

Soon you can be controlling money, instead of having money control you.

Increase money in

For many people, this is the most appealing way to fix a broken budget. After all, if you increase the amount of money coming in, you can still enjoy the benefits of spending it.

This approach is reasonable, and it has a potential problem. When their income increases, many people continue to spend more than they make. Their money problems persist, even at higher incomes. You can avoid this dilemma by managing your expenses, no matter how much money you make.

There are several ways to increase your income while you go to school. You can get scholarships and grants. You can borrow money, inherit it, or receive it as a gift. You can sell property, collect income from investments, or use your savings.

Other ways to increase your money supply include lotteries and theft. These alternatives are risky and could easily distract you from your life as a student.

Start by making money the old-fashioned way: Earn it.

Part-time jobs

If you work while you go to school, you can earn more than money. Working helps you gain experience, establish references, and expand your contacts in the community.

Regular income, even at minimum wage, can make a big difference. Look at your monthly budget to see how it would be affected if you worked just 15 hours a week (times 4.3 weeks a month) for only $5 an hour.

A job also will demonstrate your work patterns. Future employers won't expect you to have been on the President's Cabinet, but they will be pleased to know that you can get along with co-workers and arrive on time every day.

Older, nontraditional students often continue to work full-time or part-time jobs when they return to school. Work and school don't have to conflict, especially if you enlist your employer as an ally in your higher education. In fact, you can find ways to make your work and your schooling complement each other. For some suggestions, see "The art of re-entry—Going back to school as an older student" on page 20.

This article suggests ways to find jobs and keep them in line with your purposes. For more ideas, see the *Career Planning Supplement to Becoming a Master Student*.

How to find a job

To get the most out of your job search, take some time to define what you want. Describe your dream job—the work you would do if you had no money worries. Then brainstorm ways to find or create that job. Including other people in your brainstorm can help you see more options. You could discover some ways to bridge your dreams with reality.

Next, make a list of your work skills. To get a full picture of your abilities, include both content skills and transferable skills. Content skills qualify you for a specific job. For example, a knowledge of accounting principles qualifies you to work as an accountant. Transferable skills can apply to many jobs, even in different fields. Examples are writing, speaking, planning, learning, budgeting, and leading meetings. Many people forget about transferable skills and short-change themselves when they write a resume. You can avoid this mistake.

With your list of skills in hand, go to the library or a career counselor and find out which jobs call for your skills. Often students fail to appreciate the vast range of jobs that are available. Taking this step can multiply your job options.

Some of the best jobs are never advertised. In fact, your best source of information about new jobs is people—friends, relatives, co-workers, and fellow students.

Ask around. Tell everyone you want a job. In particular, tell people who might be able to create a job for you. Many jobs are created on the spot because a person with potential simply shows up and asks. Some students create their own jobs—everything from lawnmowing services to computer consulting.

Make a list of several places that you would like to work. Include places that have advertised jobs and those that don't. Then go to each place on your list and tell someone at each place that you would like a job. This will yield more results than depending on the want ads alone.

The people you speak to might say there isn't a job available, or that the job is filled. That's OK. Ask to see the person in charge of hiring and tell her you want to work.

She will probably say she doesn't have a job

available. No problem. Ask to fill out an application or leave a resume to be considered for future job openings. Then ask when you can check back.

Before you leave, tell her you are a student. Explain why you would like to work there. Briefly tell why you would be an excellent employee, that you are trustworthy, loyal, courteous, kind, obedient, cheerful, thrifty, brave, and so on. Offer to start work anytime ("Today, if you need me!").

Now she sees you as more than an application in a file. You are a living, breathing human being. The next time you meet, you won't be strangers.

Finally, remember to check back, the sooner the better.

You can use a resume as a calling card, something that will remind a potential employer of who you are. A resume is a summary of your work history, education, and references. To get the most impact, make your resume professional-looking, concise, and easy to skim. Stress your accomplishments and skills in ways that will grab the employer's attention.

Visual impact counts. For just a few dollars, a local print shop can typeset, proofread, and print your resume. Have it printed on heavy, rich-looking paper. Avoid getting too fancy, but let the printer set some small headlines.

The interview is the most important part of a job search. When speaking to the prospective employer, remember that people like to talk about themselves. Before the interview, research the company you're approaching. During the interview, ask questions.

Also, respect the interviewer's time. Avoid rambling and ask for the job. That shows you know time is money.

According to one estimate, people recall about 20 percent of what they hear during a conversation and about 90 percent of what they feel. The impression you leave at an interview will depend much more on how you act than on what you say. Be relaxed, confident, and eager. Lighten up, enjoy yourself. If you do, so will the interviewer, and that will increase your chances for a job.

Job hunting is like prospecting for gold. You dig a lot of holes and uncover a lot of rocks before hitting pay dirt. Eventually, you will find work. Before you start your search, set a quota. Tell yourself you will continue the search until you have spoken to at least 100 people—or some other number you can live with.

After two or three interviews you may get tired of hearing people say "We don't have an opening," or, "We already filled that job." At this point, consider your quota—the number chosen before you had your first few rejections. If you ask enough people, someone will say, "Yes!"

The first job you get might not be perfect. If it doesn't conflict with school, consider taking it anyway. Work hard, and make a good impression. It's easier to find a job when you already have one.

How to find another job

Your new job may not be the "executive position" you originally had in mind. It can be a steppingstone to something closer to the executive suite.

First, determine whether you really want to change jobs. Make a list of the benefits of your present job. ("It pays $5.50 an hour. It's close to where I live. I can study on the job.") Then list the disadvantages. ("I have to wear a chicken costume. The boss is grouchy. It pays $5.50 an hour.")

If the disadvantages outweigh the benefits, continue your search. You have an income now, so you have less pressure to take the first job you find. After comparing the advantages and disadvantages of your current job, you will have a more accurate picture of the job you are looking for.

You can use the same techniques to find a new job that you used to find the old one. You also can use contacts that you develop on your current job. You might even find a better job with the same company. That is one reason it pays to do your best, even in a job you don't like.

Keep it in perspective

When you are a student, the purpose of a job is to support you and your educational goals. If the job is in your career field, great. If it is meaningful and contributes to society, great. If the job involves working with people you love and respect, fantastic. If not—well, remember its purpose.

It's also easy to let a job eat up time and energy you need for your education. You can avoid this by managing your time effectively. To get started, choose several time management techniques from Chapter Two. Then decide how you will use them. You're more likely to avoid conflict between work and school if you write long-term plans, keep a semester or quarter calendar, create a weekly plan, and prioritize your to-do lists.

That might sound like a lot of work. It probably will take you only a few minutes a day, and it can save you hours.

Decrease money out

Learning how to control your expenses is a powerful tool for managing money—even more powerful than increasing your income.

There are many ways to decrease the amount of money you spend. Pick from the following list those ideas which best fit your situation. By continually monitoring your money flow, you can determine how to decrease what you spend.

1. Look to the big-ticket items. Changing your own oil or clipping coupons might save you hundreds of dollars. Your choices about which car to buy and where to live can save you tens of *thousands* of dollars. When you look for places to cut expenses, look to the items that cost the most. That's where you can have the most impact on your budget.

2. Use the telephone. You can save time, gasoline, and money. Find out in advance which store has what you want at the right price.

3. Comparison shop. Prices vary and on big items, like cars, the differences can be significant. Also, wait for sales. This is one way to control impulse buying. Almost everything goes on sale sooner or later. Make sure sales offer genuine savings.

If you plan to buy a big item, such as a stereo or car, leave your checkbook at home. Look at all the possibilities, then go home and make your decision when you don't feel pressured by salespeople or your own desire.

Shop at second-hand stores, thrift stores, or garage sales.

4. Be aware of quality. The cheapest product is not always the least expensive over the long run. Sometimes, a slightly more expensive item is the best buy. There is no correlation between the value of something and the amount of money spent to advertise it. Inspect your purchases carefully and see if they are well-made.

5. Keep receipts. If the product turns out to be defective, your complaint carries more weight when you have proof of purchase.

6. Complain. If you didn't get your money's worth, start with the person who sold you the item and work your way up until you are satisfied. Go to the top if necessary. If you have been treated unfairly, contact your Better Business Bureau. If you can't find it in the telephone book, call the local Chamber of Commerce.

Make your complaint specific: date, amount, location, problem.

7. Use coupons. Newspapers and magazines carry clip-out coupons. Beware of misleading coupons—ones that offer widgets for $11.95 when, down the street, you can buy generic widgets for $8.95.

8. Cook for yourself. This one simple idea could save many a sinking budget. Most students would be shocked to learn how much money they spent at fast-food restaurants in a year.

At the grocery store, shop for nutrition and food value. Fresh produce, whole grains, and other foods are not only better for you than processed food, they cost less—a lot less. Cooking for yourself doesn't take much time if you plan in advance.

9. Plan your wardrobe in advance. Stick to one or two color schemes. Find items that you can mix and match with other items. That maroon sharkskin belt looks fantastic in the store, but what can you wear with it? And when?

Shop for next year's clothes at end-of-the-season sales. If you do decide to go along with the latest fad, buy cheap. The style may go out of fashion before the item wears out.

10. Conserve energy. To save money on utility bills, turn out the lights. Keep windows and doors closed in winter. Avoid loss of cool air in summer. When you wash dishes or take a bath in winter, leave the hot water in the sink or tub until it is cool. The heat is exchanged in the room rather than warming the sewer for half a block. In cool weather, dress warmly and keep the house at 68 degrees or less. In hot weather, take cool showers and baths. Leave central air conditioning at 74 degrees or above.

11. Keep your housing costs reasonable. Sometimes an apartment a little farther from school or a slightly smaller house will be much less expensive. Also, carefully compare the cost of living when utilities are not included in rent.

You can keep rent or house payments down by sharing your living space with others. Then you can split the costs. Also look for opportunities to house-sit. Some people will allow a responsible person to live in their house rent-free while they are away. In some cases, they will actually pay someone to house-sit.

Be a good tenant. Pay your rent on time and treat rental property with respect. Landlords appreciate good tenants and often give a break in rent or deposits to someone they trust.

Offer to do repairs or maintenance in exchange for reduced rent. Ask the owner of each place you rent for a favorable reference. These can come in handy when you move.

12. Pay cash. To avoid interest charges, deal in cash. If you don't have the cash, don't buy. Buying on credit makes it more difficult to monitor spending. You can easily bust next month's budget with this month's credit purchases.

If you do use credit, pay off the balance immediately. Finance charges on credit cards are high—often an annual percentage rate of 18 percent or more. If you do accumulate a large credit card balance, ask your bank about a "bill-payer" loan with a lower interest rate. You can use this loan to pay off your credit cards. Then make a promise to never accumulate a balance on your credit card again.

13. Fix things yourself. Many repair or service jobs are easy when you take the time to look into them. Ask friends for help. It's cheaper (and more fun) to buy a friend lunch or treat him to a movie than to pay a repair shop.

14. Notice what you spend on "fun." Blowing your money on fun is fun. It is also a fast way to ruin your budget.

When you spend money on entertainment, ask yourself what the possible benefits will be and whether you could get the same benefits for less money. You can use magazines for free at the library. Libraries might loan music tapes and videotapes—for free. Instead of meeting at a bar, meet at a friend's house where there is no cover charge.

Free entertainment is everywhere. It usually isn't advertised, so search it out. For more ideas, see "Free fun" on page 283.

15. Use public transportation or car pools. A car can be the biggest financial burden in a student's budget. The purchase price is often only the tip of the iceberg. Be sure to include the cost of parking, insurance, repairs, gas, oil changes, maintenance, and tires. When you add up all those items, you may well find it cheaper to take the bus or a cab.

16. Postpone purchases. When you are ready to buy something, wait a week—even if the salesperson pressures you. What seems like a necessity today may not even cross your mind the day after tomorrow. If this seems like a hardship, give yourself a small reward for waiting, and write yourself a reminder note to reconsider the purchase in a week.

17. Shop on a full stomach. Being hungry for food is not just an enticement to buy food. We tend to "want" when we're hungry, and that wanting can extend to anything that is for sale.

18. Avoid snacks. This may sound like a suggestion from a prison guard in northern Siberia. It's not. It is sound advice for the person looking for ways to decrease spending. Snacks typically cost more per nutritional unit than any other food. It is easy to spend several dollars a week, a quarter at a time.

19. Leave your cash in the bank. Avoid carrying cash. If you see money every time you open your wallet, you get the impression you have money to spend.

20. Create a budget. Sound the trumpets, wave the banners, and get this one on videotape. Budgeting is the most effective way to manage your expenses. Budgets allow you to tell the truth about the way you spend money and how you want to change that. When you budget, you take a First Step with money.

The exercises in this chapter are designed to help you create a budget. When you have a budget, you'll know how much is available for food, housing, transportation, entertainment, and other categories of expense. Keep a record of your spending in each category, aiming to keep that spending close to the amount you budget. Or, put the money you budget for each category in a separate envelope—one envelope for food, one for entertainment, and so on. When you see the cash in an envelope is getting low, you'll know to watch your spending in that category.

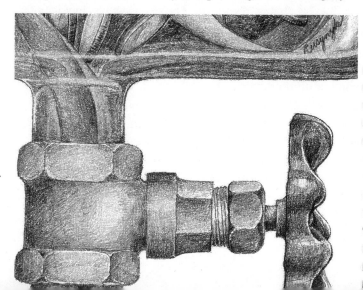

We live like royalty

"But I *really* don't have enough money. You don't know what it's like to get by on what I make."

Suggesting that money worries are unnecessary upsets some people. That's not the intention. The point is this: Frustration about not having enough money will not get you more money, nor will it help you to spend less.

If you want to eliminate money worries, keep reading. This chapter is full of ideas on handling money problems. This book is also full of ideas on handling frustrations in general. The Power Processes can be applied to your relationship with money. You can ease the frustration by being here now, detaching, surrendering, letting go of your pictures of how much money you ought to have, loving your frustration to death, or looking at how you create your money woes. It is all work and calls for the courage to look inward.

You can also consider alternatives to the thought, "I don't have enough." Some of those alternatives include: "I have money I haven't even spent yet," "I deserve money and have as much as I need," "I am rich", or "I live like royalty." These thoughts, when repeated constantly, can change how you feel about money. They can open you up to new possibilities for

making and saving money. Consequently, these thoughts can affect how much money you actually have.

Some people can't say to themselves, "I live like royalty." They can't see the riches they possess. They truly do "create it all" by their selective perceptions, and they are choosing to create scarcity.

Step back in time just 100 years and imagine how a king or queen might have lived. These ruling monarchs would have enough to eat. Several times a year, they would have a feast. In their food would be spices from the four corners of the earth. These people would eat until they were stuffed. And after a meal, they could summon entertainment with the snap of a finger. If they wanted music, a clap of the hands would bring forth dozens of songs. If they wanted humor, they could summon the court jester. If they wanted variety or drama, they could watch the actors of the court.

Transportation was no problem. Horses were always ready and a driver would chauffeur the king or queen from kingdom to kingdom in a matter of days or weeks.

Dress was lavish. Monarchs wore the finest cloth—-smooth, colorful, clean. Unlike the clothes of lesser mortals, the royal wardrobe kept its owners dry and warm. The king and queen got new clothes at least once a year and never had to wear anything that was full of holes.

Their house was a castle. It was clean, dry, and had warm fireplaces in many rooms. The inhabitants were safe from nature and relatively safe from intruders.

In short, these people lived a royal existence.

And they didn't have it nearly as good as most people in North America today.

It's worth it

A college education is one of the most durable and worthwhile investments you can make. It's one of the safest investments possible. When you are clear about what you want, education is usually the surest way to get it.

Education is a unique purchase. It is one of the only things you can buy that will last your lifetime. It can't rust, corrode, break down, or wear out. Education can't be stolen, burned, repossessed, or destroyed. Education is a purchase that becomes a permanent part of you. Once you have it, no one can take it away.

Investing money in your training and abilities is a sure bet. Money invested in land, gold, oil, or stocks can easily be lost. When you invest in yourself, you can't lose. Over their lifetimes, college graduates can expect to earn between $1.2 million and $2.75 million, while high school graduates can expect from $860,000 to $1.87 million.

Education pays off in salaries, job promotions, and career satisfaction. It is also worth investing in again and again as circumstances change and you update your skills.

Higher education has been suggested as the source of everything from better health to happier marriages.

The list of benefits continues:

- *You can earn more money*
- *You can continue to learn, building on the foundation of your education*
- *You can continue to experience personal growth*
- *You can enjoy improved social status*
- *You can experience more self-confidence*

- *You can grasp world events with more ease*
- *You can have more economic and social opportunities*
- *You can be better equipped to be a parent*
- *You can learn how to learn— and how to thrive on change*
- *You can enjoy more physical comfort*

- *You can enjoy increased flexibility on the job (with tight supervision less likely)*
- *You can enjoy improved retirement benefits*
- *You can have greater travel opportunities*
- *Your children are more likely to get farther in their education*

In short, education is a good deal.

Exercise #31
Education by the hour
Determine exactly what it costs you to go to school. Fill in the blanks. Use totals for a semester, quarter, or whatever term system your school uses.

Tuition $_____
Books $_____
Fees $_____
Transportation $_____
Clothing $_____
Food $_____
Housing $_____
Entertainment $_____
Other (insurance, medical, etc.) $_____
Subtotal: $_____
Salary you could earn per term $_____
if you weren't in school
Total (A): $_____

Figure out how many classes you attend in one term. This is the number of your scheduled class periods per week multiplied by the number of weeks in your school term. Put that figure here as

Total (B):_____

Divide the number of classes Total (B) into the Total (A) and put

that amount here: $_____

This is what it costs you to go to one class one time.

You can pay for it

It is often possible to receive assistance in paying for school when you can't pay for it yourself. Financial aid is almost always available in one form or another. Where you get help depends on your background and needs. Take an active role and investigate your options until you find a way to pay for your education.

Taking an active role in financial aid includes determining total costs (tuition, fees, living expenses, travel, books, supplies, etc.); actively searching for various types of funding (work, savings, relatives, scholarships, loans, grants); understanding everything before you sign; completing forms accurately and on time; notifying your school or lender of changes in address, financial condition, or attendance; and being aware of refund policies.

Set up a strategy

Financing your education is most useful when it includes a master plan for the big picture. Instead of looking at just one term, consider the entire time you will be in school.

A plan for paying for your entire education makes staying to the end a more realistic possibility. If you start every term wondering where you are going to get the money, you are more likely to drop out.

A master plan includes a clear picture of your income and expenses. It is a long-term budget listing how much you need to complete your education and where you plan to get the money. Use the budgeting system described in this chapter.

Sticking to a budget is particularly important if you receive a large grant or loan at the beginning of the school year. It is tempting to spend the money on something besides education. Hundreds of dollars intended for your education could go a long way toward buying a car, stereo, clothes, camera, video equipment, parties, and ski vacations. Not only would you be short for the next term, you might have to pay back the money without benefit of a completed education.

Once you know precisely how much you need, get help finding the money. Every college has someone to assist with this.

For a copy of the "Federal Student Aid Fact Sheet," write to:
U.S. Department of Education
Office of Student Financial Assistance
Washington, D.C. 20202-5464

Or call the Federal Student Aid Information Center tollfree at:
1-800-333-INFO

You can also get help from publications in financial aid offices and most public and college libraries.

Find...

You can find money for your education from the Federal Government, most state governments, parents, other relatives, banks, and the college or school you attend. Programs vary and are available for students with differing needs. The programs also change. Be sure to get the most current information. Look for money in the following places.

1. Pell Grants, based on need, are awarded by the school you attend and are financed by the Federal Government. This is the largest federal student aid program. Pell Grants provide a foundation of financial aid to which aid from other sources may be added. The Department of Education guarantees that each participating school will receive enough money to pay the Pell Grants of its eligible students. Money received through a Pell Grant does not have to be repaid.

2. Supplemental Educational Opportunity Grants (SEOG) are designed to add to other forms of financial aid. There is no guarantee that every eligible student will be able to receive an SEOG. Money is limited and application deadlines are critical.

3. College work-study (CWS) gives you a chance to earn money to help pay for your educational expenses. Your pay will be at least the current Federal minimum wage and may also be affected by the type of work you do and the skills required. Jobs may be on or off campus. Your financial aid administrator can assign work hours based on your class schedule, your health, and your academic progress.

4. Perkins Loans are available directly from a school that has received money for this purpose. These long-term loans are based on financial need and have low interest rates. The loan is repaid in monthly payments after you complete your education.

5. Stafford Loans are low interest loans made by a lender such as a bank, credit union, or savings and loan association. They are insured by a guarantee agency in each state and reinsured by the Federal Government. Like Perkins loans, these are repaid in monthly payments after you complete your education.

6. PLUS Loans and *Supplemental Loans for Students (SLS)* are made by lenders such as banks, credit unions, or savings and loan associations. They have variable interest rates, adjusted each year. PLUS loans are for parents who want to borrow to help pay for their children's education. SLS loans are for student borrowers. You don't have to show financial need for either loan and, generally, repayment of principal and interest begins 60 days after the last loan disbursement. If a deferment applies (including a deferment for being in school), repayment of principal can be postponed.

7. Scholarships are available through most colleges for outstanding performance in athletics, academics, or the arts. Fraternal, service, educational, and social societies like the American Association of University Women, Elks, Rotary, Kiwanis, Sertoma, or Lions often provide grants that don't have to be repaid for local students.

8. The Veterans Administration has money available for some veterans and their dependents. The War Orphans Educational Assistance, Air Force Aid Society, and Army Educational Assistance programs are set up for children of military personnel.

9. Active military personnel can take advantage of financial aid programs by contacting their local personnel office.

10. Company assistance programs, provided by employers, offer financial aid for employees to attend school while working.

11. Social Security payments are available up to age 18 for unmarried students with a deceased parent or a parent who is disabled or drawing Social Security benefits.

12. State vocational rehabilitation offices usually have financial assistance for people with visual impairments, with hearing or speech difficulties, or with other physical disabilities.

13. The U.S. Bureau of Indian Affairs has financial aid available for Native American students.

14. The local branch of your state employment office provides information about two government programs which are set up to train the unemployed. These programs are JTPA (Job Training Partnership Act) and WIN (Work Incentive). Both provide money for going to school.

15. Relatives often provide financial help for a dedicated student. Someone who would be reluctant or unwilling to lend you money for a car, a new business, or a trip to the South Pacific might be honored to help you get an education. A sincere, straightforward request is never insulting.

16. Personal savings comprise the bulk of money spent on higher education. Use money from savings accounts, bonds, stocks, or trusts set up by others to support your education.

17. Employment is another way students can get additional money. Working in a job related to your future career field can supplement your education as well as your finances.

18. Sell something. Find something you need less than an education and sell it. This may be an option of last resort, but it is an option. Consider the money you have tied up in a car, motorcycle, horse, piano, house, or hobby.

...money

Exercise #32
Where does all the money go?

Money is easy to lose track of. It likes to escape when no one is looking. And usually, no one is looking. That's why the simple act of observing money can be so powerful, even if that is the only thing you do to manage money.

This exercise is an opportunity to observe how money flows into and out of your life. You will record all the money you receive and spend over the course of one month. This is no small task. It requires commitment to carry a pen and a Money Monitor and to use them, even when it's inconvenient. Doing so can give you power. Here's how to tap that power:

1. Tear out the Money Monitor form on the following page. You can make photocopies of the form to use it each month.

2. On the left-hand side of the form there is a column marked "Money In." Record here all the money you receive during the course of a month. Include money from jobs, family, loans, veterans' benefits, and any other sources. For example, if you take money out of a savings account, write it down as "Money In." The "Money In" column is divided into two sub-columns. Record the date you get the money, where the money came from (under "Date/Note") and the amount. (See the example below.)

3. Record "Money Out"—the money you spend—by categories. Under "Money Out—Categories" record rent, phone bills, utility bills, car payments, credit card payments, and any other bills you pay every month. Other categories might include food, transportation, entertainment, savings, and clothing. Many people have enough categories to fill two or three pages of a Money Monitor. If an expense item doesn't fit into a category, put it in a "miscellaneous" category. It is important to record everything you spend. Write down the date you spent it, a brief description of what you spent the money on, and the amount you spent. (See the example below.)

4. Record your "Money In" and CMoney Out" every day for the next month. Under "Amount" you also can record how you paid for the item by using simple codes—"$" for cash, "chk" for check, and "cc" for credit card. A handy way to keep track of cash spent is to fold a 3x5 card over the cash in your wallet. Every time you take out a bill to buy something, you will see the card. Record the expense on the 3x5 card and write it in your Money Monitor later.

5. At the end of the month, add up all of the columns. Then use these totals to construct a budget in Exercise #33.

After you create a monthly budget, you can use these Money Monitors as a navigational device to keep yourself headed in the direction of your budget. After a few months of recording Money In and Money Out—income and expenses—you're likely to notice patterns. You can develop your own style of making money work for you rather than against you.

MONEY MONITOR

MONEY IN		MONEY OUT— CATEGORIES		
		Entertainment		Car- gas,
DATE/NOTE	AMOUNT	DATE/NOTE	AMOUNT	DATE/NOTE
Savings	$500	2/1 Fox Lounge	5.00	2/4 Gas
Grant	350	2/15 6pk	3.50	2/11 Gas
Tax Refund	300	2/16 Movie	4.00	2/18 Gas
Job	200	2/19 Cards	3.00	2/19 Oil
Uncle Jim	500	2/22 Union Movie	4.00	2/22 Gas
Loan	1000	2/27 Hall Inn	3.00	2/27 Gas
	$2850.		22.50	

MONEY MONITOR

MONEY IN		MONEY OUT— CATEGORIES													
DATE/NOTE	AMOUNT	DATE/NOTE	AMOUNT	DATE/NOTE	AMOUNT	DATE/NOTE	AMOUNT	DATE/NOTE	AMOUNT	DATE/NOTE	AMOUNT	DATE/NOTE	AMOUNT	DATE/NOTE	AMOUNT

MONEY MONITOR

MONEY IN

DATE/NOTE	AMOUNT

MONEY OUT— CATEGORIES

DATE/NOTE	AMOUNT	DATE/NOTE	AMOUNT	DATE/NOTE	AMOUNT	DATE/NOTE	AMOUNT	DATE/NOTE	AMOUNT

MONEY MONITOR

MONEY IN

DATE/NOTE	AMOUNT

MONEY OUT— CATEGORIES

DATE/NOTE	AMOUNT	DATE/NOTE	AMOUNT	DATE/NOTE	AMOUNT	DATE/NOTE	AMOUNT	DATE/NOTE	AMOUNT	DATE/NOTE	AMOUNT	DATE/NOTE	AMOUNT

The monthly budget

Use this exercise to develop a plan for spending your money month-to-month. Complete the Money Monitor (Exercise #32) before doing this exercise. Figures from month-to-month usually change because of periodic payments such as tuition, so revise this as needed. Complete this monthly budget prior to doing the long-term budget in Exercise #34.

1. Tear out the Budget worksheet on the following page. You can photocopy it before you begin to use this form every month.

2. At the top of the form under "Money in from:" list all your sources of income from your Money Monitor. In the left-hand column, write down where the money came from. In the middle column, write down the amount.

3. Under "Money out to:" list all the "Money Out" categories, titles, and totals from your Money Monitor. List the amounts in the middle column. (See the example below.)

4. Add up all the "Money in from" items and write the total in the box labeled "Total cash income." Add up the "Money out to:" items and write the total in the box labeled "Total cash expenses."

5. Subtract total cash expenses from total cash income, and write the result in the box labeled "Money left" under the "This month" column. This is your monthly surplus—or deficit.

6. Now you can decide how much surplus you want next month or how large a deficit you can survive. (Unless you are a government, you probably can't run a deficit for long.) You also can set a goal to come out dead even—zero surplus and zero deficit—if you include in your "Money out" categories money you set aside for savings and emergencies. When you have determined your goal, write it in the box marked "Money left" under the "Next month" column.

7. Next, adjust your "Money in from" categories (income) and your "Money out to" categories (expenses) to meet your goal for next month. For example, if you ran a $50 deficit last month and you want to run a $50 surplus next month, increase income by $100, reduce expenses by $100, or do some combination of both.

You might decide to work 10 more hours to earn $50 more next month. Then you could cut your entertainment budget by $20, your food budget by $15, and your clothing budget by $15.

Write the amounts for your adjusted budget categories in the column labeled "Next month." Then add them all up to make sure you will reach your goal.

Other budget tips: Use old receipts, utility bills, cancelled checks, and credit card records as sources of information for your budget. Also, remember to include any unusual expenses you can predict, such as tuition, medical bills, automobile licenses, car repairs, and vacations.

Each month, examine the previous month's Money Monitor and use that information to refine your budget. Be realistic about what money is likely to come in and go out. Then stick to the budget.

Money in from:	This month	Next mon
1. SAVINGS	#150	# 200
2. Grant	100	100
3. Tax refund	90	0
4. Job	320	370
5. Uncle Jim	300	300
6. LOAN	200	200
7.		
8.		
9.		
10.		
Total cash income	$1,160	$ 1,170

Money out to:		
11. Entertainment	#30	#25
12. Car	40	40
13. Clothing	0	50
14. Laundry	10	10
15. Food	152	160
16. Phone	30	25
17. Household	15	20

BUDGET_____/_____/_____
<small>DATE</small>

Money in from:	This month	Next month	
1 _____	_____	_____	
2 _____	_____	_____	
3 _____	_____	_____	
4 _____	_____	_____	
5 _____	_____	_____	
6 _____	_____	_____	
7 _____	_____	_____	
8 _____	_____	_____	
9 _____	_____	_____	
10 _____	_____	_____	
Total cash income	$	$	Total in (add 1-10)

Money out to:	This month	Next month	
11 _____	_____	_____	
12 _____	_____	_____	
13 _____	_____	_____	
14 _____	_____	_____	
15 _____	_____	_____	
16 _____	_____	_____	
17 _____	_____	_____	
18 _____	_____	_____	
19 _____	_____	_____	
20 _____	_____	_____	
21 _____	_____	_____	
22 _____	_____	_____	
23 _____	_____	_____	
24 _____	_____	_____	
25 _____	_____	_____	
26 _____	_____	_____	
27 _____	_____	_____	
28 _____	_____	_____	
29 _____	_____	_____	
30 _____	_____	_____	
31 _____	_____	_____	
32 _____	_____	_____	
33 _____	_____	_____	
34 _____	_____	_____	
35 _____	_____	_____	
36 _____	_____	_____	
37 _____	_____	_____	
38 _____	_____	_____	
39 _____	_____	_____	
Total cash expenses	$	$	Total out (Add 11-39)
Money left	$	$	From Total In subtract Total Out

BUDGET_____/_____/_____
DATE

Money in from:

	This month	Next month
1		
2		
3		
4		
5		
6		
7		
8		
9		
10		

Total cash income $ ___ $ ___   Total in (add 1-10)

Money out to:

11		
12		
13		
14		
15		
16		
17		
18		
19		
20		
21		
22		
23		
24		
25		
26		
27		
28		
29		
30		
31		
32		
33		
34		
35		
36		
37		
38		
39		

Total cash expenses $ ___ $ ___   Total out (Add 11-39)

Money left $ ___ $ ___   From Total In subtract Total Out

Planning for the future

The benefits of taking control of your money are cumulative. Planning now paves the way for fewer money worries in the future.

Savings

You don't have to wait until you finish school to begin saving for the future. Even if you are in debt, living in a dorm on a diet of macaroni, you can begin saving today. It's worth it. Saving now helps you establish a good credit rating in the future.

You can save for short-term goals (a new winter coat), mid-term goals (a down payment on a car next year), or long-term goals (a down payment on a house in several years).

You also can put money aside for emergencies. A guideline for economic survival is to have savings equal to three to six months of living expenses. Build this "nest egg" first. Then save for major purchases, such as a house, car, your child's education, retirement, or an expensive vacation. Keep in mind that living expenses usually grow as we get older. That means the nest egg needs to increase, also.

Savings can include liquid investments such as insured savings accounts, certificates of deposit, and savings bonds. (The word *liquid* means that you can turn these investments into cash quickly.)

See your banker or an independent, certified financial planner for advice on how to save. In general, avoid getting investment advice from someone who has something to sell, such as a stockbroker.

Use the Money Monitor and Budget Worksheet in this chapter to set up a regular program for savings. Budget money for savings just as you budget money for going to the movies. Even a small amount of money set aside each month can grow rapidly. If you saved just $30 each month in an account that pays 8 percent interest compounded monthly, you'd have $10,450 in 15 years.

The biggest benefit of starting to save right now is practice. If you get into the *habit* of saving, you are more likely to do it when you can afford to put away more than $30 a month.

Savings are one of the most effective ways to take control of your money. If you want to reach your financial goals, save at least 10 percent of your monthly take-home pay for as long as you work. And if you can save more, do so.

Investments

Investing is risky. Avoid it until you have that nest egg—enough savings to meet your expenses for three to six months, even if you lose your job. It's also wise to invest only after saving money for the major purchases mentioned above.

If you do have money to invest, consider something safe, like no-load mutual funds or blue chip stocks and bonds. Plan to spend a lot of time studying investment alternatives.

Sensible investing requires extensive homework. Avoid taking a friend's advice on how to invest your hard-earned money. Only risk money you can afford to lose. Keep the grocery money.

Insurance

Once you have insured your health and your life, it's usually possible to stay insured even if you develop a major illness. For that reason, it is a wise investment for the future to insure yourself now.

Buy health, auto, and life insurance with high deductibles to save on premiums.

There are basically two kinds of life insurance: term and whole life. Term insurance is the least expensive. It pays if you die, and that's it. Whole life is more expensive. It is a savings and investment plan in addition to paying if you die. Under a typical whole life policy, you could collect a pension when you retire in addition to having your life insured.

You may get a higher return on your money if you buy the lower-priced term insurance and invest the extra dollars in something other than insurance. This is not always true, however. Some new policies, called "universal life," combine features of term and whole life insurance. Benefits vary from policy to policy, so study each one carefully.

All insurance is not alike, so shop with more than one agent before you decide. Ask questions about anything you don't understand. If the agent can't answer your questions to your satisfaction, then get another agent.

Insurance is available for your possessions even if you don't own a house. Check the cost of renter's insurance. It can cover your belongings against fire or theft.

If you drive at all, car insurance is a must. Shop around—premiums vary considerably. Also ask for safe driver or good student discounts.

Contracts

Be careful. Before you sign anything, read the fine print. If you are confused, ask questions and don't stop asking until you are no longer confused.

Be leery of someone who says: "Oh, this is just the standard lease arrangement. I wouldn't try to pull the wool over your eyes. You look too smart for that."

After you sign a contract or lease, read the entire document again. If you think you have signed something that you will regret, back out quickly and get your release in writing. Purchase contracts in many states are breakable, if you act quickly. For example, the buyer might be allowed to back out within three days, with no penalty.

If you can't get out, get legal help immediately. If you have little money, inquire at any attorney's office or look in the phone book for a legal aid office. Legal aid attorneys offer free or low-cost assistance to people who meet certain income guidelines.

Be particularly careful of long-term purchase agreements. That beautiful cookware might cost you only 72 cents a day, but if you have to make payments for three years, it will cost you $788.

Know the total cost before joining book clubs or record clubs.

Credit

A good credit rating is a worthy objective. If you don't already have one, you can begin to establish a credit rating now. Borrow a small amount of money and pay it back on time. Consider borrowing for the next major purchase you make. Start now to demonstrate you can be trusted to make all of your payments, and that you can make them on time.

Credit cards are also a way to establish a credit record. Get a bank credit card, an oil company credit card, or a major department store card. Use it only for necessary items that you have enough cash to buy anyway. Keep track of how much you spent and save the equal amount in cash.

Pay off the entire credit card balance each month. An unpaid balance is a sure sign that you are spending more money than you have.

Utility companies also influence your credit rating. Pay your telephone, gas, electric, and water bills on time. The temptation is to let big companies wait for their money. Don't do it. Develop a credit rating that will support your borrowing large amounts of money, if you ever need it.

With your utility company, explore "budget plans" for monthly payments that fluctuate, such as those for heating your home. These plans average your yearly expenses so you pay about the same amount each month. That makes it easier to budget monthly.

To keep your financial net worth from decreasing, borrow no more to buy something than it's worth after you buy it. Say that you borrow $10,000 to buy a $10,000 car. The moment you drive it off the lot, it's a used car. Already the car's actual value may only be $8,000. A wiser strategy is to borrow only $8,000 or less.

By the same logic, it's not wise to borrow money to pay for a vacation. Your trip to Florida has little value to anyone else after you take it. It's hard enough getting people to look at your slides of the beach, let alone try to sell them a used vacation.

An education, on the other hand, is a durable investment that offers a worthwhile return. Borrowing money to pay for school makes sense. Even then, aim to pay part of your education bills from your own savings. That's one more step to financial peace of mind.

Exercise #34
The long-term budget

A long-term budgeting works very much like the monthly budget.
Do Exercise #33: "The monthly budget" before you do this one.

1. Use a copy of the Budget Worksheet and title the colums as "Draft Budget" and "Final Budget" to represent either a year or the length of one school term. (See the example on this page.)

2. Write down the same income and expense categories you used in Exercise #33: "The monthly budget." Now, under the column "Draft budget," predict the totals for each category.

3. List any unusual income or expense items you can predict, such as lump-sum grants (money in) or tuition payments (money out).

4. Total the "Money in" and "Money out" items, subtract the total expenses from the total income, and write the result in "Money left."

5. Don't panic. It is common to have more money going out than coming in the first time you make a long-range projection. The effectiveness of this exercise may be finding out that you are spending more than you have. If that is the case, try it again using the "Final budget" column. Re-work your budget until Money Out is less than Money In. Be realistic and don't cut necessary expenses.

When you have figured out a workable plan, write your revised projections in the right-hand column that you labeled "Final budget." (See the example below.)

BUDGET 1 / 15 / 92 DATE	Draft budget ~~This month~~	Final budget ~~Next month~~
Money in from:		
1. SAVINGS	$1000	$1200
2. GRANT	1100	1000
3. TAX refund	100	100
4. Job	2500	2800
5. Uncle Jim	600	600
6. LOAN	2000	2500
7.		
8.		
9.		
10.		
Total cash income	**$ 7,300**	**$ 8,200**
Money out to:		
11. Entertainment	$350	$300
12. Car	500	450
13. Clothing	400	400
14. Laundry	150	120
15. Food	2000	1900
16. Phone	350	300
17. Household	200	250
18. Tuition	3000	3000
19. Books	500	500

Exercise #35

What are you worth?

Net worth is an accounting term that refers to the difference between what you own and what you owe. The goal of most companies is to have their net worth increase even when they take on more debt. This is a reasonable goal for individuals as well.

1. Under assets, list everything you own that is worth anything. This can include money you have in the bank in checking accounts, savings accounts, bonds, or certificates of deposit. Also include money owed to you.

Include the value of your car, house, stocks, boat, and other personal property. Don't forget clothes, jewelry, appliances, and hobby equipment.

To determine the value of these items, estimate what you could get for them if you had to sell them quickly. Be realistic. This amount is often a fraction of what you paid for the item. Don't use the amount you paid or the replacement cost.

2. Under liabilities, list everything you owe. Include money you owe to mortgage companies, banks, credit card companies, department stores, individuals (including relatives), and credit unions. Don't forget school loans.

3. Total the assets first and then liabilities. Compute your net worth by subtracting total liabilities (Total 2) from total assets (Total 1). This is your financial worth, as seen from a banker's point of view.

You can repeat this exercise every few months to get a picture of how your financial worth is changing.

FINANCIAL STATEMENT _3_ / _8_ / _____
DATE

Assets:

1	Checking	$52.25
2	Savings	250.00
3	1982 Chevette	900.00
4	Clothes	350.00
5	Jewelry	125.00
6	Stereo	175.00
7	Camera (New)	100.00
8	Weights	35.00
9	Bicycle - 10:speed	50.00
10	Textbooks ($10 ea. - 10 books)	100.00

Total assets $2137.25.   Total 1 (add 1-10)

Liabilities:

11		
12	Uncle Jim + interest	$1050.00
13	Student Loan	2000.00
14		
15		

FINANCIAL STATEMENT ____/____/____
DATE

Assets:

1 _____ _____
2 _____ _____
3 _____ _____
4 _____ _____
5 _____ _____
6 _____ _____
7 _____ _____
8 _____ _____
9 _____ _____
10 _____ _____

Total assets | $ | Total 1
(add 1-10)

Liabilities:

11 _____ _____
12 _____ _____
13 _____ _____
14 _____ _____
15 _____ _____
16 _____ _____
17 _____ _____
18 _____ _____
19 _____ _____
20 _____ _____
21 _____ _____
22 _____ _____
23 _____ _____
24 _____ _____
25 _____ _____
26 _____ _____
27 _____ _____
28 _____ _____
29 _____ _____
30 _____ _____
31 _____ _____
32 _____ _____
33 _____ _____
34 _____ _____
35 _____ _____
36 _____ _____
37 _____ _____
38 _____ _____
39 _____ _____

Total Liabilities | $ | Total 2
(Add 11-39)

Net worth | $ | From Total 1
subtract Total 2

FINANCIAL STATEMENT____/____/____
_{DATE}

Assets:
1 _____ _____
2 _____ _____
3 _____ _____
4 _____ _____
5 _____ _____
6 _____ _____
7 _____ _____
8 _____ _____
9 _____ _____
10 _____ _____

Total assets | $ | Total 1 (add 1-10)

Liabilities:
11 _____ _____
12 _____ _____
13 _____ _____
14 _____ _____
15 _____ _____
16 _____ _____
17 _____ _____
18 _____ _____
19 _____ _____
20 _____ _____
21 _____ _____
22 _____ _____
23 _____ _____
24 _____ _____
25 _____ _____
26 _____ _____
27 _____ _____
28 _____ _____
29 _____ _____
30 _____ _____
31 _____ _____
32 _____ _____
33 _____ _____
34 _____ _____
35 _____ _____
36 _____ _____
37 _____ _____
38 _____ _____
39 _____ _____

Total Liabilities | $ | Total 2 (Add 11-39)

Net worth | $ | From Total 1 subtract Total 2

Free fun

Sometimes, it seems that the only way to have fun is to spend money. Not true. Aside from free entertainment available through your school and community, your imagination is the only limit on free fun. Many of these ideas may sound crazy. Pick a few that sound fun and experiment. Add your own ideas.

Exercise
Visit a pet store
Ride elevators
Take a candlelight bath
Grow a beard
Start a club
Write a letter—continuing story letters or
    mirror-readable-only letters
Play board games
Have an egg toss
Give a massage
Reread old letters and journals
Sing loudly
Climb trees
Test drive new cars
Look at the babies in a maternity ward
Kick a rock down the street
Paint scenes on your windows
Write a poem
Give a haircut
Learn to juggle
Adopt a grandparent, little brother or sister, etc.
Bicycle
Play cards
Throw a popcorn and television movie party

Window shop
Arm wrestle
Write to Ann Landers
Go puddle stomping
Make yourself breakfast in bed
Hike
Watch sunrises or sunsets
Skip
Kiss
Build a snowman
Call a friend (not long distance)
Tickle
Pillow fight
Plan a slumber party
Sleep outside
Read
Start a water balloon fight
Watch birds
Dress up
Open all your cabinets, and drawers, then close them
Look at old photographs
Draw
Make wild flower crowns
Roast marshmallows
Listen to music
Dance
Catch fireflies
Watch people
Whittle
Whistle
Stretch
Take a nap
Fill a friend's car with balloons (blow them up first)
Have a goofy scavenger hunt
Peel an orange, keeping the peel in one piece
Star gaze
Short sheet beds
Skip stones
Play tag
Weed a garden
Wash and wax your car
Giggle
Scratch a back
Go fishing
Fly a kite
Throw a house-cleaning party
Go to the library to read or listen to tapes
Start a comedy improvisation group
Get involved in a political issue
Join intramural sports
Walk
Build a snow sculpture

Journal Entry #74
Discovery Statement

Reflect on what you want from an education that makes it worth the investment. You are likely to spend several thousand dollars, maybe even tens of thousands of dollars, getting educated. Write about what's in it for you.

Spending money on education is worth it for me because I can get. . .

I can also get. . .

Journal Entry #75
Discovery Statement

Exercises #32, #33, #34, and #35 all dealt with you and your money. You were given a chance to look at your financial worth, your current spending habits, getting and spending money, and short- and long-term budgets. Write about what you learned concerning each area.

Having completed the financial statement that listed my assets, liabilities, and net worth, I learned that I . . .

Having completed the Money Monitor, giving me a picture of how I manage money, I learned that I. . .

I also learned that I. . .

Having completed the long-term budget, I learned that I. . .

Having completed the monthly budget, I learned that I. . .

If you're in trouble

Financial problems are common. You can handle money problems in a way that protects a good credit rating. If you get in over your financial head, here is a strategy.

1. Get specific data. Complete the following exercises in this chapter:

Exercise #32: "Where does all the money go?" (page 271)
Exercise #33: "Monthly budget" (page 274)
Exercise #34: "Long-term budget" (page279)
Exercise #35: "What are you worth?" (page 280)

If you have trouble collecting this information, get some help. A bookkeeper or an accounting student can usually help.

2. Be honest with creditors. It's best to let people know in advance if you can't pay them. They may not be happy, but they will appreciate knowing about the problem. Suggest a payment schedule. Determine the amount you are sure you could pay every month and ask if that would be workable for your creditors. Most would rather receive something each month than risk never getting paid.

3. Go for credit counseling. Most cities have agencies with professional advisers who can help straighten out your financial problems. They may even contact creditors for you. Go prepared. Take all your bills, loans, and other obligations. Take the data mentioned in step #1 above.

4. Change your spending patterns. Spending money is a habit similar to eating food. It is not easy to change. If you have a history of overspending (or under-earning), know that change is possible and sometimes slow. Congratulate yourself on small improvements and stick to effective techniques for money management.

Journal Entry #76
Discovery Statement

Much about life has nothing to do with money. On a separate sheet of paper, brainstorm a list of areas in your life that are unaffected by money. Remember, a brainstorm is a quick, long list of whatever comes to mind.

After the brainstorm, circle those items that really don't have anything to do with how much money you have. Then write a Discovery Statement concerning money.

Concerning money in my life, I learned that I. . .

The process is always the same

PEOPLE OPERATE LIKE HOLOGRAMS. Holograms are three-dimensional pictures made by using lasers and a special kind of film. You can cut holographic film into tiny pieces and reproduce the entire image from each piece. Each piece contains the whole.

Scientists have observed this same principle at work in biology, physics, sociology, politics and management, as well as in individual human behavior.

Biologists know that the chromosomes in each cell are the blueprints for that entire organism. Careful study of any one cell can show a plan for the entire body.

Pollsters can survey a few people and determine how millions of people feel about an issue.

A student who skips one assignment in English Literature is more likely to skip another. If he hasn't prepared for any of the last three classes, he is unlikely to be prepared for final exams. How someone reacts in a traffic jam might tell how he handles stress in general. If a man is attentive and thorough in washing the dinner dishes, he is probably detail-oriented at work.

When you carefully observe one part of your life, you gain insight into the way you conduct other parts of your life. And if you change your behavior in one small area, your behavior may change in several other areas.

Changing a small behavior is similar to the principle of a "trim tab." A trim tab is a small rudder at the end of a large rudder on a plane or a ship. Air pressure or water pressure can exert tremendous pressure on the large rudder, making it difficult to move. That's where the trim tab comes in. This small rudder is easier to move. Because of its location and leverage, it turns the larger rudder just as the larger rudder turns the ship or the plane.

That's what can happen when we make small changes in our behavior. For example, take a student who uses two note-taking techniques from Chapter Five in biology class on Monday. This student is more likely to use the same techniques in history class on Tuesday. And those note-taking techniques are related to the reading techniques he might decide to use Tuesday night, which are related to the time

management techniques he will use Wednesday to get a head start on his political science paper.

Within a few weeks that one act—using two note-taking techniques during one biology class—can shift the course of his career as a student.

This example is not an exaggeration. If anything, it understates the power of seeing our natural tendency to live in patterns, to act out of habit. When we see our patterns, we can use small actions to make big changes.

The key is being able to look at the details and see the patterns. You can use the Discovery Statements in this book to do that. Look beyond the specific study technique you are writing about and see your whole life reflected in your response to an exercise or a suggestion. Discover what that small insight tells you about how you live the rest of your life. An objective look at one item in your personal catalog of behavior is like putting your eye to a keyhole. Suddenly, a whole new room appears, and what you see is you.

When you discover a behavior you don't like, you can rearrange the whole pattern by changing one small part of your life. If you have a habit of being late for class, and if you want to change that process, be on time to one class. As soon as you change the

old pattern by getting ready and going on time to one class, you'll likely   find yourself arriving at all of your classes on time. You may even start arriving everywhere else on time.

The joy of this process is watching one small change ripple through your whole life.

If you know that you are usually nervous, you don't have to change how you react in all situations at all times. Just change your nervous behavior in one setting. Like magic, watch the rest of your nervousness lessen, or even disappear.

By looking closely at the little things you do, you can discover yourself. Modify one or two of those little things, and watch your whole life change.

Fred Smith,

a graduate of Yale, is the founder and CEO of Federal Express Corporation.

A Business Visionary Who Really Delivered, *reprinted by permission from Nation's Business, November, 1981. Copyright 1981 U.S. Chamber of Commerce.*

Frederick W. Smith may have a common last name, but he is a most uncommon man. What other American business leader of today had a revolutionary idea and converted it into a company that, starting from scratch and with heavy early losses, passed the $500 million revenue mark and had a 10 percent net profit margin in a few years?

Or founded such a company in his 20's and is guiding it toward a distant maturity at the ripe old age of 37?

What other American business leader with so brilliant an idea first wrote it out in a college paper that was graded C? Or says that the people with the greatest impact on him have been a poorly educated sergeant whom he led in combat and a science professor who liked to buzz a university stadium in a fighter plane?

What other. . .?

This could go on and on.

Fred Smith is chairman and chief executive officer of Memphis-based Federal Express Corporation, an air cargo firm that specializes in overnight delivery door-to-door, using its own planes.

To put it another way, Fred Smith is Federal Express.

Smith, a Memphis native whose father became a millionaire after founding a bus company and whose grandfather was a Mississippi riverboat captain, got his revolutionary idea in the 60's while majoring in economics and political science at Yale.

Technological change had opened a radically new transportation market, he decided. The proliferation of computers and similarly intricate equipment—and the impracticality of stocking multitudes of expensive and rapidly obsolescent parts at offices and plants all over the country—posed an enormous logistics problem.

"Steamboats and trains were the logistics arm of the Industrial Revolution's first stage," he says. "Trucks became a good logistics arm later—and still are because of their flexibility. But moving the parts and pieces to support the Electronics Age requires very fast transportation over long distances. I became convinced that a different type of system was going to be a major part of the national economy. . ."

Smith spelled it out in an overdue economics paper. To cut cost and time, packages from all over the country would be flown to a central point, there to be distributed and flown out again to their destinations—a hub-and-spokes pattern, his company calls it today. The flying would be late at night when air lanes were empty. Airports used would be in sizable cities, and trucks would carry packages to their final destinations, whether in those cities or in smaller communities. Equipment and documents from anywhere in the U.S. could be delivered anywhere in the U.S. the next day. . .

For the benefit of business history, it would be nice to have that college paper today. But who saves college papers, particularly those done in one night and branded mediocre? Smith says the professor— he doesn't name him—apparently didn't think much of either his concept or the way he laid it out. "Anyway," he says, "to a ne'er-do-well student like myself, the grade was acceptable."

He says one reason he was no scholastic superstar was that many courses he had to take didn't interest him. Other things did. He and two faculty members resurrected a long-dormant flying club at Yale. One of his cohorts was Professor Norwood Russell Hansen.

"Russ taught the psychology of science—how science was developed," Smith says. "I was a friend of his, not one of his students. He had a big impact on me because of his outlook on life. He was a great singer and a pianist of virtual concert talent. He rode a motorcycle, and he had a World War II fighter plane that he flew all over the place. He buzzed the Yale Bowl from time to time. He marched to the beat of a different drummer. . ."

Smith went to Vietnam as a platoon leader. . .

"A lot of the people in my platoon had an influence on my life," he says. "The one who made the strongest impression was my platoon sergeant, Jack Jackson, a black guy who had been in the Marines about 14 years and was not very well educated. He lost his life in Vietnam later.

"Sgt. Jack was probably the wisest man I have ever met. He had a wisdom about what people who aren't officers think and want. That has stood me in good stead since as a manager.

"Ordinarily, kids who go to Yale—some of them work on construction gangs for the summer, big deal!—don't really get to know the kind of people who fill your gas tank."

Such people, Smith says, are "enormously important" to a company's success, and at Federal Express, to make sure they realize he realizes it, he has done some "iconoclastic things. . ."

"I spend much time trying to find out what our employees think," Smith says. . .

Will he be successful in future undertakings? Says Arthur C. Bass, vice chairman: "A few years ago, some of us used to let off steam in the afternoon by playing basketball on a court behind an apartment house. It was amazing—no matter who had the ball and no matter where Fred was on the court, if Fred's side needed to score to win, he would get the ball and make the winning basket. That's the way he is in the business world."

QUIZ

1. Name at least four sources for money to help students pay for their education.

2. When listing work skills, you can list both content skills and transferable skills. What is the difference?

3. Describe at least three ways to decrease your expenditures while you are in school.

4. The only purpose for having a part-time job while you are a student is to get experience in your career field. True or false. Explain your answer.

5. How can you avoid getting into financial trouble when you use credit cards?

QUIZ
C O N T I N U E D

6. If you are in financial trouble, which of the following strategies is LEAST likely to help:

  (A) Begin to monitor and budget.
  (B) Borrow additional money.
  (C) Be honest with creditors.
  (D) Go for credit counseling.
  (E) Change your spending patterns.

7. According to the text, borrowing a small amount of money to pay for a vacation is a good way to establish credit. True or False. Explain your answer.

8. How is investing in your education safer than investing in land, gold, oil, or stocks?

9. A First Step approach to managing money is to:

  (A) realize that you probably don't have enough money.
  (B) know that money management is a rather complicated matter.
  (C) tell the truth about how much you have and how much you spend
  (D) all of the above
  (E) none of the above

10. How are our lives today similar to how kings and queens lived 100 years ago? Describe at least three ways.

Journal Entry #77
Discovery Statement

Review what you learned in this chapter about your relationship to money. Then complete the following sentence:

In reading and doing this chapter, I discovered that I . . .

_____

_____

_____

Journal Entry #78
Intention Statement

Describe a new strategy you will use to manage money and how you intend to use it.

I intend to . . .

_____

_____

_____

Journal Entry #79
Discovery statement

Review the intentions you wrote in Chapter 9 about improving your health and check to see if you have acted on them. Write about how acting (or not acting) on these intentions has changed your view of your current state of health.

I discovered that I . . .

_____

_____

_____

_____

_____

_____

_____

_____

_____

_____

_____

Chapter 11 Resources

Not I, but the city teaches.
SOCRATES

*The only man who is educated is the man who has learned
how to learn; the man who has learned how to adapt and
change; the man who has realized that no knowledge is secure,
that only the process of seeking knowledge gives a
basis for security.*
CARL ROGERS

Every problem has a gift for you in its hands.
RICHARD BACH

Journal Entry #80
Discovery Statement

From this chapter, I want . . .

In this chapter . . .

Mountains of gold are located near you—information, answers to your questions, and free services. Many students don't realize they exist. ***Supercharge your education*** is about how to find them.

Library: The buried treasure says you can begin by excavating the wealth of facts and ideas in the library. You might be surprised by all the gold in this mountain of information.

Most people try to hide their mistakes, forgetting that mistakes contain the seeds of success. This chapter suggests that you can find ***Ten reasons to celebrate mistakes.***

Forty-seven miles from town and out of gas? Six chapters of analytic geometry to comprehend before tomorrow's midterm exam? Don't sweat the small stuff. Find out how to cut your current problems to size by reading ***Power Process #11: Find a bigger problem***. In the spirit of "Ideas are tools," this chapter also reminds us that there are times to ***Find a smaller problem.***

The telephone can bring information, products, and services to your door. ***Magic machine*** suggests how to change this everyday technology from a nuisance into an opening to the world.

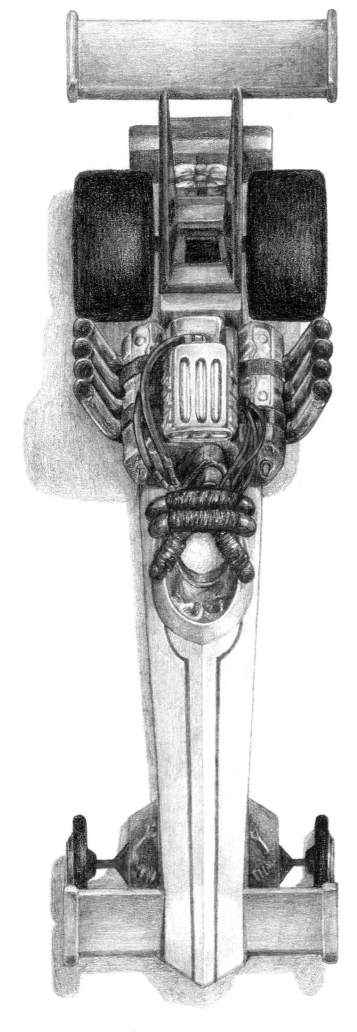

Supercharge your education

A SUPERCHARGER INCREASES THE AIR SUPPLY to an internal combustion engine. The difference in power can be dramatic.

You can make just as powerful a difference in your education by using all the resources available to students. In this case, your "air supply" is comprised of people, organizations, services, publications, and activities.

Of all these resources, people are the most important. You can isolate yourself, study hard, and get a good education. When you establish relationships with faculty, staff, fellow students, employers—anyone with interests related to your own—you can get a great education.

One of the most valuable resources we have is the mistakes we make. Many people think of their mistakes as tragedies to conceal. That prevents them from learning from experience. As this chapter points out, mistakes are some of the most powerful teachers we have. When we get past the fear of making mistakes, we can take risks and reach for mastery.

Unfortunately, resources at many schools go largely unused because students never take the time to learn about them. These students are content to feed an adequate air supply to their educations, and that's fine. The alternative is to pour on the oxygen by actively researching your school and community for resources you can use to accomplish your goals. The following list of on-campus and off-campus resources can be the basis for the beginning of that research.

Supercharge your education with on-campus resources

1. Student organizations. Explore fraternities, sororities, service clubs, veteran's organizations, religious groups, sports clubs and political groups. These groups can be sources of friends, fun, and intellectual development.

2. Student government. It can be a good training ground for leadership and teamwork. The dynamics of student politics are mirrored in most large organizations, and many employers recognize this. They are looking for job applicants who have demonstrated an ability to work with people, organize people, and motivate people. That's what politics is about.

3. The school catalog. This often overlooked resource is the rule book for the game of education. It usually contains course descriptions and requirements for graduation. Sometimes catalogs have information about faculty, financial aid, accreditations, goals and objectives, school history, student services, admissions policies, grading practices, student organizations, and academic calendars. It is a handy resource to use when planning long-term educational goals.

4. Job placement offices. Non-students often have to pay to get these kinds of services, which are available free to most students. Placement offices can help you find part-time employment while you are in school and the first job of your new career when you graduate. (Some continue the service for job changes down the road.)

5. Counseling centers. The emotional pressure of school can be intense. The good news is, many schools have free or low-cost counseling services. Academic counseling is often available. If you need help that is not available at your school, a dean's office or student health center can refer you to the appropriate community agency.

6. The registrar. Your school records are kept here. See the registrar for information about transcripts, changing grades, changing majors, transferring credits, and dropping or adding classes. You might use the registrar's office after graduation, too, if employers or other schools require transcripts or proof of graduation. It pays to know the registrar's procedures at your school.

7. The financial aid office. Money can be confusing, especially for the student using a combination of loans, scholarships, and grants. Some students drop out of school thinking they can't afford it, when financial aid was in fact available. Make a friend in this office.

8. Alumni organizations. They aren't just for graduates. Alumni publications and the actual living and breathing alumni themselves can be good sources of information about the pitfalls and benefits of being a student at your school.

9. Tutoring. Even if you think you are hopelessly stuck in a course, there is often a way out. Tutoring usually is free. It is available through academic departments or special tutoring centers.

10. The student health clinic. It often provides free or inexpensive treatment of minor problems.

11. Chapels. They are usually open to students of any religion. They are quiet places to pray or meditate.

12. Child care. Check with the early-childhood education department. Child care may be provided at your school for a reasonable cost.

13. Car pooling maps. Bulletin boards can provide information on getting across town or across the country.

14. The school newspaper. A good one provides information about school policies, politics, social activities, sports, jobs, and more. You can advertise in it, too, if you need a job, a roommate, or a ride to Dubuque. Larger schools also may have their own radio and television stations.

15. School security. School police departments often can tell you what's safe and what's not. They can also provide information about parking, bicycle regulations, and traffic rules. Some security agencies will provide safe escort at night for female students.

16. Arts resources. Schools often have their own museums, art galleries, observatories, and special libraries. Music practice rooms, with pianos, are often available to all students, not just music majors.

17. Athletic centers. Gymnasiums and field houses are not just for athletes. Schools usually open weight rooms, swimming pools, indoor tracks, basketball courts, and racquet-sport courts to all students.

Supercharge your education with community resources

1. The Chamber of Commerce. It can provide information about local attractions, clubs, organizations, activities, museums, galleries, libraries, and businesses. Larger chambers of commerce have committees that deal with specific issues, such as the environment or economic development. These can be good sources of information for term papers. Chambers of commerce also can provide general information about your community's economy and specific information about local businesses. That information might help you find a job.

2. Churches and synagogues. People are happy to welcome fellow worshippers who are away from home. You can attend to your spiritual needs and make friends, too.

3. Specialty clubs and organizations. Whether your interest is public speaking (Toastmasters) or conservation (the Sierra Club), you can usually find a club full of people with your interests. A list of local organizations and clubs is usually available from the chamber of commerce.

4. Consumer credit organizations. If you've really blown your budget, consider an organization such as Consumer Credit Counseling. These non-profit groups offer free assistance to people with severe financial problems. Remember, no matter how bad your financial picture, you are probably in better shape than most governments. Do not despair. Get help.

5. Off-campus counseling. If you can't get help for a problem at school, assistance is usually available in the community. Job service offices can provide career counseling. You can get help for other problems through rehabilitation offices, veterans' outreach programs, church agencies, private clinics, social service agencies, or area mental health clinics.

6. Child care. Day care for children is provided by private and public organizations. Some places charge for child care based on your income. Girls Clubs and Boys Clubs offer child care, guidance, and recreation opportunities for young people.

7. Health care. Health care centers provide inexpensive birth control, gynecological exams, disease diagnosis and treatment, vaccinations, and care for pregnant women and sick children.

8. Hot lines. The telephone can save your life during a crisis. Professionals or trained volunteers are often available 24-hours a day, whether the problem is physical abuse, AIDS, suicidal feelings, rape, or another difficult situation.

9. Legal advice. Legal aid services provide free or inexpensive assistance to low-income people.

10. Local residents. People who have spent their lives in your community know the best restaurants, the most fascinating second-hand stores, and the secluded hiking spots close to town. If you are a live-in student from out of town, cultivate friendships with students who commute.

11. Money. In a real emergency, you can turn to the Salvation Army, the Red Cross, local churches, or a county relief agency. Be prepared to document the exact nature of your problem. Be specific about why it is an emergency.

12. Local newspapers. They list community events and services that are free or inexpensive. These include outdoor concerts, art showings, hobby and crafts shows, amateur sporting events, auctions, etc. Reading a local newspaper also is a good way to get a feel for the rhythm and texture of a new city.

13. Public transportation. Buses, trains, trolleys, and subways are money-saving alternatives to owning and operating a car. People with handicaps are often provided special transportation services.

14. Recreation. City or county recreation departments, YWCAs, YMCAs, and other organizations provide free or inexpensive ways to exercise and have fun.

15. Support groups. They exist for just about everything. You can find people with problems similar to yours who meet every week to share suggestions, information, and concerns. These include but are not limited to groups for the overweight, for single parents, for abusive parents, for parents with twins, for newly-widowed people, for alcoholics, drug addicts, terminally ill people, women who have had breasts removed, people who have had open-heart or colon-rerouting surgery, families of drug addicts or alcoholics, women who are abused, nursing mothers, Vietnam veterans, and parents who have lost a child.

16. Governments. City, county, and state governments often have programs for students. If you have questions or problems regarding the federal government, contact your senators or representatives. They usually have local offices, which are listed in local telephone directories under the federal government listings.

If you are not sure of the name of your senator or representative, call the mayor's office, the local offices of political parties, the Chamber of Commerce, your local newspaper, the news department of your local TV station, or find the information at the library.

17. Political parties. They always want volunteers. Working for a candidate you believe in is one way to make a difference in the world. It also is a good way to learn organizational skills and meet people with similar interests.

18. Community education. Many local school districts and other organizations offer community education classes. Through them, you can learn about anything from tax planning and ballroom dancing to woodworking and writing a will.

Exercise #36

What's available to you?

Review the section of the article "Supercharge your education," dealing with on-campus resources and place a check by the resources that are available where you attend school. Put a line through those not available at your school. If you're not sure—great. The purpose of this exercise is for you to discover resources. Ask around, call someone, find out which you can use. If you are aware of resources not listed, write them in the margin of this book.

This resource list will be one place to look when you need to find help you haven't needed in the past.

Exercise #37

I have to. . .

This exercise is about obligation and limitations. We often limit ourselves when thinking about what we have to do or what we think we can't do. Look back to Power Process #5: I Create It All on page 140.

Part 1

Take a look at all aspects of your life (family, friends, school, work) and complete each of the following sentences with whatever comes to mind.

I have to. . .

I ought to. . .

I should. . .

I can't. . .

I really must. . .

I just couldn't. . .

I am not able to. . .

I have to. . .

I can't. . .

I shouldn't. . .

Part 2

Review each of the previous sentences, cross off the first two or three words, and replace them with one of the following groups of words:

"I want to. . ."

"I don't want to. . ."

"I choose to. . ."

"I choose not to. . ."

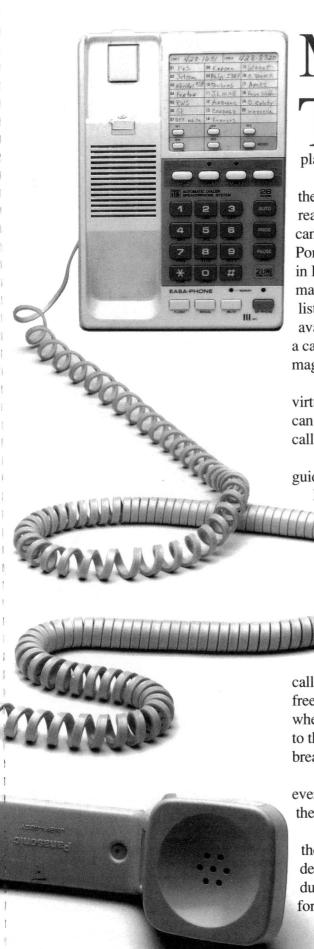

Magic machine

There is a magic machine very close to you. You can use it as often as you like. It has miraculous qualities. This machine can send words, pictures, charts, and drawings to almost any place in the world within seconds.

Your writing can be seen and your voice heard anywhere on the planet almost instantly—and for only a few cents. You can reach out and touch someone in New Zealand, Peru, or India. You can connect with a group of friends in Chicago, Ft. Lauderdale, or Portland. You can get information about current weather conditions in Denver or stock market quotations in Japan. You can use these magic machines to research history, order new products on sale, listen to music, or wake you up in the morning. These machines are available to nearly everyone and you can use one in your home, in a car, in an airplane, and even when you're out riding horses. This magic machine is the telephone.

Cellular phones, fax machines, and computer data bases virtually allow you to have the world at your fingertips. The phone can save hours of shopping, miles of walking, and reams of paper. A call can give you information, advice, comfort, or friendship.

The white page directory and the Yellow Pages are detailed guides to your community. The Yellow Pages are indexed to quickly locate the nearest pizza parlor or dog groomer. Use it to find out who sells fire extinguishers or fertilizer. In a snap you can discover who can complete your tax return or paint your car. If you can't find it yourself, call information or a library and ask for help. Your library may have a copy of *Dial An Expert*, a consumer's guide to expertise available by phone, or similar books.

Lots of companies, colleges, universities, and non-profit organizations offer hotlines and help lines. By calling these numbers and others like them, you can get information free or for a nominal charge. These range from grammar hotlines—where you can get advice on how to handle a dangling participle—to the Astronomy Hotline, where you can keep track of fast-breaking celestial events.

Businesses and government agencies receive thousands of calls every day. They want you to call. That's why their numbers are in the book.

And that's not all. In addition to being able to perform all of these miracles, telephones can set the tone of your living room decor. They can look like an antique collector's item or a mallard duck. Hang them on your wall or carry them in your pocket. Watch for fashion colors, see-through covers, and flashing neon lights.

This magic machine is a marvelous resource.

Library:
The buried treasure

Books. That's what most people imagine when a library is mentioned. Books occupy a lot of space in a library, but they are only part of what is really there.

Most libraries have books. Many also have records, art work, maps, telephone directories for major cities, audio-visual equipment, newspapers, microfiche, microfilm, and audio and video cassettes. You may also find computers and computer software, slide programs, film strips, magazines, dictionaries and encyclopedias of all varieties, research aids, computer searches, and—people.

Libraries range widely in size. Most have the same purpose. They exist to help you find information—facts, opinions, or ideas.

Getting familiar with the resources and services in a library is crucial to the success of most students. It can enhance your reading skills, expand your vocabulary, increase your self-confidence, and save you time. Even more valuable for some is the convenient, comfortable, quiet, and dependable atmosphere for studying.

THE BEST RESOURCE IS NOT MADE OF PAPER

People who work in libraries are trained explorers. They know how to search out information that might be located in several different places. They can also act as a guide for your own expedition into the data jungle. Their purpose is to serve you. Ask for help.

Most libraries have a special reference librarian who can usually let you know right away if the library has what you need. He may suggest a different library or direct you to another source, such as a business, community agency, or government office.

You can save hours by asking.

ANY BOOK YOU WANT

Most libraries now have nearly every book you could ever want through a service known as interlibrary loan. This sharing of materials gives even the smallest library access to millions of books. Just ask that the book be ordered from another library. Keep in mind that this usually involves a small fee and could take anywhere from a few days to a few months. It pays to plan for this time when doing research.

PERIODICALS

Which magazines and newspapers a library carries depends mostly on the location and purpose of the library. A neighborhood branch of a public library may have copies of the local paper and magazines right from the grocery store aisle. A library in a business school is more likely to have the *Wall Street Journal* and trade journals for accountants and business managers. Law libraries subscribe to magazines that would probably bore the socks off a veterinarian.

REFERENCE MATERIAL

The library catalog lists books available in that library and their location. These listings used to be kept on cards, and in some libraries they still are. Today many libraries catalog their materials on computer or microfilm.

A computerized catalog gives you a little more flexibility in searching for materials. For example, you can type in a key word and ask the computer to search for all listings with that word. Some of these systems will also allow you to see if the title is on the shelf or checked out. They may even allow you to put a hold on a book or recording.

In any case, the catalog is an alphabetical listing that is cross-referenced by subject, author, and title. Each listing carries the author's name, the title, the publisher, the date of publication, the number of pages and illustrations, the Library of Congress or Dewey decimal system number (for locating the book), and sometimes a brief description of the book.

Books in Print is a list of most books currently in publication in the United States. Like the card catalog, it is organized by subject, author, and title. (Note that this resource is not a guide to the materials in any particular library.)

The Reader's Guide to Periodical Literature catalogs articles found in many magazines. Searching by subject, you can find titles of articles. The magazine name, date, and page numbers are usually listed. If you want an older magazine, many libraries require that you fill out a form requesting the magazine so it can be retrieved from storage in closed stacks.

Other guides to what has been recently published include: *New York Times Index, Business Periodicals Index, Applied Science and Technology Index, Social Sciences Index, Accountants' Index, General Science Index, Education Index, Humanities Index,* and *Art Index.* These indices help you find what you want in a hurry.

More recently, such indices have become available on microfilm or compact disk. These include *Magazine Index, Business Index, InfoTrac, Newsbank,* and *Medline.* The information these sources provide is the same as the traditional bound indices. Yet many people find them quicker and easier to use, and often they are more current than printed indices.

Abstracts are publications that summarize current findings in specific fields. You can review condensed versions of specialized articles by reading, for example, *Chemical Abstracts, Psychological Abstracts,* or *Sociological Abstracts.*

Pamphlets and clippings are usually stored in file cabinets organized by subject.

Exercise #38
Catalog reconnaissance

Look at every page in your school catalog—quickly. Notice what is new, interesting, or puzzling. Locate your major program description and notice the courses you are required to take for graduation. Find out more about courses you know nothing about. If you see that you have to take Macro Economics to graduate, find out how that differs from Micro Economics and Accounting.

Locate the major program that is the most different from yours. Look through the courses students in that major are required to take. Pick out a course that looks interesting, even though it is different from anything you ever thought you'd take. Find out more about that course.

This section contains information from the U.S. Government Printing Office, state and local governments, and newspaper and magazine clippings.

Facts about virtually anything you can imagine are waiting in almanacs and publications from government departments such as Labor, Commerce, and Agriculture.

The U.S. Government Printing Office is the largest publisher in the world. *The Monthly Catalog* of its printings takes up several feet of shelf space.

Resources listed in indices or *Reader's Guide* but not available at a particular library are usually available through interlibrary loan for a small fee.

General and specialized encyclopedias are also found in the reference section. Find what you want to know about individuals, groups, places, products, words, or other books. Specialized examples include: *Cyclopedia of World Authors, Grove's Dictionary of Music and Musicians, Encyclopaedia of Religion and Ethics, Encyclopedia of Associations, Thomas Register of American Manufacturers,* and *Encyclopedia of World Art.*

Dictionaries of all sizes and specialties are also available in the library. Technical disciplines (medicine, computer science, engineering) often have their own dictionaries.

Of special value to your writing projects is the thesaurus, a type of dictionary. This is one place to check for words that have a similar meaning to the word you look up (synonyms). Instead of standard definitions, a thesaurus provides fast relief when you just can't think of the word you want.

Computer networks now provide information and resource materials to most libraries. DIALOG, ERIC, ORBIT, and BSR are four major electronic information vendors, and each network contains several dozen data bases. Up-to-the-minute reports (stock prices set in the past 15 minutes, yesterday's *New York Times* stories) can be retrieved almost instantly on a computer terminal.

Ironically enough, one place to learn about electronic researching is with some old-fashioned reference books. These include the *Encyclopedia of Information Systems and Services* and *Directory of Online Databases.*

SOME USEFUL THINGS TO KNOW

To save research time, plan a strategy. That means asking pointed questions about your topic and knowing what kind of information you're looking for.

Say that the purpose of your paper is to persuade students to use personal computers. Begin by asking typical questions a reader might: What can a computer really do for me? How much do they cost? Can't I get along fine without one?

Next, choose, in general, what type of sources you want to consult and in what order. For help in completing this step, ask a librarian. If you're still unsure about what you're looking for, explain to the librarian the context of your paper. Describe the subject and purpose of the questions you want to answer.

Use the index in the back of books or last volume of encyclopedias to save time when searching for information.

Look in the front of reference materials for guidelines on how to use them. Often this section will tell you what abbreviations mean, and how the entries in that volume were selected.

Look for the most specific items first. Then generalize if needed. For example, if you are looking for a user's manual for a particular word processing program, look under the name of that program. If that doesn't work, then look under the more general category of "word processing."

Use magazines for purposes other than researching a paper. Use them to find tips for how to quit smoking, build bookshelves, or knit a sweater. You can also find product ratings that provide valuable information about major purchases, such as a car or stereo.

Remember that any specific subject has a corresponding set of specialized reference materials. For example, if you're looking for an introduction to the thought of Spinoza, the philosopher, you can look in the *Encyclopedia of Philosophy.*

Keep in mind the full range of sources for finding facts. Many of these were mentioned above: encyclopedias, indexes, the library catalog, computer databases, magazines, and journals. You can also use abstracting services, which summarize published and unpublished articles on paper, microfiche, or microfilm. An example is ERIC (the Educational Resources Information Center), which specializes in information on education.

Look through non-print materials. These include audio and videotapes, videodiscs, films, slides, and filmstrips.
Other information sources are outside the library. They include corporations and professional organizations, museums, and historical societies. You can also write or talk directly with people who know a lot about a given subject. Often a librarian can guide you to such resources in the community.

The library exists for your benefit, waiting only for you to use it. Happy treasure hunting.

Exercise #39
Find it

Most libraries have the answers to the following questions. Go exploring. If you search for the answer and can't find it on your own, ask one of the librarians for help.

1. What are a dozen words that mean about the same thing as the word "power"?

2. What is the Library of Congress number (which is used to locate books in many libraries) for the novel **1984** *by George Orwell? (Give the Dewey decimal number if that is the system used in your library.)*

3. Is the book **Lazy Man's Guide to Enlightenment** *still in print? If so, who is the publisher?*

4. What are three magazine articles, published since last year, that discuss methods to prevent or treat cancer?

5. Who manufactures nails and tacks? List three companies you could contact if you wanted one million nails made to your specifications.

6. What computer search capabilities are available at two libraries you can use? List the names of the two libraries and briefly describe information they can access directly by computer.

Ten reasons to celebrate mistakes

MANY PEOPLE ARE HAUNTED BY THE FEAR OF FAILURE. *Most of us fear making mistakes or being held responsible for a major breakdown. We fear that mistakes could cost us grades, careers, money, or even relationships.*

It's possible to take an entirely different attitude toward mistakes. Rather than fearing them, we could actually celebrate them. We could revel in our redundancies, frolic in our failures, and glory in our goof-ups. We could marvel at our mistakes and bark with loud laughter when we blow it.

A creative environment is one in which failure is not fatal. Businesses, striving to be on the cutting edge of competition, desperately seek innovative changes. Yet innovation requires risk-taking—and along with it, the chance of failing.

This is not idle talk. There are real places where people celebrate mistakes. Management consultant Tom Peters gives these examples:

• One marketing director at Pizza Hut ended up with $5 million dollars in unused sunglasses when a sales promotion scheme backfired. (The sunglasses were specially designed for viewing the movie Back to the Future, Part 2.) He was promoted soon afterward, and the company's profits still increased 36 percent that year.

• The chief executive officer of Temps & Co., a temporary services firm, opens some meetings by asking managers to describe their biggest mistakes. The person with the "best" mistake gets a $100 prize. One of the winning mistakes was typing a social security number in the place of the dollar amount and cutting a multimillion-dollar paycheck.

• At its First Annual Doobie Awards, the Public Broadcasting System honored prominent mistakes made by its members. Nominees included an executive whose "improved" time sheets required three sign-offs instead of one. "It's a way of not taking ourselves too seriously," said one senior vice president of the award. "It gets a message across. . .that it's okay to try and fail." Here are some solid reasons for celebrating mistakes—10 of them, to be exact.

1. Celebration allows us to notice the mistake. Celebrating mistakes gets them out in the open. Mistakes that are hidden cannot be corrected. It's only when we shine a light on a mistake and examine it that we can fix it.

This is the opposite of covering up mistakes or blaming others for them. Hiding mistakes takes a lot of energy—energy that could be channeled into correcting errors.

2. Mistakes are valuable feedback. A manager of a major corporation once made a mistake that cost his company $100,000. He feared that his boss would fire him. When his boss found out, he responded, "Fire you? I can't afford to do that. I just spent $100,000 training you." Mistakes are

part of the learning process.

Not only are mistakes usually more interesting than most successes—they're often more instructive.

3. Mistakes demonstrate that we're taking risks. People who play it safe make few mistakes. Making mistakes gives evidence that we're stretching to the limit of our abilities, growing, risking, and learning.

4. Celebrating mistakes reminds us that it's OK to make them. When we celebrate, we remind ourselves that the person who made the mistake is not bad—just human.

This is not a recommendation that you set out to make mistakes. Mistakes are not an end in themselves. Rather, their value lies in what we learn from them. When we make a mistake, we can admit and correct it.

5. Celebrating mistakes includes everyone. It reminds us that the exclusive club named the Perfect Performance Society has no members. All of us make mistakes. When we notice them, we can work together. Blaming others or the system prevents the cooperative efforts that can improve our circumstances.

6. Fear of making mistakes can paralyze us. This fear might frighten us into inaction. We could become afraid to do anything for fear of blowing it. Celebrating mistakes helps us move into action and get things done.

7. When we celebrate mistakes, we set an example. We model the idea that mistakes are OK. We back up our words about the value of mistakes with action.

8. Mistakes occur only when aiming at a clear goal. We can express concern about missing a target only if the target is there in the first place. If there's no target or purpose, then there's no concern about missing. Making a mistake affirms something of great value—that we have a plan.

9. Mistakes happen only when we're committed to making things work. Systems work when people are willing to be held accountable. Openly admitting mistakes promotes accountability.

Imagine a school where there's no concern about

quality and effectiveness. Teachers usually come to class late. Residence halls are never cleaned and scholarship checks are always late. What's more, the administration is in chronic debt, students seldom pay tuition on time, and no one cares.

In this school, the word "mistake" would have little meaning. Mistakes become apparent only when people are committed to improving the quality of an institution. Mistakes go hand-in-hand with a commitment to quality.

10. Celebrating mistakes cuts the problem down to size. On top of the mistake itself, there is often a layer of regret, worry, and desperation about having made the mistake in the first place. Not only do people have a problem with the mistake, they have a problem with having *made* the mistake.

When we celebrate mistakes, we eliminate that layer of concern. When our anxiety about making a mistake is behind us, we can get down to the business of correcting the mistake.

POWER PROCESS #11:

Find a bigger problem

MOST OF THE TIME we view problems as barriers. They are a source of inconvenience and annoyance. They get in our way and prevent us from having happy and productive lives. When we see problems in this way, our goal becomes the elimination of problems. This point of view is flawed. It is impossible to live a life without problems. Besides, they serve a purpose.

The word "problem" stems from the ancient Greek word "proballein" which means "to throw forward." Problems are opportunities to participate in life. Problems stimulate us and move us forward.

When problems are seen this way, the goal becomes not to eliminate them, but to find problems that are worthy of us. Worthy problems are those that draw on our talents, move us toward our purpose, and increase our skills. The challenge is to tackle those problems that provide the greatest benefits for ourselves and others.

Problems seem to follow the same law of physics that gases do. They expand to fill whatever space is available. If your only problem for the entire day is to write a follow-up letter to a job interview, you can spend the whole day finding paper and pen, thinking about what you're going to say, writing the letter, finding an envelope and stamp, going to the post office, and then thinking about all the things you forgot to say.

If, on that day you also need to shop for groceries, the problem of the letter shrinks to make room for another problem. If you also want to buy a car, it's amazing how quickly and easily the letter and the grocery shopping are finished. One way to handle little problems is to find bigger ones.

Remember that the smaller problems are still to be solved. The goal is to do this with less time and energy.

Bigger problems are not in short supply. Consider world hunger. Every minute of every day, 21 people die because they don't have enough to eat. Each day, 35,000 people die of hunger or hunger-related diseases. Each year 13 million people die because they don't have enough food.

Consider the devastating effects of alcoholism. One of every four people in the United States is directly affected by her own drinking or the alcoholism of someone in her family. Consider nuclear war that threatens to end life on the planet. Child abuse, environmental pollution, human rights violations, drug abuse, street crime, energy shortages, poverty, and wars throughout the world await your attention and involvement. You can make a contribution.

Considering bigger problems does not have to be depressing. In fact, it can be energizing—a reason for getting up in the morning. Taking on a huge project is a tool for creating passion and purpose.

Perhaps your little voice is saying, "That's crazy. I can't do anything about those kinds of problems," or "Everyone knows that hunger has always been around and always will be, and there is nothing anyone can do about it." These thoughts prevent you from taking on bigger problems.

Realize that you can make a difference. Your thoughts and actions can change the quality of life on the planet.

This is your life. It's your school, your city, your country, and your world. Own it. Treat it with the same care you would a prized possession.

The surest way to be sure that your problems are worthy of your talents and energies is to take on bigger ones. Take responsibility for problems that are bigger than you are sure you can handle. Then watch your other problems shrink.

...or a smaller one

THIS IDEA APPEARS TO CONFLICT with the Power Process "Find a bigger problem." Like all the ideas in this book, "Find a smaller problem" is offered in the spirit of "ideas are tools." These ideas are not true or false, good or bad. Keep in mind that different jobs call for different tools.

It's easy to feel overwhelmed when faced with a huge task—writing a thesis, studying for a final, choosing a career, finding a job. By telling ourselves how difficult such things are, we can feel disempowered.

One response is to give up—quit. Another is to resign ourselves to drudgery and dive into the work with a deep sigh, always feeling the weight of a monumental job. And after accepting responsibility for it, we may feel obligated to handle the entire job alone. Whenever this happens, we are less effective. Our feelings of being overwhelmed are reinforced.

"Find a smaller problem" is really another way of combining the Power Process "Be here now" with a time management tool known as "divide and conquer." It works this way: Divide a gigantic project into many small jobs. Rather than worrying about the huge problem, ignore it for now. Turn your attention to a specific little job until it is complete, carefully attending to details. Do the same with the next small job, and the next.

The role of planning is critical. Finding a smaller problem is not the same as finding busy work. Without planning, we can end up completing jobs of low priority. That can sabotage the project. If we plan effectively, the small jobs we do are those most critical to the big picture.

Using this procedure, we can string a number of successes together, one after another. Success breeds success. Not only are we accomplishing many important tasks—we're building a pattern of improving skills. When we look up from our work to see the huge job we were faced with—poof! The job has shrunk. Our problem may have even disappeared. That's the power of finding a smaller problem.

Lauren Elder,

a professional artist in the Bay Area, graduated with honors in fine arts from UCLA. She later worked for three and a half years as a counselor in a halfway house for mental patients.

From **And I Alone Survived,** *copyright 1978 by Lauren Elder with Shirley Streshinsky. Reprinted by permission of the author.*

Good Lord. He wasn't even sure if his ten-year old daughter knew he was going flying today. Didn't he make any contingency plans for her? It all seemed so haphazard, so slipshod. No flight plan. Nobody knows where we are. I don't even know where we are, I thought. There was nobody to sound the alarm.

It hit me then: I am on my own. Jay couldn't take care of me, and I couldn't expect him to. We were in this together. We could help each other, but there had to be balance. . .

. . .So much for Plan A, I said to myself. What is Plan B? Clearly, I would have to settle for an alternative course of action. Then I remembered the second line of defense—the rocks. What we had was a pile of very hot granite rocks that would give off heat for a time, maybe for a long time. The heat would last longer if I could get the rocks into a small, protected space out of the wind. I decided to load them into the tail section of the plane, the part that had partially split off from the main body. It was a small aluminum cone just big enough for two bodies and a store of heated granite.

"If we get in there," I said to Jay, "I mean, if we pile some rocks into the tail of the plane—" I knew I had asked him the question several times before, but clearly the idea bothered me. "If we pile in all those rocks and ourselves in after," I started over again, "do you suppose we might tip it over? " I could imagine the plane tumbling down the mountain.

"It's okay," he said with unconcealed annoyance. "It's anchored. The wing tip is dug in. The wheels too." He answered as if by rote. There was a tape-recorded quality to his voice, and it gave me the bizarre feeling that in some way he wasn't there.

The thought crossed my mind: Is he leaving? Leaving, slipping away. Could something be wrong with him that I didn't understand?

No, I told myself firmly. I had survived the crash and so had Jay. All I had to think about was keeping warm. Jay said the plane was solidly anchored. I sincerely hoped he was right.

I squeezed sideways through the tiny baggage door and kicked

out some flimsy plastic dividers used to separate the compartment. Our feet would be near the bottom, where the fuselage narrowed at the tail of the plane, and our heads would be at the top. The roof had split open, exposing the rear passenger seat; but if we curled as low as we could, we would be well enough protected.

"We've got to pile as many rocks into the tail as we can," I ordered as I climbed back out. "There's enough room for the two of us, and we've got to fill the leftover space with stones. Maybe they'll get us through what's left of the night."

Jay said nothing, and he did not move. I resisted the urge to say something cutting. It would take too much energy, and I had to gather the stones.

I began to grope in the dark, feeling for the hot, oil-blackened stones. I smelled flesh singeing, felt the stinging rocks. The hotter the better, I thought. My left arm was of little use, but I managed to get several rocks into the tail. A fingernail bent back and broke off, and my fingers were smashed and charred; but it was the price I had to pay, I told myself. The rocks were all the insurance we had. . .

It seemed forever, but it was worth it, because the added heat was immediately noticeable. The air in the section was almost warm, and I was content that I had done all I could do. With that thought I pulled my silk scarf over my face and curled into a fetal position. Lauren, I congratulated myself, you really are smart.

That is how I felt—smart. I don't mean intelligent or bright or any of the usual meanings of the word. I mean, simply, that given a certain set of conditions, I had chosen the proper sequence, I had made optimum use of the possibilities presented. I had put the puzzle together in the time allotted.

QUIZ

1. How are a supercharger for an internal combustion engine and resources available to students alike?

2. What information can you find at the registrar's office?

3. How can you obtain a book that is not available at your library?

4. The Reader's Guide to Periodical Literature:
    (A) catalogs articles found in many magazines by subject.
    (B) usually lists the magazine name, date, and the page numbers of articles.
    (C) provides indices on microfilm or compact disk.
    (D) A and B.
    (E) None of the above.

5. There are several reasons to celebrate mistakes. Which of the following is NOT one?
    (A) Mistakes are valuable feedback.
    (B) Mistakes demonstrate that we're playing it safe.
    (C) Mistakes demonstrate we are committed to making things work.
    (D) Celebrating mistakes reminds us that it's OK to make them.
    (E) Celebrating mistakes demonstrates that we are setting an example.

QUIZ

C O N T I N U E D

6. The Chamber of Commerce can be a good source of information for term papers. True or False. Explain your answer.

7. Problems can be a positive force in your life. True or false. Explain your answer.

8. What does "find a smaller problem" mean and how can it be useful?

9. What characteristic of a master student does Lauren Elder demonstrate? Explain your choice.

10. Where can you find information about United States Government publications?

Journal Entry #81
Discovery Statement

Describe one new thing you learned from this chapter.

　　I discovered that I . . .

_____

_____

_____

_____

Journal Entry #82
Intention Statement

Review the list of things you wanted to get from this chapter. Did you get what you wanted? If not, then describe what you will do to get what you wanted.

　　I intend to . . .

_____

_____

_____

Journal Entry #83
Intention Statement

Of the dozens of resources reviewed in this chapter, pick one or two you want to use. Consider various resources in the library, at your school, or around your community, and make an intention to use something you haven't used in the past.

　　I intend to . . .

_____

_____

_____

_____

Journal Entry #84
Discovery Statement

Spend a few minutes reflecting on Power Process #10: "The process is always the same." Choose one small behavior of yours and describe how that behavior is repeated in other things you do.

　　I discovered that I . . .

_____

_____

_____

_____

Chapter 12

What next?

Learning is not a task or a problem—it is a way to be in the world. Man learns as he pursues goals and projects that have meaning for him.
SIDNEY JOURARD

Think wrongly if you please, but in all cases think for yourself.
DORIS LESSING

Live as if you were to die tomorrow.
Learn as if you were to live forever.
GHANDI

Journal Entry #85
Discovery Statement

From this chapter, I want . . .

In this chapter . . .

By working through this book, you've learned a lot about how to succeed in school. And everything you've learned so far pales when compared to what is available.

Becoming a master student is not a one-term process. It continues for life. *Now that you're done—Begin* suggests how personal discovery and growth can become a habit.

Attitudes underlie every tool we bring to success in school and careers. Learn how to work with them effectively in *Attitudes, affirmations, & visualizations* and *Attitude replacements*.

Knowing what you want to do in your career helps you know with equal clarity what you want in school. *Career planning—Begin now* suggests how you can gain this benefit today.

Most people go through life concentrating on what they want to do and what they want to have. There's a more basic path to those goals that's often missed. Learn about it in *Power Process #12: Be it.*

Knowing how to succeed in school fills you with satisfaction. And when you're full, it's natural to spread the wealth a little. Contributing to others increases your satisfaction even more. Learn how in *Contributing—the art of selfishness.*

Now that you're done— Begin

IF YOU USED THIS BOOK, if you actively participated in reading the contents, writing the journals, doing the exercises, and applying the suggestions, then you have had quite a journey. You are on a path of growth toward becoming a master student. Now what? What's the next step?

The world is packed with opportunities for master students. If you excel in adventure, exploration, discovery, and creativity, you will never lack for possibilities. If you want to continue to grow, continue to learn how to learn, the choices are endless.

You are on the edge of a universe so miraculous and full of wonder that your imagination at its most creative moment cannot encompass it. Paths are open to lead you to worlds beyond your wildest dreams.

If this sounds like a pitch for the latest recreational drug, it may be. The drug is adrenaline, and it is automatically generated by your body when you are growing, risking, and discovering new worlds inside and outside of your skin.

This book has started the process of discovery and intention which can be a powerful tool in assisting you to get exactly what you want out of life. Following are several ways to reinforce that discovery and intention process.

"...use the following suggestions to continue..."

1. Keep a journal. Buy a bound notebook in which to record your private reflections and dreams for the future. Get one that will be worthy of your personal discoveries and intentions.

Write in this journal daily. Record what you are learning about yourself and the world. Write about your hopes, wishes, and goals. Keep a record of significant events. Consider using the format of Discovery Statements and Intention Statements you learned in this book.

2. Take a seminar. Schooling doesn't have to stop at graduation, and it doesn't have to take place on a campus. Workshops start each week in most cities about everything from cosmetology to cosmology. Use workshops to learn skills, understand the world, and discover yourself. Learn cardiopulmonary resuscitation (CPR), attend a lecture on developing nations, or take a course on assertiveness training.

3. Read, watch, and listen. Dozens of books related to becoming a master student are recommended in the bibliography on page 336. Ask friends and instructors what they are reading. Sample a variety of newspapers and magazines. None of them have all of the truth; most of them have a piece of it.

In addition to books, many bookstores and publishing houses offer audio and video tapes on personal growth topics.

Record your most exciting discoveries in an idea file.

4. Take an unrelated class. Sign up for a class that is totally unrelated to your major. If you are studying to be a secretary, take a physics course. If you are going to be a doctor, take a bookkeeping course.

You can discover a lot about yourself and your intended future when you step out of old patterns. In addition to formal courses offered at your school, check into community education classes. These are a low-cost alternative that offer no threat to your grade-point average.

5. Travel. See the world. Visit new neighborhoods. Travel to other countries. Explore.

Find out what it looks like inside buildings you normally have no reason to go into, museums you think you have little interest in, cities that are out of the way, forests and mountains that lie beyond your old boundaries, and far-off places that require planning and saving to reach.

6. Get counseling. Solving emotional problems is not the only reason to visit a counselor, therapist, or psychologist. These people are excellent resources for personal growth. You can use counseling to look at yourself and talk about yourself in ways that may be uncomfortable for anyone except a trained professional. Counseling offers a chance to talk about nothing but yourself without anyone thinking you are rude.

7. Form a support group. Just as a well-organized study group can promote your success in school, an organized support group can help you reach goals in other areas of your life.

Today, people in support groups help each other lose weight, stay sober, cope with chronic illness, recover from emotional trauma, and overcome drug addiction.

Groups can also brainstorm possibilities for job hunting, career planning, parenting, solving problems in relationships, promoting spiritual growth—for reaching almost any goal you choose.

8. Find a mentor—or become one. Seek the counsel of experienced people you respect and admire. Use them as role models. If they are willing, ask them to be sounding boards for your plans and ideas. Most people are flattered to be asked.

You can also become a mentor. If you want to perfect your skills as a master student, teach them to someone else. Offer to coach another student in study skills in return for childcare, free lunches, or something else you value. A mentor relationship can bridge the boundaries of age, race, or culture.

9. Redo this book. Start by redoing one chapter or maybe just one exercise. If you didn't get everything you wanted from this book, it's not too late.

You can also redo portions that you found valuable. Redo the quizzes to test your ability to recall certain information. Redo the exercises that were particularly effective for you. They can work again. Many of the exercises in this book can produce a different result after a few months. You are changing, and your responses change, too.

The Discovery Wheel can be useful in revealing techniques you have actually put into practice. Redo the Journal Entries. If you keep your own journal, refer to it as you rewrite the Journal Entries in this book.

As you redo the book or any part of it, reconsider techniques that you skimmed over or skipped before. They may work for you now. Modify the suggestions or add new ones. Redoing this book can refresh and fine-tune your study habits.

Another way to redo this book is to retake your student success course. People who do that often say the second time was much different from the first. They pick up ideas and techniques they missed the first time and gain deeper insight into things they already know.

Exercise #40
Do something you can't

You can accomplish much more than you might think you can. Few significant accomplishments result when people stick to the familiar. Risk yourself.

Pick something that you don't know how to do and do it. Choose something you think you can't do and do it.

Be smart. Don't pick something that will hurt you physically, such as flying from a third-floor window.

This exercise has three parts.

Part 1
Select something that you have never done before, that you don't know how to do, that you are fearful of doing, or that you think you probably can't do. Describe below the thing you have chosen.

Part 2
Do it. Of course this is easier to say than to do. This exercise is not about easy. It is about discovering capabilities that stretch your self-image.

In order to accomplish something that is bigger than your self-perceived abilities, use all the tools you have. Develop a plan. Divide and conquer. Be willing to be a fool. Stay focused. Use all available outside resources. Let go of self-destructive thoughts.

Part 3
Write about the results of this exercise in your journal if you choose to start one.

Attitudes, affirmations & visualizations

"I have a bad attitude." People say this as if they were talking about the flu. An attitude is certainly as strong as the flu, but it isn't something you have to succumb to or accept.

Some people see their attitudes the way they see their height or their eye color. "I may not like it, but I might as well accept it."

Acceptance is certainly a worthwhile approach to things you cannot change. Acceptance is not necessary when it comes to attitudes. If you have an attitude that you don't like, change it. You may have to go through life being too short or too tall. You don't have to live your life with an attitude that doesn't work.

Attitudes are powerful because they create behavior. If your attitude is that you're not very interesting at a party, then your behavior will probably match your attitude, and you can act like a bore. If your attitude is that you are fun at a party, then your behavior is more likely to be fun. Soon you are the life of the party. All that has to change is attitude.

You can change your attitudes by regular practice with affirmations and visualizations.

Affirm it

An affirmation is a statement describing what you want. The most effective affirmations are personal, positive, and written in the present tense.

Affirmations have an almost magical power. They are used successfully by athletes and actors, executives and ballerinas, and tens of thousands of people who have succeeded in their lives. Affirmations can change your attitudes and behaviors.

To use affirmations, first determine what you want, then describe yourself as if you already had it. For example, if you decide you want a wonderful job, you might write: "I, Susan Webster, have a wonderful job. I respect and love my colleagues and they feel the same way about me. I look forward to going to work each day."

Or, if money is your desire, you might write: "I, John Henderson, am rich. I have more money than I can spend. I have everything I want, including a six-bedroom house, a new sports car, a 200-watt stereo system, and a videotape recorder with a satellite dish receiver."

What makes the affirmation work is detail. Use brand names, people's names, and your own name. Involve all your senses—sight, sound, smell, taste, touch. Be positive. Instead of saying, "I am not fat," say, "I am slender."

Once you have written the affirmation, repeat it. Practice saying it aloud several times a day. This works best if you say it at a regular time, such as just before sleep or just after waking up.

Sit in a chair in a relaxed position. Take a few deep and relaxing breaths, and then repeat your affirmation with emotion. It's also effective to look in a mirror while saying the affirmation. Keep looking and repeating until you are saying your affirmation with conviction.

Visualize it

It would be difficult to grow up in our culture without hearing that practice improves performance. The problem is that most of us limit what we consider practice. Effective practice can occur when you are not moving a muscle.

You can improve a golf game, a tennis serve, or your skiing ability while lying in bed. You can become a better driver, speaker, or cook while sitting silently in a chair. In line at the grocery store, you can improve your ability to type or take tests. This is all possible through visualization—the art of seeing yourself be successful.

Here's how. Decide what you want to improve, and write down what it would look like, sound like, and feel like to have that improvement. If you are learning to play the piano, write down briefly what you would see, hear, and feel if you were playing skillfully. If you want to improve relationships with your children, write down what you would see, hear, and feel if you were communicating successfully.

A powerful visualization includes not only seeing but other sense channels as well. Feel the physical sensations. Hear the sounds. Note any smells, tastes, textures, or qualities of light that accompany the scene in your mind.

Once you have a sketch of what it would be like to be successful, practice in your imagination—successfully. Rehearse in your mind. Include as many details as you can. Always have your practices be successes. Each time you toss the basketball, it will swish through the net. Every time you invite someone out, he will say yes. Every test will have an A on the top. Practice at least once per day.

You can also use visualizations to replay errors. When you make a mistake, replay it in your imagination. After a bad golf shot, stop and replay it in your head. Imagine yourself making that same shot again very successfully. If you just had a discussion with your lover that turned into a fight, replay it successfully. Get all your senses involved. See yourself calmly talking it over together. Hear the words, and feel the pleasure of a successful interaction.

Visualizations and affirmations can restructure your attitudes and behaviors. Be clear about what you want and then practice.

ATTITUDE REPLACEMENTS

You can use affirmations to replace a negative attitude with a positive thought. There are no limits other than your imagination and practice. Here are some ideas to stir your imagination. Modify them to suit your individual hopes and dreams, and then add practice. The article "Attitudes, affirmations, and visualizations" explains how to use these attitude replacements.

I, _____, am healthy.

I, _____, have abundant energy and vitality throughout the day.

I, _____, exercise regularly.

I, _____, work effectively with many different kinds of people.

I, _____, eat wisely.

I, _____, plan my days and use time wisely.

I, _____, have a powerful memory.

I, _____, take tests calmly and confidently.

I, _____, am a great speller.

I, _____, fall asleep quickly and sleep soundly.

I, _____, am smart.

I, _____, learn quickly.

I, _____, am creative.

I, _____, am aware of and sensitive to people's moods.

I, _____, have relationships that are mutually satisfying.

I, _____, work hard and contribute to other people through my job.

I, _____, am wealthy.

I, _____, know how to play and have fun.

I, _____, am attractive.

I, _____, focus my attention easily.

I, _____, like myself.

I, _____, am liked by other people.

I, _____, am a worthwhile person even though I am _____.

I, _____, have a slim and attractive body.

I, _____, am relaxed in all situations including _____.

I, _____, make profitable financial investments.

I, _____, have income that far exceeds my expenses.

I, _____, live a life of abundance and prosperity.

I, _____, always live my life in positive ways for the highest good of all people.

Exercise #41
Reprogram your attitude

Affirmations and visualizations can be used to successfully reprogram your attitudes and behaviors. Use this exercise to change your approach to any situation in your life.

Step 1
Pick something in your life that you would like to change. It can be about anything—relationships, work, money, or personal skills. Write a brief description of what you choose to change.

Step 2
Write how you would like your choice in Step 1 to change. Be outlandish. Write down your greatest wish about how you would like it to be. Imagine you are about to ask your fairy godmother for a wish you know she will grant. Be detailed in your description of how you want it to be.

Step 3
Here comes the fairy godmother. Use affirmations and visualizations to start you on the road to creating exactly what you wrote about in Step 2. Below, write at least two affirmations that describe your dream wish. Also, briefly outline a visualization that you can use to picture your wish. Be specific, detailed, and positive.

Step 4
Put them to work. Set up a schedule of practice. Determine a time and place when you can practice your new attitudes. Set the first time to be right now. Then set up at least five other times that you intend to practice your affirmations and visualizations.

I intend to relax and practice the affirmations and visualizations for at least five minutes on the following dates and at the place(s) given.

	Date	Time	Location
1.			
2.			
3.			
4.			
5.			

Career planning— Begin now

A satisfying and lucrative career is often the goal of education. It pays to clearly define both your career goal and your strategy for reaching it. Then you can plan your education effectively.

Career planning is an adventure that involves exploration. There are dozens of effective paths to planning your career. The Career Planning Supplement to Becoming a Master Student *offers many suggestions on this subject and guides you to more.*

You can begin career planning now by remembering three basic ideas.

You already know a lot about your career plan

When people learn study skills and life skills, they usually start with finding out things they don't know. That means discovering new strategies for taking notes, reading, writing, managing time, and the other subjects covered in this book.

Career planning is different. You can begin by realizing how much you know right now. You've already made many decisions about your career. This is true for young people who say, "I don't have *any* idea what I want to be when I grow up." It's also true for mid-life career changers.

Take the student who can't decide if he wants to be a cost accountant or a tax accountant and then jumps to the conclusion, "I'm totally lost when it comes to career planning." It's the same with the student who doesn't know if he wants to be a veterinary assistant or nurse.

These people forget that they already know a lot about their career choice. The person who couldn't decide between veterinary assistance and nursing already ruled out becoming a lawyer, computer programmer, or teacher. He just didn't know yet whether he had the right bedside manner for horses or people. The person who was debating tax accounting versus cost accounting already knew he didn't want to be a doctor, playwright, or taxicab driver. He did know he liked working with numbers and balancing books.

In each case, these people have already narrowed their list of career choices to a number of jobs in the *same* field—jobs that draw on the same core skills. In general, they already know what they want to be when they grow up. So do you.

Find a long list of occupations. (One source is *The Dictionary of Occupational Titles*, a government publication available at many libraries.) Using a stack of 3x5 cards, write down about 100 job titles, one title per card. Sort through the cards and divide them into two piles. Label one pile "careers I've

definitely ruled out for now." Label the other pile "possibilities I'm willing to consider."

It's common for people to go through a stack of 100 such cards and end up with 95 in the "definitely ruled out" pile and five in the "possibilities" pile. This demonstrates that they already have a career plan in mind.

Career planning is a choice, not a discovery

Many people approach career planning like panning for gold. They keep sifting through the dirt, clearing the dust, and throwing out the rocks. They are hoping to strike it rich and discover the perfect career.

Other people believe they'll wake up one morning, see the heavens part, and suddenly know what they're supposed to do. Many of them are still waiting for that magical day to dawn.

We can approach career planning in a different way. It can be the bridge between our dreams and the reality of our future. Instead of seeing a career as something we *discover*, we can see it as something we *choose*. We don't find the right career. We create it.

There's a big difference between these two approaches. Thinking that there's only one "correct" choice for your career can lead to a lot of anxiety: "Did I choose the right one? What if I make a mistake?"

Viewing your career as your creation helps you relax. Instead of anguishing over finding the right career, you stay open to

possibilities. You choose one career today, knowing that you can choose again later.

Suppose that you've narrowed your list of possible careers to five, and you still can't decide. Then just choose one. Any one. Many people will have five careers in a lifetime anyway. You may be able to do all your careers, and you can do any of them first. The important thing is to choose.

One caution is in order. Choosing your career is not something to do in an information vacuum. Rather, choose *after* you've done a lot of research. That includes research into yourself—your skills and interests—and a thorough knowledge of what careers are available.

Career planning materials and counselors can help you on both counts. You can take skills assessments to find out more about what you like doing. You can

take career planning courses and read books about careers. You can contact people who are actually doing the job you're researching and ask them what it's like. You can also choose an internship, summer job, or volunteer position in a field that interests you. There's no end to resources for gathering information about yourself and the job market.

After all the data has been gathered, there's only one person who can choose your career: you.

This decision does not have to be a weighty one. In fact, it can be like going into your favorite restaurant and choosing from a menu that includes all your favorite dishes. At this point, it's tough to make a mistake. Whatever you choose, you can enjoy it.

You can change your mind

Career planning is not a once-and-for-all proposition. Rather, career plans are made to be changed and refined as you gain new information about yourself and the world. Career planning never ends. If your present career no longer feels right, you can choose again—no matter what stage of life you're in. The process is the same, whether you're choosing your first career or your fifth.

"Yes," says the skeptic. "But what if I spend two years going to school and then discover I'm in the wrong field? Think about all the time I'll waste!"

There are three responses to this. First, you might be killed in an earthquake or struck by lightning in those same two years.

But it's unlikely. It's also unlikely that you'll choose a career that's totally off-base for you as long as you do your homework in career planning. Remember that you're working on the difference between your top four or five career possibilities—not the 95 cards you put in the "definitely not" pile.

Second, there is some risk associated with career planning, just as there's risk in being alive. Risk cannot be totally avoided. People change. Circumstances change. The idea of facing 30 fourth graders for 270 days each year, which sounded so good 10 years ago, may not be as appealing to you today.

Third, if you are a master student, learning, growing, and benefiting from every experience, there's no such thing as a waste.

Journal Entry #86
Intention Statement

Even if you are not sure of your career preference, write a career plan right now. Include three elements: a career title, a list of steps you can take to prepare for that career, and a timeline for reaching that career goal.

Your plan might be incomplete or tentative. No problem. You can change this plan later—even throw it out and start over. Career planning is a continual cycle of discovery and feedback.

The point is to dive into the process and make career planning a lifelong habit. This habit can radically affect the quality of your life.

You can plan now, with no further research. Go ahead. There's nothing to lose and lots of space to write. Make an outline, do a mind map—use any format you like. Discover what you already know.

Mind map, outline, or write your career plan below:

POWER PROCESS #12:

Be it

"**B**E IT" IS THE ULTIMATE POWER PROCESS. All of the techniques in this book are enhanced by this Power Process. The idea is that getting where you want to *be* by what you *do* or by what you *have* is like swimming against the current. HAVE ⇨ DO ⇨ BE is a tough journey. It's much easier to go the other direction—BE ⇨ DO ⇨ HAVE. To get what you want, be it.

If you can visualize where you want to be, if you can go there in your imagination, if you can *be* it, then you have set yourself up to achieve your goal. You can soon *have* and *do* what you want. This is true because, as human beings, we subconsciously create whomever we *think* we are.

Usually, we work against nature by trying to have something or do something before being it. That's the hard way. All of your deeds (what you do) won't get you where you want to be. Getting all the right things (what you have) won't get you there, either.

Take the person who wants to master tennis. He buys an expensive racket and a stylish tennis wardrobe. Yet after a year of lessons, he still can't consistently return a serve. Having the right things didn't accomplish his goal.

Frequently we hear about people who did everything right and still didn't make it. Life didn't work out to their expectations. What went wrong is usually very subtle. "He lost the match even though he played a good game. Something seemed to be wrong. His technique was fine, but each swing was just a little off."

Two people tell the same joke in what seems to be the same way, yet one person brings a smile, and the other person has you laughing so hard your muscles hurt. The difference in how they tell (do) the joke is imperceptible.

When a successful comedian tells a joke, he does it from his experience of already being funny. Laughter results from being funny, not from doing anything. And that's the difference.

This last Power Process contains the same message that began the book. "This book is worthless." Only now, the idea is carried a step further. Techniques in this book can indeed be worthless <u>if</u> you operate with the idea that you are an ineffective student. Even if you consistently apply all the techniques presented, you are likely to subtly sabotage your success.

For example, if you consider yourself stupid in math, you are likely to fail at math. If you are convinced you have a poor memory, chances are that practicing memory techniques won't improve your memory much.

As human beings, we change ourselves by changing our thoughts *about* ourselves. Great achievements happen as the result of subtle choices that start from "be."

If you want to experience more success in school, then start from the idea that you are a master student right now, lacking only a few skills that come with practice.

If you want a fulfilling career, begin from the idea that you have many options and are already on the way to a job you love.

Use affirmations and visualizations to plant these ideas firmly in your subconscious.

This is not mere positive thinking or emotional cheerleading. "Be it" works best when you take a First Step—when you tell the truth about your current abilities. Telling the truth about where you are does not limit what you can *be*.

Starting from *be* doesn't guarantee anything. It is still necessary to take action to get what you want. But when you start from a mind-set of being, your actions become much more natural and on target. Then your body is not fighting your subconscious idea of what is possible.

Begin your journey toward becoming a master student by being a master student. Get what you want naturally. Use your subconscious powers.

Flow with the natural current of BE ⇨ DO ⇨ HAVE.

If you want it, be it.

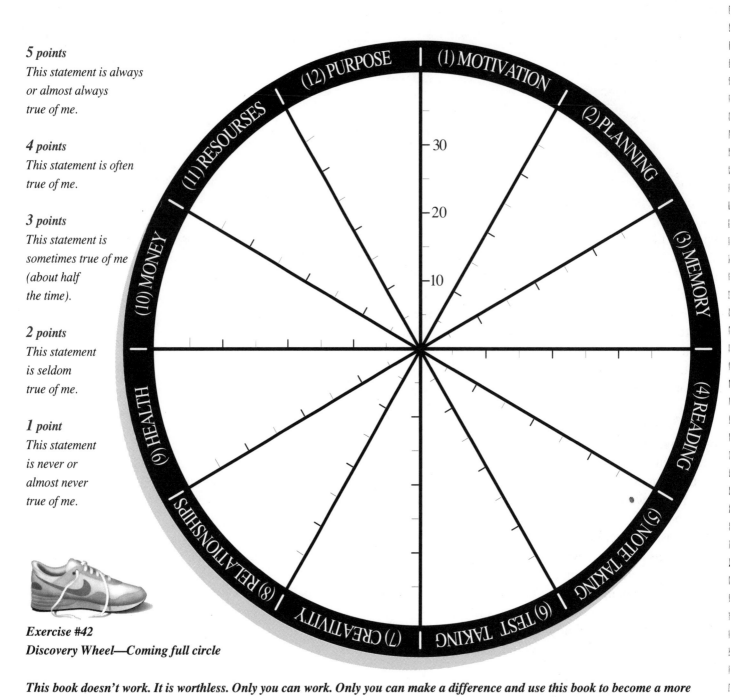

5 points
This statement is always
or almost always
true of me.

4 points
This statement is often
true of me.

3 points
This statement is
sometimes true of me
(about half
the time).

2 points
This statement
is seldom
true of me.

1 point
This statement
is never or
almost never
true of me.

Exercise #42
Discovery Wheel—Coming full circle

This book doesn't work. It is worthless. Only you can work. Only you can make a difference and use this book to become a more effective student.

The purpose of this book is to give you the opportunity to change your behavior. Just because something seems like a good idea doesn't mean that you will put it into practice. This exercise gives you a chance to see what behaviors you have changed on your journey to becoming a master student.

Answer each question quickly and honestly. Record your results in the Discovery Wheel, and then compare it with the wheel you produced in Chapter One. Your scores may be lower here than on your earlier wheel. That's OK. Lower scores might result from increased self-awareness and honesty—a valuable asset.

The scores on this Discovery Wheel indicate your current strengths and weaknesses in becoming a master student. The last Journal Entries in this chapter provide space for writing about how you intend to change. As you complete this self-evaluation, ask yourself how you want to change. Your commitment to change allows you to become a master student.

1. _____ I start each school term highly motivated, and I stay that way.

2. _____ I know what I want to get from my education.

3. _____ I enjoy learning.

4. _____ I study even when distracted by activities of lower priority.

5. _____ I am satisfied about how I progress toward achieving goals.

6. _____ Studying is important and I allow adequate time for it.

7. _____ I am excited about the courses I take.

8. _____ I have a clear idea of the benefits I expect to get from my education.

_____ Total score (1) Motivation

1. _____ I periodically refine my long-term goals.

2. _____ I regularly define short-term goals.

3. _____ I write a plan for each day and each week.

4. _____ I assign priorities to what I choose to do each day.

5._____ I plan review time so I don't have to cram before tests.

6. _____ I plan regular recreation time.

7. _____ I adjust my study time to meet the demands of individual courses.

8. _____ I have adequate time each day to accomplish what I plan.

_____ Total score (2) Planning

1. _____ I am confident in my ability to remember.

2. _____ I remember people's names.

3. _____ At the end of a lecture, I can summarize what was presented.

4. _____ I apply techniques that enhance my memory skills.

5. _____ I can recall information when I'm under pressure.

6. _____ I remember important information clearly and easily.

7. _____ I can jog my memory when I have difficulty recalling.

8. _____ I can relate new information to what I've already learned.

_____ Total score (3) Memory

1. _____ I preview and review reading assignments.

2. _____ When reading, I underline or highlight important passages.

3. _____ When I read, I ask questions about the material.

4. _____ When I read textbooks, I am alert and awake.

5. _____ I relate what I read to my life.

6. _____ I select a reading strategy to fit the type of material I'm reading.

7. _____ I take effective notes when I read.

8. _____ When I don't understand what I'm reading, I note my questions and find answers.

_____ Total score (4) Reading

5 points

This statement is always or almost always true of me.

4 points

This statement is often true of me.

3 points

This statement is sometimes true of me (about half the time).

2 points

This statement is seldom true of me.

1 point

This statement is never or almost never true of me.

1. _____ When I am in class, I focus my attention.

2. _____ I take notes in class.

3. _____ I am aware of various methods for taking notes and choose those that work best for me.

4. _____ My notes are valuable for review.

5. _____ I review class notes within 24 hours.

6. _____ I distinguish important material and notice key phrases in a lecture.

7. _____ I copy material the instructor writes on the board or overhead projector.

8. _____ I can put important concepts into my own words.

_____ Total score (5) Note taking

1. _____ I feel confident and calm during an exam.

2. _____ I manage my time during exams and I am able to complete them.

3. _____ I am able to predict test questions.

4. _____ I can examine essay questions in light of what I know and come to a new and original conclusion during a test.

5. _____ I adapt my test-taking strategy to the kind of test I'm taking.

6. _____ I understand what essay questions ask and can answer them completely and accurately.

7. _____ I start reviewing for tests at the beginning of the term and review regularly.

8. _____ My sense of personal worth is independent of my test scores.

_____ Total score (6) Test taking

1. _____ I have flashes of insight, and solutions to problems appear to me at unusual times.

2. _____ I plan writing assignments, create first drafts, and revise them to get clear final drafts.

3. _____ When I get stuck on a creative project, I use specific methods to get unstuck.

4. _____ I know how to prepare and deliver effective speeches.

5. _____ I use brainstorming to generate solutions to a variety of problems.

6. _____ I am confident when I speak before others.

7. _____ I see problems as opportunities for learning and personal growth.

8. _____ I am willing to consider different points of view and alternative solutions.

_____ Total score (7) Creativity

1. _____ I develop and maintain mutually supportive relationships.

2. _____ I am candid with others about who I am, what I feel, and what I want.

3. _____ Other people tell me that I am a good listener.

4. _____ I communicate my upset and anger without blaming others.

5. _____ I am aware of my cultural biases and open to understanding people with different backgrounds.

6. _____ I am able to learn from various instructors with different teaching styles.

7. _____ I have the ability to make friends and create valuable relationships in a new place.

8. _____ I am open to being with people I don't especially like in order to learn from them.

_____ Total score (8) Relationships

1. _____ I have enough energy to study and still fully enjoy other areas of my life.

2. _____ I exercise regularly.

3. _____ My emotional health supports my ability to learn.

4. _____ If the situation calls for it, I have enough reserve energy to put in a long day.

5. _____ I accept my body the way it is.

6. _____ I notice changes in my physical condition and respond effectively.

7. _____ I am in control of the alcohol and drugs I put into my body.

8. _____ The food I eat contributes to my health.

_____ Total score (9) Health

1. _____ I budget my money and I am in control of my personal finances.

2. _____ I am confident that I will have enough money to complete the education I want.

3. _____ I have a clear picture of the financial resources available to me to pay for my education.

4. _____ I can make a little money go a long way.

5. _____ My education supports my long-range financial goals.

6. _____ I repay my debts on time.

7. _____ My sense of personal worth is independent of my financial condition.

8. _____ I make regular deposits to my savings account.

_____ Total score (10) Money

Journal Entry #87
Discovery Statement

Comparing the Discovery Wheel in this chapter with the Discovery Wheel in Chapter One, I learned that I . . .

_____

_____

_____

_____

_____

_____

1. _____ I can effectively use libraries to find the resources and information I want.

2. _____ I am aware of the services offered by my school and know how to use them.

3. _____ I use my job or other activities outside of school as learning experiences.

4. _____ I take on projects that can make a difference in other people's lives.

5. _____ I know where to get help in my community for a variety of problems.

6. _____ My relationships with friends, family, and others support my educational goals.

7. _____ I think of my mistakes as valuable opportunities to learn.

8. _____ I see the world's problems as opportunities for me to participate and contribute.

_____ Total score (11) Resources

1. _____ I see learning as a lifelong process.

2. _____ I relate school to what I plan to do for the rest of my life.

3. _____ I learn by contributing to others.

4. _____ I revise my plans as I learn, change, and grow.

5. _____ I am clear about my purpose in life.

6. _____ I know that I am responsible for my own education.

7. _____ I take responsibility for the quality of my life.

8. _____ I am willing to accept challenges even when I'm not sure how to meet them.

_____ Total score (12) Purpose

I also learned that I . . .

_____

_____

_____

_____

_____

_____

_____

Contributing:
The art of selfishness

THIS BOOK IS ABOUT CONTRIBUTING TO YOURSELF—about taking care of yourself, being selfish, and filling yourself up. The techniques and suggestions in these pages focus on how to get what you want out of school and out of life. One of the results of all of this successful selfishness is the capacity for contribution, for giving to others. Contributing is what's left to do when you're satisfied—filled up—and it completes the process.

People who are satisfied with life can share that satisfaction with others. It is not easy to contribute to another person's joy until you experience joy. The same is true for love. When people are filled with love, they can more easily contribute love to others.

Our interdependence calls for contribution

Every day we depend on contribution. We stake our lives on the sensibilities of other people. When you drive, you depend on others for your life. If a driver in the oncoming lane crosses into your lane, you might die. You depend upon the sensibilities of world leaders for your safety.

People everywhere are growing more interdependent. A plunge in the U.S. stock market reverberates in markets across the planet. A decrease in oil prices gives businesses everywhere a shot in the arm. A nuclear war would ignore national boundaries and devastate life on the planet. Successful arms negotiations allow all people to sleep a little easier.

In this interdependent world, there is no such thing as win/lose. If others lose, their loss directly affects us. If we lose, it is more difficult to contribute to others. The only way to win and to get what we want in life is for others to win, also.

A caution

The idea of contributing is not the same as knowing what is best for other people. We can't know.

There are people, of course, who go around "fixing" others. "I know what you need. Here, do it my way." That is not contribution. It often causes more harm than good and can result in dependence on the part of the person we are "helping."

True contribution occurs only after you find out what another person wants or needs and then determine that you can lovingly support him to have it.

How you can begin contributing

The world will welcome your gifts of time, money, and talent. The advantages of contributing are clear. When we contribute, the whole human family benefits in a tangible way. Close to home, contributing often means getting involved with other people. This is one way to "break the ice" in a new community and meet people with interests similar to your own.

When you've made the decision to contribute, the next step is knowing how. There are ways to contribute in your immediate surroundings. Visit a neighbor, take a family member to a movie, or offer to tutor a roommate. Or you can begin by reading about campus and community resources in the article "How to supercharge your education." Look for ways you can contribute to the organizations mentioned. An additional benefit to volunteer work is that it is a way to explore possible career choices. Consider the following organizations:

Big Brothers and Big Sisters provide friendship and guidance to children who might have only one parent. Girls Club, Boys Club, Girl Scouts, and Boy Scouts of America all need large numbers of volunteers.

Sierra Club, Greenpeace, Audubon Society, the World Wildlife Fund, and similar organizations are dedicated to protecting the environment and endangered species.

Amnesty International investigates human rights violations. It assists people who are imprisoned or tortured for peacefully expressing their points of view. You can participate in letter writing campaigns.

Hospitals and hospice programs often depend on volunteer help to supplement patient care provided by the professional staff. Museums and art galleries need interested people to conduct tours and provide supervision.

Nursing homes welcome visitors who are willing to spend time listening and talking with lonely people.

Political parties, candidates, and special interest groups need volunteers to stuff envelopes, gather petition signatures, and distribute literature.

The American Red Cross provides disaster relief. Local community care centers use volunteers to feed homeless people.

Service organizations like Cosmopolitan, Zonta, Jaycees, Jayceettes, Altrusa, Kiwanis, Lions, American Association of University Women, Sertoma, Business and Professional Women, and Rotary want members who are willing to serve others.

Tutoring centers offer opportunities for competent students to help non-English-speaking people, grade school and high school students, and illiterate adults.

Churches of all denominations want volunteers to assist with projects for the community and the world.

World hunger groups want you to help feed starving people and to inform all of us about the problems of malnutrition, food spoilage, and starvation. These groups include Oxfam America, CARE, and The Hunger Project.

Our environmental problems are so serious that there's a chance the earth will be uninhabitable in 30 years. And there are so many nuclear warheads right now that if only 10 percent of them were accidently detonated, human life might no longer exist. Over 18 million people die each year from hunger or hunger-related diseases.

The techniques and strategies in this book make no difference in all this. However, *you* can make a difference. You can use these techniques to work with others and choose a new future for our planet.

Journal Entry #88
Discovery Statement

Recall a time when you contributed—for example, when you volunteered your time for an important cause or a worthy group. Write details of the contributions you made and how you felt afterwards.

Journal Entry #89
Intention Statement

Review the list of organizations in the article "Contributing—the art of selfishness." Choose one or two organizations which interest you. Also, think about people in your life to whom you could give time, money, or something of yourself.

Make a commitment to contribute. Make the commitment detailed and time-specific.

I intend to contribute . . .

Exercise #43

This book shouts:

Use me!

Becoming a Master Student *is designed to be used for years. The success strategies presented here are not likely to become habits overnight. There are more suggestions than can be put into action immediately. Some of what is discussed may not apply to your life right now, but may be just what you could use in a few months.*

Plan to keep this book and use it again. Imagine that your book has a mouth. (Visualize the mouth.) Your book has arms and legs. (Visualize them.)

Now, picture your book sitting on a shelf or table that you see every day. Imagine a time when you are having trouble in school and struggling to be successful as a student. Visualize your book jumping up and down and shouting, "Use me! Read me! I may have the solution to your problem, and I know I can help you solve it."

This is a memory technique to remind you to use a resource. Sometimes, when you are stuck, all you need is a small push or a list of possible actions. At those times, hear your book shout, "Use me!"

Other ideas for getting lasting value from **Becoming a Master Student** *include:*

* *Keep it on the coffee table, in the kitchen, or in the bathroom.*
* *Keep it near your bedroom night stand.*
* *Loan the book to someone else, then talk about it with that person.*
* *Teach your favorite suggestions from this book to your friends and family.*
* *Tear out specific articles and share them with family or friends.*
* *In your calendar or appointment book, schedule periodic times to review the book.*

Raul Julia,

after receiving four Tony
nominations for performances
on Broadway, appeared in
many films including *One
From the Heart, The Morning
After, Moon Over Parador,
Tequila Sunrise, Kiss of the
Spider Woman, Havana,
Presumed Innocent,* and
Romero. He is also active in
The Hunger Project which is
an international organization
committed to the end of
hunger on the planet by the
year 2000 as an idea whose
time has come.

I've always known I was an actor. I acted in my first play
when I was five years old. The play was in Spanish and I was the
devil competing with a student, a farmer, and a hunter to capture
the heart of a fair maiden. During the opening performance, I
remember choosing to let go and risk being foolish. I fell to the
floor and started rolling all over the stage like I was having a fit.
No control. Everyone was stunned because this was not in the
script. Suddenly I got up and started saying my lines. I've been
acting and taking risks ever since.

I am committed to acting. Many years ago I had to choose
between doing what I loved—acting—or going into my father's
restaurant business in Puerto Rico. Choosing an acting career was
a financial risk and besides, being a successful actor in the United
States was as unlikely as being a prince in a fairy tale. I chose to
do what I loved, no matter what. What's the point of doing
anything you don't love? It's not worth it.

Sometimes acting is very tedious and tiring. Giving a
natural performance in the midst of all the technology of film
making is challenging. To help me over these barriers, I look at
why I'm doing it. I love acting and I'm very excited about
making movies. And there's more to it. It's called The Hunger
Project. Getting in touch with my work in The Hunger Project
carries me through.

I was attracted to The Hunger Project in 1977, when for
the first time in my life, I realized that we could actually end
hunger on the planet.

I feel I have a responsibility beyond myself and my family
to others who are starving. I have the good fortune to be able to
feed my family. I imagine myself looking for work, not finding
any, and not being able to provide food. This is happening right
now for many people. All that is needed to end this tragedy is the
commitment of people like you and me.

My commitment to end hunger inspires my acting. When
I'm tired, disgusted, bored, or just don't feel like it, I remember
that the more successful I become, the more of a difference I can
make. Since I am now committed to something more than self-
gratification, my work becomes finer. I am still learning and
growing, of course, and contribution brings a different quality to
my work.

Many of my high school Jesuit teachers had been tortured
while they were imprisoned in China. The General of the Jesuit
order had been at Hiroshima when they dropped the bomb. The
primary thing I learned from the Spanish Jesuits is that a hero is
someone who goes beyond himself to make a difference for
other people.

Going beyond yourself includes going beyond your
cultural background. It is best to educate yourself about your
background, be proud of who you are, and be accurate and
knowledgeable when you communicate about it. Be an example.
Regardless of where you come from, regardless of your
background, you can succeed. The more you achieve and the
better you can communicate, the more people will respect and
understand you.

Once you are knowledgeable and proud of your culture,
you can go beyond yourself and become whatever you want to be.
Transcending your background allows you to be free and proud.

I don't go around waving a flag saying that I am "Mr.
Puerto Rico." I have that background and I am proud of it. I love
Puerto Rico, I love my culture, and I love my background. But
before anything else, I am a human being. My cultural heritage is
in the background. I am first a human being who happened to be
born into that background. If we can see it that way, we can
appreciate the diversity and, at the same time, enjoy our heritage
even more. Then we don't need to use it as a shield in competition
or as a prejudicial label.

The planet is small enough. It is time to put all that cultural
and nationalistic kind of flag waving in the background. It is now
time for everyone on the planet to be human beings together.

1. Briefly discuss the meaning of "Now that you're done-begin."

2. Which of the following affirmations does *not* follow the suggestions for an effective affirmation?

    A) I have a healthy, fun, respectful relationship with my in-laws.
    B) I am an artistic person.
    C) I will stop putting off math assignments.
    D) I speak clearly and concisely.
    E) All of the above are affirmations.

3. Explain how career planning can be a process of choosing instead of a process of discovery.

4. What are three responses given for the argument that making the wrong career choice will waste time?

5. Power Process #12 carries the idea "This book is worthless" one step further. Explain what this means.

6. Using the Power Process "Be it" eliminates the need to take action. True or False. Explain your answer.

7. If your scores are lower on the Discovery Wheel the second time you finish it, that means your study skills have not improved. True or False. Explain your answer.

8. Explain what Raul Julia learned about the meaning of "hero."

9. Contributing to others does *not* involve:

   (A) telling people the best way for them to change.
   (B) finding out what they want or need.
   (C) determining if you can help them get what they want.
   (D) giving your time, talent, or money.
   (E) making sure that you experience satisfaction also.

10. List at least four ways you can continue on your path of becoming a master student after completing this book.

Journal Entry #90
Discovery Statement

Review the Intention Statements throughout this book. They appear at the end of every chapter as well as throughout each chapter. See if you have been keeping your agreements with yourself. See if you have been getting what you said you wanted.

If you are consistently not doing what you said you would do, or if you are not getting what you said you wanted, examine what you have been saying. You might be saying you want one thing, when you actually want something else.

On reviewing past Intention Statements, I learned that I . . .

_____

_____

_____

_____

_____

Journal Entry #91
Intention Statement

Hundreds of tools, techniques, hints, processes, and suggestions for being a successful student have been presented in this book. At the end of each chapter you have been asked to make a commitment to experiment with a suggestion or two.

Quickly review this book and choose a few more techniques that you can be counted on to use. Make sure your promises are time-specific and achievable. Also include a reward for keeping your promises.

Intention	Time/Date	Reward
I will . . .		

Journal Entry #92
Intention Statement

Consider the benefits of doing this book one year from now. Imagine what you could gain by rereading the material, rewriting the Journal Entries, and redoing the exercises.

Also consider the cost of redoing the book. You would spend hours reading, writing, and experimenting. You might feel uncomfortable looking at some aspects of yourself or discovering that you created your circumstances.

Once you have thought about the potential costs and benefits of redoing this book, write down your intention. Be specific about completion dates and the extent of your review.

I intend to . . .

_____

_____

_____

Congratulations —
You have completed a journey through a book that is designed to be the start of an Adventure in becoming a master student.

Dave Ellis

Bibliography

GOALS:
American Personnel and Guidance Association. *Career Decisions*, Washington, DC: American Personnel and Guidance Association, n.d.

Bolles, Richard Nelson. *What Color is Your Parachute?* Berkeley, CA: Ten Speed Press, updated annually.

Ellis, Dave, Lankowitz, Stan, Stupka, Ed, and Toft, Doug. *Career Planning Supplement to Becoming a Master Student*, Rapid City, SD: College Survival, 1990.

Satir, Virginia. *Making Contact*, Berkeley, CA: Celestial Arts, 1976.

Sher, Barbara with Gottlieb, Annie. *Teamworks! Building Support Groups That Guarantee Success,* New York, NY: Warner, 1989.

Sher, Barbara with Gottlieb, Annie. *Wishcraft: How to Get What You Really Want,* New York, NY: Ballantine, 1979.

Sinetar, Marsha. *Do What You Love, The Money Will Follow*, New York, NY: Dell, 1987.

U.S. Department of Labor. *The Occupational Outlook Handbook*, Washington, DC: Government Printing Office, n.d.

U.S. Department of Labor. *The Directory of Occupational Titles*, Washington, DC: Government Printing Office, n.d.

HEALTH AND SAFETY:
Cousins, Norman. *Anatomy of an Illness As Perceived by the Patient*, New York, NY: Bantam Books, 1981.

Johnson, Vernon E. *I'll Quit Tomorrow*, New York, NY: Harper & Row, 1980.

Robbins, John. *Diet For A New America*, Walpole, NH: Stillpoint, 1987.

Ryan, Regina Sara and Travis, John W., M.D. *Wellness Workbook: A Guide to Attaining High Level Wellness*, Berkeley, CA: Ten Speed, 1981.

Silber, Sherman J., M.D. *How Not to Get Pregnant: Your Guide to Simple, Reliable Contraception*, New York, NY: Scribner, 1987.

Vickery, Donald M., M.D, and Fries, James, M.D. *Take Care of Yourself: The Consumer's Guide to Medical Care*, Reading, MA: Addison-Wesley, 1986.

Whittemore, Gerard. *Street Wisdom for Women: A Handbook For Urban Survival*, Boston, MA: Quinlan Press, 1986.

Yoder, Barbara. *The Recovery Resource Book*, New York, NY: Fireside, 1990.

LEARNING TOOLS:
Barzun, Jacques & Graff, Henry F. *The Modern Researcher*, New York, NY: Harcourt Brace Jovanovich, 1977.

Blanchard, Kenneth & Johnson, Spencer. *The One Minute Manager*, New York, NY: Morrow, 1983.

Buzan, Tony. *Use Both Sides of Your Brain*, New York, NY: Dutton, 1974.

James, William. *Talks to Teachers on Psychology and to Students on Some of Life's Ideals*, New York, NY: Norton, 1958.

Matheson, Maureen, ed. *College Handbook*, New York, NY: College Board, 1983.

Pauk, Walter. *How to Study in College*, Boston, MA: Houghton Mifflin, 1974.

Ries, Al and Trout, Jack. *Positioning: The Battle for Your Mind*, New York, NY: McGraw-Hill, 1980.

Rogers, Carl. *Freedom to Learn*, Columbus, OH: Merrill, 1982.

Ruggiero, Vincent Ryan. *Critical Thinking Supplement to Becoming a Master Student*, Rapid City, SD: College Survival, 1989.

MATH AND SCIENCE:
Kogelman, Stanley and Warren, Joseph. *Mind Over Math*, New York, NY: Dial Press, 1978.

Mallow, Jeffry V. *Science Anxiety: Fear of Science and How to Overcome It*, New York, NY: Thomond, 1981.

Tobias, Sheila. *Succeed with Math: Every Student's Guide to Conquering Math Anxiety*, New York, NY: College Board, 1987.

MEMORY:
Brown, Alan C. *Maximizing Memory Power*, New York, NY: Wiley, 1986.

Higbee, Kenneth L. *Your Memory—How It Works and How to Improve It*, Englewood Cliffs, NJ: Prentice-Hall, 1977.

Lucas, Jerry, and Lorayne, Harry. *The Memory Book*, New York, NY: Ballantine Books, 1975.

MONEY AND CONSUMER:
Department of Energy. *The Car Book*, Pueblo, CO: Consumer Information, n.d.

Elgin, Duane. *Voluntary Simplicity*, New York, NY: Morrow, 1981.

Porter, Sylvia. *Slyvia Porter's Your Financial Security*, New York, NY: Avon, 1990.

MULTICULTURAL AWARENESS:
Beckham, Barry, ed. *The Black Student's Guide to Colleges*, Hampton, VA: Beckham House, 1984.

Condon, John C. and Yousef, Fathi S. *Introduction to Intercultural Communication*, New York, NY: Macmillan, 1975.

NONTRADITIONAL STUDENTS:
Burke, Anna Mae Walsh. *Are You Ready: A Survival Manual for Women Returning to School*, Englewood Cliffs, NJ: Prentice-Hall, 1980.

Hecht, Miriam and Traub, Lillian. *Dropping Back In: How to Complete Your College Education Quickly and Economically*, New York, NY: E.P. Dutton, 1982.

Katz, Montana and Vieland, Veronica. *Get Smart! A Woman's Guide to Equality on Campus*, New York, NY: Feminist Press, 1988.

PERSONAL DEVELOPMENT:
Bach, Richard, *Illusions: The Adventures of a Reluctant Messiah*, New York, NY: Delacorte, 1977.

Bandler, Richard & Grinder, John. *Frogs into Princes: Neuro-Linguistic Programming*, Moab, UT: Real People, 1979.

Benson, Herbert & Klipper, Miriam Z. *The Relaxation Response*, New York, NY: Avon, 1976.

Bloomfield, Harold, et.al. *How to Survive the Loss of a Love*, New York, NY: Bantam Books, 1977.

Buber, Martin. *I and Thou*, New York, NY: Scribner, 1970.

Castaneda, Carlos. *A Separate Reality*, New York, NY: Pocket Books, 1981.

Corey, Gerald. *I Never Knew I Had a Choice*, Monterey, CA: Brooks-Cole, 1982.

Covey, Stephen R. *The Seven Habits of Highly Effective People*, New York, NY: Simon & Schuster, 1989.

Emery, Stuart. *Actualizations: You Don't Have to Rehearse to Be Yourself*, Garden City, NY: Doubleday, 1978.

Frank, Victor. *Man's Search for Meaning*, New York, NY: Simon & Schuster, 1970.

Gawain, Shakti. *Creative Visualization*, Mill Valley, CA: Whatever, 1978.

Golas, Thaddeus. *The Lazy Man's Guide to Enlightenment*, Palo Alto, CA: Seed Center, 1972.

James, Muriel and Jongeward, Dorothy. *Born to Win*, Reading, MA: Addison-Wesley, 1971.

Keyes, Ken, Jr. *Handbook to Higher Consciousness*, Berkeley, CA: Living Love, 1974.

Maltz, Maxwell. *Psycho-Cybernetics*, New York, NY: Pocket Books, n.d.

Maslow, Abraham. *Toward a Psychology of Being*, New York, NY: Van Nostrand Reinhold, 1968.

Miller, William A. *You Count-You Really Do!*, Minneapolis, MN: Augsburg, 1976.

Pirsig, Robert. *Zen and Art of Motorcycle Maintenance*, New York, NY: Bantam Books, 1976.

Rajneesh, Bhagwan S. *Journey Toward the Heart*, New York, NY: Harper & Row, 1980.

Robbins, Anthony. *Unlimited Power*, New York, NY: Simon & Schuster, 1986.

Satir, Virginia. *Peoplemaking*, Center City, MN: Hazelden, n.d.

Solly, Richard and Lloyd, Roseann. *Journey Notes: Writing for Recovery and Spiritual Growth*, Center City, MN: Hazelden, 1989.

Waitley, Dennis E. *The Psychology of Winning*, cassette, Chicago, IL: Nightingale-Conant, n.d.

Williams, Paul. *Energi*, New York, NY: Warner Books, 1980.

Zimbardo, Philip G. *Shyness—What It Is, What To Do About it*, Reading, MA: Addison-Wesley, 1977.

READING:
Adler, Mortimer and Van Doren, Charles. *How to Read a Book*, New York, NY: Touchstone, 1972.

Gilbart, Helen W. *Pathways: A Guide to Reading and Study Skills*, Boston, MA: Houghton Mifflin, 1982.

Rial, Arlyne F. *Speed Reading Made Easy*, Garden City, NY: Doubleday, 1985.

REFERENCE:
Bartlett, John G. *Bartlett's Familiar Quotations*, Boston, MA: Little, Brown, 1980.

Davies, Peter, ed. *The American Heritage Dictionary of the English Language*, New York, NY: Dell, 1982.

McCutcheon, Randall. *Can You Find It?* Minneapolis, MN: Free Spirit, 1989.

Osborn, Susan. *Dial An Expert: The Consumer's Sourcebook of Free & Low Cost Expertise Available By Phone*, New York, NY: McGraw-Hill, 1986.

Strunk, William, Jr. and White, E. B. *The Elements of Style*, New York, NY: Macmillan, 1979.

Wurman, Richard Saul. *Information Anxiety*, New York, NY: Doubleday, 1989.

RELATIONSHIPS:
Driekurs, Rudolf and Soltz, Vicki. *Children: The Challenge*, New York, NY: Dutton, 1964.

Gordon, Thomas. *Parent Effectiveness Training: The Tested New Way to Raise Responsible Children*, New York, NY: New American Library, 1975.

Keyes, Ken, Jr. *A Conscious Person's Guide to Relationships*, Coos Bay, OR: Living Love, 1979.

Keyes, Ken, Jr. *The Hundredth Monkey*, Coos Bay, OR: Vision, 1982.

Lerner, Harriet G. *Dance of Anger*, New York, NY: Harper & Row, 1989.

Montagu, Ashley. *The Natural Superiority of Women*, New York, NY: Macmillan, 1974.

U.S. Department of Education, Office for Civil Rights. *Sexual Harrassment: It's Not Academic*, Washington, DC: 1988.

TIME:
Lakein, Alan. *How to Get Control of Your Time and Your Life*, New York, NY: New American Library, 1974.

Winston, Stephanie. *Getting Organized*, New York, NY: Warner, 1978.

WRITING:
Cheney, Theodore A. Rees, *Getting the Words Right: How to Revise, Edit & Rewrite*, Cincinnati, OH: Writer's Digest, 1983.

Elbow, Peter. *Writing with Power: Techniques for Mastering the Writing Process*, New York, NY: Oxford University, 1981.

Goldberg, Natalie. *Writing Down the Bones: Freeing the Writer Within*, Boston, MA: Shambhala, 1986.

Murray, Donald M. *Write to Learn*, New York, NY: Holt, Rinehart & Winston, 1987.

Progoff, Ira. *At a Journal Workshop*, New York, NY: Dialogue House, 1975.

Rico, Gabriele Lusser. *Writing the Natural Way*, Los Angeles, CA: J.P. Tarcher, 1983.

Roth, Audrey J. *The Research Paper: Process, Form, & Content*, Belmont, CA: Wadsworth, 1989.

Ueland, Brenda. *If You Want To Write: A Book About Art, Independence and Spirit*, St. Paul, MN: Graywolf, 1987.

Index